RECLAIMING THE AMERICAN RIGHT

BACKGROUND

Essential Texts for the Conservative Mind

RECLAIMING THE AMERICAN RIGHT

The Lost Legacy of the Conservative Movement

Justin Raimondo

with a new introduction by George W. Carey

ISI Books
Wilmington, Delaware

Raimondo, Justin.

    Reclaiming the American right : the lost legacy of the conservative movement / Justin Raimondo ; with an introduction by George W. Carey.—[2nd ed.]—Wilmington, Del. : ISI Books, 2008.

        p. ; cm.
        (Background series)

        ISBN: 978-1-933859-60-6
        First published in 1993 by the Center for Libertarian Studies.
        Includes bibliographical references.

        1. Conservatism—United States. 2. United States—Politics and government. 3. Political culture—United States. 4. Right and left (Political science) I. Carey, George Wescott, 1933–2013. II. Title. III. Series: Background series (Wilmington, Del.)

JC573.2.U6 R35 2008   2007941668
320.52/0973—dc22   0805

ISI Books
Intercollegiate Studies Institute
3901 Centerville Road
Wilmington, DE 19807-1938
www.isibooks.org

CONTENTS

CRITICAL ESSAYS

FOREWORD

Patrick J. Buchanan

W HAT HAPPENED TO THE AMERICAN RIGHT? What became of a
movement once so united and disciplined it could deliver the
presidency, consistently, to the Republican Party?

That the old house is divided, fractured, fallen, is undeniable.
The great unifier, Ronald Reagan, is gone. The Cold War that brought
conservatives together is over. With the Berlin Wall down, the captive
nations free, the Evil Empire dissolved and subdivided, many on the
Right have stacked arms and gone home. Once there, they have discovered that we come from different neighborhoods, honor different
heroes, believe different ideas. To understand the new rifts on the Right,
scholars have begun to research its history, explore its roots. Latest to
do so is Justin Raimondo, who, in this book, argues that conservatism
is a cause corrupted and betrayed. His is a story of heroes and villains,
heresies and excommunications, faithfulness and betrayal—a veritable
Iliad of the American Right.

Raimondo's book goes back sixty years to the days when the Old
Right first rose in rebellion against the New Deal and FDR's drive to
war. Believers in limited government and nonintervention, the Old
Right feared involvement in a second world war would mean permanent

disfigurement of the old republic, and a quantum leap in federal power that could never be reversed.

But history is written by the winners.

And these men lost it all: jobs, careers, and honored places in their nation's memory. But they never lost their principles. Garet Garrett, John T. Flynn, Frank Chodorov—who has heard of this lost platoon of the Old Right? They went down fighting and ended their lives in obscurity, resisting the clamor to sign up for the Cold War.

Theirs, declares Raimondo, is the lost legacy. And the failures of conservatism are traceable to the Right's abandonment of that legacy. Beginning in the midfifties, the Right was captured and co-opted by undocumented aliens from the Left, carrying with them the viruses of statism and globalism.

First in from the cold, Raimondo writes, came the Communists, refugees from Stalin's purges, the Hitler Pact, and Moscow's attack on the Baltic republics and Finland. First among these was James Burnham, ex-Trotskyite of whom Orwell wrote that he worshipped power. Burnham went on the masthead of *National Review* from its founding in 1955, to become grand strategist of the Cold War. He would be awarded the Medal of Freedom by Ronald Reagan himself. But, Raimondo argues, Burnham was never a true conservative; indeed, was barely tolerant of conservatives. A Machiavellian after renouncing Marxism, Burnham preached "American Empire" as the necessary means to combat Communist empire and was first to call for the creation of a "democratic world order."

A second wave of migrants was the neoconservatives. Though Trotskyite, socialist, or Social Democrat in their youth, by the mid-sixties they were JFK-LBJ Democrats orphaned by a party dedicated to the proposition that Vietnam was a dirty, immoral war. In 1972, they signed ads for Richard Nixon, a man not widely cherished among their number in his Alger Hiss and Helen Gahagan Douglas days.

With Reagan's triumph, the neocons came into their own, into his government and his movement. Raimondo echoes the Old Right journalist who calls the neocons the cow-birds of conservatism, migratory fowl that wait for birds to build their nests and lay their eggs, then swoop down, barge in, and kick the first birds out. If conservatism has failed, he writes, it is "because a Trojan horse inside the movement has been undermining the fight against big government. Since the mid-fifties . . . these interlopers have acted as a Fifth Column on the Right: conciliating the welfare state, smearing their Old Right predecessors, and burying the real story of how they came to claim the mantle of conservatism."

And today? "Two traditions stand head-to-head, contending for the future of the . . . movement. One piously holds out the promise of enterprise zones from South Central Los Angeles to Mogadishu, while the other dares utter the forbidden phrase, *America first!*" Written in defense of, and in the style of, the dead lions of the Old Right, whom Justin Raimondo reveres, *Reclaiming the American Right* is not about olive branches; it is about conflict, about taking back the movement, about taking back America. Richly researched, beautifully written, passionately argued, *Reclaiming the American Right* is targeted at the new "generation of conservative theorists and activists (that) yearns to get back to first principles and get in touch with its roots." Many will call this the revisionist history of the Right, but even those who work for consensus need to understand how those who do not believe, feel, and think. And the timing is perfect. For, suddenly, all the new issues before us, Bosnia, Somalia, foreign aid, NAFTA, intervention, immigration, big government, sovereignty, bear striking resemblance to the old.

Introduction to the 2008 Edition

George W. Carey
Georgetown University

I STILL REMEMBER MY KEEN DISAPPOINTMENT a few years back when the university bookstore informed me that Justin Raimondo's *Reclaiming the American Right* was out of print. I knew from past surveys that students had consistently ranked it among the most stimulating and rewarding of all the required readings in my course on modern American conservative thought. I realized as well that its unavailability would create a significant void that could not be filled. No other work could match Raimondo's sympathetic and comprehensive portrayal of the leading lights of the Old Right. Nor has any other single work chronicled so thoroughly the reactions of leading Old Right figures to the abrupt and arguably revolutionary changes in the American political order brought about by Franklin D. Roosevelt and his New Deal. Moreover, Raimondo's treatment of the sources and ideology of neoconservatism and the emergence of the New Right open up perspectives for thinking about the future course of American politics not to be found elsewhere.

These remain among the reasons why, even fifteen years after its first appearance, this republication of *Reclaiming the American Right* will be most welcomed. Among those works that deal with the roots of modern American conservatism, the directions it has taken, and the troubling issues that confront it today, Raimondo's merits a special and lofty status.

It is not possible in this brief introduction to survey all of the ground covered by Raimondo. Nor could any survey do justice to his main arguments. For this reason, I confine myself to indicating why his work is significant and to assessing its place in the realm of modern American conservative thought.

TO SAY THAT FUNDAMENTAL QUESTIONS concerning the meaning of conservatism have arisen in recent decades would be an understatement. To be sure, no era has been free from disputes over precisely what conservatism signifies, but today's disputes revolve around its very essence. When a Republican administration, widely portrayed as perhaps the most conservative in our history, practices fiscal irresponsibility, promotes policies that expand the size of government, advances the centralization of federal authority, and launches a "preventive" war—that is, acts in a manner one might expect of liberal Democratic administrations—there is good reason to believe that something is terribly amiss, that somehow and at some point in time those principles and tenets which once formed the core of conservatism have been altered or abandoned. Such, at least, is the conclusion of many of my acquaintances in the academic community and elsewhere who have long considered themselves conservatives. Not unlike other commentators who have written to this issue, they believe that the word "conservative" has been applied to policies and actions that are, in fact, alien and antagonistic to what were once widely understood to be its basic tenets. Some fight this development by working for a restoration of the original understanding of conservatism; others have surrendered, in the sense that they now seek another word or term to characterize their beliefs.

This state of affairs is what makes this book uniquely interesting and its republication so timely. While many, if not most, have come to realize the full dimensions of the crisis within American conservatism only recently, they come as no surprise to those familiar with Raimondo's analysis. He details how the militant anticommunism of

New Right—fanned by the late William F. Buckley and the editors of *National Review*—opened the gates for the invasion of the Right by the neoconservatives, who, in turn, repudiated Old Right values and principles. On his showing, for instance, we can see how and why interventionism, including the doctrine of "preventive war," has now come to be associated with conservatism, and why, moreover, if neoconservatives have their way, we can anticipate additional foreign interventions in pursuit of unattainable ideological goals such as the eradication of "evil."

Raimondo maintains that the values, principles, and goals of the Old Right—which, as the subtitle informs us, constitute "The Lost Legacy of the Conservative Movement"—represent the core of conservatism and form a benchmark for assessing and evaluating the direction it has taken. While a goodly portion of the book offers an engaging and informative treatment of the lives and thought of intellectual leaders among the Old Right such as Garet Garrett, John T. Flynn, Rose Wilder Lane, Frank Chodorov and Isabel Paterson—individuals unknown to most of today's conservatives—the strength of Raimondo's approach, and what serves to make his arguments so formidable, resides in the fact that the New Deal era, that period in which the Old Right emerges, is both a convenient and natural starting point for discovering the roots of modern American conservatism. The New Deal fundamentally transformed American political and economic culture. As Robert Nisbet, a leading traditional conservative, observed, the New Deal represents "a great watershed not only in twentieth-century American history but in our entire national history."[1] The New Deal can legitimately be viewed as "founding" the American nation anew on principles at odds with those underlying the original founding. For this reason, if no other, it was bound to engender responses involving appeals to values presumably embedded in the American political tradition.

Most, if not all, traditional conservatives today share the basic concerns of the Old Right and would join Raimondo in his repudiation of the neoconservatives. They would, however, view modern American conservative thought from a wider perspective, one that points to serious tensions between them and the Old Right. In Raimondo's approach and analysis, these tensions arise from the fact that he writes from a libertarian perspective and that, in addition, most of the leading figures of the Old Right were also libertarian—or at least very sympathetic to libertarian values. In light of the long-standing division between libertarians and traditional conservatives on philosophical grounds,[2] a crucial question arises: Can the roots or basic principles of American conservatism be derived principally from libertarian reactions to the New Deal? A related concern, perhaps of even greater significance, relates to the differences between libertarians and traditionalists over the character of the American political tradition and, thus, the meaning and interrelationship of central values, such as "liberty" and "equality," embodied within it.

These issues arise from the evolution of conservative thought. Raimondo, from my vantage point at least, is correct in asserting that in the early 1950s the New Right eclipsed the Old. During this period, however, with the publication of Russell Kirk's *The Conservative Mind* (1953),[3] modern American conservatism also began to take a direction largely distinct from that of the New Right. To be sure, Kirk and other traditional conservatives viewed the Soviet Union as a threat to Western civilization, but they can hardly be considered an integral part of the New Right that Raimondo describes. Kirk, for instance, was never as one, philosophically speaking, with the principal editors of *National Review.* At the very least, by linking conservatism to Edmund Burke and to the main intellectual currents in the broader Western tradition, Kirk's work transcended the issues involved in the Cold War—i.e., those concerns that preoccupied the New Right.[4] Likewise, his approach pointed to and embraced new dimensions of conservative thought well beyond those central to the libertarians of the Old Right. Indeed, the seemly unbridge-able philosophical divide between libertarians and traditionalists can be viewed as the outgrowth of this new and more comprehensive view of conservatism. As Nisbet stated, Burke can be regarded as the "father" of modern conservatism in large part because he rejected the "individual-istic perspective" of society that undergirds libertarian thought.[5]

In light of these developments, what can be said about the "legacy" of the Old Right? What is the relationship, if any between more traditional, Burkean conservatism and the libertarianism of the Old Right, other than their incompatibility with neoconservatism?

By way of answering these questions we should note that Raimondo is not mistaken in characterizing the responses of the Old Right to the New Deal as "conservative," even though they do spring from libertarian values. As Raimondo suggests, the Old Right and conservatism, at least until the early 1950s, were virtually one and the same; up to this point in time there simply was no awareness of deep divisions within the ranks of those opposed to expansive government, centralization, executive war-making powers, and the like. I know from personal experience that those of us in the Chicago area who relished the editorials in Colonel McCormick's *Chicago Tribune* considered ourselves true "conservatives" and were so considered by our liberal counterparts. Likewise, at the 1952 Chicago Republican Convention, there was no question about which candidate was the conservative in the contest for the presidential nomination between Senator Taft and General Eisenhower.

The consensus that existed during this period may well account for the fact that over the last fifty years traditional conservatives have embraced and, in some cases, have even given new meaning to and justification for the principles and concerns expressed by the Old Right. Certainly, they would be loathe to abandon that which for a generation served to define conservatism, if only because to do so would—as is the case with the neoconservatives—bring their own authenticity into question. But it is also the fact that traditionalists, consistent with their understanding of conservatism, view the policies and actions of the New Deal period and beyond in essentially the same light as the Old Right. It is no surprise to find that in 1967, long after Old Right conservatism was a spent force, Russell Kirk lauded Robert A. Taft's conservatism and his principled opposition to unchecked presidential powers and centralization of political authority,[6] while Raimondo, for similar reasons, regards Taft as a major political figure of the Old Right. Nor is it surprising that traditionalists readily join the Old Right's condemnation of the major centralizing policies of the New Deal, albeit on the distinctly nonlibertarian Tocquevillian grounds that they have "atomized" individuals by undermining the status of intermediate social groups and associations.[7]

Raimondo's treatment invites the reader to think about the currents of thought within conservatism and their relationships to one another by raising anew the difficulties of reconciling libertarianism and traditional conservatism. Whatever differences might exist on this score should not obscure the vast areas of substantial agreement. Raimondo and traditionalists perceive essentially the same problems confronting the American republic. These problems include wisely delineating America's role in the world, an issue that promises to become more acute in the years ahead. On this matter, especially with the end of the Cold War, there exists a virtual "fusion" among traditionalists and libertarians in their opposition to costly and counterproductive interventionist foreign policies. Closely connected to this issue are still others involving the constitutional separation of powers. Traditionalists clearly share the fears of the Old Right concerning the steady growth of presidential power, particularly the president's presumed authority to unilaterally commit the nation to war. They share concerns as well about the ever-expanding welfare state, its costs, and its enormous bureaucracy that generates countless rules and regulations. To this must be added their mutual antipathy toward the political centralization resulting from the breakdown of federalism. In sum, to go no further, on operational and policy grounds there are a wide range of crucial concerns, many of them perennial, shared by libertarians and traditionalists. And in our present age, at least, these areas of agreement far outweigh the philosophical differences between the two groups.

Raimondo's achievement, on the one hand, is to remind us that the principles and values of the Old Right should occupy a central place in contemporary American conservatism. On the other hand, it is to show not only why they do not occupy such a place, but also how and why conservatism is now widely perceived to stand against much of what the Old Right fought so valiantly for. This is no small accomplishment, and it is one good reason why this provocative book will always occupy a significant position among those volumes dealing with the course and character of American conservatism.

Introduction

> *Before true conservatives can ever take back the country,*
> *they are going to have to take back their movement.*
> —*Patrick J. Buchanan*

AFTER A DECADE IN POWER, why has the conservative movement failed to make a dent in the growth of big government? After taking over the Republican Party in the sixties, and then capturing the White House in 1980, conservatives are baffled to discover that the power of the federal government to tax, regulate, and invade every aspect of our lives has not lessened but increased over the last decade. Bewildered, frustrated, and demoralized, the men and women of the Right are asking themselves, *What went wrong?*

This haunting question cannot be answered unless conservatives are willing to confront the ghosts of their intellectual ancestors. Before they can understand what is happening to their movement in the nineties, conservatives must reexamine their past—and learn the secret of their true history. The purpose of this book is to uncover it.

But before we start digging, it is necessary to examine the current crisis on the Right—an identity crisis that began with the spectacular breakup of the Soviet empire. Before the Great Revolution of 1989–91, which overthrew communism in Eastern Europe and the Soviet Union, the Right marched in virtual lockstep, united on the top priority of a global crusade against Marxism-Leninism. Today, the conservative movement is united on *nothing*, not even the traditional conservative credo of limited government. The nineties have seen the growing dominance of a new faction on the Right, the neoconservatives; Fred Barnes of the *Weekly Standard* has aptly dubbed them the "Big Government conservatives." Instead of railing against the corruption of the Republic and the depredations of the New Deal and the Great Society, they are comfortable with the legacy of FDR and seek not to repeal it but only to trim it around the edges. "Big Government conservatives" don't want to roll back—or, God forbid, abolish—the welfare state, but only to modify it, modernize it, and make it more efficient. In this view, the American state is much like its European cousins; it is provider, as well as protector and policeman, not only of its own mean streets but of the entire world.

This is the opposite of the view taken by the Old Right, that coalition of libertarian and conservative writers, publicists, and politicians who united against the Roosevelt revolution, opposed U.S. entry into World War II, and decried the permanent war economy. For reasons that today's neoconservative intellectuals dismiss as "nativist," the Old Right used to argue in terms of an American exceptionalism, a largely unspoken but all-persuasive assumption that the New World is and ought to be exempt from the vicissitudes ordinarily visited upon the Old. In doing battle with the New Deal, partisans of the Old Right such as Rose Wilder Lane campaigned for an embargo on the European import of statism:

> [D]uring half a century, reactionary influences from Europe have been shifting American thinking onto a basis of socialistic assumptions. In cities and states, both parties began to socialize America with imitations of [the] Kaiser's Germany: social welfare laws, labor laws, wage-and-hour laws, citizens' pension laws and so-called public ownership.
>
> Eleven years ago this creeping socialism sprang up armed with Federal power, and Americans—suddenly, it seemed—confronted for the first time in their lives a real political question: the choice between American individualism and European national socialism.[1]

Introduction

It was the great Old Right polemicist and editor Garet Garrett who—in the crystalline prose of *The American Story*—expressed this sentiment in its purest form:

> The American Revolution was a pilot flame that leaped the Atlantic and lighted holocaust in the Old World. But its character was misunderstood and could not have been reproduced by any other people. It was a revolution exemplary.[2]

This American exceptionalism animated the Right's case for limiting the power of the state, both at home and abroad, right up until the U.S. entered World War II. Based on the bedrock American political values of individualism, anti-statism, and the kind of foreign policy envisioned by Washington in his Farewell Address, the laissez-faire credo of the Old Right was founded on this reverence for "a revolution exemplary." Even as late as the midfifties, the idea of a conservative globalism seemed unthinkable, for this would cut out the very heart of the American conservative soul, the nationalism that was unlike any other. Unique in that it was founded neither in ancient folk dances, nor religion, nor ethnicity, but in an abstract and revolutionary idea inextricably bound up with the American character: the idea of liberty.

Garrett's *The American Story* was published in 1955. It was the last echo of what had once been a mass movement. By that time, the Old Right of Garrett, Senator Robert A. Taft, and John T. Flynn was no more. In its place rose what came to be called the "New" Right, the birth of which can be traced to the founding of *National Review* in 1955. Like the Old Right, it was a coalition of many components, but with one essential difference: the center of gravity was radically shifted. In place of the Old Right's American exceptionalism, derided by the New Rightists as outdated "isolationism," there was the new anticommunist messianism. The onset of the Cold War dictated a new conservative movement that was willing to endorse and lead a global crusade on the scale of the one just concluded.

What gave the New Right its peculiar coloration was that the first recruits to this movement came from the ranks of the disaffected Left. As John Judis notes in his biography of William F. Buckley Jr.,

National Review's masthead was heavily weighted with former left-ists preoccupied with fighting communism. Besides [James] Burnham, [Wilmoore] Kendall, and [Willi] Schlamm, the contributors included Max Eastman, Morrie Ryskind, Ralph de Toledano and former Communists Frank Meyer, Freda Utley, and Eugene Lyons.[3]

This was the first of three invasions from the Left, loosely grouped along generational lines, that would eventually detach the conservative movement from its moorings in American political culture and transform it into something unrecognizable—something which closely resembled that heretofore impossible creature, the globalist of the Right.

The irony is that, at the very moment conservatives declared their intention to launch a worldwide crusade against the menace of Marxism, this same European virus had worked its way through the crusader's armor and into the bloodstream of the conservative movement.

The New Right reflected its origins; it was an inverted mirror image of the faith that these renegades had rejected and now hated with the special venom of the disillusioned. The ex-Communist recruits to conservatism waged their battle with all the ferocity they had once invested in their fight against a "decadent" and "exploitive" capitalism. Their war of retribution consumed them and dominated the movement with which they now found themselves aligned.

The results were catastrophic for the future of conservatism, for the content of their ideology had indeed changed, but not, in many cases, its *form*. Their outlook remained universalist and globalist, imprinted with the European mind-set that could not imagine or allow the limits of power. This new conservatism was hostile to the idea of an American exceptionalism that claimed immunity to the disease that had decimated Eastern Europe and was threatening Asia. According to the New Right, no nation could be immune to the Communist menace; what was required was not complacence, or "isolationism," but a war to the death—a total war in which we dared not hesitate to use the same methods employed by the Communists. In this way, the war against totalism itself took on the characteristics of a totalist creed.

The exemplar of this obsession was James Burnham, the ex-Trotskyist professor and author of *The Managerial Revolution, The Machiavellians, The Suicide of the West,* and other books, whose ideas came to exert such a decisive influence on the New Right. Burnham's contribution to Cold War conservative ideology consisted of its central thesis: that the Manichaean struggle between communism and the West should take precedence over everything, even liberty. In his view, the Third World War had already begun and the U.S. was losing. The only thing to be done, therefore, was to immediately reorient U.S. policy along the lines of a concerted and merciless counterattack. Having given up Marx for Machiavelli, he was not overly concerned with the effects of this monomania on the American republic or on the conservative psyche.

If Burnham represented the first wave of disaffected Marxist intellectuals who jumped ship on the eve of World War II and wound up dominating the postwar conservative movement, then the second wave came in the late sixties and early seventies—and again a war was the catalyst. Just as the outbreak of World War II led Burnham and others to a reappraisal of basic principles, so the Vietnam War and the cultural revolution of the sixties led to another influx of ex-leftist recruits into the conservative coalition.

Repulsed by the New Left and motivated in large part by the desire to be nearer to power, a group of disgruntled liberals centered around Norman Podhoretz's *Commentary* magazine and Irving Kristol's *The Public Interest* began to attack the "adversary culture" of the Left and to seek an alliance with conservatives. Here was a new generation of the disillusioned: liberals and assorted Social Democrats, who had often been radical leftists in their youth, finding that they had more in common with *National Review* than with *Ramparts*. A heterogeneous crowd to be sure, ranging from self-proclaimed neoconservative Irving Kristol to the ostensibly "socialist" followers of Max Shachtman in Social Democrats, USA, the extreme right-wing of the Socialist International. The only constants in this diverse constellation appeared to be a militant anti-Stalinism, and an abiding interest in raising up the common man and in fostering "democracy."

Propelled by the Vietnam War and the nihilism of the ultra-Left, this small but well-positioned clique of intellectuals eventually found itself in the conservative camp. There ensconced, they developed a theory of government which owes much to James Burnham's theory of the managerial revolution. Like Burnham, the neoconservatives posited the rise of a new class that was neither capitalist nor socialist, but a new supranational elite based on the rule of bureaucrats, administrators, lawyers, politicians, and the professional class, who would manage if not own outright the means of production. Socialism had failed, but the laissez-faire capitalism of an earlier era was finished as well.

Having long ago given up their faith in socialism, the neoconservatives yet retained a residual distaste for capitalism. The title of a collection of Kristol's essays, *Three Cheers for Capitalism*, sums up their view of the free market. Instead of untrammeled free enterprise, the neoconservatives stand for a modified capitalism which allows for a significant degree of government intervention.

However much Kristol, Nathan Glazer, Daniel Patrick Moynihan, and others attacked the failure of the Great Society, it was the takeover of the Democratic Party by the "left-isolationist" McGovernites that really animated the neoconservatives. However much they differed among themselves as to what degree of government intervention in society was permissible or desirable, one thing was constant: a hard-line anticommunism with a globalist perspective.

This second infusion of fresh recruits from the Left soon coalesced into a political tendency in its own right. By the eighties the neoconservatives enjoyed wide influence among the core institutions of the conservative movement. Since the collapse of the Scoop Jackson wing of the Democratic Party, most neocons had, by default, wound up in the GOP. By the end of the decade they established themselves as the brain trust of the so-called "Big Government conservatives."

Their brand of conservatism, or "democratic capitalism" as they call it, rejects laissez-faire and would retain the "reforms" of the New Deal almost wholly intact. Far from abolishing the welfare state, the neocons want to take it over and use it to "empower" people, employing conservative means to achieve liberal ends. The fact that ostensibly conservative politicians such as Jack Kemp are now beginning to echo this New Age psychobabble is clear evidence that the political culture, and especially the language of politics, is thoroughly corrupted. Today's "mainstream" conservatives are no longer talking about the proper *limits* of power, but only of the best and most efficient way for government to *empower* its citizens: that is, to invest them with all the newly minted "civil rights" which they have recently acquired—the "right" to housing, medical care, education, and jobs, plus the democratic right to vote the nation into penury. Whereas once the Right would have scoffed at such a weird conception, today it is applauded by some alleged conservatives. This is a sad commentary on a defeated, degenerated, and thoroughly Europeanized conservative movement, domesticated by power and finally neutralized by a Fabian incursion from the Left.

There has been no equivalent of Marxist ideology on the Right, no overarching system that defined the commonality of American conservatism; and this is even truer today, with the end of the Cold War and the dissolution of the old conservative consensus. The lack of any such ideology has been one of the chief complaints of the neoconservatives, and the subject of a debate between Russell Kirk and Irving Kristol some years ago at a Heritage Foundation seminar. According to Kirk, Kristol

> and various of his colleagues wish to persuade us to adopt an ideology of our own to set against Marxist and other totalist ideologies. Ideology, I venture to remind you, is political fanaticism: at best it is the substitution of slogans for real political thought. Ideology animates, in George Orwell's phrase, "the streamlined men who think in slogans and talk in bullets."[4]

In Kirk's view, "all ideologies are anti-religions, or inverted religions"; the very concept of ideology is blasphemous and dangerous. It is blasphemous because, as Dr. Gerhart Niemeyer put it, "All these presume that man could create himself, implying that he is not a creature, dependent on God, but the master of his own soul and destiny." It is dangerous because a belief in the perfectibility of man is often married to the idea that the State must do the perfecting.

The traditionalist antipathy to ideology put the neoconservatives in an excellent position. It gave them the intellectual advantage of a positive program as against the aloof mysticism of a few, like Kirk, that could only appeal to a few rarefied souls. Having surrendered the vital realm of ideology to various and sundry ex-Leninists, what was left of the old conservative movement slowly faded out of the picture.

While the conservative mainstream was content to meander along in the old way, the neocons were incubating the third generation of their little band in the think tanks, magazines, and activist organizations of the Right. This third wave seeks to finally replace what they regard as the nativist mythology of American exceptionalism with a new conservatism, one that is mildly statist, fulsomely "democratic," and aggressively globalist—with emphasis on this last. The battle cry of these ideologues is "global democracy." Some, like Francis Fukuyama, proclaim the "end of history" and the inevitable triumph of Western liberalism. Others, like Joshua Muravchik, want to help the end of history along a bit and urge the U.S. government to launch a campaign to "export democracy." Thus the seeds of a new universalism, a new totalism, are even now growing in the ashes of the old, sprouting in the core institutions of the conservative movement.

The co-optation and corruption of the Right means that the American political dialogue is now decisively tilted in favor of statism. For if conservatives are committed to a globalism that sets no limits on the exercise of power, either at home or abroad, then the dialogue becomes a monologue. In that case, the American character cannot save the republic—nothing can.

Yet there are hopeful signs. When the Berlin Wall fell, it sent a seismic shock clear across the Atlantic. From one end of the American political spectrum to the other, old assumptions were shaken and old orthodoxies crumbled. Certainly the death of communism has had a devastating effect on the Left, on the domestic scene as well as abroad. Except for American academics and the "Soyuz" group in the Russian Parliament, no one is a Marxist-Leninist anymore. Yet it isn't only or even chiefly on the Left that the collapse of communism has wreaked devastation. The Right is today embroiled in an internecine struggle every bit as vicious as the ancient blood feuds coming to the surface in the postcommunist Balkans. The Cold War consensus, which once cemented the various conservative constituencies into a united front against communism, is finished, and all the old divisions and antagonisms have suddenly reasserted themselves. The American Right has been shaken to its very foundations, and conservatives are split into rival factions based on polar opposite reactions to the sudden absence of an overwhelming external threat.

The challenge to the neocons comes from rebels who call themselves paleoconservatives. The prefix *paleo* is derived from the Greek word *palaio*, which means ancient. As Llewellyn H. Rockwell Jr., president of the Ludwig von Mises Institute, a leader in this new movement, put it, the rebel paleocons are

> cultural traditionalists who reject the egalitarian movements that have wielded their way through America. They share the Founding Fathers' distrust of standing armies, look to the original American foreign policy of isolationism as a guide to the post–cold war era, and see the welfare state as a moral and Constitutional monstrosity.[5]

The paleoconservative response to the Kremlin's downfall, like that of most Americans, was a sense of overwhelming relief. They genuinely looked forward to postcommunist quiescence, and when George Bush rallied the country to the cause of the "New World Order" and against the alleged threat posed by Saddam Hussein, they dissented—and not so politely.

The neoconservatives have responded to the death agony of communism quite differently. They are thrilled by the sight of their old enemies, the Stalinists, tossed on the dustbin of history—and, at the same time, the sight of it makes them distinctly uneasy. Unlike their paleo distant cousins, they saluted when Bush raised the banner of the New World Order. They jumped at the chance of embarking on an open-ended quest to make the world orderly, safe, and even democratic; indeed, they were more royalist than the king before, during, and after the war against Iraq, urging Bush to strike as soon as Saddam invaded Kuwait and lamenting the fact that Stormin' Norman did not march all the way to Baghdad. They feel the lack of some overwhelming danger, some Satan with a sword, and look for new enemies, new crusades, new reasons to pour billions and blood into building an American Empire on which the sun never sets.

Now that totalitarian socialism is dead, will conservatives return to their roots as the great defenders and preservers of the unique American character or will they chase the will-o-the-wisp of global democracy and a "New World Order"? How this debate is resolved will be determined by how conservatives answer the question asked at the beginning of this chapter: What went wrong with the conservative movement? How is it that, after a decade of Reaganism, big government is not only undiminished but growing faster than ever before?

The temptation is to look for some variable, such as certain personnel decisions, bad advisors, or the personality of Ronald Reagan, which could explain the failure of conservatives to achieve their political goals. There is no evidence that Reagan was hostile to those goals, although some of his appointments displeased conservative activists. Many of his advisors in later years were chosen from the ranks of the Eastern Liberal Republican Establishment. Yet the question remains: how did these advisors infiltrate the most conservative administration in recent memory? There was only one way to do it: by burrowing into the conservative movement itself. The problem, then, predates Reaganism. The answer to our question is not to be found in the history of the Reagan administration, but earlier in the history of the conservative movement in America.

This book examines that history from a new perspective and presents a radical new thesis: that conservatism failed because a Trojan horse inside the movement has been undermining the fight against big government. Since the midfifties, for over forty years, these interlopers have acted as a Fifth Column on the Right—conciliating the welfare state, smearing their Old Right predecessors, and burying the real story of how they came to claim the mantle of conservatism.

Two traditions stand head-to-head, contending for the future of the conservative movement. One piously holds out the promise of enterprise zones from South Central Los Angeles to Mogadishu, while the other dares utter the forbidden phrase, *America first!* It is an old argument, using language that seems to echo the past.

The America First Committee, main opponent of U.S. entry into World War II, was dissolved on December 11, 1941, more than half a century ago. Smeared, subjected to government repression, and ultimately defeated, the America Firsters are mentioned in passing in American history textbooks, if at all, as either crankish obstructionists or outright Nazi sympathizers. Now the same forbidden phrase is heard once more in the land and the smearmongers are at it again—recycling old libels and raving that some tinpot Third World dictator is the reincarnation of Adolf Hitler.

Today's paleoconservatives are the continuators of the America First wing of the conservative movement, which has a long and distinguished history. They can count among their intellectual ancestors such towering (and, in some cases, half-forgotten) figures as Garet Garrett, Senator Robert A. Taft, John T. Flynn, Frank Chodorov, and Rose Wilder Lane. These names mean little or nothing to modern conservatives, who have lost touch with their heritage. As a new generation of conservative theorists and activists yearns to get back to first principles and to get in touch with its roots, blasting through the historical blackout on this subject is an all-important task, and the main purpose of this book.

Another subordinate but related purpose, equally important in understanding what went wrong with the conservative movement, is an examination of the history of the small but influential sect of neoconservatives. Although a few articles and books have been written on this subject, the history of the neoconservatives, like that of the Old Right, is also not generally known. If the prehistory of the paleos can be traced back to the Old Right and the period preceding World War II, then the origin of the neoconservatives is to be found in that same period, the so-called Red Decade of the thirties. The difference is that the neocons' antecedents are to be found on the far left, in the movement of Marxist dissidents founded by the American followers of Leon Trotsky.

The history of the modern conservative movement in America is really the history of two movements. The Old Right, the original Right, was nationalist, populist, and fundamentally libertarian. The Cold War

Right, dominated in large part by ex-leftist converts to conservatism, was militantly internationalist, increasingly elitist, and largely indifferent to free-market economics—indifferent, indeed, to virtually everything but the crusade against communism.[6] Starting out at opposite ends of the political spectrum, these two movements eventually came to meet and merge. The end result of this long process, which began in the midfifties and was completed by the time the eighties rolled around, was the transformation and betrayal of the American Right. What was betrayed, and by whom, is the theme and substance of this book.

1

James Burnham:
From Trotsky to Machiavelli

> *In a lifetime of political writing, James Burnham [showed] only one fleeting bit of positive interest in individual liberty; and that was a call in* National Review *for the legalization of firecrackers!*
> —*Murray N. Rothbard,*
> The Betrayal of the American Right, 1970

THE INTELLECTUAL CRISIS OF SOCIALISM preceded the political and military collapse of the socialist bloc by more than fifty years. Ever since the 1917 Bolshevik Revolution, the Left has suffered numerous setbacks—the Moscow Trials, the Hungarian revolt, the revelations of Stalin's crimes—each one setting off a wave of defectors. Over the years, the intellectuals among them have coalesced into a potent ideological force. What characterizes this otherwise diverse fraternity is that, for the most part, they started out in the Third International and wound up in the camp of Ronald Reagan via the Fourth—the Fourth International, that is, stillborn rival to Stalin's Comintern, founded by Leon Trotsky after his expulsion from the Soviet Union. Trotsky's schismatic sect never achieved a mass following and went into decline after his assassination, in 1940, by a Stalinist agent. For a brief moment during the thirties, however, Trotskyism was a fad that swept through the radical intelligentsia of Manhattan and environs and corralled quite a few.[1]

By taking refuge in the doctrines of Trotsky, who taught that the Russian party had been taken over by a "bureaucratic caste," these leftist intellectuals could hold on to their core beliefs even as the Moscow trials were going on. The Revolution, said Trotsky, had been betrayed, and the only thing left to do was to build a new International, reclaim the banner of authentic communism, and overthrow the bureaucrats so that true socialism could be unleashed. The Trotskyites made a great show of denouncing the Stalinist terror, rightly claiming that hundreds of thousands went into Stalin's prisons and never came out. What they neglected to say was that Trotsky's policy, had he won, would have been no less bloodthirsty. The only difference was that he would have chosen different victims, and, perhaps, executed them at a more leisurely pace.

Those who still retained their faith in socialism, but were profoundly affected by the sight of the purges and the show trials, were naturally attracted to the Trotskyist movement. Trotsky's problem, however, was that while he insisted on the distinction between anti-Stalinism and anti-Sovietism, in practice these two were often blurred. In an important sense, the Fourth International became a kind of halfway house between communism and reconciliation with bourgeois society. A whole bevy of intellectuals in retreat from communism parked themselves in the Trotskyist organization for some months or years at a time. Long after abandoning Marxism and Socialism, these types retained their Stalinophobia. Their fixation intensified with the years, the one constant encompassing careers that started out in the Trotskyist youth group and ended up in the conservative movement.

Intellectual defectors from communism have always played a key role in the modern conservative movement. Up until the Great Revolution of 1989, there was always a spot on the right-wing lecture circuit for ex-Communists, who enthralled conservative audiences with lurid tales of internal subversion directed by Kremlin masterminds. Benjamin Gitlow, a top leader of the Communist Party from its founding, was one of the first to go that route, and was followed by many others, a great number of whom eventually found themselves on the staff of the *National Review.* Whittaker Chambers was one; Frank S. Meyer, the conservative polemicist and theoretician of "fusionism," was another. Freda Utley and Eugene Lyons, both ex-Communists, were also on the NR staff at its birth, along with ex-leftists Max Eastman and Ralph de Toledano. These, then, were the precursors of today's neoconservatives, who made careers out of destroying what they had once fought to build, and whose lifelong obsession colored the modern conservative movement in its formative years.

But there are some striking differences, as well as obvious similarities, between these disparate figures. The ex-Stalinists, who came directly into the anticommunist movement from the Kremlin-loyal Communist Party, such as Frank S. Meyer, for the most part became genuine conservatives, even if of an idiosyncratic sort. Meyer, once a top Communist official, was the progenitor of the old "fusionist" school of conservative thought, which sought to fuse the best features of conservatism and libertarianism.

On the other hand, the great majority of those who came in from the anti-Stalinist Left, usually one sort of Trotskyist or another, were an altogether different breed. They retained more of their old allegiances and stubbornly resisted rejecting the central moral and political premises of collectivism. The conversion of the ex-Trotskyist intellectuals to the conservative cause was—with a single important exception—a long process extended over many years. Instead of jumping over to the other side of the political spectrum, this group of mostly New York–based intellectuals—such as Max Shachtman, who was one of the three original founders of the American Trotskyist movement—slowly worked themselves over from the Far Left, sidling up to the Social Democracy, then worming their way into the Democratic Party. By the time the sixties came around, Shachtman was supporting the Bay of Pigs invasion and the Vietnam War. His ex-comrades on the left contemptuously dismissed him as a "State Department socialist," but his commitment to socialism never truly dimmed, although it was radically modified.

The Trotskyist Phase

The key to understanding the motive power behind the Long March of the neoconservatives from one end of the political spectrum to the other is to be found in an obscure but pivotal event. On September 5, 1939, at a meeting of the National Committee of the Socialist Workers Party, the Trotskyist Party in the U.S., James Burnham and Max Shachtman began a factional struggle against Trotsky and the party leadership that was to end, less than a year later, in a split. This mini-event was set off by a big event, namely, the signing of the Hitler-Stalin Pact and the opening shots of World War II.

One the eve of the war, the American Trotskyists, considered somewhat fashionable up until that point, suddenly found themselves in a difficult position. Although they had always enjoyed the advantages of being considered "idealists," Communists who nevertheless could afford the luxury of denouncing the crimes of Stalin, there was a hitch with the Hitler-Stalin Pact: Trotsky stubbornly insisted that the Soviet Union must be defended, "against the Stalinists and in spite of the Stalinists."

As the Soviets, in league with the Nazis, attacked Poland, Finland, and gobbled up the Baltic states, being a Trotskyist was no longer so attractive. The intellectuals recruited in bulk at the height of the Moscow Trials defected in droves. Most notable and visible of these was James Burnham, a top Trotskyist leader and theoretician, who taught philosophy at New York University and was to become one of the most influential figures of the American Right, the great-grandfather of today's neoconservatives.

When Burnham, as a member of the Socialist Workers Party National Committee, rose to challenge Trotsky, he set off a factional explosion, the momentum of which eventually hurled him and his circle to the other end of the political spectrum. From Trotskyism to Reaganism is a long way to travel; the "Big Bang" that sent them on their way was World War II. "It is impossible to regard the Soviet Union as a workers' state in any sense whatever," declared Burnham at that fateful meeting. "Soviet intervention [in World War II] will be wholly subordinated to the general imperialist character of the conflict as a whole and will be in no sense a defense of the remains of the Soviet economy."

The orthodox Trotskyists, led by James P. Cannon and energetically supported by Trotsky, argued that the Fourth International had always defended the USSR against the threat of capitalist restoration, and they saw no reason to change course. The Soviet Union, though degenerated, was still a "workers' state": the "gains of October," though besmirched and endangered by the Stalinists, were still essentially intact and had to be defended.

Burnham had come into the Trotskyist movement via A. J. Muste's American Workers Party, which fused with the Trotskyist organization (then known as the Communist League of America) in December of 1934. As a leader of the AWP, Burnham was co-opted onto the National Committee of the new organization and absorbed into the Trotskyist movement. As a leading figure in the anti-Stalinist left, a respected intellectual who often graced the pages of *Partisan Review*, the avant-garde literary journal of modernist Marxism, Burnham was an important acquisition for the Trotskyists.

He was a loyal member of the Fourth International from 1934 until the winter of 1939–40, and in that time he rose to occupy an important place, especially in the New York organization. For five years, he went along with the twists and turns of the Trotskyist leadership, entering the Socialist Party in 1936, when the Trots conducted a factional "raid" on the party of Norman Thomas. Burnham then dutifully joined the SWP when it reconstituted under its own banner in 1937. He was willing to play ball with the Socialist Workers Party as long as it looked like Trotskyism might be the coming thing; that is, until the outbreak of World War II.

The irony is that, less than a year before, Burnham and Shachtman had coauthored an attack on former fellow-traveling intellectuals such as Sidney Hook, Eugene Lyons, and Max Eastman for the party theoretical magazine, *New International*, entitled "Intellectuals in Retreat," and foretelling their own apostasy with preternatural accuracy. The article ridiculed what it called the "League of Abandoned Hopes" as hopelessly flighty petit-bourgeois intellectuals, fly-by-night operators who had abandoned the USSR in its darkest hour. In describing the

Eastman-Lyons-Hook pattern, they foreshadowed their own. At first, the apostates denied their renegading by bringing up essentially peripheral arguments, such as the validity of dialectical materialism and abstract quibbles about "democracy" and "freedom"—which, of course, the authors dismissed out of hand. But all of this is irrelevant, said Burnham and Shachtman during their orthodox phase, because what it really came down to was the Soviet Union, the "Russian question." The "main intellectual disease from which these intellectuals suffer may be called Stalinophobia, or vulgar anti-Stalinism," they wrote. This affliction was generated "by the universal revulsion against Stalin's macabre system of frame-ups and purges. And the result has been less a product of cold social analysis than of mental shock; where there is analysis, it is moral rather than scientific and political."[2]

Nine months later came the shock of the Hitler-Stalin Pact. The two main currents of Socialism, National Socialism and International communism, merged into a military and political alliance, and suddenly the macabre specter of "Communazism" was looming over the rubble that was Europe. Under the impact of these events, Burnham and Shachtman took out a joint membership in what they had once mockingly referred to as the "League of Abandoned Hopes," with Burnham as chief theoretician and Shachtman as his attorney and chief factotum. They refused to defend the Soviet Union in this war or any other because, they said, it had degenerated into a phenomenon that had become indistinguishable from Hitlerism—into a new form of class society which they called "bureaucratic collectivism," competing with capitalism for control of the world.[3]

As the Red Army rolled into Poland, crushed the Baltics, and attacked neutral Finland, it was obvious to the Burnham-Shachtman group—about 40 percent of the SWP membership, including most of the intellectuals and virtually all of the youth—that the military alliance of the two totalitarian powers was more than just an alliance of convenience. A certain ideological affinity was at work here, and events gave new impetus to this perspective.

Up until the U.S. entry into the war, this view of the Soviet Union in left-wing circles had been confined to a few "ultra-lefts," the anarcho-syndicalists, the followers of the German theorist Karl Korsch, and the Italian Bordigists, who contended that the Soviet Union had reverted to capitalism. This theory had only a small following, and understandably so. As Stalin "liquidated" the kulaks and all vestiges of private property and liberalism, it was difficult to argue that capitalism was being reborn. However, the Shachtman-Burnham faction had come up with a new variation of the old "ultra-left" argument, which combined the Trotskyist theory of the Kremlin oligarchy as a caste of Stalinist Brahmins with Burnham's innovation: the bureaucracy, he claimed, represented a new class based not on private property but on collectivized property forms.

This challenge to party orthodoxy upset the orthodox Trotskyists and outraged Trotsky himself, who was sitting in his fortified compound in Coyoacán, Mexico, embattled and nearing the end of his long struggle to build the phantom "Fourth International." There had already been a few attempts on the old revolutionary's life, and soon a Stalinist agent provocateur would succeed where the others had failed. It was the last battle of Trotsky's life, and he attacked Burnham as if he knew it. In several open letters the old revolutionary declared his contempt for the bourgeois professor, who dared question the mystic dogma of dialectical materialism. "Educated witch-doctor" was among the more temperate epithets hurled from Coyoacán.

Nor did Burnham restrain himself. His answer to the founder of the Red Army, "Science and Style," marked his break with the Marxist movement.[4] In this article, he exhibited all of the symptoms of the "disease" he had warned readers of the party theoretical magazine against: disbelief in the dialectic and a "Stalinophobia" that equated the Soviet regime with Hitler's Germany. Although at the time he protested that "[i]t is false that we reject Marxian sociology," soon he would reject Marxism completely.

The Theory of the Managerial Revolution

A mere three months after penning "Science and Style," having just spoken from the platform of the new party he had helped to organize with Shachtman, Burnham dropped off his letter of resignation with the secretary at the Workers Party headquarters. "The faction fight in the Socialist Workers Party, its conclusion, and the recent formation of the Workers Party have been in my own case the unavoidable occasion for the review of my own theoretical and political beliefs," he wrote. "This review has shown me that by no stretching of terminology can I any longer regard myself, or permit others to regard me, as a Marxist." Marxism could no longer contain the limits of Burnham's evolving worldview. "Not only do I believe it is meaningless to say that 'socialism is inevitable' and false that socialism is 'the only alternative to capitalism'; I consider that on the basis of the evidence now available to us a new form of exploitive society (what I call 'managerial society') is not only possible as an alternative to capitalism but is a more probable outcome of the present period than socialism."[5]

This is the origin of the theme and title of Burnham's famous book, *The Managerial Revolution* (1941), in which he propounded his view that a new form of class society, spearheaded by a new elite, was virtually unstoppable. According to Burnham, the new ruling elite is made up of administrators, technicians, scientists, bureaucrats, and the myriad middlemen who have taken the means of production out of the hands of the capitalists. This bloodless coup occurred by virtue of the fact that the managers administer and therefore have come to control the production process. "In the earlier days of capitalism," we are told, "the typical capitalist, the ideal of ideologists before and after Adam Smith, was himself his own manager so far as there were managerial functions." But all this ended by "the growth of large-scale public corporations along with the technological development of modern industry," which has "virtually wiped such types of enterprise out of the important sections of the economy," except for marginal "'small businesses' which are trivial in their historical influence."[6]

Burnham's understanding of entrepreneurship and how markets develop, although somewhat improved after he became a conservative, never really went too far beyond this crude analysis. Perhaps we ought not to hold it against the author of *The Managerial Revolution* that he failed to foresee the influence of such companies as Apple Computer.

Yet his book is in fact a whole series of very specific predictions, most of which turned out to be wrong.

Burnham's essential insight—that the war would accelerate a world-wide statist trend in Europe and the United States—is a theme that ran through much political writing at the time. On the left, Bruno Rizzi and Rudolf Hilferding were forerunners of Burnham; but this analysis was not limited to dissident Trotskyists. The same theme was expressed on the prewar right by such writers as John T. Flynn, who, like Rizzi, compared the New Deal to German National Socialism and Italian Fascism.[7] In the case of Burnham, some essential error blurred his vision of the future, and so distorted his sense of reality that he felt confident enough to predict the victory of Hitlerism. Aside from a tendency to exaggerate everything, what blinded him was his understanding of politics as a "science," like physics or chemistry. This is the philosophical legacy of Marxist materialism, which Burnham never abandoned; he merely peeled off the Marxist veneer. What remained was the theory of "managerial society," which purported to be unconcerned about such trivialities as "whether the facts indicated by this theory are 'good' or 'bad,' just or unjust, desirable or undesirable—but simply [concerned] with whether the theory is true or false on the basis of the evidence now at our disposal."[8]

Appropriating the language of science, Burnham identified managerial society with modernity. The rise to power of the new managerial class, he maintained, was necessitated by objective developments, namely, the increasing complexity and scale of modern production and advancing technology.

Throughout this work, and in his future writings, Burnham assumed the Olympian detachment of the objective seeker after truth. "I am not writing a *program* of social reform, nor am I making any *moral* judgment whatever on the subject with which I am dealing." To hear him tell it, Burnham is concerned only to "elaborate a *descriptive* theory able to explain the character of the present period of social transition and to predict, at least in general, its outcome."[9]

Writing during the latter half of 1940, Burnham predicted the triumph of the Thousand Year Reich, the postponement of the Russian-

German confrontation until after Britain's inevitable defeat, and the imminent breakup of the Soviet Union. George Orwell, in his penetrating analysis of *The Managerial Revolution*, focused on the flaw in Burnham's method:

> [A]t each point Burnham is predicting *a continuation of anything that is happening.* Now the tendency to do this is not simply a bad habit, like inaccuracy or exaggeration, which one can simply correct by taking thought. It is a major mental disease, and its roots lie partly in cowardice and partly in the worship of power, which is not fully separable from cowardice.

In the cool tone of the dispassionate scientist, Professor Burnham described the efficiency of the Nazi form of managerialism in terms verging on admiration. "The Nazi success, year after year, can only be explained by the ever-increasing weakness of the capitalist structure of society." Out of the rotting remnants of decadent capitalism is born that harbinger of the managerial future, Nazi Germany. "Internally, Germany still remains in its early stage," wrote Burnham:

> However, it was impossible to complete the internal revolution without at once going over to the more grandiose external tasks of the managerial future. Excluding Russian from consideration here, Nazism has given Germany, we might say, a head start over the other great powers in getting ready for the managerial world system.[10]

In the winter of 1940, when it looked as if Hitler would almost certainly conquer the whole of Europe, Burnham portrayed the Nazis as the agents of progress, and even defended them against charges of decadence:

> There are many who call Nazi Germany decadent because its rulers lie a great deal, are treacherous, break treaties, exile, imprison, torture, and murder worthy human beings. . . . But it is not at all a fact that such actions are typical of decadence. . . . Indeed, if historical experience establishes any correlation in this matter, it is probably a negative one: that is, the young, new, rising social order

is, as against the old, more likely to resort on a large scale to lies, terror, persecution.[11]

Without once mentioning the doctrine of racialism throughout a long chapter on "The German Way," Burnham's ostensibly value-free description of Nazi managerialism is subverted by the undertone of adulation: "A rising social class and a new order of society have got to break through the old moral codes just as they must break through the old economic and political institutions. Naturally, from the point of view of the old, they are monsters. If they win, they take care in due time of manners and morals."[12]

Burnham's vision was anything but value free. As Orwell said, "Power worship blurs political judgment because it leads, almost unavoidably, to the belief that present trends will continue. Whoever is winning at the moment will always seem to be invincible." This certainly seems to be a recurring theme in Burnham's career. When collectivism of the Left looked as if it might be winning, he was a Leninist; when Hitler was the master of Europe, he was awed into reverence for managerialism, Aryan-style; when the United States stood astride the postwar world, with a monopoly on nuclear weapons, he called on the Americans to set up a world empire.

Certain that totalitarianism, leader worship, and a regime of unrelenting cruelty were the wave of the future, Burnham wrote that

> the [Allied] nations discover that they can compete in war with Germany only by going over more and more, not merely to the same military means that Germany uses, but to the same type of institutions and ideas that characterize German society. This somewhat ironic relations holds: the surest way, the only way, to defeat Germany would be for the opposing nations to go over, not merely to institutions and ideas similar to those of Germany, but still further along the managerial road than Germany has yet gone.[13]

While Burnham's prediction was that the immediate postwar world would be dominated by Germany, Japan, and the United States, this miscalculation did not alter the basic thrust of his theory: the world was witnessing the victory of a new managerial class which had already taken power in the Soviet Union and, after the war, would be triumphant in the U.S. as well. For the U.S., in the aftermath of World War II, *had* indeed moved in the direction of Germany, albeit not to the extent imagined—or implicitly urged—by the author of *The Managerial Revolution.*

Burnham did not mourn the alleged death of capitalism. He had nothing but contempt for the American businessman, whom he saw as a greedy, shortsighted creature, richly deserving of imminent extinction. Even in the act of proposing to mount an all-out struggle against their mortal enemies, the Communists, Burnham could not help but sneer at the American capitalists, who can only

> repeat the traditional capitalist symbolic ritual of "liberty," "free enterprise," "the American way," "opportunity," [and] "individual initiative." They repeat it sincerely, as their fathers repeated it before them. But the ritual has lost its meaning and its mass appeal. Before the centralizing, statizing power of the managerial revolution, the institutions of American society, the Constitution, the vision of the Founders, and the spirit of 1776 are swept away like so much litter.[14]

Burnham's power-worshipping mentality is epitomized in his subsequent book, *The Machiavellians: In Defense of Freedom.*[15] "In *The Managerial Revolution,*" writes Burnham, "I tried to summarize the general character of the revolution. I did so . . . primarily in institutional, especially in economic terms. I propose here to redefine the nature of the revolution through the use of the Machiavellian principles."[16]

In spite of its title, *The Machiavellians* indicates a softening of Burnham's position. While still heralding the implacable march into the managerial future, the author stopped to at least examine the fact that such a development bodes ill for human freedom. He admits that "it would be absurd to deny" how much advancing managerialism "darkens the prospects of freedom for our time. Nevertheless, I am not yet convinced that they are sufficient to make freedom impossible." Besides, we are told, "Freedom does require that all economic power should not be centralized, but there are other means than capitalist property rights to prevent such centralization." Despite this minor modification, the essential contours of the theory of the managerial society remain intact. In *The Machiavellians*, Burnham still projects a society that is neither socialist nor capitalist, and he attacks both the Marxists and the conservatives as purveyors of "myths that express, not movements for political liberty, but a contest for control over the despotic and Bonapartist political order which they both anticipate."[17]

Here he steps out of his role as mere chronicler of the inevitable to dispense advice to the new ruling elite:

> There would seem to be no theoretic reason why sections of the elite should not be scientific about political affairs. If our reference is to the governing elite, we are asking whether rulers can rule scientifically; and the answer would seem to be that, up to a certain point, they can.[18]

Instead of denying that "the primary real goal of every ruling group is the maintenance of its own power and privilege," a truly scientific elite would "recognize it frankly, and take appropriate steps to insure power and privilege."[19]

Burnham's sudden defection from Marxism, and his subsequent odyssey which led him to join the staff of the leading journal of the anticommunist Right, is not as inexplicable as it first appears. There is a continuity in his thought, a constant theme. Trotskyist communism posited a revolution betrayed and a parasitical ruling caste sprung from but also in conflict with collectivized property forms. Shachtman went a little farther down the same road and posed the question of whether the bureaucracy was in fact a new exploiting class; Burnham took the theory of bureaucratic collectivism still farther, positing a Machiavellian creed which denied all "utopias" and sought only to modify the behavior of the ruling managerial elite in a more "scientific" direction. Burnham's political trajectory, from revolution to reconciliation with the ruling class, in the space of less than five years, encapsulates the experience of a whole generation of ex-leftists, who moved rightward more slowly but steadily during the fifties and were finally driven out of the Left completely in the sixties. Burnham was the first neoconservative, and the purest in the sense of being the most explicit and consistent.

National Review *and the Anticommunist Crusade*

After his break with the Workers Party, Burnham lingered for a short while in the ranks of those anticommunist liberals who were associated with the Congress for Cultural Freedom and with the *Partisan Review* crowd. As long as he confined himself to a call for rolling back communism and outlawing the American Communist Party, he was considered extreme but still within the bounds of rational discourse. The split with liberals such as James T. Farrell, Dwight Macdonald, and Daniel Bell came over the issue of Joe McCarthy. Burnham did not openly come out for "Tail-Gunner Joe," but he attacked the Senator's leftist critics and defended the concept that governments have the right and even the duty to investigate internal subversion. In 1953, Burnham resigned from the American Committee for Cultural Freedom, the liberal anti-communist front financed largely by the CIA, declaring that while he was not a McCarthyite, nor was he an "anti-anti-McCarthyite." Sentiment against Burnham had been building in the ACCF for months, and he had been under attack by some members who criticized him for writing the introduction to a book that accused American scientists of relaying secret information to the Soviet Union. Burnham replied that his critics had

> failed so far to realize that they are, in political reality, in a united front with the Communists, in the broadest, most imposing united front that has ever been constructed in this country.[20]

Isolated from the intellectual circles in which he had formerly flourished, Burnham retired to his home in Kent, Connecticut, to write a book for the *Reader's Digest*, defending the congressional investigation into Communist activities. When William F. Buckley Jr. came to visit him in late 1954, Burnham welcomed the suggestion that he join the staff of a new conservative magazine. As senior editor at *National Review*, Burnham played a pivotal role, taking on a good deal of the day-to-day editorial tasks. For the next twenty-three years he was a decisive influence on what was to become the fountainhead of American conservatism.

In his *National Review* column, "The Third World War," Burnham turned his elegant, angular prose to the task of outlining an unrelenting but ruthlessly realistic strategy for meeting the Communist challenge. The title of his column is taken from the opening of his 1947 polemic, *The Struggle for the World*,[21] wherein he comes to grips with the errors of *The Managerial Revolution*, which were by that time quite glaring. The triumph of tripolar totalitarianism had been averted. Instead, the struggle for the world was reduced to two powers, the United States and the Soviet Union. The Third World War, as the logical outgrowth of the Second, had begun.

The Struggle for the World develops this contention into a full-blown justification for a U.S. world empire. Without mentioning his earlier prediction of a tripartite world of mega-states, Burnham presents two proposals for the postwar bipolar world: first, the merger of the United States and Great Britain, with the latter in a subordinate role, and second—incredibly—a preventive war against the Soviet Union.

The existence of nuclear weapons and the unique nature of the Communist enemy, he argued, made it imperative for the U.S. to use its nuclear monopoly to impose a "World Federation" on "at least enough of the world to dominate effectively the major questions of world politics." He freely admitted, however, that "[a] federation . . . in which the federated units are not equal, in which one of them leads all others, to however slight a degree and holds the decisive instrument of material power is in reality an empire." Naturally, the word "empire" will not be used, he says, but

> [t]he reality is that the only alternative to the communist World Empire is an American Empire which will be, if not literally worldwide in formal boundaries, capable of exercising decisive world control.

> Nothing less than this can be the positive, or offensive, phase of a
> rational United States policy.[22]

Before the clarion call for a "New World Order" was sounded in
1990 by a Republican president, there was Burnham's declaration that
the U.S., in 1946, had two choices: a "world imperial federation with
a monopoly of atomic weapons" or else another devastating world war
that might destroy both superpowers.

Conspiracy theorists of the Right have traditionally blamed the
Council on Foreign Relations for coming up with the expression "New
World Order," but in fact it was Burnham who, with unusual prescience,
first coined the phrase:

> It will be useful to give a name to the supreme policy which I
> have formulated. It is neither "imperial" nor "American" in any
> sense that would be ordinarily communicated by these words. The
> partial leadership, which it allots to the U.S., follows not from any
> nationalist bias but from the nature and possibilities of existing
> world power relationships. Because this policy is the only answer to
> the communist plan for a universal totalitarianism, because it is the
> only chance for preserving the measure of liberty that is possible for
> us in our Time of Troubles, and because it proposes the sole route
> now open toward a free world society, I shall henceforth refer to it
> as *the policy of democratic world order.*[23]

While Burnham's prediction that "a new war in the full sense,
and in a comparatively short time, is very probable," was wrong, his
insight that the United States might well embark on a quest for empire,
or world dominion, was uncannily accurate, right down to approximat-
ing the phrase employed by George Bush to describe the goal of U.S.
foreign policy.

True, it is not quite a *democratic* world order—certainly the emir
of Kuwait does not qualify as a democrat—but that would have bothered
Burnham as much as it apparently bothered the Bush administration.

Neither Capitalism nor Socialism

The globalist ideologues who today tell us that we must establish a Pax Americana, by force of arms if need be, owe a great debt to James Burnham, who was the first to openly advocate their program for the post–Cold War world. This debt was readily acknowledged by John O'Sullivan, the editor of *National Review*, who replaced Buckley in 1990. In a long paean to Burnham, published in the magazine's thirty-fifth anniversary issue, O'Sullivan was clearly looking for precedents for the new conservative globalism, searching for a theoretical peg on which to hang conservative support for the Iraq war, and hoping to find it in Burnham. "The best new world order we can reasonably hope for," declares O'Sullivan, at the end of his long, rambling essay,

> is that the U.S. . . . may be persuaded to go beyond a narrow interpretation of its national interest. . . . America's position in such a system would be similar to that of a medieval king in a feudal society: the sole sovereign with a recognized monopoly of force, but reliant for levies of both troops and money upon powerful barons. . . . Such a system would not be perfect, but, as Burnham himself might have said, it would certainly be an improvement on the totalitarian Dark Ages from which we have only just emerged.[24]

If this is the best new world order we can hope for, then perhaps we can do without. To compare the chief executive of the American Republic to a medieval king is bad enough; to add dependence on a council of foreign barons would be obscene if it weren't so absurd.

O'Sullivan's program of British-style imperialism has limited appeal to Americans, whatever their political coloration. If American conservatives were going to have the "New World Order" shoved down their throats, then the editor of *National Review* was determined to find some way to make it all go down smoothly. He had to discover some American precedent for a globalism of the Right, and certainly Burnham fit the bill.

O'Sullivan's attempt to resurrect Burnham's ghost, in defense of a globalist doctrine profoundly alien to American conservative thought, failed because Burnham, who believed neither in liberty nor transcendence, was no more a conservative than he was a Trotskyist, as anyone who skims through *The Managerial Revolution*, *The Machiavellians*, and even *The Struggle for the World*, and some of the later works will readily discover. Neither in his method, a crude form of mechanical materialism, nor in his politics, was James Burnham any sort of conservative, either traditionalist or libertarian. As one who would bring "science" to politics, he had no use for transcendence. As for liberty, Murray Rothbard put it well in his unpublished manuscript, *The Betrayal of the American Right*. Discussing the strong authoritarian trend at *National Review*, Rothbard writes,

> At the opposite pole from the Catholic ultras, but at one with them in being opposed to liberty and individualism, was James Burnham, who since the inception of *National Review* [was] its cold, hard-nosed, amoral political strategist and resident Machiavellian. . . .In a lifetime of political writing, James Burnham has shown only one fleeting bit of positive interest in individual liberty: and that was a call in *National Review* for the legalization of firecrackers![25]

Burnham's views were a constant source of conflict at *National Review*. In spite of the fact that the magazine had consistently mocked the policies of Dwight Eisenhower, in 1956 Burnham argued that NR ought to endorse him. In his biography of Buckley, John Judis quotes Neal Freeman as saying that in 1964, Burnham "had been subtly but persistently reminding the editorial board of the hidden virtues of Nelson Rockefeller."[26] In any conservative's book, the chapter entitled "The Hidden Virtues of Nelson Rockefeller" is going to be *very* short.

None of this seems to bother O'Sullivan, at least not much. Perhaps he assumes that most of his readers will not have read the books he cites, except perhaps for *The Suicide of the West*, a standard anticommunist tract. Still, there is always the danger that his more inquisitive readers may have stumbled across *The Managerial Revolution* or will be impelled to pick it up on his recommendation. Thus he is forced to downplay the importance of the book as bearing "the marks both of

Burnham's recent Marxism and of the period in which it was written." To say that a book bears the mark of the period in which it is written is to tell us nothing, for surely every book bears this mark. As for the effects of the author's cast-off Marxism, this would make sense if *The Managerial Revolution* stood in contrast to his later works. But in fact they are all of one piece: *The Machiavellians, The Struggle for the World, The Coming Defeat of Communism*, and the rest. All are suffused with a single theme, and that is the supremacy of power.

O'Sullivan even falsely states that "Burnham therefore explicitly retracted his predictions of a new world order in *The Managerial Revolution*." Far from retracting the conclusions reached in that seminal work, Burnham merely modified and refined them over the years, as his preface to the 1960 Midland Books edition makes eminently clear. In spite of what he called a tendency to be overly "schematic," too "rigid and doctrinaire," he stood by his basic thesis. While allowing for the possible retention of some capitalist property forms—though in a distinctly subordinate role—even at that late date he was able to write,

> Throughout the world, indeed, informed and thoughtful men have come to a double realization: first, that the capitalist era, in anything like the traditional meaning . . . is drawing to a close, or may even be regarded as finished; but second, that it is not to be replaced by socialism. . . . If these two negative facts are accepted, there then remains a double positive task: from a theoretical standpoint, to analyze the precise nature of this present historic transition . . . [and] from a human and practical standpoint, to act in such a way as to promote those variants of the new order that permit us that minimum of liberty and justice without which human society is degraded to merely animal existence.[27]

This was the essence of Burnham's view: if liberty were to exist at all, then it would have to be the bare minimum. In Burnham's malevolent universe, man's inevitable station in life is just a cut above slavery—and he had better learn to be grateful that he isn't totally at the mercy of his masters. In any case, Burnham assures us, the growth of state power is unavoidable, with the clear implication being that conservatives would be well-advised to abandon their futile efforts to stop it and focus their energies on the real threat posed by communism.

In *The Coming Defeat of Communism*, which was in effect a program for the implementation of the principles outlined in *The Struggle for the World*, Burnham bares his contempt for the American businessman.[28] Aside from being "ignorant, abysmally ignorant about what communism is," a condition none too surprising, this is the least of his sins. "Very many businessmen do not know the difference between a communist and an anarchist, democratic socialist, or mere eccentric dissident," scolds Burnham. "They pick up a pompous phrase like 'socialism is the half-way house to communism,' and imagine that by repeating it they are being profoundly philosophical."[29]

Defending Hubert Humphrey, the Reuther brothers, and labor leader John L. Lewis against the Right, Burnham turned his fire on the "greedy" capitalists, whose "monstrous incomes and profits have an antagonizing and demoralizing effect upon the workers, and the rest of the poorly or normally paid members of society, in this country and throughout the world. These income statistics are emotional explosives handed gratuitously to the communist propaganda machine." Another villain is the businessman who stupidly resists the trade union attempt to extort tribute. "Some of the businessmen, plain and simple reactionaries, are absolutely anti-union," lamented Burnham.[30]

This book, written over a decade after his formal break with Marxism, cannot be so easily dismissed as the remnants of a recently shed ideological skin. How easily these phrases—"greedy" capitalists, "monstrous incomes and profits"—could be lifted out of context and dropped onto the pages of some Trotskyist jeremiad! Although now a man of the Right, Burnham still spoke the language of egalitarianism, in which all profits beyond some ineluctable minimum are "monstrous." No plain and simple reactionary, Burnham had nothing but contempt for the crude and grasping American entrepreneur, who was apparently too dull to recognize his own best interests.

In his attitude toward business and the mysterious exigencies of the market, Burnham shared the general view held by most American intellectuals: it was all dreadfully vulgar and distasteful. This equation of commercialism with philistinism is deeply embedded in European political culture but alien to America. It was the intellectuals who imported this foreign affectation to our shores; certainly most if not all of the intellectuals who graced the pages of *Partisan Review* were imbued with it. In moving rightward, Burnham did not discard it but carried it with him into the conservative movement, where its echoes are to be found today in the calls emanating from the neoconservative camp for a "socially responsible" and "democratic" capitalism.

Hailing the rise of the new managerial classes—the engineers, soldiers, government bureaucrats, and other "professionals" whose status had been elevated by World War II—Burnham decided that he didn't really need the businessmen, especially if they insisted on opposing such political innovations as "the Reconstruction Finance Corporation, the Export-Import Bank, the International Bank for Reconstruction and Development, the Marshall Plan, the Securities and Exchange Commission, and the Federal Deposit Insurance Corporation"—in short, the whole structure of the welfare-warfare state built up by Roosevelt and extended by Truman. "I do not wish to imply that I think that all of these and of the other major changes of this period have been 'good.' But most of them have been almost inescapable adaptations to the quickly changing world in which we are living." In a footnote, he berates Wendell Wilkie for "having made his public reputation as the representative of Commonwealth & Southern in battling [the] TVA. I wonder how many stockholders of Commonwealth & Southern have reflected on the fact that their properties . . . are now paying dividends, and are immeasurably better off as a direct result of the area development brought about by TVA?"[31]

In Burnham's totalistic view, *everything* had to be subordinated to the fight against international communism: even capitalism itself. Capitalism was, at any rate, doomed, according to the theory of the managerial revolution, and hardly worth fighting for.

What, then, was the West supposed to be fighting for? In a word: *power.* Summing up the career of James Burnham, ideologue, which telescoped in many ways the progression of a whole generation of intellectuals from Left to Right, we can point to a single theme dominating all the phases of his evolution: the manipulation of power by an elite. Like most of the intellectuals of his generation, as Orwell pointed out, Burnham was fascinated by power and possessed by the desire to wield it. This is the leitmotif of his life's work.

O'Sullivan attempts to defend Burnham against Orwell's charges by citing a letter in which Orwell agrees that the trend is toward centralism and planning "whether we like it or not." Correctly explaining this by noting that both men were socialists, he writes that Orwell "remained a curious kind of cranky, unsystematic British socialist," while "Burnham evolved into a curious kind of American conservative." Curious indeed, as one examines the record of Burnham's written works, and certainly for the time. In our time this sort of conservatism is still curious, but no longer quite so unfamiliar. The seed planted by Burnham—and the other defectors from communism who were soon to follow him in droves—has sprouted and flourished to such an extent that it now threatens the delicate ecology of the conservative movement.

O'Sullivan presents us with a choice of Burnhamite visions: the three super-states of *The Managerial Revolution*, based on the three major trade blocs led by the U.S., Japan, and Germany; or else the U.S.-led World Empire of *The Struggle for the World*—with the former based on protectionism and the latter on free trade.

O'Sullivan does not reveal why it would be impossible to have a tripartite world based on relatively free trade—or what would prevent subsidies and trade barriers from distorting the economic structure of his U.S.-led World Empire. Surely our allied "barons" would demand something as the price of their allegiance. But all this is beside the point: O'Sullivan's argument is just a diversion from the emptiness at the core of the new Burnhamite dispensation. What he is evading is the answer to the question, *Why* should America take on the burden of empire, now that communism has collapsed, when the natural inclination of those who do not live in Washington, D.C., is to go back to their own affairs, back to economic matters and concern for community and family?

As the manifesto of post–Cold War conservatism, O'Sullivan's essay is fatally flawed. If Burnham is the best the "New World Order" conservatives can come up with, the sole or even the major precedent for a globalism of the Right, then the effort is doomed to failure. Burnham, although intimately connected with *National Review,* was always the outsider, a permanent guest in the house of the Right, who was barely able to tolerate what he no doubt considered the curiously archaic and even primeval customs of his conservative hosts.

Globalism of the Right

It is true, as O'Sullivan says, that James Burnham was prescient in many ways; his predictions concerning the internal weaknesses of the Soviet Union in *The Coming Defeat of Communism* were for the most part accurate. But, in an important sense, he missed the boat even in this area. While correctly pointing to the vital national question as the Achilles heel of the Soviet Union, and while citing endemic economic problems, Burnham did not believe that the masses of the Communist bloc, left to themselves, would ever revolt, or, if they did, that their struggle could be anything other than sporadic and ineffective.

Containment or Liberation, The Suicide of the West, and much of Burnham's published writings after *The Struggle for the World* were devoted to developing a vast and detailed plan, coordinated on a world scale, to eradicate the Communist menace. In every sphere of social and political activity, from the labor unions to the cultural front, Burnham urged the U.S. government to organize the cadres of the counterrevolution into a kind of Anticomintern, devoted to spreading the doctrine of the "democratic world order" by word and deed. This huge apparatus, supported not only by tax dollars but by U.S. military might, would have a fighting chance to defeat the enemy, but only if U.S. policymakers recognized the nature of the threat and immediately acted to meet it.

The vast apparatus of official anticommunism, the creation and expansion of which Burnham spent much of his life urging, has outlived its adversary. Today, although this giant machine is dormant, it is not demobilized. The Voice of America, the National Endowment for Democracy, and the like live on. This is due to the fact that these bureaucracies, like all such agencies, are not without their constituencies, the special interest groups that lobby on their behalf and save them, year after year, from the budget-cutter's axe.

Now the very existence of the "pro-democracy" bureaucracy is being called into question. After all, if there is no enemy, then the war is over—right? Wrong, say the neoconservatives. Instead of dismantling the network of political apparatchiks that waged the Cold War on the ideological front, we ought to greatly expand it *precisely because* we find ourselves, as Charles Krauthammer puts it, at the "unipolar moment." With no enemy and therefore no obstacle in our path, now is the time to act before that moment passes. The post–Cold War world, they argue, is the perfect opportunity for the U.S. to make its bid for empire.

It is the old Burnhamite idea of a "democratic world order," revived and refurbished—but with a new twist. The neocon credo of "exporting democracy" is Burnhamism minus the scenery, i.e., minus the threat of implacable communism looming in the background. What is left is the fascination with power and Burnham's original vision of a managerial elite in the saddle on a world scale.

Certainly most Americans would scoff at the idea of an American Empire and remain unmoved at the prospect of a "New World Order." But the neocons think they have figured out a way around this. As Burnham predicted, these would-be Caesars do not openly call for an empire; only the haughty Krauthammer dares to name what he is advocating. Instead, in what is the ultimate irony, they pose as champions of "democracy." Rather than seeking to build an empire, which the American people would not long tolerate, the advocates of the new globalism claim to be "exporting democracy." This is the new myth in the name of which the world-savers and would-be world planners empty our wallets and fill their coffers; the new rationale for the existence of countless think tanks and the cushy jobs that go with them; the latest code word for a frankly imperial policy, unrestrained by either modesty or common sense.

The proper goal of U.S. foreign policy is not to protect and defend the people of this country, say the democratists; it is to extend our system to the rest of the globe. It is a temptation that will be the undoing of the

American republic. Such a policy would have to mean constant wars, an attendant confiscatory taxation, and political and economic centralization. In addition, what greater threat to our form of government exists than the clandestine machinations of American intelligence agencies engaged in political intrigues, all carried out under the shroud of official secrecy? Yet Burnham and his league of embittered ex-Leninists flourished in the atmosphere of secrecy and conspiracy with which the CIA cloaked its activities. Indeed, Burnham worked as a consultant for the CIA. He was a founder and leading light of the CIA-financed International Congress for Cultural Freedom and its U.S. affiliate, the American Congress for Cultural Freedom, which provided a base for so many liberal anticommunists during the fifties.

This affiliation is the organizational link between two generations of leftist intellectuals moving rapidly rightward. Many of today's neo-conservatives were yesterday's liberal anticommunists who, unwittingly or not, played the CIA's game. But this allegiance, while not irrelevant, is potentially misleading. For in the end it is ideology that connects the generations, a common origin in the same troublesome brand of schismatic Trotskyism that blew apart the Socialist Workers Party on the eve of World War II and enjoyed an independent existence longer after that event.

It is therefore instructive for those who would understand what is happening to the conservative movement to examine the history of the anti-Stalinist Left. Before we can begin to see how and why the original ideology and goals of the American Right have become corrupted, it is necessary to examine the roots of that corruption in a strain of leftist ideology that seems to carry within itself some mutating power, some crucial gene that transformed a generation of American intellectuals, and may yet succeed in rendering the conservative movement unrecognizable.

2

Max Shachtman: Journey to the West

> I will support American imperialism when hair grows on
> the palm of my hand!
> —Max Shachtman, 1940, some thirty years
> before supporting Richard Nixon
> and the Vietnam War on "Marxist" grounds

MORE THAN ANY OTHER SINGLE figure on the anti-Stalinist
Left, Max Shachtman represents the evolution of a generation of revolutionary Marxist intellectuals into the most implacable
foes of the Soviet Union. His political career, after the break with
Trotsky and Burnham's sudden defection, was a long, tortuous zigzag
away from Marxism, a twenty-year journey to the West.

Max Shachtman was born on September 10, 1904, in Czarist
Russia, shortly before his family emigrated to the U.S. He grew up in
a socialist household; his father was active in the tailors union and a
supporter of the Socialist Party. Young Max developed an interest in
Marxism at the age of sixteen, when he enrolled at the City College of
New York. He soon lost interest in college, however, and dropped out
to join the revolutionary movement.

But it wasn't as easy as that. Those were the underground days of
the Communist Party, when Communists lived in fear of arrest and no
stranger could easily penetrate its defenses. He tried to make contact
with the party by going to the left-wing public meetings in Central Park,

but without success. Young Shachtman had to settle for the Workers Council, a CP front set up to persuade the Socialist Party to join the Third International. This group, nominally independent of the CP, soon gave up the pretense of a separate existence, and Shachtman was finally admitted to the Communist Party. At the age of nineteen, he worked for the party's youth group in Chicago, where he helped put out the CP's youth paper, *Young Worker*. He was a dedicated party man, living on a subsistence salary, ready and willing to take on any task the party might assign—such as in 1923, when he acted as a courier for Moscow's gold, carrying funds for the party youth group directly from Moscow on his way back from the Fifth Plenum of the Communist International.[1] Returning to New York, he was assigned to the International Labor Defense as editor of the *Labor Defender*, where he worked in close association with James P. Cannon.

In 1928, when Cannon returned from the Sixth Congress of the Comintern, he had in his hands a document by Trotsky containing the apostate's criticisms of the Stalinists. Trotsky had by this time already been drummed out of the Russian Party and was living in exile in Alma Alta. But somehow this document, Trotsky's criticism of the Stalinist draft program, had been translated into English and distributed to the Comintern delegates through a bureaucratic mix-up. Cannon read it, was instantly converted to Trotskyism, and managed to smuggle the document back to the States, where he began to recruit a Trotskyist faction inside the American Communist Party. This had to be done in secret, of course: at that point, the campaign against the "Trotskyite wreckers" had been going on for years and Trotskyism was a crime punishable by immediate expulsion. Shachtman and Martin Abern were Cannon's first converts. Even as Trotsky was going down to defeat in the Soviet Union and thousands of Oppositionists were being rounded up and sent to slave-labor camps, these three determined to raise the banner of the Left Opposition in the United States.

Proceeding with caution, they circulated Trotsky's document to likely prospects one at a time, because they didn't have a mimeograph machine and they couldn't afford to have it typed up. And they had to be very careful, so as not to arouse any suspicion. One by one they recruited new initiates, until, through some indiscretion on the part of one of the comrades, they were found out.

Founders of American Trotskyism:
Three Generals without an Army

Brought up on charges before the Political Committee, the three of them, Shachtman, Cannon, and Abern, were expelled on October 27, 1928. But they had expected it, and a week later they came out with the first issue of their Trotskyist newspaper, *The Militant*.[2]

The Stalinists contemptuously called them the "Three Generals Without An Army," a phrase that captures their almost complete isolation. Arrayed against them was the entire apparatus of the Communist International—the American section of which controlled five daily newspapers, dozens of magazines, and a score of labor unions. The heresy of the "renegade Trotskyites" was continuously denounced, while the CP effectively sealed off its members from the heretics. Those associating with the Trotskyists were immediately expelled; resolutions were introduced condemning Cannon, Shachtman, and Abern in all party cells. Those who voted against it or even asked questions were also kicked out. Trotskyist meetings were visited and broken up by gangs of Stalinist hooligans.

Totally cut off from the party that had been their world, the "Three Generals Without an Army" gathered a small group around them. They soon ran into a brick wall. In the Soviet Union, Stalin was carrying out his "left turn," collectivizing the land, "liquidating" the kulaks, launching an industrialization program, and generally doing all the things the Trotskyists had been urging.

By this time, Trotsky had been exiled from the Soviet Union and sent to the Turkish island of Prinkipo, where he got in touch with his American co-thinkers. Shachtman came to visit him, and thus began a political collaboration which was to last until the outbreak of World War II. When Trotsky arrived in Tampico, Mexico, on January 9, 1937, Shachtman was there to greet him and his wife Natalya. Shachtman's book, *Behind the Moscow Trials*, was one of the earliest voices raised on the left against Stalin's terror.[3] In 1938, he chaired the founding Congress of the Fourth International, held in Paris.

Shachtman was the pyrotechnical orator and theoretician of the American Trotskyist movement. He had a facility for argument, an almost uncanny ability to defend one position with references to the Marxist classics, and then turn around and take the opposite view, footnoting it with different quotations. His slashing wit, occasionally off-color, could be a formidable political weapon. In 1934, as the Trotskyists (then known as the Communist League of America) were merging with A. J. Muste's American Workers Party, Shachtman debated CLA member Tom Stamm over the right approach to take to their new comrades-in-arms, the AWPers. At the time, an ultra-left faction supported by Stamm was determined to immediately undertake a "Bolshevization" program, while Shachtman and Cannon urged a more reasonable approach. As Alan Wald relates, Shachtman compared the new party to

> "a baby that has to be nursed." "Yes," Stamm replied, "but nursed at the left breast of revolutionary Marxism and not at the right breast of conciliationism and centrism." To this Shachtman retorted that he certainly favored nursing at the proper breast, "but at a breast and not at an organ of the body that's designed for other functions."[4]

Trotsky had a great affection for Shachtman, considered him brilliant, if a bit on the flighty side, and was saddened by the fact that his favorite American disciple deserted him as war clouds loomed. In a letter to Shachtman, Trotsky wrote,

> If I had the possibility I would immediately take an airplane to New York in order to discuss with you for 48 or 72 hours uninterruptedly. I regret very much that you don't feel in this situation the need to come here to discuss the questions with me. Or do you? I should be happy.[5]

Neither East Nor West: The Theory of the Third Camp

Alas, Shachtman did not feel the need, or, at least, not enough to make the trip. Less than a year later, Trotsky was dead and Shachtman had begun the next phase of his remarkable evolution, that of the leading figure on the American anti-Stalinist left. After Burnham's resignation from the Workers Party, Shachtman's only competition for the title was James P. Cannon, the guardian of Trotskyist orthodoxy. But Cannon was an organization man, definitely not an intellectual, who had derided the Burnham-Shachtman group as a bunch of petit-bourgeois dilettantes who did not dirty their hands with the gritty realities of the class struggle. The Cannonites gathered almost no support from the group of anti-Stalinist New York-based intellectuals who had been attracted to Trotskyism and independent Marxist politics before the war. On the other hand, Shachtman brought under the wing of the Workers Party virtually an entire generation of Manhattan-based leftist writers and academics. What it lacked in numbers, the Workers Party more than made up for in sheer intellectual firepower. The roster of Shachtmanites who later rose to prominence reads like a roll call of leading literary and academic luminaries: Irving Kristol, Gertrude Himmelfarb, Seymour Martin Lipset, Martin Diamond, Irving Howe, Michael Harrington, James T. Farrell; the list goes on.

Although the Workers Party started out with a relatively free internal life, full of vigorous debate, the Leninist theory of organization, which Shachtman still paid fealty to, led inevitably to splits over virtually every disagreement. During the forties there was a series of expulsions and defections, all of them to the Right. Shachtman pronounced anathemas on them, one after another, in thick internal bulletins; and yet he slowly moved in the same direction himself, without acknowledging (at least in print) the change in his views.

The first to go were the "Shermanites," the followers of one Philip Selznick. In those days they had the charmingly archaic custom of taking party names, so that Selznick was known as Sherman. He had joined the Socialist Party youth group at CCNY when it came out in favor of Trotskyism, and sided with Shachtman and Burnham in the dispute with Cannon. Sherman held a few private meetings with the defector Burnham and then organized a faction inside the Workers Party, which described itself as "revolutionary anti-Bolshevik" and looked to the Socialist Party as a vehicle for accomplishing a "social overturn." The editor of the official Shermanite organ, *Enquiry*, was Irving Kristol, later to become the most visible of the neoconservatives. Other prominent Shermanites included Kristol's wife and comrade, Gertrude Himmelfarb, Lipset, Diamond, and Jeremiah Kaplan, found of the Free Press. Insisting on their revolutionary credentials, the Shermanites' worldview was summed up by Alan Wald as a "revolutionary outlook . . . coupled with a thoroughgoing concern for the maintenance and extension of the practices and institutions of democracy." In the pages of *Enquiry*, Kristol excoriated Sidney Hook's prewar stance, and the editors denounced "political support for the present war, organized by reactionary forces and deepening the totalitarian trend."[6]

The Shermanites went into the Socialist Party, whereupon the founding cadres went on to build careers in academia and the world of letters. Sherman, by this time having reverted back to Selznick, abandoned his "revolutionary anti-Bolshevik" theories and became a Cold War liberal. In 1952, the Rand Corporation published Selznick's *The Organizational Weapon: A Study of Bolshevik Strategy and Tactics*. As to the subsequent political evolution of the other Shermanites, much more will be said, but first let us follow the story of Max Shachtman to the very end. For it enacts, in slow motion, the very same intellectual odyssey on which the Shermanites, whom he once denounced as "weaklings," had embarked.

In 1949, the Workers Party changed its name to the Independent Socialist League (ISL), and this coincided with the further development of Shachtman's theory of bureaucratic collectivism. The Soviet bureaucracy had become more than just a new exploiting class. In Shachtman's view, Stalinism had become the barbarism predicted by Trotsky if World War II should fail to topple the Soviet bureaucrats and open the way to true socialism. The spectacle of Stalinism triumphant in Eastern Europe and spreading its tentacles into Asia and Africa was, for Shachtman, a development that necessitated a new course: an alliance with the West against the Stalinist menace. By the fifties, it was clear that the "Third Camp" position upheld by the Shachtmanites was completely untenable; there was no force that could or would interpose itself between East and West, no third alternative to the totalitarian brutality of the Kremlin except the imperfect but democratic United States. This change took place over a period of almost a decade, in which Shachtman and the ISL still spoke in the incantatory language of classical Marxism while orienting themselves more and more toward Social Democracy.

By the end of the decade, the ISL was reduced to a small sect. Moving rapidly rightward, Shachtman then broke with Michael Harrington, Irving Howe, and Hal Draper; Harrington and Howe both joined the Democratic Socialist Organizing Committee, later the Democratic Socialists of America, while Draper helped organize the International Socialist Clubs, which were instrumental in setting up the Peace and Freedom Party. Shachtman, meanwhile, had dissolved his group into the Socialist Party–Social Democratic Federation, and outflanked both Harrington and Howe on the right when the war in Vietnam became the defining issue. Shachtman defended the U.S. troop presence and support to the South Vietnamese on "Marxist" grounds. His group, in its final incarnation, reconstituted itself as the Social Democrats, USA, aligned itself with the Democratic Party, and wielded much influence in the AFL-CIO, where Shachtman loyalists Tom Kahn, Donald Slaiman, and Sam Fishman held major positions. Another influential Shachtmanite was black socialist and civil-rights leader Bayard Rustin, who, together with his mentor, set up the A. Philip Randolph Institute. Carl Gershman, a member of Social Democrats, USA—once head of the neocons' favorite government agency, the National Endowment for Democracy—was Jeane Kirkpatrick's assistant during her tenure as U.S. ambassador to the United Nations. Shachtman became an important adviser to such notables as Walter Reuther, Albert Shanker, and I. W. Abel, as well as Hubert Humphrey and Senator Henry "Scoop" Jackson. In the 1972 Democratic primaries, while the left-Shachtmanites grouped around Harrington and Howe supported McGovern, those loyal to their leader backed Jackson. In the November election, Shachtman and his group—which was still affiliated with the Socialist Party—backed Nixon for president. For all its apparent strangeness, "Socialists for Nixon" makes a kind of twisted sense. Nixon instituted wage and price controls, and certainly his anti-Stalinist credentials were impeccable.

It may seem unusual that a book ostensibly devoted to examining the history of the American Right should devote so many pages to analyzing the career of a figure who, for all the fierce anticommunism of his later years, remained a socialist to the end. The reason is that Shachtman is the bridge that links two generations, two waves of disillusioned leftist intellectuals, many of whom eventually wound up in the conservative movement. Although he never wrote a book-length exposition of his theory of bureaucratic collectivism, this concept as Shachtman came to interpret it had an enormous influence on the evolution of the anticommunist liberals of the fifties—who were soon to become the anticommunist neoconservatives. From Trotsky to Shachtman to Reagan is a long road to travel, and these ideological marauders, tired of their restlessness and longing for power, have settled quite comfortably into the conservative camp. They sit on the boards of directors of the leading conservative think tanks, inhabit the editorial boards of leading conservative publications, and dispense millions in grants to deserving scholars and scholarly institutions. *Enquiry*, voice of the "revolutionary anti-Bolsheviks" of the Shermanite tendency, may be long dead, but the Shermanites seem to have reconstituted themselves in the form of the American Enterprise Institute.

A study of Max Shachtman's life and work, then, is worthwhile to those who wish to understand what is happening to the conservative movement in the nineties. His brand of what his leftist critics called "State Department socialism" was central to the development of left-wing anticommunism in the fifties and sixties, and the neoconservatism of the seventies and eighties.

The Theory of Bureaucratic Collectivism

Shachtman's theory of bureaucratic collectivism is broadly outlined in an early essay, "Is Russia a Worker's State?"[7] In it, he explains that "our analysis must necessarily take issue with Leon Trotsky; yet, at the same time, base ourselves largely upon his studies. . . . Most of what we learned about Russia, and can transmit to others, we learned from Trotsky." Making his bow in the direction of the Old Man, as they used to call him, Shachtman analyzes Trotsky's last articles on the Russian question, the issue that led to the 1940 split and the formation of the Workers Party. He homes in on a haunting passage, which, written as it was a few months before Trotsky's death, is grounds for believing that the Old Man may have been changing his mind on this vital matter. He quotes it in full, and it is worth reviewing here, if only for its luminous sense of tragic grandeur:

> The historic alternative, carried to the end, is as follows: either the Stalin regime is an abhorrent relapse in the process of transforming bourgeois society into a socialist society, or the Stalin regime is the first stage of a new exploiting society. If the second prognosis proves to be correct, then, of course, the bureaucracy will become a new exploiting class. However onerous the second perspective may be, if the world proletariat should actually prove incapable of fulfilling the mission placed upon it by the course of development, nothing else would remain except openly to recognize that the socialist program based on the internal contradictions of capitalist society, ended as a Utopia. It is self-evident that a new "minimum" program would be required—for the defense of the interests of the slaves of the totalitarian bureaucratic society.[8]

Trotsky concluded, however, that there was no data to compel him to renounce the prospect of socialist revolution. Shachtman agrees, while noting that his mentor had finally admitted to the theoretical possibility that the Soviet bureaucracy was a new exploiting class, in spite of the fact that property had been collectivized. But that, says Shachtman, is exactly the point: the Soviet bureaucracy is a new exploiting class precisely *because* all property is collectivized, that is, owned by the state and controlled by the Soviet *nomenklatura*.

Against Burnham's concept of a managerial class rising on a global scale, Shachtman rules out that such a "division of labor" meant the rise of a new exploiting class in the United States:

> Even though this tendency to separate out of the capitalist class . . . a group of managers and superintendents is constantly accentuated under capitalism, this group does not develop into an independent class. Why? Because to the extent that the manager . . . changes his "relations to property" and becomes an owner of capital, he merely enters into the already existing capitalist class. He need not and does not create new property relations.[9]

In the case of a society based on collectivized property forms, says Shachtman, it is quite a different story. The Bolshevik Revolution of 1917 took place in a backward country, not in the industrialized West, as Marx originally envisioned. Under primitive conditions, the Russian revolutionaries had to turn to the managers, whether Communists or Czarists or Mensheviks, in order to build a new state on the ruins of the old. The Kremlin bureaucracy

> was becoming increasingly different in *quality* from the "hired hands" of the workers' state as well as from any kind of bureaucratic group under capitalism. While this division of labor does not transform the social system under capitalism, it does tend to create a new class in a state reposing on collectivized property, that is, in a state which is itself the repository of *all* social property.[10]

The socialist revolution, which was supposed to have abolished classes, led instead to the creation of a new and ruthlessly efficient exploiting class, one just as brutal and expansionist as the capitalists, if not more so. Shachtman speaks of the Soviet "lust for expansion" and brushes aside the arguments of orthodox Marxists, who demand to know what economic forces drive this imperialist impulse. "Stalinist imperialism is no more like capitalist imperialism than the Stalinist state is like the bourgeois state," he replies. Bureaucratic collectivism is a new kind of creature under the sun, a brand-new horror with a "lust to extend its domination over the peoples of the weakened and more backward countries."[11]

At the beginning of the forties, when those words were written, Shachtman's conception of the "Third Camp"—of building a revolutionary socialist alternative against both the capitalist West and the Stalinist empire—was at least theoretically possible. As the fifties dawned, Stalinist imperialism had gobbled up Eastern Europe and was lapping at the shores of the West; by the middle of the decade, it had absorbed China and was infiltrating into other parts of the Third World. Shachtman stoutly maintained his Third Camp position through the Korean War, but this soon became untenable. To begin with, there *was* no Third Camp. In addition, the Stalinist bureaucracy, far from being an abhorrent but temporary relapse, was firmly in the saddle in the Eastern bloc and seemed to be on the march not only in Western Europe but also in the Third World. Therefore, the Shachtmanites concluded, it was time to opt for what Trotsky had called a "minimum program" required "for the defense of the interests of the slaves of the totalitarian bureaucratic society": alliance with the imperfect but democratic West against the totalitarian enemy. And so Shachtman—who once declared that he would "grow hair on the palms of [his] hands" before he would capitulate to U.S. imperialism—finally made the plunge, dissolved the ISL, and followed in the footsteps of Burnham, the Shermanites, and so many others.

This conception of Stalinism as something unprecedented, an unmitigated evil that had to be fought as the "mortal enemy of Socialism," as the ISL program put it, was the ideological cornerstone of anticommunist leftism in the fifties. As Irving Howe, once editor of the ISL's *Labor Action*, put it,

> For the few of us who still considered ourselves Socialists—that is, for those who had experienced the debacle of socialism as a central event in their lives—an unqualified and principled opposition to Stalinism was a first premise. It meant more than a political judgment; *it meant an effort to salvage the honor of the socialist idea.* Confronting the postwar growth of Soviet power and the possibility that communist rule might reach as far as Western Europe, we had

to ask ourselves: does it still make sense to keep saying, as the Left often had, "a plague on both your houses"?[12]

Cold War Liberalism and the CIA

While Howe and a few others managed to maintain their intellectual independence, the rest of the anti-Stalinist left and the liberal intellectual milieu rushed straight into the arms of the CIA. Although the participants in the American Committee for Cultural Freedom (ACCF) and its international affiliates later disclaimed all knowledge of the CIA connection, there is much evidence that the connection was at least *suspected* by a number of major players. I refer the interested reader to Christopher Lasch's account of the ACCF affair in his essay "The Cultural Cold War: A Short History of the Congress for Cultural Freedom."[13] Whether the substantial group of anti-Stalinist leftist and liberal intellectuals knew they were being used by the CIA or not is mildly interesting, but largely irrelevant. The real point is that they were now willing, even eager, to be of service to the very government they had once vowed to overthrow. By that time, these mostly New York–based writers and academics had given up sectarian leftist politics and come up in the world; they were paid well to write for CIA-funded periodicals like *Encounter* or its German and Italian equivalents, and they did not ask too many questions. At one time or another, the ACCF included such notables as Norman Thomas, Sidney Hook, James T. Farrell, Arthur Schlesinger Jr., Irving Kristol, Lionel and Diana Trilling, and Daniel Bell. In the ACCF, they met up with their old friend James Burnham, who was the far right-wing of the anticommunist Popular Front. (If any one of the ACCF members knew about the CIA connection, it was undoubtedly Burnham.)

At first, the ACCF was a truly broad group, encompassing a large contingent from the Right: Burnham, Max Eastman, Ralph de Toledano, and John Chamberlain. But with the rise of Joe McCarthy and the subsequent polarization of the American intellectual community, the Committee split, with Burnham and the Right leaving in 1954. The Center, led by Daniel Bell and Irving Kristol, was reluctant to condemn McCarthy by name. To Kristol, he was "a vulgar demagogue" who was nonetheless an "unequivocal anti-Communist—unlike all too many of his critics, whose main preoccupation seemed to be anti-anti-Communism." Their criticism of McCarthy was that he was an amateur and ought to leave it to the experts—such as themselves—to do the necessary job. Christopher Lasch pinpoints the true meaning of the ACCF's view of McCarthyism as freelancing without a license: "The student of these events is struck by the way in which ex-communists seem always to have retained the worst of Marx and Lenin and to have discarded the best. The elitism which once glorified intellectuals as a revolutionary avant-garde now glorifies them as experts and social technicians." Lasch concludes that "many intellectuals were more attracted to Marxism in the first place as an elitist and antidemocratic ideology than as a means of analysis."[14] Having rejected Marxism, or at least the Leninist version, there remained the fascination with power. In daring to attack the army and the Voice of America, McCarthy was attacking the ACCF's benefactor and chief backer, the U.S. government, and for that he was denounced as a "cultural vigilante." In a series published in the *New York Times*, and later reprinted by the Committee as a pamphlet, "Heresy, Yes—Conspiracy, No!" Sidney Hook deplored the efforts of some to discredit the "reforms" of the New Deal, such as progressive education and the federal withholding tax as evidence of Communist and leftist infiltration of the U.S. government at the highest levels. His chief objection, however, was that these "vigilante" activities did not have the sanction of "our government."

The late Sidney Hook, a founder and the first chairman of the ACCF, was the paradigmatic neocon. A distinguished philosopher, Hook started out his political career as an open sympathizer of the Communist Party. Even after his philosophical views were denounced in the party's theoretical organ, Hook offered to meet with party officials and work out their differences. But the Stalinists would have none of it and they threw him out, whereupon he allied with A. J. Muste's American Workers Party and wrote its revolutionary manifesto. James Burnham came into the AWP at about the same time. The AWP, an attempt to "Americanize" the European virus of Marxism, soon merged with the (Trotskyist) Communist League of American, a merger which Hook greatly facilitated. Although Hook declined to join the new party, the Workers Party of the United States, he cooperated with the Trotskyists in 1935, when they decided to enter the Socialist Party. In 1936, he put his name to a joint statement with the Trotskyists in support of Norman Thomas for president. In the thirties, both he and James Burnham were the subjects of a hate campaign whipped up by the Hearst papers. A rally of 2,500 was organized by the Trotskyist youth organization to protest the witch-hunt and defend the right of professors to hold dissident political views. Twenty years later, this same Professor Hook would write a book calling for the expulsion of Communist professors from the nation's schools, defending the Smith Act on the grounds that, if prosecution of speech alone was improper, then so too was the Sherman Anti-Trust Act and all attempts to regulate interstate commerce. Communism, he proclaimed, is not like other political movements: It is by its very nature a conspiracy, acting under the orders of a foreign power. Thus Hook fell into line as the Cold War dawned, just as he had given up his previous opposition to "imperialist wars" and climbed on the bandwagon in all-out support for World War II. Eventually he wound up, with Shachtman, in the Social Democrats, USA—the only other political group he ever joined outside of his fling with the American Workers Party—declaring to the end that he was a socialist. With Shachtman, he was an active member of that small but apparently influential group, Socialists for Nixon. In 1980 Hook endorsed Ronald Reagan, who reciprocated by sending greetings to Hook's eightieth birthday party. In spite of his profession of continuing faith in the secular religion of socialism, Hook, the prototypical neocon, was welcomed in conservative quarters, where he was a fixture at the Hoover Institution.

It is clear that at the height of the Cold War, the CIA made a decision to utilize liberal and socialist "fronts" in its worldwide crusade against communism. When the story of the CIA-ACCF connection came out, CIA veteran Tom Braden, who ran the agency's cultural activities, revealed the nature and extent of the agency's true role—and its contempt for the bought-and-paid-for intellectuals it had manipulated with apparent ease. At a time when the ACCF group was frantically trying to distance itself from any knowledge of, or responsibility for, the CIA-ACCF connection, Braden set out the agency's perspective in the *Saturday Evening Post*.[15] His article is an account of the fight against the Communists in the European trade unions, in which Jay Lovestone and Irving Brown, two former Communists, played a key role. Lovestone had been the leader of the American Right Opposition, followers of Nicolai Bukharin. It was not so surprising, then, that the rest of the independent Left was also the object of interest on the part of the U.S. government. "To a man of Braden's background and inclinations," notes Lasch,

> the idea of supporting liberal and socialist "fronts" grew naturally out of the logic of the cold war. During World War II, Braden served with the OSS—next to the communist movement itself the most fruitful source, it would appear, of postwar anticommunism *(the same people often having served in both)*.[16]

The CIA was touting Hook, the Socialist Party leader Norman Thomas, and their counterparts abroad because it had by that time settled on a policy of penetrating the anti-Stalinist left, not just in this country but on a global scale. The CIA strategy was to build a "Third Force," socialist but democratic, as a bulwark against communism. Quoting Braden, Lasch tells us that

> Braden is under the impression that this combination was almost irresistible to the Europeans, at whom the CIA's cultural program was directed. "The fact, of course, is that in much of Europe in the fifties, socialists, people who called themselves 'left'—the very people whom many Americans thought no better than Communists—were the only people who gave a damn about fighting Communism."[17]

If the Shachtmanites were disappointed that their mythical "Third Force" did not spring up to save the honor of socialism, then perhaps it could be said that they settled for the only alternative: a "Third Camp" artificially created by U.S. covert operations and a vast infusion of U.S. taxpayers' dollars.

The discovery of the CIA connection destroyed whatever credibility the Committee had once had, and it soon disappeared. But the core group that had served as the nucleus of the organization remained intact. This group later came to be known as the neoconservatives.

The Rise of the Neoconservatives

Much has been written about them, mostly invective by their estranged comrades on the left. On the Right, the coming of the neocons has been received with a kind of mute acceptance. Who are these famed creatures, the stuff of so much legend? This, of course, is a subject of endless dispute and deep mystery, since only a few members of this mystic fraternity, notably Irving Kristol, have "come out of the closet," so to speak, and actually admitted that such a label could reasonably describe their views.

Grouped around *Commentary* magazine, and later around a whole constellation of periodicals such as the *Public Interest*, by the eighties the neocons had developed a critique of modern society which, while reconciled to capitalism, was nevertheless concerned with what it termed the "cultural contradictions" of the capitalist system. This point of view is best summarized by Michael Novak in *The Spirit of Democratic Capitalism*. Capitalism, we are told, leads to "the corruption of affluence." We have managed to produce the wealthiest society on the face of the earth, but there is a worm at the center of the apple and that is the possibility that, in the midst of all this wealth, people will actually start enjoying themselves. "Thus the system's ironical momentum heads toward hedonism, decadence," and narcissism. "Instead of seeking discipline, citizens seek 'liberation.' Instead of saving, individuals borrow and spend. Instead of committing themselves to hard work, citizens live for week-ends."

Horror of horrors! That anyone should possibly live primarily in and for those completely private moments of pure enjoyment, which give life meaning—instead of acting like capitalist Stakhanovites, and giving up weekends for the "cause" of producing, laboring, and "saving" for some unspecified national purpose—is a sin almost too horrible for the neocons to contemplate. Why? Because "the economic system depends upon a sense of duty . . . but it also emits siren calls of pleasure." Those who listen to the siren song of consumerism and hedonism, which is the inevitable consequence of capitalist society, are responsible for the symptoms of decline and cultural rot we see all around us: "Productivity falls; debts grow; inflation roars; the system stagnates."[18]

The neoconservatives are not out to convince Joe Six-pack that he ought to adopt the neoconservative program. Instead, their writings often take the form of an open letter to the rich and powerful, alternately scolding and coaxing them into the neocons' idea of better behavior. Thus, Novak writes of the second greatest danger to the soul of capitalism, second only to hedonistic weekends:

> *Advertising and moral weakness.* The leaders of the economic system permit advertising to appeal to the worst in citizens. They encourage credit-card debt, convenience purchasing, the loosening of restraint. Their workers, their customers, and they themselves—following such solicitations—reap the whirlwind.[19]

Economic freedom leads to cultural rot; such bourgeois decadence as "convenience purchasing" corrupts the workers; the contradictions inherent in the nature of capitalism lead inevitably to its destruction. Where have we heard all this before? In fact, the inflation Novak blames on American workers is caused by government debasing of the currency and has nothing to do with the consumers' virtue or lack of it. American productivity is falling because government is seizing and redistributing the wealth, not because workers look forward to weekends. As for debt, government itself is the biggest debtor, and we are all the poorer for it. If the system stagnates, then it breaks the chains of regulation, lifts the burden of taxes, and stops hectoring the working men and women of this country.

The neoconservatives are not interested in challenging or undoing the "reforms" responsible for such economic dislocations, which are the very bedrock of the modern welfare state—or, as they like to call it, the social security state. Far from challenging the status quo, the neocons have advised business interests to submit and adapt, rather than fight. The New Deal cannot be repealed, say the neoconservative mentors of big business, nor would that be a desirable result even if it were possible. Instead, what we need is a government that knows what the necessary requirements of "the good society" are—and one, moreover, that has no bones about legislating it into existence. As Kristol says, "[t]he basic principle behind a conservative welfare state ought to be a simple one: wherever possible, people should be allowed to keep their own money—rather than having it transferred (via taxes to the state)—*on condition that they put it to certain defined uses.*"[20]

Thus, what attracted certain intellectuals to the Leninist program—the idea that intellectuals constitute an elite which, alone, is fit to rule—is the very same impulse that drove them into the ranks of the neoconservatives: the desire to wield the whip—for "the good of society," of course.

Combined with this cultural critique of capitalism, which bemoans the loss of the society of status and the subjection of the workers to the temptations of the market, the neocons defend the welfare-warfare state; that is, they defend not only the domestic legacy of the Roosevelt revolution, but also its interventionist foreign policy. This is really the heart of the neoconservative program: a sense of the rightness of America's ultimate destiny as the inheritor of a world empire.

At the End of History: Muravchik, Krauthammer, Fukuyama

In the neoconservative lexicon, the key word is *Democracy*. Whereas individual rights and even the phrase "property rights" was once the battle-cry of the conservative movement, now we hear only about the glories of Democracy. Yes, I do mean to capitalize the word, for it has taken the place of Marxism in the hearts of these third-generation Shachtmanites. This is the new secular religion of the powerful and well-funded neoconservative movement, and its insignia are everywhere. As Paul Gottfried, professor of politics at Elizabethtown College, remarked,

Thus it is possible, while walking on Connecticut Avenue in North-west Washington, to encounter a phantasmagoria of neoconservative magazines and advertisements for lectures, all having titles with the word "democracy" or "democratic." The four sister philanthropic foundations [Olin, Scaife, Bradley, and Smith-Richardson] have funded, singly or jointly, all the following advocates of world democracy: Institute on Religion and Democracy, Institute for Democracy in Eastern Europe, Bradley Institute of Democracy and Public Values, Institute for Liberty and Democracy, the partly public National Endowment for Democracy, the friends of the Democratic Center in the Americas, Gregory Fossedal's tribute to global democracy, *The Democratic Imperative*, a center for "democratic" journalism at Boston University, and the magazine *Studies in Democracy*.[21]

What is this "democracy"? It is *social* democracy, albeit of a sterner variety than we are used to seeing, and it has global ambitions now that communism is dead. With its great archenemy, the Third International, utterly defeated, the Second International is moving to, as Irving Howe put it, "reclaim the honor of socialism." With even the alleged leading spokespersons for the Right calling for a "conservative welfare state," it is clear that what the Bolsheviks lost the Fabians gained. Instead of a debate over whether or not we ought to have socialized medicine, today the debate is over what form federally mandated national health insurance should take. Rather than argue over whether or not we ought to have a tax hike, the American dialogue has degenerated into a contest of pressure groups haggling over *which* taxes to raise. What has really disappeared, however, is any discussion of foreign policy.

On one side, we have liberal internationalists who want to uplift the starving masses of Somalia to the level of the worst American slum and bring "democracy" to the long-suffering people of Botswana. On the other, we have conservative internationalists who see the U.S. as a kind of medieval king, attended by the barons of Europe. These two visions are merely variations on a single theme of Empire, the Napoleonic versus the British model, with no real difference between them except, perhaps, one of temperament. Whatever their tactical disagreements, both share a common premise: that the U.S. ought to acknowledge and even formalize its global ambitions. Both left and right internationalists invoke the incantatory power of the magic word "democracy" to justify any and every U.S. intervention. Thus the new Caesarism is dressed up in "democratic" clothing.

With such a formidable array of foundations and think tanks, all continuously churning out theses on the wonders of Democracy, the neocons have constructed an elaborate theoretical edifice which bears all the marks of its origins. It is a kind of inside-out Trotskyism-of-the-Right, whose partisans claim that it is not only our sacred duty but also in our interests to spread democracy far and wide. The best example of this group is Joshua Muravchik, a resident scholar at the American Enterprise Institute, whose book *Exporting Democracy* makes the case for a starry-eyed internationalism that can only be described as Napoleonic.[22] Muravchik's manifesto of the new millenarianism is a call for the U.S. to lead a world "democratic" revolution. How? Although the author has many good things to say about the benefits of outright invasion and occupation, as in the case of the MacArthur regency in Japan, he realizes that this is not really an option in the present political atmosphere. His solution is to set up an international grouping of democratic parties—funded by the U.S. taxpayers, of course—to guide the revolution to victory on a global scale. Instead of sneaking around with covert actions, as in the past, Muravchik believes the U.S. should openly fund and organize a Democratic International.

Muravchik's argument is that once a nation achieves a state of democracy—which he defines as simple "majority rule"—it will lose the desire and the ability to aggress against its neighbors. Both history and common sense disprove this idea. To begin with, the democratic process is not enough to confer sainthood on an entire nation; in fact, it may encourage the growth and eventual dominance of trends not at all conducive to peace. In addition, how does Muravchik's Law of Harmonic Convergence account for the fiercely aggressive and expansionist Athenian democracy, which planted scores of colonies and engaged in a series of wars which decimated the Greek city-states, or the ancient Roman republic, which became an enormous empire? Great Britain was a parliamentary democracy by the time it reached the apex of its imperial ascendancy. In modern times, the prime example of a belligerent democracy is that of the United States itself. After extending itself from sea to shining sea, the American republic engaged in hundreds of overseas adventures, overt and covert, large and small.

For all the palaver about "Democracy," the tradition represented by Muravchik and his fellow neocons has little to do with the spirit of 1776. Although it is never explicitly stated, in practice the first loyalty of the member parties of Muravchik's Democratic International would not be to their native land, but to their benefactors in Washington. A supranational movement, loyal and one might even say subservient to foreign masters, whose cadres are motivated by a vision of world revolution—does any of this sound familiar?

Far from being an extremist, Muravchik is a moderate compared to his fellow neocon Charles Krauthammer, the syndicated columnist. Krauthammer's vision of a Pax Americana is even more explicit: he wants to "integrate" with Europe and Japan in a "super-sovereign" entity which is "economically, culturally and politically hegemonic in the world." The "new universalism," he opines, "would require the conscious depreciation not only of American sovereignty but of the notion of sovereignty in general. This is not as outrageous as it sounds."[23]

It is naturally not at all outrageous to the inside-the-Beltway intelligentsia, who spend their time designing "new architectures" and agitating for a new Imperium to build them. It is not an outrage for those who see government as the end-all and be-all of productive human activity, and the bigger the better. Such a conception is the big government "ideal" brought to its logical and monstrous conclusion: a world government whose tentacles reach into every corner of the world and every aspect of our lives.

The leftist origin of the neoconservative mind-set is underscored by their enthusiasm for the "endism" of Francis Fukuyama, who—capturing perfectly the spirit and style of these latter-day Mensheviks—imported Hegel into the pages of the *National Interest*. As Krauthammer put it, "The goal is the world as described by Francis Fukuyama. Fukuyama's provocation was to assume that the end [of history]—what he calls the common marketization of the world—is either here or inevitably dawning; it is neither. The West has to make it happen. It has to wish and work for a super-sovereign West economically, culturally, and politically hegemonic in the world."[24]

At the height of the tumult in Eastern Europe, it was virtually impossible to read an article about the rise of Gorbachev and the end of the Cold War without running across a reference to "The End of History," Fukuyama's famous essay. An analyst for the Rand Corporation and a former State Department official, Fukuyama set forth a startling thesis: that the crisis of the Communist bloc was part of a "larger process at work, a process that gives coherence and order to the daily headlines." What we may be witnessing," he announced,

> is not just the end of the Cold War, or the passing of a particular period of postwar history, but the end of history as such; that is, the end point of mankind's ideological evolution and the universalization of Western liberal democracy as the final form of human government.[25]

Fukuyama's thesis is an application of the ideas of Alexandre Kojève, a Russian émigré and Hegelian scholar whose series of seminars given in Paris during the thirties proved influential on both sides of the European political spectrum. Seeking to rescue Hegel from the Marxists, and citing the German philosopher's *Phenomenology of Mind*, Kojève proclaimed the rather quirky Hegelian idea that history had "ended" at the Battle of Jena in 1806. Napoleon's victory, having "actualized the principles of the French Revolution," settled for all time the question of what principle governed human societies. In his view, the liberal revolutions in the West prefigured the advent of a "universal homogenous state," in which peace and democracy would reign supreme. Turning Marxism on its head, Kojève made it clear that this superstate is none other than the United States: "One can even say that, from a certain point of view, the United States has already attained the final stage of Marxist 'communism,' seeing that . . . all the members of a 'classless' society can from now on appropriate for themselves everything that seems good for them."[26] Fukuyama's vision expresses perfectly the neoconservative view of world and national politics. At the "end" of history, at home and abroad, left and right are abolished, along with all "extremism," and the "Vital Center" reigns supreme. As the living embodiment of Democracy, the United States polices a world in which all traces of nationalism are mercilessly crushed. On the home front, the great enemy is nationalism of the American variety—although it is never called that, "isolationism" being the preferred epithet.

Krauthammer's quarrel with Fukuyama is over means, not ends. Just as Lenin berated orthodox Marxists who relied too heavily on the alleged inevitability of socialism, so Krauthammer is worried that "endism" will lead to complacency in pursuit of world dominion. At "the end of history," as the U.S. stands astride the world, these third-generation neocons preach a new globalism that is messianic, universalist, and utterly subversive of the American character. In the name of a mutant "conservatism," they exhort us to abandon the Republic and openly make the case for Empire. Disoriented by the end of the Cold War, some conservatives, such as former perennial presidential candidate Jack Kemp, have gone along with the new messianism. But the sea change effected by the Soviet collapse changed the political context and fundamentally altered the terms of the policy debate. As liberal columnists hardly let a day go by without calling for the bombs to fall on Belgrade, and liberals in Congress and even in Hollywood call on President Clinton to jump into the Bosnian quagmire, Kemp's fervently globalist effusions have distanced him from most conservatives. Just as American liberals are now following their natural inclination to utilize the centralizing, statizing effects of war and preparations for war to advance the collectivist agenda, so, in the absence of Soviet power, the essentially nationalist orientation of American conservatives is reasserting itself. Conservatives, too, are getting back to their roots. Freed by the end of the Cold War, they are beginning to understand that the crisis of their movement goes much deeper than the failure of this or that politician or policy initiative. It is not a question of recovering from a temporary setback, but of recovering their lost legacy—the true history and traditions of the conservative movement in America.

3
GARET GARRETT:
EXEMPLAR OF THE OLD RIGHT

If you say, "I am first of all an American," you have to be
careful. It may be misunderstood. You might have said, "I am
for America first." And the American who says that will be
denounced in his own country and by his own government.
— Garet Garrett, Chicago Tribune, 1943

F OR MANY YEARS, THE OLD Right has been relegated to the memory
hole by those who have a vested interest in promoting the utterly
false and pernicious idea that there was no indigenous life on the Right
worth considering before the founding of *National Review*. The fact
is, however, that the so-called "New Right" of William F. Buckley Jr.,
intellectually dominated by the first generations of ex-Communists and
ex-Trotskyists, did not triumph in a vacuum. They displaced the Old
Right of Senator Robert A. Taft, John T. Flynn, and Garet Garrett, which
fought Roosevelt and the rise of the modern welfare-warfare state. Since
they came together in the great Old Right mass movement of 1940–41,
the America First Committee, they might be called the America First
generation. As far as today's conservatives are concerned, they are the
Forgotten Generation.

The accepted view—pushed by both neocons and liberals—has
been that the Old Right consisted of nothing but reactionaries, nativ-
ists, and anti-Semites, and that before Bill Buckley there was nothing

but Darkness and Old Night.[1] This is a contemptible lie which rests on prejudice and ignorance of primary sources. It is a scandal that the true history of the prewar American Right is today distorted beyond recognition or else completely unknown. As the end of the Cold War and rise of the paleocons awakens conservatives to the need to get back in touch with their Old Right roots, it is time for "movement" conservatives to rediscover the legacy of an American nationalism which is anti-statist, anti-interventionist, and in favor of laissez-faire. If the Right is to regain its bearings in the post–Cold War world, this rich inheritance must be rediscovered and reevaluated. For now that the Cold War consensus has been broken and the issue of what role America ought to play in the world is once again an open question on the Right, it is high time that the conservative critics of globalism were revived, remembered, and given the honor that is their due.

The Old Right was that loose grouping of intellectuals, writers, publicists, and politicians who vocally opposed the New Deal and bitterly resisted U.S. entry into World War II. This summarizes the two first principles of the Old Right worldview: less government at home and strict adherence to the Founders' admonitions against foreign adventures and entangling alliances. It is a calculated risk to describe the Old Right as nationalist, but one that must nevertheless be taken. The risk is that the reader will think in terms of the Prussian model: statist, militaristic, obscurantist. This would be a gross error. The truth is that the Old Right represented a distinctively *American* phenomenon, which owed nothing to the Old World and was, in all essential ways, the exact opposite of its European counterpart. It was a nationalism of an unprecedented kind, based not on blood and soil and the need to expand, but on a tendency toward introversion, an impulse to draw back from the world and its endless quarrels. This was not a narrow, backward-looking nationalism, but a forward-looking pride of place that had nothing in common with the tribalism of the Europeans. Pride not only of place, but of spirit; the anti-statist spirit that sparked the American Revolution and was suspicious of power, not progress.

In chronicling the rise of the neoconservative tendency and the long journey to the West experienced by so many anti-Stalinist intellectuals, we have necessarily been immersed in the traditions of European statism: Hegel and Marx, the varieties of Leninism and their American offshoots. Such a study has made it necessary to examine the more exotic varieties of Trotskyism and delve into the history of such obscure sects as the Socialist Workers Party and the Independent Socialist League.

This exoticism is wholly removed from the experience of most Americans, never mind most conservatives; it is the product of the Old World, of a specifically European perspective. By European I mean not the legacy of ancient Greece, the Renaissance, and the Enlightenment, but *modern* Europe, the Europe of the Weimar Republic and the Bolshevik Revolution, a dark Europe dominated by the looming shadows of twin totalitarianisms.

Poisoned by the European virus, America's intellectual community became an adversary subculture, with its own mores and politics, and veered off in a direction completely at variance with the rest of the country. While the millions were reading the *Saturday Evening Post*, with its celebratory view of the American experience, tight little cliques of New York intellectuals were poring over copies of *Partisan Review*, which gloried in its status as a European colony, an outpost of sophistication in a Rotarian desert.

Partisan Review versus the *Saturday Evening Post* is a useful dichotomy. Unlike the anguished fiction of the avant-garde, which usually centered on the sufferings of a sensitive intellectual at the hands of capitalist philistines, the fiction of the *Post* featured the copybook virtues: thrift, honesty, loyalty, industry, piety, and especially "Americanism," a synonym for pride in American genius and the unprecedented productive power of American business. These were the Old Right virtues, which had transformed a nation formerly based on agriculture into the world's industrial powerhouse and which the intelligentsia despised. While the radical intellectuals who read and contributed to *Partisan Review* were agitating for a socialist America, denouncing the tyranny and backwardness of the bourgeois family and deploring the crassness of all things commercial, the readers of the *Saturday Evening Post* were enjoying stories about the two things most people like to fantasize about: success and romance. During the twenties, many of these tales were written by a key figure of the Old Right, whose brilliant but now forgotten career marks the rise and fall of what was once a popular mass movement.

The Young Journalist

Garet Garrett was born in February of 1878, the son of a tinker, and spent his boyhood in Burlington, Iowa. Young Edward Peter Garrett, as he was then known, became a printer's apprentice and worked in that capacity for local newspapers. Before he was twenty, he hopped a freight car for Chicago and then on to Cleveland, Ohio, where he worked for the *Cleveland Recorder.* Moving on to Washington, D.C., he made the leap from printer to journalist, serving as correspondent and night editor at the *Washington Times*, where he covered the White House of President William McKinley, and changed his name to Garet Garrett.

In January of 1900 he was married to Bessie Hamilton of Washington. Soon after the wedding, the couple left for New York City, where Garrett embarked on what would turn out to be a long and illustrious career.[2] But success was not instantaneous. The first three years of his residence in New York City did not yield a newspaper job; indeed just what he did during this period is a bit of a mystery. Finally, in 1903, he joined the staff of the *New York Sun* as a financial writer. For the next few years he wrote financial news articles for the *New York Times*, the *Wall Street Journal,* and the *New York Evening Post.* But there was no real opportunity for an ambitious writer to make his reputation in that arena, as the notices of new stock issues and bits of gossip rarely sported a byline.

At the age of twenty-seven, young Garrett was restless and ambitious. In his personal life, there was a change: in 1905, he divorced Bessie, his first wife. In his professional life, there was also change, as he branched out to write for new markets. Under the pen-name John Parr, he contributed to the so-called "muckraking" press, such as *Everybody's Magazine*, an outlet for the kind of business exposés that were popular at the time. But there was a big difference between Garrett and left-wing muckrakers such as Ida Tarbell and Upton Sinclair; Garrett's prose was almost entirely descriptive. He never prescribed government action as the cure-all for society's ills, as the others did, but merely advised the small investor against the lure of speculating in Wall Street stocks. In his early pieces, Garrett warned the average investor to stay away from speculation, but he was clear about the distinction to be made between amateur gambling and

> the kind of legitimate speculation which seeks to anticipate great economic changes. Legitimate speculation has its translation into prices, too, but it takes, first, original capital in some reasonable proportion to the profits expected, and secondly, the treatment of exceptional opportunity with correct imagination.[3]

His first book, *Where the Money Grows*, was a tour of Wall Street types—speculators, traders, bankers, and "wolves" who operated on the margin of legality.[4] Most interesting were the "invisibles," the mysterious big players—referred to only as "they"—whose inscrutable actions accounted for sudden large movements in the stock market. It was a journalistic account, not overburdened with financial arcana, written with grace and style. A reviewer for the *Nation* noted the book and commented that "it would be interesting to see the writer's graceful wit applied to broader themes."[5] This somewhat fictionalized account, in which he presented a series of archetypal Wall Street characters, was the prelude to the more ideological novels that were to come.

Garrett left the *Evening Post* to become editor of the *New York Times Annalist*, a new weekly financial supplement which published market quotations, editorials, and news of Wall Street. In 1914, he was listed in *Who's Who in America* (and thereafter until his death in 1954).

In 1915, the *New York Times* sent him to Germany, where he reported,

> When you are in Berlin you may have the strange sensation of being farther from the war than you were in New York. . . . One reason for this is that you thought it would be very different and expected

to feel the nearness of war. Then you are struck by the absence of the symbols and accessories of patriotism. It is partly that. There are no flags waving. One may be in Berlin for a fortnight without once seeing a German flag. There is a saying that life is so completely regulated in Germany that the people wait for the Government to say when the flags shall come out and go in.[6]

While his dispatches from Berlin evinced no sympathy for either side, his description of the situation hinted at his isolationist temperament:

> You get the feeling in Europe that the people are mad and begin to know it, as if they had suddenly come awake in an asylum, all shouting together that they are sane but unable to prove it. . . . There must be a way out. Everybody keeps saying so, as if it were something that had to be true, without any reasons why. And although Americans are disliked . . . most Germans think the initiative for peace will come from the United States.

It was unimaginable to young Garrett that America should become involved in the conflict; it was a war of the Old World, an internecine affair and, presumably, none of our business.

Garrett returned from Germany in January of 1916, restless and longing for a change. The *Times* was cramping his style; there was, in his view, no room for creativity. Soon thereafter, he submitted his resignation and took a job as financial editor of the *New York Tribune*.

When the war broke out, he dutifully supported the war effort—although not out of any special love for our allies, who seemed to him rather shiftless. Garrett was on the *Tribune* staff for the duration of the war. When peace came, his restlessness again manifested itself. In November 1919, he resigned his position and decided to take up the writing of fiction. He immediately began to write short fiction for the *Saturday Evening Post*.

The first story was "Red Night," in which a famous entrepreneur is ambushed at home by a left-wing anarchist whom he had helped to put in prison. After lulling his captor with a long lecture on the benefits of the capitalist system, the entrepreneur gains the upper hand by wielding an unloaded gun. The allegory is clear enough: capitalism will outsmart the radical agitator and ultimately triumph. In August of the same year, "A Gilded Telegrapher" told the story of a stock-market trader whose office telegrapher was passing information to a syndicate of rival businessmen.[8] The employer found him out, passed along false information, and ruined his unscrupulous competitors. In the end, the telegrapher was forgiven and allowed to return to his old job, while the syndicate was utterly ruined. Moral: the market punishes dishonesty and rewards virtue. Other stories with a Wall Street background followed.

The Blue Wound: *A Futuristic Vision*

In 1921, G. P. Putnam's Sons published Garrett's first novel, *The Blue Wound*, which was really an essay on politics, economics, and the human condition.[9] The stage is set when an unknown writer appears in the office of a newspaper editor and asks for work space in order to complete his story. For years, the writer had been trying to track down a man by the name of Mered who was supposed to be responsible for causing the Great War. He finds his mystery man in London, where the quasi-godlike Mered takes the writer on a trip through space and time, beginning in prehistory and ending in New York City in the year 1950.

The Blue Wound is, in fact, a history of the human race as seen from a godlike height. The interrelated themes of the novel reflect Garrett's view that the nature of the capitalist system flowed directly from the natural inequality of man. Just as men were unequal in their natural abilities, so they were unequal in their willingness to defer immediate pleasures in order to build up capital. Few were willing to do it. The result was a conspiracy of debtors eager to repudiate their debts, a tendency which persisted not only among individuals but also among nations. The result was inflation, debt moratorium, or bankruptcy.

Garrett outlines the basic problem in the fifth chapter, "The Wages of Thrift," which examines the psychology and ultimate consequences of egalitarianism in a style reminiscent of Shirley Jackson's famous short story, "The Lottery." Mered and the narrator come upon a village of twelve houses. As they watch, a man issues forth from one house, knocks on the door of another, and a second man appears. These two go off to knock on the door of a third, and so on, until eleven are gathered together, "masked in a kind of rude hood with openings only for the eyes." Gathering in front of the twelfth house, they call out for the head of the household to appear. He emerges and is confronted with the demand of his hooded neighbors that he and his family take up such possessions as they can carry and immediately leave the valley. "What have we done?" asks the twelfth man. The villagers reply:

> "As for what you have done, we do not ourselves clearly understand the nature of the thing, and we are too simple to examine it deeply."
>
> But "Have we not been industrious?" asks the twelfth man. "Have we not shared your hardships and tasted your sorrows?"
>
> "It is true as you say. You have done all of these things. Nevertheless, you must go."
>
> "But why?"
>
> "What we know," the hooded villagers reply, "is this: in the beginning we were all co-equal and free. Then the time came when we began not to be free. All of us were in debt to you. It was not much at first—only one tenth of our produce, or in the extreme case one fifth. But your claims increased. It now is one quarter of our produce which you require from us each year, and we are no longer free. You say it is the law. We do not understand the law. We wish to be again as we were, all equal together, with no one having rights in the produce of another or putting a cloud upon the land of his neighbours. However, we are come not to parley but to execute the sentence. Make haste, please, and do as we have said. And you are never to return."[10]

When the narrator complains to his guide that he does not understand the scene he has just witnessed, Mered answers: "Nor do they."

> "The expelled family," he went on saying, "was from the first the most industrious and the most efficient. Its wick was the last to

flicker out at night and the first to be lighted in the morning. The
exiles were not bad neighbors. They were only desperate workers.
They bore their share of the hardships and were kind in their min-
istrations, but they avoided the festivities of leisure which the others
enjoyed, and toiled instead. For this they were rather looked down
upon. However, they had always a surplus, and when others were in
want they loaned freely, though invariably with the stipulation that
it should be returned with increase, that is, with interest.[11]

Thus was capitalism born of inequality. While "[f]ew are willing to
toil beyond their immediate needs in order to be able to lend," the fact
is that "many are willing to pledge future toil for immediate pleasure."
Capitalism reflected the natural inequality of man for the simple reason
that "lenders are few and borrowers are many." In the end, however,
the majority had the power to liquidate their debts by force—a sword
of Damocles which was likely to fall sooner or later.

Garrett believed that if the inequality of individuals leads to civil
war, then the inequality of nations is likely to spark endless conflict on
an international scale. Developed nations import raw materials and sell
the finished goods to less developed, less industrialized nations, and
this leads to exploitation. In addition, the developed nations compete
among themselves for markets to exploit, and this leads to wars. Garrett
believed that World War I had been fought by the colonial powers to
expand their foreign markets; this was the impulse which determined
the foreign policy of the combatant nations, especially England and
Germany. The solution, says Garrett speaking through Mered, is self-
containment:

> In place of the disastrous idea of economic necessity, which is
> fictitious, there must come the ideal of self-containment. A *self-
> contained people cannot be economically exploited by others. A
> self-contained people will not think it necessary to exploit the toil of
> others.* For the uses of this ideal it is necessary to perceive clearly
> two facts: First—No people can afford to exploit the products of
> inferior toil and import the products of prefer red toil in return,

since by so doing they are doomed to bear the heavy end of the
yoke. Second—A skilled nation cannot afford to hire its drudgery
to be performed by others, for although it may grow rich by the
exchange its own civilization will not endure. The power to destroy
it will presently rest in the hands of those who fill its belly and the
bellies of its machines.[12]

The Blue Wound is the outraged reaction of an American nationalist to the tragedy of World War I. Turning away from Europe with
revulsion, Garrett sought to save the U.S. from suffering the fate of other
empires stretched too far and wide. The envious conspiracies of other
nations had humbled them, in the end, and all in the same way: the
colonizers became dependent on the colonies, and therefore vulnerable
to attack. The umbilical cord, stretched over oceans, was cut. Essential
supplies, raw materials to feed the people and fill the iron bellies of the
new machine civilization were embargoed and the imperial capital fell.
A similar fate awaited the U.S., warned Garrett, unless it looked to the
ideal of a self-sufficient republic.

This theme is dramatized in the novel's final chapter, set in New
York City in 1950. The city is a modernistic wonder filled with moving sidewalks and monorails. Beneath the surface, however, the old
problems fester. Expensive manufactured goods are shipped abroad in
order to buy cheap basic materials; America has become dependent on
the world. Germany, still intent on revenge for the humiliations of the
Great War, has patiently bided its time. The Germans having learned
their lesson in the last war, have become economically self-sufficient
through the development of technology, and are at last ready to strike.
They declare economic warfare on America, initiating an economic
boycott which is soon joined by the other nations of the world. In the
end, New York City is attacked by German super-weapons and the
Second Great War is begun.

The Blue Wound is the manifesto of as thoroughgoing an American
nationalist as ever set pen to paper. Thinking it might be possible to
insulate the United States from the European madness, Garrett also
warned against the tide of slave labor washed up on our shores, immi-

grants who performed the drudgery disdained by the natives. This was a deep reservoir of resentment waiting to be tapped; a volcanic possibility whose eruption was only a matter of time.

Not only the resurrection of Germany but also the rise of the Japanese Empire is projected in Garrett's fantastic novel. In a chapter on the rise of Japan as a modern power, he traces the history of that island

> where the people were so quaint and naïve and blithesomely sad that the heart yearned and a mist rose in the eyes, not out of pity, but as it is with one sometimes in beholding a wistful landscape.[13]

Here is Garrett's autarchic utopia, the symbolic image of a lost Golden Age. "Life in these islands was leisurely and immemorial," he writes. "People took it seriously and touched it lightly." This wise people readily embraced the central fact of existence—the necessity of work—and thus their attitude toward life was that "they were indifferent to its discomforts, fancifully aware of its beauties, grateful for its benefits, and otherwise much centered in themselves and enthralled by the nature of their journey."

But Western intervention put them on a different road. The introduction of foreign manufactured goods destroyed indigenous industries. Eventually all the natives had left to sell was their labor, and their infinite adaptability. Through a prodigious effort, they began to develop their own industries and their ability to defer immediate pleasure for future success served them well. When they finally reached the point of challenging their former oppressors, the Western powers, they announced that all imports would henceforth be subject to a special tax.

> "[W]e wish to do as you do in your own countries. We shall lay an import tax, please, upon foreign merchandise until such time as we are industrially strong and skilled enough to compete with you as equals. We thank you for having opened our eyes to these possibilities."

The "free traders" of the West object:

> "But don't you see," said the foreigners, "that by putting a tax on the things you buy from us you will only be making them dearer to

yourselves. Take matches. We are selling you matches for a penny a
hundred. Now suppose you lay upon them an import tax of a penny
more. Then everybody will have to pay two pennies for a hundred
matches. Where is the sense of that?"

The Japanese elders reply:

It is true, as you say, that the first effect would be to make matches
dearer. But we perceive that there are two interests among us. On one
hand lies the interest of the individual, whose advantage is served by
the present cheapness of things; on the other hand lies the interest of
the people, whose future is at stake. These two interests we find to
be antagonistic, for the reason that the life of the individual is brief
and discontinuous whereas the life of the people is continuous and
forever. Thus, it is better that the individual for the present should
pay two pennies a hundred for matches if thereby it becomes possible
for the people in the future to have industries of their own.[14]

This sentiment, ostensibly expressed by the Japanese, is clearly
shared by Garrett. It expresses the classic Old Right case for protectionism, advanced not as an economic argument but as a cultural and
even a moral stance by the new nationalists as represented, for example,
by the U.S. Industrial Council.[15] Instead of arguing the issue on its
merits, some free traders dismiss these arguments out of hand as being
completely outside the conservative tradition. But in fact, Garrett was
hardly alone in this. Exhibit A is Senator Robert A. Taft, who supported
the idea of "scientifically fixed" tariffs, while opposing high tariffs and
sectional "log-rolling."

There is, however, one big difference between Garrett and today's
right-wing protectionists: while the neonationalists demand a bigger
share of the world market for U.S. manufacturers, Garrett wanted as
little to do with world markets as possible.

[W]hat you call international trade is a dangerous and turbulent
relation between, on the one side, that eight or ten per cent of the
human race which is efficient and skilled and has reserved to itself
the preferred labor, and, on the other side, the inert and unskilled

> people, fit only to perform the drudgery. It is a turbulent relation because the unskilled chafe under the yoke, and are continually threatening to revolt. It is a dangerous relation because the materials produced by this unwilling labor are essential to the existence of the over-people, so that in the end absolute power over the few rests in the hands of the many who toil complainingly and multiply. Civilization is ultimately put on the defensive.[16]

This is not so much an argument in favor of tariffs as it is a polemic against mercantilism and imperialism. America, he warned, must not go the way of Europe's decadent colonial empires.

The Twenties: U.S. Foreign Policy and the War Debt

Garrett saw the world of the twenties as filled with forbidding omens. This fear of imminent danger, this sense that the country was fast approaching a turning point, is expressed in his articles as well as his fiction. The great "war to end all wars" had planted the seeds of another conflict, and the cause was economic. The Allies had imposed reparations and then loaned the Germans the money to pay it back—earning a high rate of interest in the bargain. Germany got out of paying reparations by inflating its currency beyond anything ever seen before. The Allies had just one goal in mind: keep the Germans afloat and thus ensure payment of their huge war debt, two-thirds of which was owed to American banks and private investors. As Germany threatened to sink into the sea of insolvency, her creditors were obliged by their own interests to rescue her. This was blackmail, pure and simple; behind it was the threat to turn Bolshevik, which a ruined Germany was likely to do. For the first time the Red Menace was being used as a justification for foreign entanglements. In a series of articles for the *Saturday Evening Post*, later published as a pamphlet, Garrett wrote,

> The red menace in all political senses is probably seven-tenths conjuration. The [German] Communists are 4,000,000 or 5,000,000 all

together. But they have no leadership. There is not one important mind among them. There is an idea in Germany that the rulers of Soviet Russia do not want Germany to go red—at least, not yet. They are too fearful of the effect it might have on her efficiency and productive power and too anxious for the present to draw upon that efficiency and power for their own needs. Whether this is true or not, the Russians would be very intelligent to take that view and to maintain in Germany merely a tin façade of Communism, numerically strong, politically weak.[17]

The debt structure created by the war was precarious and unsupportable. The one thought in the German mind was to get out of paying reparations, which wounded their pride; the one thought of our former allies in the great Wilsonian crusade was to get out of paying their war debts to the United States. American loans to Europe were not investments, or at least good investments, although that is what we told ourselves in the beginning. Garrett thought that "beyond all considerations of an economic or financial character, there is pressing upon us all the time that sense of obligation to save Europe." This same motive

> seized us deeply during the war. It carried us into the war. We were going to save Europe from Germany, the German people from the Hohenzollerns, little nations from big ones, all the people from the curse of war forever.[18]

The Wilsonian crusade did not survive the war. "What survived," said Garrett, "was a continuing sense of obligation to save Europe." And what did we gain by it? The hatred of our ex-Allies, who told the Germans that if only London and Paris could stop making these onerous debt payments to Uncle Sam, they could cancel Germany's war reparations. Were we saving Europe, asked Garrett, or were we setting her up for an even grislier fate? Washington was right to warn us against foreign entanglements; we were impoverishing ourselves so that Europe could put its people on the dole and build up its armaments in preparation for another war.

The domestic implications of the postwar economic order were equally ominous. In Garrett's view the war had "profoundly altered the significance and status of American industry."

> Formerly it had been privately owned and privately managed; and when and if it happened that private ownership was unable to keep rhythm and order in it, finance intervened. But finance was private, too. Government as a rule touched it gingerly or hardly at all, except to regulate its social behavior.
>
> But during and after the war industry came to be regarded as an attribute of state power, almost as clearly such as the military establishment. And why not? Security, independence, national welfare, economic advantage, diplomatic prestige—were not all as dependent upon efficient machine industry as upon an army or navy? Mechanized warfare had done this.
>
> The new way of thinking about industry, therefore, was basically political. A factory thereafter would be like a ship—a thing to be privately owned and privately enjoyed only in time of peace, always subject to the mobilization for war.[19]

The series of articles on the question of the war debt was a project close to the heart of George Horace Lorimer, editor of the *Saturday Evening Post,* and their collaboration on this project led directly to Garrett's long association with the magazine. He continued to write articles on financial and other matters for the *New Republic,* but soon branched out into fiction again with a remarkable novel, *The Driver,* a *Post* serial,[20] later issued as a book by E. P. Dutton.[21]

The Driver: *The Entrepreneur as Hero*

When Garrett warned the readers of his financial-advice columns that small investors ought to stay away from stock speculation, he qualified this by saying that there is another kind of speculation, which amounts to entrepreneurial foresight. In the case of the ordinary mortal, speculation is just gambling; but the hero of *The Driver,* Henry Galt, had a burning vision of what railroads would be, *must* one day be, and, imbued with this vision, his speculation was only a means to a much larger creative end.

In many ways *The Driver* bears an almost uncanny resemblance to the much more famous *Atlas Shrugged*, by Ayn Rand—and the resemblance consists of more than just the fact that the main characters of both novels share the same first name. Like Rand's monumental novel, Garrett's book is a paean to the American industrialist and a sustained polemic against the enemies of capitalism. In fact there are so many similarities between the two books, that it would not be unreasonable to make the claim that Garrett's now forgotten novel was a seminal influence on Rand.

Henry Galt, a Wall Street speculator, is a man of genius with an obsession: railroads. In *The Driver,* Galt endures scorn, indifference, and persecution by both his fellow businessmen and government; his wife and children are snubbed by "society," and he is brought up on charges of violating the Sherman Anti-Trust Act. In Rand's book, the industrialist Henry Rearden, inventor of Rearden Metal, is subjected to a similar series of trials, both private and public; here, again, there is more than just a similarity of names. Rand's Rearden and Garrett's Galt both are meant to exemplify the best qualities of the American businessman, to present the entrepreneurial virtues as a moral and even aesthetic ideal.[22]

The Driver opens on a scene that is at once ominous and comical, on Easter Sunday in a small village in Ohio, in the "fourth year of the soft Money Plague, 1894":

> The sky is low and brooding, with an untimely thought of snow. Church bells are ringing. They sound remote and disapproving. Almost nobody is mindful of their call. The soul may miss its feat; the eye of wonder shall not be cheated. The comic god has published a decree. Here once more the sad biped, solemn, ludicrous and romantic, shall mount the gilded ass. It is a spectacle that will not wait. For weeks in all the newspapers of the country the fact has been advertised in a spirit of waggery. At this hour and from this place the Army of the Commonweal of Christ will set forth on foot in quest of the Economic Millennium.[23]

The purpose of this army is "to demand from Congress a law by which unlimited prosperity and human happiness might be established on earth." The commander of this ragtag army, Jacob S. Coxey, is described in utterly unheroic terms:

> The type is well known to inland communities—the man who believes in perpetual motion, in the perfectibility of human nature, in miraculous interventions of the deity, and makes a small living shrewdly. He might be the inventor of a washing machine.

The banner of the Commonweal of Christ, adorned with a painted Christ head, reads, "PEACE ON EARTH: GOOD WILL TO MEN—DEATH TO INTEREST BEARING BONDS!"[24]

Throughout the novel, this farrago of economic nostrums and crankism is called "Coxeyism," the idea that something may be gotten for nothing. "The thing," says Garrett, "is Russian—'a petition carried in boots,' a prayer to the government carried great distances by peasants on foot." Coxey's army, ridiculed by the press, is the subject of much public discussion. "People laugh openly and are secretly serious."

Much of the rest of Garrett's life was taken up with debunking the varieties of Coxeyism—from the half-articulated yearnings of left-wing populists to the fully articulated statism of the New Deal, which was Coxeyism in power.

In his next novel, Garrett celebrated the prodigious achievements of the American steel industry. The title of *The Cinder Buggy: A Fable in Iron and Steel* gives a fairly good summation of its subject.[25] *Satan's Bushel* is Garrett's answer to the Coxeyite demands for federal aid to the farmer. In the form of an allegory, he demonstrates how the market could deal with the great agricultural surplus which was driving farmers off the land.[26]

A Critique of Radicalism

Garrett's final novel, *Harangue: The Trees Said to the Bramble, "Come Reign Over Us,"* is a frontal assault on the growing menace of socialism, an exposé of the types that made up the radical movement of the day.[27] His fictional Freeman's League was modeled on the Non-Partisan League of North Dakota, which dominated the politics of that state in the early part of the century. The NPL advocated state ownership of banks, terminal elevators, and packing houses. By 1919, it had seized control of the state government and begun to implement its program.

In Garrett's novel, the Freeman's League takes over an unnamed Western state, renames it New Freedom, and starts to implement the socialist program. Led by a mini-Stalin by the name of Capuchin, the league is ultimately undone by the economic impossibility of its schemes. The burden of taxation crushes the people; the state-owned bank soon goes broke and is unable to finance the fantastic social-welfare programs Capuchin has promised. All the while, a crusty old banker known as "Anxious" Plainto becomes the Thomas Paine of the counter-revolution. Plainto writes pamphlet after fiery pamphlet exposing the true state of New Freedom's finances, and predicting that it will end with the nationalization of all land. As this Midwestern version of the Bolshevik Revolution begins to unravel, the radical hard core of the league, a thinly disguised version of the Industrial Workers of the World, resorts to violence. Plainto is assassinated by the IWW, the people of New Freedom rise up against the tyrant, and the league is destroyed.

Garrett examines the various types attracted to the socialist cause— the socialist intellectual, the rank-and-filer, the rich patrons—effectively lampooning the guilt-ridden heiresses, the weak and basically dishonest intellectuals, and the power-mad demagogues who make up the cadre of the socialist movement. The major theme of this work is the essential insight of the Old Right: that American radicals were partisans of the Old World transplanted in the soil of the New. This graft could not take unless the American character was somehow corrupted. Speaking through one of his characters, Garrett says,

> The people are not radical here. They are conservative. The soil is young, the hour is young, opportunity is young. Radicalism in this country is a pale ferocity; a personal attitude disguised as a social intention. If you are really radical there is something the matter

with you. There was nothing the matter with the people of New Freedom. They were too young to have anything the matter with them. They had no impulse to destroy anything. What they did want they did want and all they wanted was increased participation in the material benefits of the order that is; which is not radicalism. Now comes a man like Capuchin, bidding them rise as peasants against the castle. They are not peasants. They are proprietors of the land they work. And there is no castle.

The proletariat. This is an Old World word, imported here. So far as it is a fact it is an Old World fact, also imported here.[28]

It is important to realize that Garrett was writing for the most widely read market of his day, the *Saturday Evening Post* and other magazines put out by the Curtis Publishing Company. His was not the voice of a small and beleaguered minority dedicated to preserving the flame of liberty and individualism, but instead reflected the great unspoken consensus of the day. Old Right politics was simply an extension of Old Right *culture*—a culture that valued achievement, hard work, self-improvement, independence, self-discipline, and the entrepreneurial spirit.

The message of Garrett's last published novel is that socialism cannot work; if it ever comes to power, it will eventually be brought down by its own inner contradictions. As a long-range prediction, it was right on the mark. In the short term, however, the specter of socialism was just beginning to haunt the world. Garrett was at the beginning of a long struggle with the bane of the twentieth century.

Although he had been concentrating on his fiction, during the early twenties Garrett also kept writing about economics in nonfiction form in the *New Republic* and the *New York Times*. In 1922, he attacked Thomas Alva Edison's proposal for the establishment of a commodity dollar, and wrote a series of articles on the necessity of a 100% gold dollar. "Governments cannot be trusted to issue paper money on good intentions," he wrote. "They must be restrained by a gold reserve." In making the case for sound money, Garrett warned against the inflationary policies of the Federal Reserve Bank:

> The Federal Reserve Board indignantly resented talk of inflation while issuing Federal Reserve currency and Federal Reserve credits in cataracts to the banks of the whole country, not only during the war but for two years thereafter. It particularly denied that we printed money to carry on the war as all the other countries did; but we did it all the same, issuing first the bonds and then the money the bonds were bought with. So naturally when the process of deflation begins everybody must deny both the fact and the responsibility, since deflation is a sequel to inflation, and inflation was said never to have taken place.[29]

Garrett was an increasingly consistent advocate of laissez-faire capitalism, but he was no apologist for big business. He attacked the Eastern Financial Establishment for pushing Congress to bail out the Europeans in the wake of World War I. "The American producer who advocates borrowing money from the American people and lending it to foreign countries in order that they may buy his goods . . . and then demands high tariffs to keep foreigners from selling to American consumers, is consistent only in minding his own profit."[30]

Garrett also wrote a series of articles on the immigration question, which was at that time a topic of great debate. Garrett and the *Post* expressed much concern that America would be engulfed in the wave of European immigrants landing on our shores. He wrote,

> Glowing through the whole history of American naturalization was the concept, mystically implicit, that citizenship is a transforming agent, acting upon the individual. However it happens to him, like salvation, it will change him.[31]

Assimilation would not come easily because the adjustment was cultural as well as economic—an idea that, in our era of political correctness, is bound to be smeared as "racist" but was, in fact, a legitimate if not prescient fear that a flood of immigrants would transform the political culture. Armed with the vote, immigrants would undermine the American tradition and, perhaps, sweep the hitherto unsuccessful Capuchins into power. Whereas the people of New Freedom were not peasants, but freeholders with an individualist tradition, this time there would be plenty of peasants—all of them armed with the vote. What Garrett and others of the Old Right foresaw was the growth of a large immigrant population as the political base of unscrupulous big-city politicians, who would buy votes and expand the power of the state—and they were absolutely right. Garrett believed that the vote should be earned; the fact of universal suffrage meant that American citizenship had to be treated as a privilege, not a right.

Turning Point: FDR and the New Deal

The crash of 1929 and the ascension of Franklin Delano Roosevelt to the presidency marked a turning point in the career of Garet Garrett and also of the Old Right. For now, the two things they had feared most—the rise of an all-powerful federal government and the acceleration of foreign entanglements—began to dominate the American stage. They fought these policies every step of the way and none harder than Garrett. The *Post*, under Lorimer, was implacably hostile to both trends, and Garrett's articles and editorials blasted away at the president. He blamed the crash of 1929 on the Federal Reserve's inflationary policy and warned of the dangers of turning to government as the solution to the crisis; it was the same poison that had caused us to get sick in the first place. In a prophetic paragraph in the June 25, 1932, issue of the *Post*, Garrett saw what the end of this "let the government do it" attitude would be:

> Increasingly, as it may seem, irresistibly, we are using public credit to create an indigent caste, indigence becoming more and more comfortable until for many it may seem a goal; then a very great dependent caste referred to as people in the "lower income ranges," who, without being indigent at all, are yet dependent upon public credit for security, for modern housing, for care in illness, protection in health, economic insurance, amusement and guidance; then a social-service caste to mind the indigent and oversee the

dependent. In all of these ways we are exchanging freedom for
something else—for security, for status, for refuge from the terrors
of individual responsibility.[32]

During the terrible "Hundred Days" in which FDR launched a
frontal assault on the American capitalist system, Garrett was in fine
form. On June 16, Congress passed the Banking Act, which instituted
federal deposit insurance, and Garrett wrote,

> So, after 130 years of American banking, we hesitate between what we
> rationally know ought to be done, and, on the other hand, love of the
> dangerous credit ecstasy, and make believe that American banking
> can be made safe of a Government guaranty of bank deposits.[33]

The inflationary and speculative fever had to be sweated out,
said Garrett; the Depression had to be allowed to take its course. The
only way out was to avoid the mistakes that had led to the debacle.
We must, he insisted, reject the false god of unlimited credit. The
only barrier to this, the gold standard, was demolished by Roosevelt in
1933–34. Garrett believed that gold was the best means of controlling
credit. He conceded that, if all gold obligations were simultaneously
called in, they could not all be honored. However, he argued, this was
irrelevant, since "bonds payable in gold are not actually paid in gold"
but in income. The purpose of the gold-backed dollar was to establish
a ratio of gold to dollars beyond which money would not be issued.
Farm from abandoning the gold standard because it was an ineffective
limit on credit, the New Deal attacked it because it was too effective.
Roosevelt, Garrett realized, longed to be freed from the constraints of
the gold-backed dollar in order to inflate the currency and redistribute
the wealth.

Instead of redistributing the wealth, the solution was to create
new wealth. Instead of limiting production and competition by setting up government-privileged cartels, Garrett advised the president
to unleash all constraints on free competition, let prices reach their
natural level—they would, he believed, not fall far—and the recovery
would be upon us.

Roosevelt certainly did not take this advice. Instead, he introduced the Social Security Act of 1935, which Garrett denounced in the pages of the *Post* as fraud, for "all the people can possibly receive from the Government in the way of benefits is their own money back, less the cost of government." The social security tax penalized employment and would lengthen the bread lines. The very idea of "social security" was a snare and a delusion because

> No government can provide social security. It is not in the nature
> of government to be able to provide anything. Government itself is
> not self-supporting. It lives by taxation. Therefore, since it cannot
> provide for itself but by taking toll of what the people produce, how
> can it provide social security for the people?[34]

Just as in his novel *Harangue*, when old "Anxious" Plainto had fought Capuchin and the Freeman's League by firing broadside after broadside at the follies of red radicalism, so Garrett now waged merciless war against the Roosevelt revolution, taking aim at the plethora of alphabet-soup agencies set up by the "brain trusters" of the New Deal.

Garrett's great philippic against the New Deal, *The Revolution Was*,[35] did not appear until 1945, but it was written in the heat of battle, in 1938. In this essay, and in two others later collected in his book *The People's Pottage*, Garrett is at his best; the prose style, with its striking simplicity and sense of tragedy, is hauntingly beautiful:

> There are those who still think they are holding the pass against a
> revolution that may be coming up the road. But they are gazing in
> the wrong direction. The Revolution is behind them. It went by in
> the Night of Depression, singing songs to freedom.[36]

Those who say that the republic is in danger "had forgotten their Aristotle," who had written of what can happen within the form when "one thing takes the place of another, so that the ancient laws will remain, while the power will be in the hands of those who have brought about revolution in the state."[37] That is what had happened: that was the essence of the New Deal—"revolution within the form."

The New Deal, Garrett contended, did not make any sense if one approached it in the conventional way, that is, if one criticized it as a contradictory program which was bound to fail—because the critic, in that case, had no real conception of its true purpose. It was fruitless to observe, for example, that the New Deal agricultural policies were to raise prices, while the National Recovery Administration (NRA) had as its ostensible goal to maintain industrial prices within certain limits. That was the point: *power* was not the point.

For Garrett, the New Deal represented "nothing that was implicit in the American scheme. It took off from a revolutionary base. The design was European." While the contradictory jumble of agencies may in some cases have had the effect of canceling each other out, "from the point of view of the revolutionary technique it made perfect sense." The so-called mistakes of that tumultuous era all had one common effect: they increased the executive power over the life of the economy and society. In order to bail us out of the distortions and dislocations caused by government intervention into one area, the nation was maneuvered into "further extensions of the administrative hand." "When you have passed a miracle," said Garrett, citing DeLawd in the stage play *Green Pastures*, "you have to pass another one to take care of it."

At a time when everyone was exulting in the idea that the New Deal would preserve our system of free enterprise, what the American business community did not realize was that it was already, as Garrett put it, "a conquered province." With the coming of the New Deal, "the ultimate power of initiative did pass from the hands of private enterprise to government. There it is and there it will remain until, if ever, it shall be reconquered. Certainly government will never surrender it without a struggle."

This essay marked a dramatic change in the tone of Garrett's writing. During the era of Harding, Coolidge, and Hoover, Garrett had been the prophet of American optimism. His book *The American Omen* presents America as a new kind of civilization under the sun, the New World as the first truly *modern* society founded in opposition to the Old World of caste and feudal privilege.[38] In a short book, *Ouroboros; or, The Mechanical Extension of Mankind*, he made the argument that capitalism was overcoming its enemies by sheer productive power, by lifting humankind higher in a few decades than every before in history.[39] In *Harangue* the American partisans of socialism had been depicted as little more than a marginal gang of misfits, dreamy-eyed intellectuals, and Wobbly *lumpen* elements, who would fall of their own weight if, by chance, they should ever find themselves in power. By 1938, however, Garrett had good reason to change his opinion. The techniques of revolution had been modified, refined, elevated into a discipline that combined aspects of art and science, and the New Deal was triumphant. In retrospect, Garrett concluded that both he and the American people had been naïve. Oliver Wendell Homes was wrong when he said, "Revolutions are not made by men in spectacles."

> Revolution in the modern case is no longer an uncouth business. The ancient demagogic art, like every other art, has, as we say, advanced. It has become in fact a science—the science of political dynamics. And your scientific revolutionary in spectacles regards force in a cold, impartial manner. It may or may not be necessary. If not, so much the better; to employ it wantonly, or for the love of it, when it is not necessary, is vulgar, unintelligent and waste-ful. Destruction is not the aim. Always the single end in view is a transfer of power.[40]

Americans, awash in material success and taking liberty for granted, had underestimated their deadliest foes. The uncouth Wobbly had been transformed into the steely-eyed young man in spectacles, the Ivy League brain truster who had graduated into the upper ranks of the emerging managerial bureaucracy. Written at the same time as *The Managerial Revolution*, Garrett's *The Revolution Was* identified and analyzed the same phenomenon as Burnham's work, but took the opposite tack. Instead of joining the march into the supposedly inevi-table managerial future, the doughty old warrior of the Old Right was determined to resist to the bitter end and go down fighting.

The New Deal was all about the transfer of power from the old capi-talist class to the new revolutionary elite. This elite was not a party:

It had no name, no habitat, no rigid line. The only party was the Communist Party, and it was included; but its attack was too obvious and its proletarianism too crude, and moreover, it was under the stigma of not belonging. Nobody could say that about the elite above. It did belong, it was eminently respectable, and it knew the American scene. What it represented was a quantity of bitter intellectual radicalism infiltrated from the top downward as a doctorhood of professors, writers, critics, analysts, advisers, administrators, directors of research, and so on—a prepared revolutionary intelligence in spectacles.[41]

The radical intellectuals grouped around the Communist Party had prepared the ground. Now that the Depression had struck down the American giant in his tracks and sent him reeling, it was time for the main strike force to launch the final assault on the citadel of Capital. "When the opportunity came a Gracchus would be needed," wrote Garrett. "The elite could produce one. And that was something the Communist Party could not hope to do."

That country squire in the White House, as John T. Flynn characterized Roosevelt in the title of his bestselling book, was the perfect American Gracchus. Having captured the seat of government, said Garrett, the president moved quickly to consolidate the revolution with the form. In a blitzkrieg assault on our traditional republican form of government, Roosevelt moved on several fronts at once. In the name of the national emergency, he moved to increase the power of the executive branch of government: "its power, that is, to rule by decrees and rules and regulations of its own making," From there, he proceeded to extend his control over the economic and political life of the nation. The effect was "to degrade the parliamentary principle," subvert the independent judiciary, violate basic civil liberties, "exalt the leader principle," and "weaken all other power—the power of private enterprise, the power of private finance, the power of state and local government."[42]

Garrett leaves aside the question of whether the New Deal had anything to do with recovery—he saves that for a later book—but instead is more interested in the question,

Where was the New Deal going?

The answer to that question is too obvious to be debated. Every choice it made, whether it was one that moved recovery or not, was a choice unerringly true to the essential design of totalitarian government, never of course called by that name either here or anywhere else.[43]

A similar theory of where the New Deal was going was developing at both ends of the political spectrum. From the left, Burnham was also proclaiming the advent of the new order:

Already in the United States, the tendency away from capitalism and toward managerial society has received a specific ideological and institutional expression. This expression, suited to an earlier stage in the process than that reached in Russia or Germany, is the "New Deal."[44]

Here are two nearly identical theories, a convergence of left and right—with one vital difference. Garrett despised the new order; Burnham exulted in it. Roosevelt's so-called brain trust was the object of the latter's sincere admiration:

These men include some of the clearest-headed of all managers to be found in any country. They are confident and aggressive. Though many of them have some background in Marxism, they have no faith in the masses of such a sort as to lead them to believe in the ideal of a free, classless society. At the same time they are, sometimes openly, scornful of capitalists and capitalist ideas. They are ready to work with anyone and are not so squeamish as to insist that their words should coincide with their actions and aims. They believe that they can run things, and they like to run things.[45]

In November of 1932, the American people voted for less government and fiscal sanity—and elected Franklin Delano Roosevelt to the presidency. Thus the first requirement of the revolutionary elite, the seizure of the executive power, was accomplished; and all with the form, according to law, in a free vote of the people.

The second requirement was to seize economic power. Toward that end, the New Dealers took the most direct route: control of money, banking, and credit. The collapse of the weaker banks had given Roosevelt a golden opportunity, and he did not hesitate. Demanding extraordinary powers to deal with the emergency, he proceeded, in a series of nine steps, to gain control of the economy by,

1. Declaring a "banking holiday," an act that effectively shut down the economy—and locked in the rich, who were forbidden to transfer funds abroad.

2. Relegating Congress to the role of rubber-stamping after the fact.

3. Directing that the government seize all the gold, on pain of fine and imprisonment. Everyone was to give up his gold, in exchange for paper money. This was presented as the patriotic duty of all American citizens. But there was one detail the brain trusters forgot to tell the people: that the paper they were handing out, which had always been redeemable in gold, was going to be drastically devalued. Roosevelt was planning to repudiate the gold standard, but he didn't show his hand until *after* the people fulfilled their patriotic duty and handed over their gold to the federal government.

4. Passing legislation authorizing the creation of three billion dollars in fiat money at the president's discretion and giving him the power to devalue the dollar by half.

5. Repudiating the gold standard. On June 5, 1933, Congress not only defrauded its own bond holders, but it invalidated the gold-redemption clause in all private contracts.

6. Changing one little word in the country's organic banking law. From the beginning until then the law was that a Federal Reserve Bank "shall" lend to a private bank on suitable security. This word was changed to "may." Thus a right became a privilege and a privilege that could be suspended at will.[46]

7. Designing a policy "to produce what may be described as monetary pandemonium." With the dollar's link to gold severed, the value of the dollar did not plummet, at least not at first, so the government decided to help it along a bit by going into the gold business. Roos-

evelt's aim, as he stated, was "to establish and maintain continuous control." In effect, the president and the secretary of the treasury sat down every day and fixed the value of gold in dollars—or, if you like, vice versa. This made no sense as monetary policy: all private lending virtually came to a halt. Why lend out any money today when there was no way to be certain what its value would be tomorrow? But as a political strategy it made perfect sense. Thus the way was paved for the government, via the Reconstruction Finance Corporation, to move into the void. Private debt was socialized. This was very popular. The result was that the capital of American finance was moved from Wall Street to Washington, D.C. Where did all the money come from? By the only means available to government: theft. As Garrett summed it up, All through the commotion of these unnatural events one end was held steadily in view, and that was a modern version of the act for which kings had been hated and sometimes hanged, namely to clip the coin of the realm and take the profit into the king's revenue.[47]

8. Committing the act of confiscation: on January 30, 1934, Congress passed a law vesting title in the government of all the gold supposedly held in trust.

9. Devaluing the dollar to 59 percent of its former value. Forty-one cents in every dollar was in effect confiscated, and put into a fund which the president used to seize control of the last vestige of private capital, the foreign exchange market.

The conquest of the economic realm was complete. Next on the agenda: the conquest of the political culture. This was no easy task. Just as the fictional Freeman's League of Garrett's 1926 novel had run up against the stubborn individualism of the American people, so the revolutionary vanguard of the New Deal might have run into the same brick wall, except the brain trusters were brainier than that. These were not the unwashed Wobbly agitators who proclaimed the dogma of red revolution from the rooftops, but the polished scions of the professional elite—Burnham's ambitious managers, "who like to run things."

They had to be careful. It was important not to directly attack the symbols and values of the established order—the Old Right culture of capitalism, individualism, and personal responsibility—since these were too deeply entrenched in the American conscience. "Instead of attacking directly those symbols of the old order to which the people are attached he will undermine and erode them by other symbols and slogans, and these others must be such as . . . to take the people off guard."

> For example, if the propagandist said, "Down with the Constitution!"—bluntly like that—he would be defeated because of the way the Constitution is enshrined in the American conscience. But he can ask: "Whose Constitution?" That question may become a slogan. And that creates an image, which is a symbol. He can ask: "Shall the Constitution be construed to hold property rights above human rights?" Or, as the President did, he may regretfully associate the Constitution with "horse and buggy days."[48]

As the New Deal forged ahead, the propaganda war escalated. The word "individualism" was not spoken without the mocking qualifier "rugged." The individual was depicted as the helpless plaything of abstract historical forces and the lure of security was held up before the people. In the propaganda onslaught which brought the New Deal to power, Garrett foresaw the use and importance of imagery in the modern art of public relations. The genius of Roosevelt and his brain trusters was in the use of the negative image to counteract the power of the positive values they wanted to destroy. Citing Roosevelt's first inaugural address, in which the president denounced the "unscrupulous money-changers [who] stand indicted in the court of public opinion," Garrett focuses on the central image of New Deal propaganda. All the other managerial ideologies had their hate objects. In Russia, it was the capitalists; in Germany, it was the Jews. Here is how Garrett described the same phenomenon in the United States:

> There was the pattern and it never changed. The one enemy, blamable for all human distress, for unemployment, for low wages, for the depression of agriculture, for want in the midst of potential

plenty—who was he? The money-changer in the temple. This was
a Biblical symbol and one of the most hateful. With what modern
symbol did this old and hateful one associate? With the Wall Street
banker, of course . . . the least attractive symbol of capitalism.

Therefore, capitalism, obliquely symbolized by the money-
changer scourged out of the temple, was entirely to blame; capitalism was the one enemy, the one object to be hated. But never was
it directly attacked or named; always it was the *old order* that was
attacked. The old order became a symbol of all human distress.

It was never the capitalist that was directly attacked. Always it was
the economic royalist, the brigand of the skyscrapers, the modern
Tory—all three hateful counter symbols. The true symbols of the
three competitive systems in which people believed were severely
let alone. The technique in every case was to raise against them
counter symbols. Thus, against the inviolability of private property
was raised the symbol of those who would put property rights above
human rights; and against all the old symbols of individualism and
self-reliance was raised the attractive counter symbol of security.[49]

A major problem confronting Roosevelt and his fellow revolutionaries was to "reconcile and attach to the revolution the two great classes
whose adherence is indispensable," namely, the industrial worker and
the farmer. The essence of the problem was that, if the planners raised
agricultural prices, the urban wage-earner suffered. Conversely, if wages
are raised, *all* prices rise. In Garrett's view, "The only solution so far has
been one of acrobatics. The revolutionary party must somehow ride the
see-saw." Having gained control of money, banking, and credit, the New
Deal planners were next in a position to "in fact redistribute the national
income almost as by a slide rule." They decided to retain the support
of labor by giving farmers outright subsidies. Then the New Dealers
delivered to the union bosses a legal monopoly of the labor supply, giving them unprecedented power. This decree also gave the violence and
intimidation practiced by the unions the cover and sanction of law. In
effect, unionism became compulsory. By keeping millions off the labor
market by means of work relief, the labor monopoly was protected.

The extension of the New Deal's power over business, labor, and agriculture was now complete. The question then arose as to whether the New Dealers were going to deepen their victory. Garrett posed the question as "What to do with business—whether to liquidate or shackle it." The problem of what to do with business had confronted the revolutionary elites of Russia and Germany. In the case of the former, business was liquidated. In the case of the latter, it was merely subsumed. Garrett speculates that Roosevelt did not entirely rule out the Russian model—at least insofar as the word "liquidate" is meant in the economic and not the physical sense—but eventually the decision was made to shackle it. Not only that, but business itself would forge the shackles and wear them proudly.

> Always in business there will be a number, indeed, an astonishing number, who would sooner conform than resist, and besides these there will be always a few more who may be called the Quislings of capitalism. Neither Hitler nor Mussolini ever attempted to liquidate business. They only deprived it of its power and made it serve.[50]

America would follow the German and Italian corporatist model. The tyranny of the Blue Eagle, symbol of the corporatist NRA, was soon toppled by the Supreme Court. "Yet business," said Garrett, "was not unshackled. After all, one big shackle for all business was clumsy and unworkable. There were better ways." And so the new instruments of power were multiplied, instead of centralized all in one agency. There were better ways, and the architects of the New Deal found them.

All rival centers of power were besieged: Congress, the Supreme Court, state and local governments. The power of Congress was usurped by the rise of administrative law; law made by the bureaucrats and the brain trusters was soon more prolific than that enacted by the national legislature.

Just as their cousins in Germany and Russia mobilized their shock troops on the eve of revolution, so the New Dealers brought their own shock troops into play when the Supreme Court struck down the NRA. Garrett could not "forget the spectacle of C.I.O. strikers, massed in Cadillac Square, Detroit, intoning with groans the slogan prepared by New Deal propagandists: 'Nine old men. Nine old men.' That was collaboration."[51]

Roosevelt's first serious defeat was his infamous attempt to pack the Supreme Court, but it was only a temporary setback: two anti–New Dealers on the Court died and the president put in two of his own. A three-pronged assault by the regulators, the courts, and the federal government soon reduced the sovereign states to mere appendages of Washington. The New Deal set up rival systems of power in the great regional projects and agencies, such as the TVA. The state capitals were subordinated to the edicts of the brain trusters.

For a while, the New Dealers maintained the façade of fiscal responsibility. It was necessary to reveal the new philosophy of unlimited public debt gradually, so as not to shock the sensibilities of the American people. Benumbed as they were, the people could still add and subtract; they could still understand that an unbalanced budget would have the same effect on the public sector as it invariably does in the private sector. As soon as Roosevelt's real policy was revealed in his second-year budget, the president turned to a new tack—what Garrett calls "the European device of double bookkeeping." This meant keeping two sets of books: the official budget and a special "emergency" budget, which would be balanced just as soon as we got on our feet—which was going to be any day now. Then, we would go back to the old way of having only a single set of books. When that line failed to convince, they switched to what Garrett calls "the investment state." Instead of being awash in debt, the American people—or so they were told—were really awash in *investments*. The debt incurred had to be measured against the glorious achievements of the New Deal; if this were done, the books would balance.

This spurious doctrine, which did not fool anybody to begin with, was a prelude to the doctrine of perpetual unlimited public debt. Instead of making excuses or trying to mask the problem, the solution, Roosevelt decided, was to admit it—and deny its significance. As Garrett put it,

> What difference did it make how big the debt was? It was not at all
> like a debt owing to foreign creditors. It was something we owed

only to ourselves. To pay it or not to pay it meant only to shift or not to shift money from one pocket to another.[52]

It was futile, said Garrett, to waste one's time opposing such a doctrine. That it was based on an economic fallacy could be demonstrated easily enough. But none of this had any relevance to the ultimate ends of the New Dealers, who denounced what they called the "fetish of solvency," because the New Deal had embraced "deficit spending as a social principle." The policy "means a progressive redistribution of wealth by will of government until there is no more fat to divide; after that comes a level rationing of the national income." The middle class, said Garrett, would be "murdered in its sleep."[54]

The final goal of the New Deal, which it accomplished in the end, was to transfer power, in the form of capital, from the private sector to the government. In innumerable ways, the federal government was diverting the wellsprings of the economy and the flow of capital to itself through the payroll tax, taxes on profits and capital gains, and the enormous concentrations of government-controlled capital, such as the Reconstruction Finance Corporation, which controlled half the world's gold. "This," said Garrett, "was an entirely new power"

> As the government acquired it, so passed to the government the ultimate power of initiative. It passed *from* private capitalism *to* capitalistic government. The government became the great capitalist and enterpriser.[54]

The victory of the New Deal was complete. The political culture of the Old Right, represented by Garrett, the *Post*, and the values both had fought to preserve had been smashed. In the end, Garrett presented no way out, and could only comment on the passing scene:

> So it was that a revolution took place within the form. Like the hagfish, the New Deal entered the old form and devoured its meaning from within. The revolutionaries were inside; the defenders were outside. A government that had been supported by the people and so controlled by the people became one that supported the people

and so controlled them. Much of it is irreversible. That is true because habits of dependence are much easier to form than to break. Once the government, on ground of public policy, has assumed the responsibility to provide people with buying power when they are in want of it, or when they are unable to provide themselves with enough of it, according to a minimum prescribed by the government, it will never be the same again.[55]

The Old Right and the Second World War

As the new deal obliterated the world he had known, Garrett's somber vision was being realized. All around him, allies and institutions he had counted on to stand up to the collectivist juggernaut were falling by the wayside. In October of 1937, his good friend and editor of the *Saturday Evening Post*, George Horace Lorimer, died. They had worked as an unusually effective team on the *Post*, existing in a kind of literary symbiosis, and Lorimer's death was a great blow, coming as it did in the midst of Garrett's greatest battle. But the editorial policy of the *Post* was unchanged, at least for the moment. Wesley Stout, a staunch anti–New Dealer and isolationist, was appointed editor, and in June of 1940 Garrett was elevated to chief editorial writer. Garrett and the *Post* continued the anti–New Deal crusade begun by Lorimer.

As the new decade dawned, the focus of Garrett's articles began to shift. Up until this point, he had concentrated on domestic affairs. As war clouds gathered on the horizon, however, he turned his sights to the international front. Garrett's first editorial in his new capacity of chief editorial writer was a call for England and France to look to their own defense. "For how long," he asked,

> did England and France watch the Germans at the work of building the most frightful war machine of all time? They knew well enough what it was for. They could have stopped it. Their resources were in every way superior. At least they could have prepared the invincible

> defense. But they were unwilling to forego in time their customary
> ways and comforts. . . . [The result was] they were not ready, and
> began calling to the great young democracy across the Atlantic to
> save them, or, if not to save them, who had been saved once before,
> to save civilization.[56]

Just as the *Post* was hitting the newsstands, the French were signing an armistice with Germany. Still Garrett held out against the rising
tide of interventionism. The war policy of the administration could
only end in disaster. He warned his readers that historians would one
day recount how

> in the one hundred and fifty-first year of its existence, the house of
> constitutional republican government was betrayed. . . . Unawares
> to the people, the exalted Executive principle could involve them
> in war. . . . If the American people may be involved in a world war
> unawares and without a specific act of Congress, then much else
> has happened to them of which also they are unaware.[57]

Garrett's invective against the president gained in intensity as
the approach to war accelerated. America, he said, had no business
defending Europe from itself. If Hitler's hordes were about to invade
the Americas, a premise that Garrett hotly disputed, then we ought to
be preparing our own defense instead of squandering millions on the
New Deal. The administration kept telling the American people that
Germany, Italy, and Japan were our enemies, but not one had made a
gesture of war.

As Roosevelt entered his third term, however, this view was held
by an increasingly beleaguered minority. In November of 1940, Garrett
sadly admitted his failure to influence the course of events:

> The thought of fortifying America, instead of saving the world, may
> have been a selfish thought, yet we loved it. The dream of keeping
> a New World of our own may have belonged to the youth of our
> destiny, yet we believed it. Say not it was impossible. An America
> strong enough to save the world was strong enough to stand alone.

> Yet this will be, whatever else, the second unselfish war in the history
> of the warlike human race. The other, too, was ours.[58]

On March 11, 1941, Congress lurched closer to war by approving the Lend-Lease Act, which turned over to the president the power to gradually drag us into the conflict. The act authorized the sale, transfer, exchange, or lease or war supplies to any country whose defense was deemed vital to American interests. When Roosevelt used the analogy of a neighbor's house catching fire and the necessity of using a hose, Garrett retorted,

> To suppose that in a world aflame on both sides of us we can protect
> our own house and put out the fire simply by going into the hose
> business in a large and profitable way—that we can make America
> the inexhaustible arsenal of democracy, save ourselves, have freedom
> everywhere in the world, destroy the principle of aggression, and at
> the same time raise the American way of life to new levels of comfort
> and well-being is dream-stuff.[59]

By September, with war a virtual certainty, the editorial policy of the *Post* underwent a shift. Instead of continuing to denounce Roosevelt's obsession with saving Europe, Garrett—perhaps under some pressure form the Curtis Publishing Company—was now saying that if the country must fight, it ought to avoid inflation and "totalitarian methods of price control and economic administration."[60]

A few months after Pearl Harbor, Garrett was no longer employed at the *Saturday Evening Post*. The editor, Wesley Stout, was also purged, along with others who had served under Lorimer. The new editor, Ben Hibbs, had edited another Curtis publication, *The Country Gentleman*; he was considered friendlier to the Roosevelt Administration. *Time* magazine reported the story of the purge as having to do with the magazine's financial condition. But Garrett knew better. In a letter to former president Herbert Hoover, he wrote, "You are perhaps aware that the [*Saturday Evening Post*] has lifted up her garments to the New Deal. Stout has walked out and so have I. . . . The change of policy begins at once."[61]

The reprisals which were visited upon leading figures of the Old Right—harassment, vilification, and deprivation of livelihoods—hit Garrett especially hard. At the age of sixty-four, after twenty years on the *Post*, Garrett was unemployed. After a long and distinguished career as a financial writer and commentator, the author of many books, he was blacklisted. As a genuine patriot, he tried to get involved in the war effort, but they did not want him.

After two years of looking for a niche, he found one at the magazine of the National Industrial Conference Board, *The Economic Record*, which was soon renamed *American Affairs*. Once filled with statistical reports on the economy, the business quarterly became a journal of commentary and opinion, a forum for Garrett to carry on the fight. There he took on Truman for continuing price controls and government-guaranteed "full employment." Still an unreconstructed America Firster, Garrett opposed the Marshall Plan as an absurdity. Europe's problems were due to her socialist ideology, which stifled economic growth. "There are," he wrote, "seventeen Marshall Plan countries."

> Now if you think of them as one whole, all dependent on the United States for aid, you get the following spiral absurdity. . . . They must export to us things we do not need and which they need themselves in order that they may earn dollars with which to buy similar things from us.[62]

At *American Affairs* Garrett began to articulate his theory of an ongoing "revolution within the form" begun by the New Deal and continued by the Fair Deal. The postwar mixed economy presided over by Truman had a high employment level, Garrett conceded, but this was due to the enormous demand held in abeyance during the war years, exports fueled by the Marshall Plan, and the cold-war economy, the latest form of government-business "partnership" spurred by our globalist foreign policy. The price of full employment was mountains of debt and the loss of liberty.

To the doughty old warrior, who had fought Roosevelt all the way, the postwar world must have seemed a bleak and unfriendly place. War had transformed the nation, and not, from Garrett's perspective, for the better. The economic life of the country, once ruled by the market, was now managed by Washington. The political culture, too, was transformed. Garrett had always considered himself a radical, in the classical liberal tradition; now that tradition was virtually extinct, and "what was conservative is radical, and *laissez-faire*, which was radical, is reactionary."[63]

In October of 1950, *American Affairs* ceased publication. In the four remaining years of his life, Garrett published three books. The first, *The Wild Wheel*, was a study of Henry Ford in which Garrett celebrated the age of laissez-faire, mourned its passing—and pointed to its assassins.[64]

"Laissez Faire did not survive the death of Henry Ford," he wrote,

> [i]t was betrayed by its friends, not for thirty pieces of silver but for debased paper money that would be legal tender for debt. Then it was stoned to death by the multitude and buried with hymns of praise for the easier life.
>
> The obsequies were performed by the government, which assumed at the graveside ultimate responsibility for the continued success, well-being, and growth of the national economy; by the government's tax collector, who was to become insatiable, and by organized labor, whose economic power against that of the employer was increased by law, deliberately, on grounds of social policy.
>
> You may like it better this way. Many people do. In any case, it was not to be argued. Only this—that if Laissez Faire had not begotten the richest world that ever existed there would have been much less for the welfare state to distribute.[65]

American Globalism in the Postwar Era

In 1951, Garrett published *Ex America*, the second in the trilogy of essays making up his book, *The People's Pottage*.[66] While reiterating many of the themes of *The Revolution Was*, *Ex America* reflected Garrett's distaste for the meager rewards of American globalism. Not that he had expected them to be anything other than paltry. Twice we had come to Europe's aid, and now we were doing it for the third time: defending her against the Communists, rebuilding her industries, opening the spigot of American abundance and letting it flow freely into the capitals of Europe in the form of loans, credits, subsidies, and handouts of every description. And yet,

> [t]he winds that blow our billions away return burdened with themes of scorn and dispraise. There is a little brat wind that keeps saying:
>
> "But you are absurd, you Americans, like the rich, fat boy who is tolerated while he spends his money at the drugstore and then gets chased home with mud on his clothes. He is bewildered and hurt, and yet he wants so much to be liked that he does it again the next day. But this is a parable and you are probably too stupid to get it. If you do you won't believe it, and so no harm is done. You will come again tomorrow."[67]

America, said Garrett, was victimized by arrogant European "allies" who feasted at our table and then berated us for having the wealth to spare. He would not apologize for America's wealth:

> Firstly, we made it all for ourselves, the hard way, by our own free labor, and the ground of it was a life of puritan thrift, self-discipline and austerity, while the rich in Europe, exploiting their own and their colonial labor, lived in dazzling wealth.[68]

And secondly, because America, for some strange reason, *had* shared her wealth with the world. In World War I, we saved Europe from the Kaiser—and in return the British repudiated their war debt. World War II brought Lend-Lease and the U.S. economy was placed at the disposal of the British Empire, all free of charge. The Marshall Plan not only rebuilt Europe, but also enabled the nations of Europe to compete with American industry for world markets.

This kind of generosity, maintained Garrett, was unprecedented; it equaled the national wealth of Great Britain, our next-richest ally, whose socialist leaders criticized us for our vulgar materialism. And still, insulting winds from Europe denounced American greed and "cultural imperialism." And still, U.S. aid kept flowing.

Garrett traced this softness for Europe to the turn of the century and "the flowering of that alien graft upon our tree of sapience called the intellectual," who "knew more than anybody else about everything and all about nothing, except how to subvert the traditions and invert the laws." Unsuited to the business world by reason of a lack of inventiveness, and relegated to a status lower than he thought his rightful due, "his revenge was to embrace Old World socialism." The American intellectuals were "received in the houses of the rich, where they dined on fine plate and denounced success. Standing on the eastern seaboard they gazed dotingly on Europe, which, they said, was twenty years ahead of America in social consciousness."[69]

The intellectuals were strangers in their own country, people who saw no special virtue in the American standard of living; in fact, they considered it a particular mark of dishonor. "All they knew about the American affair—all they wanted to know—was what was wrong with it." Having abdicated the task of articulating a distinctively American culture, the intellectuals "began to import political ideas from Europe. This was reversal. Until then, for more than one hundred years, Europe had been taking ideas from us," but now the transmission belt was moving in the other direction. From Germany, the idea of social security; from England, the ideas of the Fabians, as well as political laborism. Garrett contrasted these imports with the homegrown individualism of Samuel Gompers, a founder of the American labor movement, who once said he would rather be shot than become a number on a social security card.

The Europeanization of the intellectuals had its impact. The American political culture, once conducive to economic freedom and limited government, began to turn. "The first great turning," wrote Garrett,

> was accomplished with the ease of a Pullman train passing from one track to another over a split-point switch. The landscape hardly

changed at all for a while, and then gradually, and when people found themselves in a new political region, there was no turning back.[70]

The first victory of the European incursion was in the battle to ratify the Sixteenth Amendment to the Constitution, mandating a progressive tax on all incomes; an idea, as Garrett observed, that was not only European but also Marxian. Once established, the redistribution principle was a mighty lever in the hands of the collectivists. In tandem with the New Deal, it uprooted the once-secure right of private property and threatened the foundations of republican government. Having seized control of money and credit, and stroked the engine of inflation through the Federal Reserve, government was now free. As Garrett explained,

> Formerly free government was understood to mean the government of a free people. But now that meaning changed. The government itself was free. Free from what? Free from the ancient limitations of money. [Government] had no longer to fear a deficit because it could turn deficit into money; the bigger the deficit the richer the government was. It had only to think billions and behold, the billions were in the Treasury.[71]

Thus freed of its earthly bonds, there was no limit to the power of government—not even a geographical limit. "Now," said Garrett, "by this new magic, it could fill its own purse and scatter beneficence not only at home but throughout the world." "For want of dollars," he speculates, "World War II would have been impossible. . . . But if dollars made it possible, still dollars did not do it. The American mind had to be reconditioned for intervention a second time in the quarrels of the world." It was the intellectuals who subverted the natural isolationism of the American people. Americans had been soured on Europe since World War I, but the intellectuals "went to work for the second crusade" because "both their convictions and their political ambitions harmonized perfectly with the new foreign policy of intervention."

On the dust jacket of *The People's Pottage*, we are told that Garrett's *Saturday Evening Post* editorials "created much bitter controversy and caused the New Deal to threaten the life of that magazine." In describing the vicious, no-holds-barred campaign to drag America into war, Garrett's bitterness is palpable:

> In the orchestration of this policy the intellectuals had the drums, the percussion instruments and the brass; the administration played the strings and the woodwinds. To the science of propaganda a new book was added. Never before in a free country, with no actually imposed forms of thought control, had the mind of a people been so successfully conditioned. In three years *isolationist* became a smear word, supposed to be politically fatal, and to say or think *America first* was treason to mankind.[72]

They had driven him out of journalism and out of the mainstream of American political life. His views, expressed in the pages of the *Saturday Evening Post*, once representative of the culture in general, were now held only by a small and rapidly diminishing minority. Yet his voice was not stilled. It grew ever more bitter, more alarmed; and yet, strangely, more lyrical with time.

Against the Cold War: Rise of Empire

Rise of Empire, the last essay of the *People's Pottage* trilogy, returns to Garrett's theme of "revolution within the form," only this time applied to the revolution in our foreign policy. "We have crossed the boundary that lies between Republic and Empire," declares Garrett in the opening sentence of his prophetic pamphlet. Like Rome, we have passed into Empire without quite knowing it. He tells the story of Octavian, who never called himself emperor and was careful to keep the republican forms intact—all the while expanding his own power at every opportunity. One day, Octavian stood before the Roman Senate and announced that the Republic was restored. "And now I give back the Republic into your keeping," he declared. "The laws, the troops, the treasury, the provinces, all are restored to you. May you guard them worthily." As Garrett tells it:

The response of the Senate was to crown him with oak leaves, plant laurel trees at his gate and name him Augustus. After that he reigned for more than forty years and when he died the bones of the Republic were buried with him.[73]

The form of the American Republic was intact, but something more fundamental had changed. The Constitution had been subverted, undermined, and finally rendered irrelevant by the growth of administrative law. Although not even Roosevelt managed to declare war all on his own—he had to wait until Pearl Harbor—Garrett laments the fact that "nine years later a much weaker President did."

If Garrett had bitterly opposed Roosevelt and fought the New Deal every step of the way, then his view of Truman and the Fair Deal was, if possible, even harsher. Compared to Roosevelt, Truman was a pygmy—and yet he managed to set the kind of precedent that FDR could have only dreamed about. The power to declare war, the once jealously guarded prerogative of Congress, was usurped when Truman initiated the "police action" in Korea, and "Congress condoned his usurpation of its exclusive Constitutional power." The president's supporters in Congress had come up with a new argument, one so audacious that not even Roosevelt had dared utter it; modern warfare, they said, made the Congressional monopoly on the war power obsolete. We might all perish waiting for Congress to debate the merits and demerits of a formal declaration. Garrett disdained this idea: "The reasoning," he snorted, "is puerile." Congress was in session as hostilities commenced; why, then, was it dependent on the newspapers for any clue as to what was happening?

The interventionists argued that the president had acted defensively. Garrett retorted that the reason Truman never asked Congress for a declaration of war was because such an action would have opened up the question of just what it was we were defending.

When Truman sent U.S. troops to Europe and some in Congress dared to protest, the Senate asked the State Department for a position paper on the matter of the executive power to send troops all over the world. The State Department drew up a document, *Powers of the*

President to Send Troops Outside of the United States, prepared for the use of the Senate Foreign Relations Committee. "This document," said Garrett,

> in the year 2950, will be a precious find for any historian who may be trying then to trace the departing footprints of the vanished American Republic. For the information of the United States Senate it said: "As this discussion of the respective powers of the President and Congress has made clear, constitutional doctrine has been largely moulded by practical necessities. Use of the congressional power to declare war, for example, has fallen into abeyance because wars are no longer declared in advance."
>
> Caesar might have said it to the Roman Senate. If constitutional doctrine is moulded by necessity, what is a written Constitution for?[74]

As we approach the year 2000, our precious find is not this long-forgotten government document, but Garrett's pellucid analysis. Unlike most conservatives, who jumped on the cold-war bandwagon, Garrett saw that the precedent set by Truman represented a mortal danger to America's republican form of government that would have significance far beyond the Korean Peninsula. It was "a forecast of executive intentions, a manifestation of the executive mind, a mortal challenge to the parliamentary principle." A decade later, in Vietnam, Garrett's prophecy was fulfilled.

Garrett's essential insight, in later years, was that the arena of power had shifted from the domestic to the international scene. It was no longer necessary to pack the Supreme Court or mobilize the union goons in support of government policies; the welfare state was an established fact. The beast raised up by the New Deal had now turned its gaze outward. In *Rise of Empire*, Garrett—never more eloquent—now directed all of his attention to what he considered to be the central issue of our time. As he defined it,

> The question is: "Whose hand shall control the instrument of war?"

> It is late to ask. It may be too late, for when the hand of the Republic begins to relax another hand is already putting itself forth.[75]

Who or what is behind this phantom hand? It is the impulse to Empire which becomes dominant as the Republic enters its death throes. But what is an Empire? What sets it apart from democracies, republics, oligarchies, any or all of which have engaged in wars of expansion and colonization but did not attain imperial status? The U.S. expanded from ocean to ocean, and still this did not yet confer on us the mark of Empire, for, as Garrett says, "Continental conquest was but the growth of a lively political organism, acting from its own center. The natural limits of it were geographic." This view, of course, is heresy by today's "politically correct" standards. The current orthodoxy is that America's very existence is an imperialistic crime, a view Garrett would have treated with the contempt it deserves.[76]

Nor, in Garrett's view, did the existence of colonial possessions prove anything at all: colonies did not make ancient Greece an Empire. "War, conquest, colonization, expansion"—these things are "political exertions that occur in the history of any kind of state that was ever known." There is something distinctive about the internal structure and dynamics of an empire, which is alien to any and all republics, and that is, first of all, the principle that "[t]he executive power of government shall be dominant."[77]

The system set up by the Founders—with its separation of powers, its built-in tension between the judicial, congressional, and executive branches—struck a balance so perfect that sovereignty was vested not in any one of them, but only in the people. If the people wanted some law the Supreme Court deemed unconstitutional, all they had to do was amend the Constitution. That was done in the case of the income tax, and "[s]o it worked," observed Garrett,

> and worked extremely well, for the Republic. It would not work for Empire, because what Empire needs above all in government is an executive power that can make immediate decisions, such as a decision in the middle of the night by the President to declare war

> on the aggressor in Korea, or, on the opposite side, a decision by the
> Politboro in the Kremlin, perhaps also in the middle of the night,
> to move a piece on the chess board of cold war.[78]

The Cold War has ended, but the executive power has not withered. The possibility of a sudden nuclear attack has faded into improbability, but the president's authority to launch a military expedition on the other side of the world, instead of being weakened, is stronger than ever. The justification for the extension of executive power may be obsolete, or forgotten, yet the principle of executive dominance does not retreat, but only advances.

How did we arrive at such a pass? Garrett traces the rise of executive power back to the turn of the century, to, first, the imposition of the federal income tax, which gave the government the money power—that is, power to redistribute the nation's wealth—and, second, to World War I. Still, the balance might have corrected itself, as it seemed to be doing during the twenties. But then came the Great Depression, the New Deal, and World War II. During the course of those twenty years, "the sphere of Executive Government increased with a kind of explosive force." Previously, the symbol of the U.S. government was not the president, but the Congress of the United States as the voice of the people. Now, the status of Congress has been considerably lowered—and it has not recovered to this day. By the time *Rise of Empire* saw print, the office of the president had become the symbol *and* substance of American power—and the first prerequisite of Empire had been fulfilled.

It is important to contrast here the great chasm that separates the Old Right from the New on this vital question of the executive power. Garrett opposed executive dominance because he was the uncompromising champion of a strictly *limited* government. Having abandoned principle in favor of power, today our "Big Government conservatives" hail the Imperial Presidency and exult in the pomp and circumstance that surrounds that bloated office.

Yet another occasion to remark on Garrett's remarkable prescience is the second sign of Empire, which has come to pass when, as Garrett put it, "[d]omestic policy becomes subordinate to foreign policy."

The growing dominance of foreign-policy goals as a central concern of the planners and policymakers was rationalized by the ideology of the Cold War. Garrett contemptuously rejected this rationale. He had the insight to see the "revolutionary technic" inherent in the nature of this new crusade:

> It needs hardly to be argued that as we convert the nation into a garrison state to build the most terrible war machine that has ever been imagined on earth, every domestic policy is bound to be conditioned by our foreign policy.[79]

The Cold War meant that foreign policy dominated the minds and plans of the power elite, because nothing less than the survival of the nation was supposedly at stake. Therefore, any sacrifice was justified in pursuit of this new overseas crusade. Freedom, solvency, the American standard of living—there was *nothing* we might not throw overboard in order to ensure our survival. Seizure of private property, conscription, a "garrison state [in which] the hungry may have to be fed not by checks from the Treasury but in soup kitchens!"—such was the future Garrett foresaw as the Cold War got going. Just as the first two world wars paved the way for the revolution within the form, so the third great crusade would bring us near to the complete dissolution of the form.[80]

He saw it all coming, in 1952, and in such detail that *Rise of Empire* has about it an air of timeless modernity. For what else are we to make of his third sign of Empire, which he described as "[a]scendancy of the military mind, to such a point at last that the civilian mind is intimidated"?[81] As General Schwarzkopf paraded down the grand boulevards of the imperial capital in a spectacle akin to a Roman triumph, one might have been tempted to think that Garrett had a genuine premonition; that he dreamed it all one mystic night, four decades before it happened.

But it didn't take mystic insight to divine where we were headed in 1952. The Cold War had to mean the rise of the national-security state, with its penchant for secrecy, its deference to the military, its ever-expanding military budgets. Garrett's predictions came true not because he was a modern Nostradamus, but because he understood the welfare-warfare state as a system, a mechanism fueled by inflation and war. As Garrett made the analogy,

> War becomes an instrument of domestic policy. Among the control mechanisms on the government's panel board now is a dial marked *War.* It may be set to increase or decrease the tempo of military expenditures, as the planners decide that what the economy needs is a little more inflation or a little less—but of course never any deflation.[82]

Just as government now had a "vested interest in the power of inflation," said Garrett, "so now we may perceive that it will come also to have a kind of proprietary interest in the institution of perpetual war."

And so it was to be a war without end. Not even the end of the Cold War, the collapse of communism, and the emergence of the U.S. as the sole superpower on earth would satisfy the ideologues of the new globalism—and Garrett foresaw this, too. When one enemy was vanquished, a new one would rise to take its place, and so the U.S. needed a permanent shield, which was a structural feature of Empire—and this was the fourth sign of Empire, which Garrett defined as "[a] system of satellite nations."[83] The vast far-flung system of local satraps, whose security and economic well-being are deemed a vital interest to the security of the United States—which today goes under the name of "New World Order"—had its origins in the Lend-Lease Act, passed nine months before Pearl Harbor. In Garrett's view, Lend-Lease was "the single most reckless delegation of power by the Congress to the President, amounting in fact to abdication."[84] On the day Lend-Lease passed, in March of 1941, the spigot was opened. By the end of the war, "Lend-Lease goods were flowing to every non-enemy port in the world"—and the torrent of U.S. aid was never cut off. The Marshall Plan, the Mutual Aid plan, the North Atlantic Treaty Organization—all were incarnations of the same deity, the god of collective security. This pernicious and dangerous doctrine was the basis of what Garrett called "the evangel of fear" promulgated by the interventionists, a fear of standing alone.

Which brings us to the fifth sign of Empire, which Garrett describes in the following way:

Fear may be understood. But a curious and characteristic emotional weakness of Empire is:

> A complex of vaunting and fear.[85]

As the United States sets itself up as the champion of a New World Order, the vaunting has taken on outrageous dimensions that perhaps not even Garrett was capable of imagining. He likened it to the feeling experienced by the passengers on the doomed Titanic, who "would not believe that a ship so big and grand could sink." Perhaps that was a premonition that may yet come true. However, the source of the fear was something he saw clearly. It was, he said,

> Fear of the barbarian. Fear of standing alone. . . . A time comes when the guard itself, that is, your system of satellites, is a source of fear. Satellites are often willful and the more you rely upon them the more willful and demanding they are. There is, therefore, the fear of offending them. . . . If they falter or fail, what will become of the weapons with which we have supplied them?[86]

"The possibility of having to face its own weapons on a foreign field," said Garrett, "is one of the nightmares of Empire." That nightmare became a reality, not too long afterward, in Vietnam, in the Middle East, and throughout the Third World.

The sixth and final insignia of Empire, which becomes visible only when it is too late to do anything about it, is that the Empire finds itself the "prisoner of history." Locked into the economic and political necessity of Empire as a system, we would at last embrace the ideas now being bandied about by the neoconservative prophets of "world dominion" and the "end of history." This goes far beyond the concept of collective security to the idea of historical inevitability, to the notion that,

> It is our turn.
> Our turn to do what?. . .
>
> Our turn to maintain a balance of power against the forces of evil everywhere—in Europe and Asia and Africa, in the Atlantic and in the Pacific, by air and by sea—evil in this case being the Russian barbarian.[87]

Our turn to "keep the peace of the world," to "save civilization," to "serve mankind." But this, he protested, is "the language of Empire," the same imperial tongue spoken by the Romans, who took seriously their civilizing mission; the Spanish, "who added salvation;" and the British, who "added the noble myth of the white man's burden." Our own contribution to the mythology has been the addition of the words "freedom and democracy," and "yet the more that may be added to it the more it is the same language still. A language of power."[88]

This is the language of George Bush and his New World Order, the language of Krauthammer and Muravchik, of the neoconservatives who clamored for wars with Iraq, and the global planners who agitate for a multi-billion dollar buyout of the Soviet Union. The sixth and final sign of Empire is all around us.

In the end, we are brought to the question, Is the process, then, irreversible? Are we prisoners of history, who have moved into the final phase of a decadent Republic which is already an Empire in everything but name? In reading Garrett's last published writings, it often seems as if he takes this for granted. But in the last section of *Rise of Empire*, wherein he maps out "the lost terrain," there is also the hint of a plan to regain it.

The "mortal enmity" of the Empire and the Republic is such that, as Garrett says, "either one must forbid the other or one will destroy the other." The key is that the central issue has never been put to a vote of the people. The emergence of America as a global power was gradually but steadily promoted by the executive power, with "slogans, concealments, equivocations, a propaganda of fear, and in every crisis an appeal for unity." It is impossible to retrace our steps, say the globalists; we cannot go back. Garrett, however, would have none of it. "Do not ask whether or not it is possible," he writes,

> Ask yourself this: If it were possible, what would it take? How could the people restore the Republic if they would? When you have put it that way you are bound to turn and look at the lost terrain. What are the positions, forgotten or surrendered, that would have to be recaptured?[89]

The first position to be retaken is a state of mind. The people must recover "the habit of decision," and this recovery would amount to "a kind of self-awakening." What better time for this reawakening than now, when whatever threat once emanated from outside our borders is virtually nonexistent? Now that the Cold War is over and the Great Satan is vanquished, it is time to think about recovering some of that lost terrain—and in considering it we have already taken a step and recovered one position that had been lost.

Again, one is struck by the applicability of Garrett's principles to the current situation. He might have been a modern journalist commenting on the war with Iraq when he wrote,

> The second height to be regained is that where of old foreign policy was submitted to public debate. How long ago that seems! And how was that height lost? There was no battle for it. The government seized it without a struggle; and now the President may say the people ought to accept the government's foreign policy without debate.[90]

Garrett bitterly attacked the idea of a "bipartisan" foreign policy, and identified the interventionists as the same New Dealers who once assured us that the Soviet Union was our faithful and heroic ally—and who then launched the Cold War against their erstwhile comrades-in-arms. Still angry over the hate campaign conducted by the pro-war party, who had smeared their enemies as agents of a foreign power—and finally silenced them—Garrett looked forward to the day when they would get their comeuppance:

> On this height, where foreign policy once more shall be debated by the people who may have to die for it, let the wind be cold and merciless. Let those be nakedly exposed to it who have brought the country to this impasse . . . [and] who petted and nourished the Russian aggressor and recommended him to the affections of the American people as a peace-loving collaborator.[91]

Here was the source of the Old Right's attitude toward that much misunderstood phenomenon known as "McCarthyism." The orthodox liberal version of this episode in American history is that McCarthyism was a natural extension of the cold-war mentality, a domestic corollary to the Korean War. But in fact many Old Rightists who opposed the Cold War were ardent McCarthyites; John T. Flynn was one, as we shall see, and the above passage from *Rise of Empire* indicates that Garrett was not unsympathetic to the cause. The reason is that Old Rightists like Flynn and Garrett came to suspect that the great enemy we were asked to mobilize against had, in large part, been built up by ourselves. We had defeated Hitler and handed the victory to Stalin—and now we were supposed to sacrifice our economy, our liberty, and the peace of the world in order to a launch a holy war against communism.

The third great height to be reconquered is the power of the public purse, and here, says Garrett, the chief enemy is inflation. In his view, "there is only one thing to do with the monster."

> It can be sickened and starved, not to death, because the life in it is immortal, but to a harmless shadow. Its food is irredeemable paper money. Sound money is its poison. Victory here cannot be unconditional. You will have to leave a guard, and then someone to watch the guard, and then keep going back to see.[92]

The great problem, as Garrett saw it, was that there would be dissension even in the ranks of the monster-slayers, some who would advise us to go easy on the monster. "Don't kill him," they would say. "'If he dies deflation will come and deflation is worse.' And this is the final height to be retaken."

For all his bitter irony, spoken in the language of tragedy, in the end there is hope. The people, Garrett said, have the possibility of choosing liberty: "The only point is that no leader has yet appeared with the courage to make them choose." What was needed was the right leadership—a development he would not see in his lifetime, but which his work might some day make possible.

Testament: The American Story

The trilogy of essays, collected together as *The People's Pottage*, was the magnificent manifesto of a movement that was dying, even as the seventy-five-year-old Garrett was beginning to run out of steam. He was ill a great deal of the time during his last years, but he never abandoned either his writing or the pleasures of life. Concerning the former, Garrett wrote one last book, *The American Story*, a history of the United States which is also his personal and political testament.[93] Regarding the latter, he married for the third time, on August 15, 1947. His new wife was Dorothy Williams Goulet, a thirty-seven-year-old widow and former journalist who had been his secretary. He had long ago retired to a farm in Tuckahoe, New Jersey, where he lived quietly with his wife and worked on his last published writings. There, on November 6, 1954, he suffered a stroke and was taken to Atlantic City Hospital, where he died.

    The American Story was published posthumously. It is the sort of history book that is not to be found in our "politically correct" schools, since it starts out with the discovery of America by Columbus and does not condemn the founding of the freest country on earth as a racist crime against humanity. Written with the narrative power of a practiced novelist, Garrett's history of the nation he loved is a vast panorama painted in the bright colors of his unique prose style. Here he visits the central themes that dominated his works—the uniqueness of the American political culture, the inherent dynamism of the American economy, the cultural basis of the technological revolution, the virtues of laissez-faire, the real story of how we got into two world wars, the evils of the New Deal, the folly of globalism. It is a magnificent portrait of the historical pageant as seen through the eyes of a giant of conservative thought.

    At the end of some chapters in *The American Story* are sections subtitled "Marginalia," in which the author permits himself more speculative space than would otherwise be possible within the constraints of the narrative. Tacked on to the very end of the book, almost like an afterthought, is a section subtitled "Apostrophe." Here Garrett takes up a familiar theme of the Old Right, the image of the immigrant tide sweeping away the cultural foundations of the American republic. But his attitude is equivocal, speculative; he speaks of the Statue of Liberty as "[t]his heroic Copper Woman, standing at the gate . . . great symbol of the immigration that changed the blood of America, maybe not for worse but certainly for better or worse."[94]

Garrett differentiates between two waves of immigration: the voluntary migration from England, Ireland, Germany, and Scandinavia, and the induced migration of cheap labor from eastern and southern Europe. As a result of the second wave, the first inner-city slums appeared. Also making their appearance were the first racial pressure groups. In a remark that is sure to get not only the Anti-Defamation League of B'nai B'rith but also the Knights of Columbus up in arms, Garrett makes it clear that he thinks the arrival of Italians, Portuguese, Greeks, Hungarians, Balkan Slavs, Poles, and Russians on American shores is a mixed blessing. "The Russian tide was heavily loaded with Jews," he writes, "and this Jew was not like the one that came with the Germans." Considered in context, however, Garrett's remark on the influx of Russian Jews was merely a commentary on the political culture of Russia, an objection based not on ethnicity but on ideology.[95]

Garrett cites a study by Carl D. Brigham, a professor of psychology at Princeton, who made a scientific analysis of army intelligence tests and presented his findings in a book. He quotes Brigham to the effect that "The representatives of the Alpine and Mediterranean races in our immigration are intellectually inferior to the representatives of the Nordic race which formerly made up about 50% of our immigration."[96]

For all this esoteric talk about the Alpine, Mediterranean, and Nordic races, there is nothing in *The American Story* to indicate racial prejudice against blacks; in fact, quite the opposite is the case. Speaking of the Declaration of Independence, he says "Morally it was a fiction because it left out the Negro slave," and on the subject of slavery, he quotes Jefferson, who predicted, "As nations cannot be rewarded or punished in the next world they must be in this. By an inevitable chain of cause and effect providence punishes national sins by national calamities." Garrett eulogized the heroic "North American red man," who would not be tamed: "Facing extinction he made one of the grand gestures in the history of mankind. He would sooner perish than be a slave."[97]

Americans, Garrett complained, no longer knew who and what they were. Fifty years after the Statue of Liberty, "*Protestant* had the sound of bigotry, *Nordic* was racialist and intolerant, *limited* government was a memory, and free, competitive capitalism had been strangled." The "Apostrophe" ends on an inconclusive note. "Wisdom," sighs Garrett, "is not a science."[98]

While Garrett does not quite live up to the "politically correct" standards of today, his views on the immigration question were an aspect of his central concern: how to preserve the political culture of the New World against the degenerating influence of the Old. It was not the corruption of the gene pool Garrett was worried about, but the corruption of the American attitude toward work and reward.

The Legacy of Garet Garrett

For as long as the Cold War lasted, there was no room on the political spectrum for anyone even close to the position taken by Garrett and his Old Right colleagues. On the left were the liberal internationalists, who wanted to fight communism with socialism both at home and abroad. On the Right were the conservative internationalists, who wanted to roll back communism by military means, even if it meant militarizing the U.S. economy.

Today, however, the world is quite different. The red dragon is slain, impaled on its own claws. The major effect of this within the United States is that the political spectrum is radically altered. Yesterday's doves have sprouted hawk feathers. Liberals who marched against the Vietnam War in the sixties supported the bombing of Iraq in the nineties, cheered the Somalia "rescue mission," and are pressuring Clinton to fulfill his campaign promise to protect the make-believe country of Bosnia-Herzegovina from Serbian secessionists.

On the other hand, yesterday's hawks have undergone a similar role reversal. Conservatives who once cheered Nixon's invasion of Cambodia and wanted to bomb Vietnam into submission were the first to raise their voices against Bush's war in the Gulf. Skepticism of the Somalian adventure was largely confined to the Right. Opposition to intervention in the Balkans is coming not from the left, but from the Pentagon and its traditional allies, conservative Republicans. As the United Nations chips away at American sovereignty and a militant internationalism has captured the imagination of the liberal punditocracy, conservatives are once again asking the questions first raised by Garrett:

> How now, thou American, frustrated crusader, do you know where you are?
>
> Is it security you want? There is no security at the top of the world.
>
> To thine own self a liberator, to the world an alarming portent; do you know where you are going from here?[99]

Garrett's great contribution, and his relevance for today, is that he posed these questions forty years before they began to loom large on the horizon. As the foreign-policy question shapes up as potentially the most divisive among conservatives, Garrett's warning that "we have crossed the boundary that lies between Republic and Empire" returns to haunt us.

The fifty-year span of Garrett's career as a writer and editor encompasses the rise and fall of the Old Right as a major factor in American politics. At the height of his influence, as George Lorimer's right-hand man, Garrett was in the vanguard of a large and combative movement, the Old Right, which launched a furious assault on the New Deal and mobilized millions against FDR's war drive. As Garrett grew old and embittered, and yet ever more eloquent and clear-sighted, so too did his Old Right confreres tend to take a dark view of the future, succumbing to pessimism as their numbers and influence declined. When Garrett retired to his farm in the midfifties, the Old Right had virtually faded from the scene, displaced by the fevered devotees of the Cold War.

In 1900, when young Garrett started his career as a journalist in Washington, D.C., covering the White House of William McKinley, that city was the capital of a republic, in which the federal government was limited in its scope and the people had not yet surrendered their heritage. When they buried him, in 1954, Washington had become the capital of a sprawling empire, the seat of a federal government with virtually unlimited power. The people had long since surrendered their heritage. Indeed, by that time they had nearly forgotten it.

Conservatives want to revive that heritage. In doing so, however, they must first recover their own lost legacy, the traditions and history of the Old Right. Cast adrift without the compass of anticommunism, conservatives looking for answers in the post–Cold War world must necessarily begin with a search for their own roots. As today's paleoconservatives uncover the relics of their half-forgotten ancestors, they will find a treasure trove in the life and legacy of Garet Garrett.

4

John T. Flynn:

From Liberalism to Laissez-Faire

> *The theory that fascism originated in the conspiracy of the great industrialists will not hold. It originated on the Left. Primarily . . . from among those erstwhile socialists who, wearying of that struggle, have turned to becoming saviors of capitalism*
> —John T. Flynn, As We Go Marching, 1944

PRIOR TO WORLD WAR I, American liberals were guided by two principles: distrust of big business and opposition to war. As the approach of World War II darkened the political horizon, the Left's hatred of capitalism overwhelmed its traditional abhorrence of war. Liberals of the *New Republic* variety, along with their radical confreres, leaped on the Popular Front bandwagon, jettisoned their anti-interventionist and antimilitarist baggage, and rode the wave of war hysteria all the way to Pearl Harbor. The war accelerated and strengthened the statist tendencies in the Left until, in a very short time, the antimilitarism of such old-style liberals as Oswald Garrison Villard seemed archaic.[1]

The career of John T. Flynn—journalist, author, and master polemicist of the Old Right—is highly unusual in that its course reveals a pattern the exact reverse of this massive and relatively rapid degeneration. Flynn started out as a liberal columnist for that flagship of American liberalism, the *New Republic*, and wound up on the far right, defending Joe McCarthy and denouncing "creeping Socialism." Now, as we have seen, this in itself is far from unique. What is unusual about Flynn is that his journey turns the familiar neoconservative odyssey on its head. Instead of being seduced by the New Deal and the Popular Front into supporting the war, Flynn was led by his thoroughgoing antiwar stance to challenge the developing state-worship of modern liberalism.

As the New Deal liberals and Popular Front radicals deserted their former antiwar position, they blazed a path that would be followed by the anti-Stalinist leftist intellectuals of the postwar period. In defecting from left to right, the pattern of their defection was virtually always the same. They almost always broke with the Left over some foreign-policy issue, itself invariably motivated by the imminence of some military conflict involving the United States. In this moment of crisis, with the whole weight of public opinion bearing down on them, the left-liberal intellectuals broke down; it was easier to go with the flow.

Certainly "go with the flow" is the one phrase in the English language that *least* describes the career of John T. Flynn. When liberal and leftist intellectuals enlisted as the propagandists of Roosevelt's war, Flynn dared to swim against the tide and became one of the central leaders of the America First Committee. For this he endured a campaign of calumny, lies, blacklisting, and the ever-present threat of government repression. Far from breaking down in a moment of crisis, Flynn rose to the occasion and became one of the outstanding founders and leaders of the movement we know today as the Old Right.[2]

An American Liberal

John T. Flynn was born in 1882, in Bladensburg, Maryland, where he grew up in a devoutly Roman Catholic family. He graduated from Georgetown Law School in Washington, D.C., but never practiced law. Instead, he switched to journalism. After a long struggle, he finally found a position in 1920 with the *New York Globe*, where he specialized in financial analysis. By the start of the thirties, his articles exposing fraud in the financial markets were featured in *Colliers, Harpers*, and other major magazines. He also wrote a series of muckraking books: *Investment Trusts Gone Wrong!,*[3] *Graft in Business,*[4] and a biography of John D. Rockefeller, titled *God's Gold.*[5]

There was little in Flynn's writing at this time that indicated his future direction. He was a conventional liberal, whose views were not out of place in that bastion of liberal orthodoxy, the *New Republic.* In 1933, he began a weekly column for the magazine, "Other People's Money," in which he campaigned for a federal investigation of banking practices. When Roosevelt swept into office, Flynn welcomed him. Flynn supported the Democratic Party platform of 1932, which called for an end to the extravagant spending of the Republicans, a balanced budget, and the abolition of the new government bureaus and commissions, which had begun to accumulate. He believed that the way to beat the Depression was to stimulate private investment, trim the rough edges of capitalism, and avoid big-spending schemes. When campaigning for president, Roosevelt had said, "I am opposed to any form of dole. I do not believe that the state has any right merely to hand out money." Big-spending projects would only be a "stopgap" measure and would ultimately fail to solve the problem of unemployment. In July of 1932, Roosevelt cited the Democratic platform, which promised "a saving of not less than 25 percent" of the cost of the federal government. Lashing out against Hoover for not reducing government expenses, the Democratic candidate said, "I accuse the present administration of being the greatest spending administration in peace times in all our history." Then he added, "On my part, I ask you very simply to assign to me the task of reducing the annual operating expenses of your national government."

But Flynn was soon disillusioned. In fact, the New Deal that Roosevelt sold to the American people in 1932 bore absolutely no resemblance to the one he immediately imposed on an unsuspecting nation. During the first hundred days of his administration, Roosevelt racked up a deficit larger than the one it took Hoover two years to produce. Worse, from Flynn's viewpoint, was the blizzard of new government agencies the president created and the billions in borrowed money that financed them. Flynn attacked the president in his *New Republic* column and in 1940 came out with a short book, *Country Squire in the White House*, in which he excoriated FDR for betraying the trust of the people who had elected him.[6]

Flynn Against the New Deal

Flynn was particularly horrified by the National Recovery Administration (NRA), which he denounced as "one of the most amazing spectacles of our times" that "represented probably the gravest attack upon the whole principle of the democratic society in our political history." With prices, wages, hours, and production quotas set by trade associations, and an industry-wide code set up to regulate every aspect of commerce, all competition would be smashed and business would ensure for itself a secure and profitable niche in the new corporatist order. This was couched in the language of liberalism, Flynn said, but was championed primarily by the Chamber of Commerce and other business groups. Flynn saw himself as the defender of true liberalism, which had been betrayed by That Man in the White House. He argued that, in supporting the New Deal, American liberals were reversing their historical position:

> While at the same time proclaiming his devotion to democracy, he [Roosevelt] adopted a plan borrowed from the corporative state of Italy and sold it to all the liberals as a great liberal revolutionary triumph. And, curiously, every American liberal who had fought monopoly, who had demanded the enforcement of the anti-trust laws, who had denied the right of organized business groups, combinations and trade associations to rule our economic life, was branded as a Tory and a reactionary if he continued to believe these things.[7]

Flynn predicted that Roosevelt's spending on vast domestic programs could not continue, for he would run out of useful peacetime projects, which at any rate could not be maintained by local government.

At the beginning of his first term, Congress had dumped $32 billion in Roosevelt's lap for "recovery," to spend as he chose. This was the source of the president's power, and he would be determined to maintain it. Suspension or even contraction of government spending would lead to an economic downturn much worse than the Great Crash and would sink his chances for reelection. But the government had borrowed up to the limit; further funds would come out of tax revenues, and this was bound to run into resistance from conservatives. The president, Flynn said, would turn to preparations for war in order to solve his dilemma, for the fantastic extravagance of the administration had reached the point of no return.

> When this point is reached in spending programs, there is always one kind of project left that breaks down resistance—which particularly breaks down resistance among the very conservative groups who are most vocal against government spending. That is national defense. The one sure and easiest way to command national assent from all groups is to ask it for national defense.[8]

World War II would be the ultimate New Deal jobs program. The Supreme Court may have declared the NRA unconstitutional, but there were other ways to militarize the economy, such as actually going to war. Roosevelt would pursue military adventure abroad to take the people's minds off their troubles at home—troubles which were not getting any better and that the New Deal was only making worse. The president had thrown off the pretense of neutrality in the war between the European empires and was now "the recognized leader of the war party." Flynn charged that "[t]here is not the slightest doubt that the only thing that now prevents his active entry on the side of the Allies is his knowledge that he cannot take the American people in yet." Though Roosevelt's enemies attacked him as a dictator, Flynn's analysis was more subtle. The president, he said, was not a dictator: he lacked the "blazing certainty" of the ideologue, and, besides, "too many people would hate him" if he played the role of the dictator, "and he could not endure that."[9] Instead, Flynn feared that the New Deal was the prelude to a new despotism, the first two or three steps in the direction of a corporatist oligarchy.

Roosevelt had breached the walls; the future oligarchs had only to step through the breach and take possession of the fortress.

Flynn was unrelenting in his assault on the president, and Roosevelt was quick to respond. After reading an attack on himself and his aide, Harry Hopkins, in the *Yale Review*, the president wrote a letter to the editor of that publication in which he declared that Flynn had become "a destructive rather than a constructive force." The president went on to say that Flynn "should be barred hereafter from the columns of any presentable daily paper, monthly magazine or national quarterly, such as the *Yale Review*."[10]

This is exactly what happened. We hear much about the alleged effect of the anticommunist blacklist at the height of the Cold War. Any number of fellow travelers and outright Stalinists have spent the greater part of the last twenty years whining and wailing about what a great injustice it was. But this was nothing compared to the blacklisting of so-called "isolationists" during the Roosevelt era. The "Smear Bund," as Flynn called it, worked tirelessly to deprive dissidents of their livelihoods and even their legal right to speak out, with the president of the United States leading the charge.

Flynn had been using his column in the *New Republic* to denounce Roosevelt's "deliberately selling to our people the baleful notion that some enemy is about to assail us." Were liberals really so "enfeebled by confusion and doubt that they [would] permit themselves to be marched off behind this fantastic banner"? He bitterly attacked the Communists, who were interested in only one thing: that the United States should enter the war "on the side of Russia." That is why the Communist Party was now engaged in "entangling this country in the politics of Europe."[11]

In joining FDR's campaign to substitute an arms program for a true economic recovery, the Left had taken the corporatist road: "The present curse of Italy and Germany is that the dictators there have made vast arms operations the medium of spending money and creating employment. You can't build battleships and make guns and war materials without putting great industries to work. The support of the economic system of both Hitler and Mussolini is the employment they have created and the income they initiate by means of the armament industry . . . but the continuation of these war preparations requires the ceaseless unloosening of war alarms upon the people. The war scare is an essential implement of the war-preparation program."[12]

This time it wasn't just the munitions makers, the economic royalists, or the Republicans who were beating the war drums: "It is being done," said Flynn, "by a Democratic administration in possession of its liberal wing."[13] The war scare and the New Deal were, in Flynn's mind, inseparable, two aspects of the same inexorable trend. "Thus," he declared,

> the great preparedness industry grows. I dare say no one can stop it. The Democrats have come around for it, and the Republicans have always been for it. The liberals favor it, the radicals favor it. Business favors it; the idealists favor it. Hence we shall have it.

But Flynn could not, and would not, reconcile himself to it:

> Here I shall merely drop this futile warning—that you cannot prepare for war without doing something to yourselves. You cannot have a war industry without a war scare; and having built it and made it the basis of work for several million men you cannot demobilize it and you will have to keep on inventing reasons for it.[14]

America First: The Battle Against Intervention

When war broke out in Europe in 1939, Flynn devoted his energies to keeping America out of the conflict. The president wanted to repeal the Neutrality Act, which imposed an arms embargo on the combatants, and sell arms to the Allies. From there, Flynn believed, it would be a short time before America was embroiled in the war.

Flynn was instrumental in forming the Keep America Out of War Congress, an association of liberals, labor leaders, and socialists such as Norman Thomas. Speaking before that group on November 10, 1940, he declared that the president was determined to get the U.S. into war indirectly by setting up a situation that would lead inevitably to war. It would then "take fifty years of research to find out how we got in." The president's policy, he said, was to divert attention away from the failure of the New Deal to get the country out of the Depression. The proposed $3 billion "defense" budget was an effort to create employment by putting the American economy on a wartime footing. Far from inevitable, the drive toward war was a "stratagem of befuddled politicians," who could think of no new excuses for deficit spending. This was the real reason for Roosevelt's scare campaign, which was supposed to justify America throwing a 300-mile belt around the Western hemisphere. Germany may have swallowed up Poland, but we had annexed "the Atlantic and Pacific Oceans."[15]

In a letter to Senator Bennett C. Clark of Missouri, Flynn warned against the specter of government repression bound to accompany the coming war. The increase in the power and visibility of the FBI as an adjunct of the military was ominous, especially when one noted that it was J. Edgar Hoover who had "carried on J. Mitchell Palmer's atrocities after the last war." The whole campaign was "a part of Roosevelt's deliberate plan to disturb the peace of mind of the American people with his spy scares and submarine scares." It was necessary "to terrify the people before they [would] authorize military expenditures."[16]

Flynn feared that America, rapidly moving toward a corporate state, would fall into a dictatorship if war came. The president had already demonstrated that the "leader principle" had usurped the Constitution when he secretly traded fifty destroyers with Britain in exchange for bases. That move was "an invasion of the rights of Congress so grave" that a Congress not already sunk in "servile submission to the executive" would "meet this usurpation promptly with impeachment proceedings."[17]

As the year 1940 wore on, the liberal war cry grew louder and more aggressive. The Committee to Defend America by Aiding the Allies, headed by a group of prominent liberals, was formed. Added to the unending barrage of propaganda emanating from the White House, the interventionists began to have an effect on the previously isolationist American public opinion.

The shift was felt in the offices of the *New Republic*. The magazine had previously rejected the Roosevelt policy of collective security, but it abandoned this position as soon as it became inconvenient. Flynn refused to abandon his antimilitarist stance just because the editors of the *New Republic* had done so, and his column became controversial. Flynn insisted that it wasn't he who had changed, but the editors of the *New Republic*; he had simply retained his antimilitarism and deep suspicion of executive power. Yet his attacks on Roosevelt were taking on a new slant. In a review of a book by Gustav Stolper, in which Stolper argued that the road to Nazism in Germany had been paved by the movement for social reform, Flynn detected the same pattern in this country: "[W]hen we get through with this last phase of the New Deal, we shall have added the elements of militarism, the shifts of power to the executive and the militant chauvinism, basing our economy on a war industry promoted by an aggressive foreign policy."[18]

As James J. Martin said in his *American Liberalism and World Politics*, by the end of 1940 Flynn was "almost a solitary voice defending what had now become a minority viewpoint. The passage of five years had seen no change of heart so spectacular as the about-face performed by American liberals in general on the subject of arms manufacture and the growth of military institutions."[19]

While American liberals, exemplified by the *New Republic*, had switched sides on the vital issues of war and militarism, Flynn, too, was undergoing an ideological transformation. His analysis of the New Deal as carrying within it the seeds of the corporatist idea had moved him out of the liberal mainstream. His column in the *New Republic* was now prefaced by an editor's note expressing his disagreement with Flynn's views. After an angry exchange of letters with editor Bruce Bliven, Flynn's column was discontinued.

His expulsion from the precincts of "respectable" liberalism seemed to energize his activism on behalf of the anti-war cause. He joined with General Robert E. Wood, of Sears, Roebuck and Co., and a group of prominent right-wingers to form the America First Committee in September of 1940. Flynn was on the national executive committee, as well as chairman of the New York chapter, and he plunged into the cause with a furious energy.

In January of 1941, he went on a national speaking tour on behalf of the AFC. At a rally in Kansas City, Missouri, Flynn declared that America "stands on the brink of war"—not a war for democracy, as the interventionists claimed, but a war "between empires" and "about imperialism." The bombing of England had changed nothing. Great Britain was merely the "biggest of all these imperialist grabbers," which had declared war on Germany not out of any great love for Poland, but because she "has an empire of her own which she seized exactly as Germany seized Poland and she sees the rise of a German empire threatening the safety" of that empire. The rise of Germany was threatening British control of the Mediterranean, which Britain needed to "hold India and millions of people in Asia and Africa in subjection." Why, he asked, should America risk her own democracy on behalf of the British Empire? The war was yet another "chapter in the long, age-old struggle of European empires about dividing up the world. . . . And it is out of this abominable world of imperialism, the scramble for dominion, the fight for trade backed by armies and guns, that I want to keep this great peaceful democratic America of ours." Flynn accused a small minority of conspiring to drag the U.S. into war, motivated by Anglophilia and a misguided attempt to preserve democracy that could end only in destroying it. If war came, predicted Flynn, then the very democratic institutions in this country that the interventionists claimed to defend would be annihilated.[20]

By this time, a smear campaign against the America First Committee, which sought to equate antiwar sentiment with support for Hitler, had already begun. The "Friends of Democracy," the ultra-interventionist pro–New Deal group led by the Reverend Leon M. Birkhead, was in the forefront of this vicious campaign. Birkhead hired John Roy Carlson as an agent provocateur and spy, whose job was to disrupt and discredit the America First movement. Carlson was an Armenian immigrant whose real name was Avedis Derounian. Using yet another alias, "George Pagnanelli," he passed himself off as an Italian and joined the isolationist movement. "Pagnanelli" pretended to be an anti-Semite, even going so far as to put out an anti-Jewish hate sheet, *The Christian Defender*, the purpose of which was to spread the calumny that the antiwar movement was anti-Jewish and pro-Nazi. While there undoubtedly was a small pro-Nazi fringe, Carlson's effort to smear all or most America First supporters with the brush of anti-Semitism was a crude lie. In his book *Under Cover*, he used the old trick of focusing on the activities of marginal bigots who are then quoted as expressing agreement with the antiwar arguments of AFC members like Flynn. The atmosphere of war hysteria and leader worship that permeated the prewar years is brought home in *Under Cover* and its sequel, *The Plotters*, where Carlson equates all criticism of the New Deal and FDR with treason and support for Hitler. The tragedy of those years was that Carlson's diatribe was put out by a major publisher and became a bestseller, reviewed in all the mass-circulation journals, while Flynn's reply, *The Smear Terror*, was privately published and received only a limited circulation.[21]

Flynn was no anti-Semite, and certainly no fascist or Nazi sympathizer. Unlike the war party, however, he was more concerned with fighting fascism on the home front than in Europe or Asia.

When Lindbergh made his famous Des Moines speech, in which he singled out the Jews as one of the three major groups pushing the country into war, Flynn was furious. Though a member of the AFC national committee and a leading light of the group, Flynn had not seen the text of Lindbergh's speech until he read it in the newspapers. Flynn wanted the AFC to publicly disassociate itself from Lindbergh's remarks, but the AFC national committee refused to do so, instead deploring what it termed "racist smears" against Lindbergh. In a letter to Lindbergh, Flynn politely but firmly reprimanded the isolationist leader. The Des Moines speech had disrupted the work of the AFC, especially in New York. While he was sure that Lindbergh was no anti-Semite, he was equally sure that attempts to introduce "shades of meaning" into the controversy would be fruitless. Lindbergh's error was that he had allowed the AFC to be "tagged with the anti-Jewish label." Yes, it was true, Flynn acknowledged, that virtually the entire Jewish population of New York backed the war drive; he agreed with Lindbergh that war was not in their interests, just as it went against the interests of the rest of the country. He went on to say that some Jewish leaders had equated all opposition to Roosevelt's interventionism with anti-Semitism, and that making the war an ethnic issue could have unpleasant consequences. "It has seemed," said Flynn, "their [the Jewish leaders'] responsibility for this should be brought home to them. But this is a far different matter from going out upon the public platform and denouncing 'the Jews' as the war-makers. No man can do that without incurring the guilt of religious and racial intolerance."[22]

On June 25, 1941, Hitler broke his nonaggression pact with Stalin and invaded the Soviet Union, and Communist parties all over the world changed their position on the war. Whereas before they had opposed U.S. intervention, which they denounced as "imperialist," now they were in favor of it. It was now a war for "democracy," a "people's antifascist struggle," and suddenly the American Communist Party and its fellow travelers were the biggest patriots on the block. Hours after Hitler's invasion of the Soviet Union, the pro-war Left in this country was agitating for aid to Stalin.

In a radio talk, Flynn pointed out that both Hitler and Stalin were enemies of the American system. He did not want "to spill the blood of one American boy to make the world safe for either Hitler or Stalin." Why, he asked, should we bleed ourselves "white with taxation," "disrupt our whole economic system," and "plunge ourselves into bankruptcy" to fight in a war "whose peace terms will have to satisfy Communist Russia?" Flynn warned that Roosevelt's interventionist foreign policy would have to mean kowtowing to Stalin—a prediction tragically fulfilled at Yalta.[23]

By the fall of 1941, the entry of the United States into the war seemed only a matter of time. Still, Flynn fought on. On September 11, Roosevelt ordered U.S. naval and air patrols to sweep all Axis warships from waters "vital" to America's national interest. Flynn appeared before the Senate Foreign Relations Committee, testifying against a proposal by Roosevelt that would allow armed merchant ships to enter combat zones. Oswald Garrison Villard and other opponents of Roosevelt's war provocations also appeared, but to no avail; the proposal carried.

Unlike some in the AFC, who gave up even before Pearl Harbor, Flynn fought to keep the U.S. out of the war right up until the very end. The AFC was dissolved after Pearl Harbor, but Flynn continued to speak out against the war hysteria. He published *The Truth About Pearl Harbor* and *The Final Secret of Pearl Harbor*, the earliest "revisionist" histories of that fateful incident.[24]

As We Go Marching: *America's Road to Fascism*

The entry of the United States into World War II completed the transformation of Flynn from a disenchanted liberal to a proto-libertarian advocate of laissez-faire and noninterventionism. Murray Rothbard describes the context in which this occurred:

> [T]he drive of the New Deal toward war once again reshuffled the ideological spectrum and the meaning of Left and Right in American politics. The left and liberal opponents of war were hounded out of the media and journals of opinion by their erstwhile allies, and condemned as reactionaries and Neanderthals. These men . . . found themselves forced into a new alliance with *laissez-faire* Republicans from the Middle West. Damned everywhere as "ultra-conservatives" and "extreme Rightists," many of these allies found themselves moving "rightward" ideologically as well, moving toward the *laissez-faire* liberalism of the only mass base open to them. In many ways, their move rightward was a self-fulfilling prophecy by the Left. Thus, under the hammer blows of the Left-liberal Establishment, the old progressive isolationists moved *laissez-faire*-ward as well. It was under this pressure that the forging of the "Old Right" was completed.[25]

Flynn's final and definitive shift from left to right was completed with the writing of his greatest work, *As We Go Marching*.[26] In this work, Flynn stepped back and tried to see the trends he had been fighting— militarism, centralism, leader worship—as the interlocking components of a system. The growth of a huge bureaucratic apparatus, the partnership of government and business, social-welfare schemes, huge public debts, and the need to resolve economic problems by creating a permanent war economy—all of these phenomena had become dominant first in Italy, then in Germany, and then in the U.S. under the New Deal. The theme of the book is that, while the U.S. was off fighting fascism in Europe, the seeds of that doctrine had already been planted in the U.S. The war would accelerate their growth.

In Italy, Germany, and the United States, the pattern was frighteningly similar. All three societies were modeled on the same basic principles: (1) the institution of planned consumption, or the spending-borrowing government; (2) the planned economy; (3) militarism as an economic institution; and (4) imperialism as a permanent policy. New Deal programs like the National Recovery Administration resembled the corporative structure of the Italian fascist state, with its great guilds organized along industry-wide lines; the economic arrangements of Hitler's Germany were similar.

Flynn's great contribution in this book was to illustrate the political dynamics of the welfare-warfare state. To garner political support from the Right for deficit spending, public-works boondoggles, and cradle-to-grave social security for the masses, the Left had turned to militarism. With peacetime conscription to soak up idle labor, there would be a permanent war economy. America's war against fascism may be won on the battlefield and lost on the home front. For "[t]he test of fascism," Flynn wrote, "is not one's rage against the Italian and German warlords. The test is—how many of the essential principles of fascism do you accept?"

American fascism is not going to have the gaudy trappings of its European cousins, but would take a more familiar form. "Fascism will come," said Flynn,

> at the hands of perfectly authentic Americans . . . who are convinced that the present economic system is washed up . . . and who wish to commit this country to the rule of the bureaucratic state; interfering in the affairs of the states and cities; taking part in the management of industry and finance and agriculture; assuming the role of great national banker and investor, borrowing billions every year and spending them on all sorts of projects through which such a

government can paralyze opposition and command public support; marshalling great armies and navies at crushing costs to support the industry of war and preparation for war which will become our greatest industry; and adding to all this the most romantic adventures in global planning, regeneration, and domination, all to be done under the authority of a powerfully centralized government in which the executive will hold in effect all the powers, with Congress reduced to the role of a debating society. There is your fascist.[27]

The theme of *As We Go Marching* is nearly identical to that of James Burnham in *The Managerial Revolution*. A new ruling class—call them managers, the "brain trust," or whatever—is seizing power all over the world. From country to country, this new ruling class utilizes similar devices in order to gain and keep power: the bureaucratization of the economy, militarism, the new international order to gain and keep power: the bureaucratization of the economy, militarism, and the rise of the centralized state apparatus. These are the instruments of the new international order, from Rome to Berlin to Washington, D.C., the dominant factors in modern society.

Burnham is cited in the bibliography of *As We Go Marching*, and the similarity between the two books is obvious. But there is one vital difference: while Burnham celebrated the rise of the new elite, Flynn was doing his best to prevent it. In Flynn and Burnham, then, we can begin to see how the two rival camps of contemporary conservatism began to develop and eventually split.

A Man of the Right

After 1945, Flynn made the formal move into right-wing circles. Working with the National Economic Council, the Committee for Constitutional Government, and America's Future, Inc., he moved to the realm of radio commentary and had both daily and weekly syndicated programs. Flynn used this platform to carry on the fight against statism and globalism. He attacked the developing Cold War and warned that a third world war would make the "Constitution and our traditional free life" a "relic of the past." It was not necessary to launch a war to annihilate the Communists; rather "the course of wisdom for the American people would be to sit tight and put their faith in the immutable laws of human nature." We must "make an end of the cold war," he said, and communism would crash on the rocks of its own inner contradictions.

Flynn staunchly opposed the "police action" in Korea, declaring that the same State Department that had handed China over to the "agrarian reformers" of the Chinese Communist Party was now leading us into an unwinnable land war in Asia. In Flynn's view, the Korean War was yet another excuse for a power grab by the executive branch, another rationale for spending billions in borrowed money that would flood the country and induce a false prosperity based on debt.

Flynn had foreseen the coming of the Cold War as early as 1944 in *As We Go Marching*.[28] What is truly remarkable is that in 1950 he clearly foresaw the Vietnam War. In his weekly radio address of July 30, he observed that Korea was not the only Asian hot spot likely to involve the United States. Vietnam, he explained to his listeners, had been in the middle of a rebellion against French colonialism. Truman had promised to aid the French, and he noted with some disquiet, "an American military mission is . . . on its way to that country." In asking "Who is next on Stalin's list?" Flynn's answer was that either Indochina or Malaysia could be the new Korea. He warned his audience that "[i]f we are preparing to make war to save Asia from dictatorships we will waste every dollar, every pound of steel and every precious life that is snuffed out in that foolish adventure."[29]

Throughout the fifties, Flynn sounded the alarm about the growing scope of U.S. intervention in Indochina. It was, he thought, only a matter of time before "the United States may have to make a decision as to whether or not it will get into another Asiatic war," probably in Vietnam. To be put in the position of defending French imperialism from the Communist-led Vietminh would be an unmitigated disaster for the United States. "Indochina is not part of the free world," he said. "It is a captive country. The captors are the French."

Flynn was a major force on the American right during the fifties through his radio broadcasts as well as books such as *The Roosevelt Myth*,[30] *The Road Ahead: America's Creeping Revolution*[31]—which became a bestseller—*While You Slept: Our Tragedy in Asia and Who Made It*,[32] *The Lattimore Story*,[33] and *McCarthy: His War on American Reds*.[34] Flynn was a staunch defender of Senator Joseph McCarthy. In his thoughtful and informative study of Flynn, Ronald Radosh attributes Flynn's defense of McCarthy to personal bitterness that distorted his political judgment. "Thinking perhaps of his own career," Radosh writes,

> and the agony he had suffered at the hands of liberals, Flynn saw triumph for McCarthy as validating his own lifelong fight. He himself, Flynn told [Senator Karl] Mundt, had had his "share on a scale equal to almost anyone's"; it had been easier to "liquidate writers than politicians." Flynn embraced McCarthy as the liberals' major foe, and in so doing, he turned against his libertarian beliefs.[35]

Radosh's idea of a "libertarian belief" in this matter is questionable. He shows nothing but disdain for Flynn's argument that McCarthy was not "investigating any man's right to be a Communist," just "whether Communists ought to be employed in the American army, the American State Department, the radar installations, atomic energy laboratories, and other government departments."[36] But nowhere does Radosh answer this vital point, except to say that

> [h]is argument implied that belief in communism was automatically equatable with commitment to acts of treason, and that therefore an individual could be deprived of employment in government jobs because of his beliefs. McCarthyism, of course, affected many more individuals, depriving them of employment in private areas and occupations. Flynn had nothing to say about their plight. He did not ask whether it was valuable to have the right to be a Communist if it meant losing one's job.[37]

Leaving aside for the moment the question of whether Communist ideology would have permitted a party member from serving the interests of a nation other than the Soviet Union, there is nothing "libertarian" about the idea that Communists have a "right" to private-sector jobs. There is nothing in libertarianism, properly understood, to prevent any employer from immediately firing one of the comrades just as soon as his or her party membership is exposed to the light of day. The conditions of liberty are fulfilled just as long as one has the right to speak out on any subject, to espouse any political belief, no matter how irrational or repulsive—but there is no corollary to this principle that insists on making the exercise of this right profitable or even painless.

McCarthy's appeal to Flynn and other Old Right stalwarts was his value as a battering ram against the statist Liberal Establishment. While it may be true that McCarthyism provided a context and rationale for the Cold War, on the other hand it turned the main thrust of the people's suspicions inward, rather than outward; toward Washington, D.C., rather than Europe or Asia. While Flynn's defense of McCarthy may do violence to the delicate sensibilities of New Deal liberals like Radosh, who would rather not entertain the thought that the Roosevelt regime was honeycombed with Communists and fellow travelers, it is hardly the case that Flynn "turned against his libertarian beliefs" in championing McCarthy. While it was not an unprincipled stand, perhaps the problem is that it was a tactical error. For the McCarthy crusade had temporarily blurred the distinctions between Old Right and New Right, which were just beginning to develop.

As the fifties wore on, Flynn was increasingly out of the conservative mainstream. The downfall of McCarthy when he dared take on the army, and the diversion of anticommunism to targets abroad, changed the political landscape. Once again, Flynn found himself back where he had been during the days of the Popular Front: an outsider railing against an overwhelmingly powerful establishment.

When *National Review* was founded, editor William F. Buckley Jr., solicited from Flynn a review of Arthur Larson's *A Republican Looks at His Party*. But when Flynn submitted a piece attacking militarism as "a job-making boondoggle" and denouncing Eisenhower for prolonging the Cold War, Buckley rejected the article. He sent $100 along with the rejection letter, stating that Flynn failed to appreciate the "objective threat of the Soviet Union," which, he maintained, poses "a threat to the freedom of each and every one of us." Flynn returned the $100, and in a note to Buckley said that he was "greatly obligated" to him for "the little lecture."[38]

Although Buckley apologized for his incredible arrogance the next day and tried to flatter Flynn by calling him "a mentor in whose writings I never cease to delight and from whose courage I draw strength," it was clear that there was no room for Flynn in the New Right of Bill Buckley and James Burnham. The old warrior Flynn, who had fought against statism and globalism all of his life, was not about to be taken in by the new brand of globaloney being pushed by Buckley and his fellow cold warriors. Communism, he realized, was an *idea*. The threat was not military but ideological, and the main danger was not to be found in Moscow, or Korea, or Vietnam, but right here at home.

Flynn ended his public career in 1960, at the age of seventy-nine. His health was failing and he retired from journalism. He died in 1964, as Buckley and his followers were eradicating the last remnants of the Old Right, his work largely forgotten. That he died isolated from the Right as well as the Left, his books neglected, his legacy unknown, is due to the fact that the history of any conflict, both military and ideological, is largely written by the victors. Neither the Buckleyite conservatives, who thought the third world war had already begun, nor the globalist liberals who idolized Roosevelt and hailed the rise of empire, had any use for Flynn.

As the Cold War draws to a close, Flynn's essential insight—that the threat to America is not to be found in any foreign capital, but in Washington, D.C.—takes on new immediacy. His analysis of the structure of the welfare-warfare state as a system based on economic planning and a permanent-war economy is vital to understanding where we are today, how we got there—and how we can get out. Along with Garet Garrett, Flynn is the great prototype of today's paleoconservatives and paleolibertarians, an exemplar of the Old Right whose life and work represent the best of a long and proud tradition.

5

THE REMNANT:

MENCKEN, NOCK, AND CHODOROV

They are obscure, unorganized, inarticulate, each one rub-
bing along as best he can. They need to be encouraged and
braced up, because when everything has gone completely
to the dogs, they are the ones who will come back and
build up a new society, and meanwhile your preaching
will reassure them and keep them hanging on. Your job is
to take care of the Remnant.

—*Albert Jay Nock*

FLYNN WAS NOT THE ONLY old-fashioned liberal alienated by the
New Deal and caught in the stampede to war. That he initially
considered himself a man of the Left, an opponent of big business and
foreign wars, was a self-image shared by other writers, editors, and publicists with roughly the same views: H. L. Mencken, Albert Jay Nock,
and Oswald Garrison Villard (editor of the *Nation*) among them.

Up until the thirties, noninterventionism had been associated with
the left side of the political spectrum, and therefore the members of
this distinguished fraternity were considered leftists. The laissez-faire
wing of the Left, led by Mencken and Nock, had bitterly attacked the
cozy partnership of Big Government and big business. Their cultural
"leftism" was highlighted by their vigorous polemics against the various movements for moral and cultural "uplift," such as Prohibition,
championed by the conservative reformers. But they also had opposed

World War I, the Treaty of Versailles, and the policy of imperialism, both American and British. Nock's *Myth of a Guilty Nation*,[1] and his central role in the publication of Francis Neilson's *How Diplomats Make War*,[2] helped turn a generation of American liberals away from Wilsonian internationalism and toward a thoroughgoing antimilitarism. The people, Nock wrote, were tired of "professional statesmen" who lied them into war, sick of "sham and sop, of guff and sanctimony; of oily volubility about liberty and humanity," It was the credo of a worldly wise liberalism, which had learned its lesson during the last war: governments and politicians were the ultimate source of all wars, and were therefore not to be trusted.[3]

The Literary Libertarians: H. L. Mencken and Albert Jay Nock

Mencken was undoubtedly the leading figure in this group. Editor and journalist, social critic and caustic commentator, Mencken founded his monthly magazine, the *American Mercury*, in 1924, and therein he and his fellow "Tory anarchists" inveighed against the militant moralists, who wanted to save the world from sin, and the equally militant Wilsonians, who wanted the U.S. to save the world from itself.

Today Mencken is seen as a man of literature, chiefly remembered as a satirist possessed of an acerbic wit. The range of his interests, and the fact that he was not a propagandist, has obscured his role as an intellectual forerunner of the Old Right. Yet Mencken held very definite and quite consistent views which can only be considered libertarian. He believed that "[a]ll government, in its essence, is a conspiracy against the superior man; its one permanent object is to oppress him and cripple him." All governments, everywhere, depend on a regime of plunder and exploitation:

> If it be aristocratic in organization, then it seeks to protect the man who is superior only in law against the man who is superior in fact; if it be democratic, then it seeks to protect the man who is inferior in every way against both.[4]

His ideal government, in his words, "is one which lets the individual alone—one which barely escapes being no government at all."

Mencken was not a political ideologue—indeed, he would have been mortified by the very idea of it—but he reflected a political trend, what had been the dominant trend in America before World War I, and that was the belief in laissez-faire and opposition to foreign entanglements. Mencken bitterly attacked big business for securing special privileges and favored positions at the public trough, but he hailed a truly free enterprise as the creator of "almost everything that passes under the general name of civilization today."

Albert Jay Nock was also a literary figure, a social critic whose scintillating essays championed the superior man against the herd. A fierce individualist, he would have been doubtful at the thought of being part of a larger movement, never mind one of the founders, but indeed this has turned out to be the case. In his thoroughgoing and systematic individualism, Nock even more explicitly than Mencken challenged the cult of statism and warned against its growing influence.

His book, *Our Enemy, the State*, a classic of Old Right libertarian thought, applied the sociological analysis of Franz Oppenheimer to the growth and development of the modern American state.[5] Oppenheimer derived the evolution of the state from marauding bands of nomadic tribesmen who preyed on peaceful agricultural communities. As Oppenheimer puts it, "[T]he cause of the genesis of all states is the contrast between peasants and herdsmen, between laborers and robbers, between bottom lands and prairies."[6] Thus evolved the two groups in society, which are defined by two antithetical methods of survival: the *political* means versus the *economic* means. Those who favor the latter method engage in productive work, that is, they labor to produce the values they need to survive and prosper. Practitioners of the former method are our latter-day marauders, who have forsaken club and spear for more sophisticated but hardly more subtle weaponry: the state apparatus. Founded on plunder and conquest, the state is no different from any ordinary gang of highwaymen, except that it has the power to enforce its monopoly on organized crime in a given geographical area. Like the ordinary criminal, the state produces nothing; its method of survival is completely parasitical.[7]

Nock applied this analysis to the history of the American republic, particularly the process that culminated in the adoption of the Constitution. He saw this as the pivotal event which set America on the road to statism, because it

> enabled an ever-closer centralization of control over the political means. For instance . . . many an industrialist could see the great primary advantage of being able to expend his exploiting opportunities over a nationwide free trade area walled in by a general tariff. . . . Any speculator in depreciated public securities would be strongly for a system that could offer him the use of the political means to bring back their face value. Any ship owner or foreign trader would be quick to see that his bread was buttered on the side of a national State which, if properly approached, might lend him the use of the political means by way of a subsidy, or would be able to back up some profitable but dubious freebooting enterprise with "diplomatic representations" or with reprisals.
>
> The adoption of the Constitution was the beginning of the conservative Counterrevolution, and big business was its vanguard. Against the farmers, and small business, the big financial interests planned and executed a *coup d'etat*, simply tossing the Articles of Confederation into the wastebasket.[8]

In contrast to the Marxian class analysis, the Nockian view defines the two great classes not as the capitalists versus the proletariat but as the rulers versus the ruled. History can be seen, said Nock, as chapters in the ongoing story of state power versus "social power," i.e., the co-operative power of voluntary associations. Far from being a system of exploitation, the free market was, in his view, a mighty bulwark *against* exploitation.

Yet Nock was no friend of big business. As the rising tide of collectivism engulfed the modern world, he lashed out at the lords of high finance who had paved the way for the New Deal. "It is one of the few amusing things in our rather stodgy world," he wrote, "that those who today are behaving most tremendously about collectivism and the Red menace are the very ones who have cajoled, bribed, flattered and bedeviled the State into taking each and every one of the successive steps that lead straight to collectivism."

> Who hectored the State into the shipping business, and plumped for setting up the Shipping Board? Who pestered the State into setting up the Interstate Commerce Commission and the Federal Farm Board? Who got the State to go into the transportation business on our inland waterways? Who is always urging the State to "regulate" and "supervise" this, that, and the other routine process of financial, industrial, and commercial enterprise? Who took off his coat, rolled up his sleeves, and sweated blood hour after hour over helping the State construct the codes of the late-lamented National Recovery Act?[9]

Mencken and Nock represented the same classical liberal "left-wing" tradition that John T. Flynn came out of: a "left" opposition to monopolism and mercantilism that was an early form of American libertarianism.

But with the coming of the New Deal and FDR's relentless drive to war, American politics reversed polarities. Suddenly opposition to government-sponsored monopolism and overseas adventurism was "right-wing," and all the Left was proclaiming the virtues of a government-business partnership and a great "war for democracy." Thus, by simply maintaining their old position, Mencken, Nock, Flynn, and other men of the Left suddenly found themselves being attacked as "right-wing extremists."

The pro-war Left lined up with conservative big business, which saw the coming conflict as the road to prosperity and profits. After Hitler invaded the Soviet Union, the Communists joined in the fun and the war whoops from the Left were virtually unanimous. In the face of this Stalinist-liberal alliance on the war question—a tactic which the Communists dubbed the "Popular Front"—the few liberal mavericks like Flynn and Villard who dared dissent were blacklisted. Flynn lost his position at the *New Republic* and ended up with the right-wing Committee for Constitutional Government. Villard lost his editorship as a direct consequence of his intransigent opposition to the war. Garrett, as we have seen, was driven off the pages of the *Saturday Evening Post* and forced to seek refuge in an obscure business quarterly. Mencken retired to write his memoirs. Nock found himself without a major platform, although he continued to write for the National Economic Council's *Review of Books.*

Mencken and Nock belong to that generation of libertarian intellectuals who saw the height of their influence in the twenties, when Mencken's *American Mercury* and Nock's weekly *Freeman* debunked the idea of a world war as a crusade for peace and democracy, and upheld the banner of laissez-faire in economics *and* in life.

But by the midthirties, the influence of the old liberals began to disappear. After the birth of the Old Right in the crucible of war and economic dislocation, and a great upsurge in the form of the America First Committee and opposition to the New Deal, the party of liberty went into decline. The war years were the nadir of the anti-statist movement in America. All-pervasive government propaganda blaring from the radio and virtually every newspaper branded any opposition to the war, to Roosevelt, and to the New Deal as little short of treason. The America First Committee was gone. And while Roosevelt was rounding up the Japanese on the Pacific Coast, he was also jailing American "seditionists." Lawrence Dennis, author of *The Coming American Fascism*—a book that explored the same themes that had won Burnham so much praise and attention in left-wing circles—was put on trial for "sedition."[10] His crime? His writings had been quoted in the publications of the German-American Bund. Dennis, who conducted his own defense, was acquitted; but others; mostly harmless cranks, were not so lucky. Just as surely as the government had invaded the economic life of the country in the name of the New Deal, so it had conquered the political culture, imposing a ruthless uniformity of thought in the intellectual sphere. The Old Right went underground for the duration.

As America emerged from the furnace of war, however, a new generation of old-style "liberals" who believed in laissez-faire and a foreign policy of America first was making its appearance. Reborn in the shadow of the emergent welfare-warfare state, greatly reduced in numbers and influence, the Old Right yet persisted and developed while remaining faithful to the ideas of its forerunners. The outstanding example of this second generation of activists was the writer and teacher Frank Chodorov. His life and career uniquely personified the style and spirit of the Old Right during the lean years of the late forties and the decade of the fifties.

Frank Chodorov: Taking on Isaiah's Job

He was born Fishel Chodorowsky, the eleventh son of Russian immigrants, in 1887. Known as Frank Chodorov from an early age, he was raised on the lower west side of Manhattan, where his parents ran a small restaurant. He graduated from Columbia University in 1907, whereupon he taught high school, married, ran a clothing factory, and went into the mail-order apparel business. The Great Depression brought his career as an entrepreneur to an abrupt halt, however, and he went into sales and promotion. Chodorov had read Henry George's *Progress and Poverty*, and in his memoirs he recalls "reading the book several times, and each time I felt myself slipping into a cause." At the age of fifty, in 1937, Chodorov became the director of the Henry George School of Social Science in New York City and the editor of its publication, the *Freeman*. Although not a continuation of Nock's periodical of the twenties, Chodorov's *Freeman* was certainly imbued with the libertarian spirit. Nock was a frequent contributor, along with Francis Neilson, who had been a coeditor of the original *Freeman*. Aside from emphasizing the land question and Georgism, the *Freeman* was pro-capitalist, anti-taxes, and staunchly anticommunist. But most of all, the *Freeman* under Chodorov's tutelage was vehemently antiwar. When Roosevelt finally succeeded in getting the United States into World War II through the back door, Chodorov asked,

> How will we emerge from the emergency? What manner of life confronts us? . . . [T]he answer that any analysis of current events brings us is that Americans of the future will be slaves of the state.[11]

Aside from the early Georgist influence, which set him on the road to developing a radical anti-statism, Chodorov was above all a Nockian. In response to the victory of the New Deal and the eclipse of laissez-faire, Nock had developed a pessimistic view that the cause of liberty was, in the long run and perhaps even longer, utterly hopeless. His philosophy and strategic vision was summed up in his classic essay "Isaiah's Job." The prophet is sent by God to warn a decadent city "what is wrong and why and what is going to happen unless they have a change of heart and straighten up." However, Isaiah is fully aware that his words will not reach most of the people. He is speaking not to the masses but to the chosen few, "the Remnant." As God explains to Isaiah, the members of this Remnant

> are obscure, unorganized, inarticulate, each one rubbing along as best he can. They need to be encouraged and braced up, because when everything has completely gone to the dogs, they are the ones who will come back and build up a new society, and meanwhile your preaching will reassure them and keep them hanging on. Your job is to take care of the Remnant.[12]

The Remnant was composed of those who managed to preserve the values of the old, prewar culture—the culture of the Old Right—against the dominant political culture. It was a fragment of the prewar world, of a culture based on sound values, and an economy based on sound money. That world was nearly vanished. Where once its spirit had pervaded the popular culture and found intellectual champions in Mencken, Nock, and their generation, in the brave new world of the postwar era, its partisans were reduced to a handful, a mere Remnant. As Charles Hamilton writes,

> When Nock wrote this essay in 1936, he saw the job going begging. A few years later, Chodorov took that job and uniquely served to maintain the tradition of what Murray N. Rothbard has called the "old American Right": that passionate belief in individual liberty which strongly opposed both the rising statist interventionism at home, and war and imperialism abroad.[13]

In the Nockian phrase, everything had indeed gone completely to the dogs, but Chodorov never wavered. Never did he bend to the prevailing winds, but stood like a rock when all about him were prostrate before the storms of war. He foresaw the war hysteria, and what would happen to dissenters, in an article published in 1938:

> Those of us who try to retain some modicum of sanity will be scorned by our erstwhile friends, spit upon, persecuted, imprisoned. . . . We must steel ourselves for the inevitable.[14]

Perhaps he had good reason to suspect that he would personally have to steel himself most of all. Soon after the bombing of Pearl Harbor, Chodorov found himself in conflict with a faction of the Georgists that opposed his antiwar stand. In the end, after five years as director of the Henry George School and editor of the *Freeman*, Chodorov went out of town for a short time—and returned to discover that he had been evicted from his office. In the March 1942 issue of the *Freeman*, the Georgists made a terse announcement to the effect that "Mr. Chodorov has retired from the editorship."

Analysis: *Voice of the Remnant*

Two years later, Chodorov would start the project that was closest to his heart: the four-page monthly *analysis*. This periodical, its modesty of form symbolized by the editor's eschewing all capital letters when referring to his creation, had an influence far out of proportion to its official circulation, which was never higher than four thousand subscribers. For six years, until 1951, Chodorov's monthly broadsides in *analysis* kept the flame of the libertarian Old Right burning—shielding and nurturing it against the winds of collectivism and Cold War that swept across postwar America. Published out of a small office in lower Manhattan, *analysis* covered a wide range of subjects, from economics to foreign policy and whatever sparked Chodorov's interest. It was an intensely personal form of journalism, which nonetheless managed to convey the sense of being representative of a larger movement—the Nockian voice of the

Remnant. However small and isolated that movement might be, still it existed in its purest form in the small but dedicated and ultimately influential readership of *analysis*.

Expressing perfectly the uncompromising spirit of this unique journalistic venture, an early issue of *analysis* was emblazoned with the headline "DON'T BUY BONDS." This advice was proffered not solely or even primarily on fiscal grounds, but on "purely moral" grounds, for "the act of borrowing against imaginary income is a fraud, no matter who does it, and when you make a loan to that borrower you aid and abet a fraud."[15] The income tax, public schools, protectionism—no icon of statist orthodoxy went unsmashed in the pages of *analysis*. In Chodorov's uncompromising view, taxation

> is highwaymanry made respectable by custom, thievery made moral by law; there isn't a decent thing to be said for it, as to origin, principle, or its effects on the social order. Man's adjustment to this iniquity has permitted its force to gain momentum like an unopposed crime wave; and the resulting social devastation is what the socialists have long predicted and prayed for.[16]

While his intellectual forebears, Nock and Henry George, were in their day considered men of the Left, even of the far-left fringe, Chodorov was in his own time relegated to the extreme right wing, a position usually identified in the public mind with Senator Robert A. Taft's wing of the Republican Party. Chodorov's opposition to government intervention in economic affairs might have passed him off as some sort of conservative of the more extreme variety, but he was not in the habit of hiding his colors. He denounced conservatives for not opposing business subsidies and attacked the two major right-wing hobbyhorses of the period, McCarthyism and the prosecution of the Cold War.

At the height of the agitation to throw Communists or suspected Communist sympathizers out of the universities—a drive, as we have noted, that was led by such neocons as the late Professor Sidney Hook—Chodorov wrote an article titled "Let's *Teach* Communism," which pointed out that "[o]ur colleges are debarred from examining the basic assumptions of Communism because, as I will attempt to show, these basic assumptions are part and parcel of what is called capitalism, the going order, and it would hardly do to bring this fact to light." In offering his idea of how a class on communism might be taught in the nation's schools of higher learning, he regretted that his proposal would never make it into the syllabus. For such a course, beginning, say, with the Marxist conception of wages as slave labor and exploitation would soon reveal an astonishing fact:

> [I]f you dig into some standard economics textbooks or examine the labor legislation of our land you will find ideas that stem from the communist notion that capital pays wages and that the hardheaded capitalist keeps them low. A minimum wage law, for instance, is based on that notion. . . . In the course I suggest, it would have to be pointed out that minimum wage laws—that all legislation dealing with labor-employer relations—are concessions to the communist conception of wages.[17]

If capitalism is exploitation, according to the followers of Marx and Lenin, then "capitalism, in practice, accepts the indictment in large chunks," and any lecturer on the subject would be obliged to point this out. An instructor engaged in the study of communism, said Chodorov, presenting his subject in a purely objective light, would be forced to confront the issue of the income tax. "Income taxes," he wrote,

> "unequivocally deny the principle of private property. Inherent in these levies is the postulate that the state has a prior lien on all the production of its subjects; what it does not take is merely a concession, not a right, and it reserves for itself the prerogative of altering the rates and the exemptions according to its requirements. It is a matter of fiat, not contract. If that is not communist principle, what is?"

A course in communist theory and practice would be profoundly subversive to the established order, not because it would turn hapless students into advocates of communism, but because they would discover the shocking fact that, to a large degree, they were already living under it.

Earlier, in 1946, he had taken on the Chamber of Commerce of the United States, which had issued an alarmist pamphlet, *Communist Infiltration in the United States: Its Nature and How to Combat It.* Agreeing with the Chamber that "these communists are a pretty bad lot, unscrupulous, ruthless, lying, and altogether Machiavellian," Chodorov wondered about the nature of the "Americanism" counterposed by the Chamber. "One wishes the Chamber had supplemented its report with a detailed description of the Americanism it is anxious to preserve. Lacking such a description, we must supply one from our knowledge of the inclinations of all chambers of commerce which flourish or have flourished in these United States."[18]

For the Chamber to gripe about the presence of Communists in our midst was, for Chodorov, an act of breathtaking hypocrisy. For a struggle against communism was, by definition, a war against government power and privilege.

> The unhorsing of privilege can be effected only by a revolt against political power *per se*, and for that enterprise the people who make up the chambers of commerce show no passion. . . . They make no demand for the abolition of all subventions, but, rather, are feverishly lobbying Congress and the local politicians for every conceivable tax aid their cupidity can invent. The purpose and practice of every organization of businessmen . . . have been to secure from political power some economic advantage for its members. Hence, the current fretfulness about the communists must be laid to the fear of competition in the control of political power.[19]

Business wears its shackles like a badge of honor and begs for more: "regulate us, fix prices, fix wages, if you will, but for the sake of 100 percent Americanism guarantee us some rate of return, or at least assure us against losses." This, maintained Chodorov, is the main danger to what is left of our liberties, and not some cafeteria conspiracy being run out of Moscow. Chodorov declared that "[t]he commies don't count. That miserable crew of Moscow-led slaves have [sic] neither the strength nor the skill to push themselves into a position of predominance. They present no competitive force. But they may, and probably will, hasten centralization by creating a fear of it."

On the issue of McCarthyism, he differed with many Old Rightists such as John T. Flynn, as well as the main current of the conservative movement. The right to disagree, to be wrong, to hold "subversive" thoughts was inviolable and could never be a crime. Today the laws were aimed at the Communists, but Chodorov knew that tomorrow they could just as easily be aimed at malcontents such as himself.

Yet when McCarthy launched his campaign to rid the government of red subversives, in the early fifties, Chodorov was declaring himself in sympathy with the senator's goals, if not his methods. In an article for *Human Events*, "McCarthy's Mistake," he prefaced his analysis of "a tactical error in his [McCarthy's] campaign" by declaring that he "didn't want to be lined up with his enemies. It is because I admire Joe . . . and count myself on his side, that I indulge an urge to lecture him." The problem with McCarthyism was that "Joe could not have done more than he did simply because he assumed that it is possible to rid the bureaucracy of Communists." Such a task could never be accomplished because bureaucracy "is the proper habitat of Communists, even as fleas belong in a dog's fur."

Chodorov Against the Empire

Chodorov stood out in any crowd of conservatives due not only to his defense of civil liberties, but also because of his foreign-policy views. As the Cold War heated up, the Anglophile elite in government and the media decided that it was time for the U.S. to take up the imperial mantle from Great Britain. Such groups as Union Now agitated for a merger of the U.S. and Britain, and were taken seriously. In 1947, as the publicists of what Henry Luce called the "American century" were blowing their trumpets, Chodorov saw what was coming:

> If you've an historic periscope in your equipment, now is the time
> to put it up. For, over the political horizon comes a view not seen

these sixteen centuries: the sunset of a world empire. . . . In a few years . . . surely within the century, what was the British Empire will be little more than the United Kingdom.[20]

However, a successor was already stirring in the wings. "In the West a lusty heir apparent is flexing his muscles," wrote Chodorov, and it seemed to him that the American Empire would follow that of Albion much as "the Byzantine Empire followed hard on the heels of Rome." Unlike Rome, this Byzantine Empire of the West was not to be founded on the principle of aristocracy, or the "white man's burden"; what was required was a modern mythology of imperialism. In days of old, said Chodorov, the ruling class simply plundered its colonies and made no bones about its predatory habits. So that everyone might partake of the spoils of victory to some degree, outright looting by common soldiers was a matter of course.

> However, such square-toed methods had to be abandoned with the advent of the printing press, which encouraged the habit of reading, which in turn aroused querulousness. Naturally, the people took to reading moralisms which flattered their egos—namely, the phrases of democracy—and lest this should stimulate any predisposition against plunder, the proper kind of reading had to be provided. Thus, propaganda was added to the arsenal of empire building.[21]

Chodorov saw the propaganda of the Cold War as a narcotic spell induced to veil the reality of plunder on an international scale. In a remark which seems preternaturally directed at the National Endowment for Democracy and its Washington-based claque of publicists and intellectuals, Chodorov wrote, "If folks new exactly what an empire is, and resolutely refused to have anything to do with the business, its advocates would have to turn to decent pursuits for a living."

Applying the Nockian class analysis to international affairs, Chodorov asked, Who profits from the new internationalism? His answer was that "if we go through with this empire-succession business, it is quite possible certain communications systems will improve their financial position, certain investment trusts will pay out bigger dividends." The drive toward war is fueled, he thought, by financial interests and other pressure groups who see in it an opportunity to secure markets, drive out competition, and make enormous profits using the U.S. government as their instrument. Were we making loans to Greece and Turkey to halt the advance of communism—or to give the price of certain banking stocks a lift? In Chodorov's view, it is impossible to see where one leaves off and the other begins: "That there is any conspiratorial connection between such a result and the loans to Greece and Turkey will always be an unprovable conjecture. Such is the genius of the cartel."

He feared that the modern international corporation, with its global reach, "facilitates an established imperialistic process." Once upon a time, when swashbuckling adventurers roamed the world, weaker states sought the protection of stronger neighbors and then became wards of a new overload. "Such things," said Chodorov,

> are not being done in these days of international protocol. The British, for instance, could hardly be expected to apply for a secondary position in the big American Union; not only is national pride against it, but the cartel system makes such a crudity unnecessary. Through the orderly process of the securities markets, American participation in the profitable oil, rubber, tin, and other concessions will be allowed to infiltrate, so that the cartel may become sufficiently American in character to warrant the protective arm of a government standing up against the Russian aggression. Through stock transfers and interchange of directorships, the transition from one flag to another is done without offense to national sensibilities or tradition. In some respects, this migration of capital is comparable to the transfer of wealth from tottering Rome to the burgeoning Byzantine Empire, in the third and fourth centuries; the modern cartel obviates the use of a moving van.[22]

Chodorov made the point that the dynamics of the modern democratic state encouraged a proliferation of pressure groups with international interests. An aggressive, expansionist foreign policy was the inevitable result of *particular* interests succeeding in getting themselves endowed with the title of "American interests." The machinations of the state in the international arena, then, were no different than on the home front: the foreign policy of the United States, in line with its domestic policy, was founded not on protecting the citizens of this country from attack, but on protecting the privileges and profits of those who had the most to gain from the right war at the right time in the right place.[23]

The "fear propaganda" that fueled the Cold War was, said, Chodorov, completely irrational. But what if Russia should succeed in conquering all of Europe, subjecting her peoples to the same system that impoverished the Soviets? Chodorov's answer was that the thing could not last because "slaves are poor producers, and we can predict the collapse of communism in Europe from lack of production." "The more the Russian state spreads itself," he said, "the weaker it must become." Chodorov argued that the best strategy would be to stay at home, conserve and stockpile our resources, and look toward a victory over communism "shaped in the nation's factories, not on the battlefields."

It was a grim future Chodorov contemplated in the August 1950 issue of *analysis*: his article, "A Jeremiad," drew a picture of a war-fighting oligarchy which has eliminated free speech, nationalized all industry, reduced the people to a subsistence level, and placed the economy on a military footing. "In short," he wrote, "the net profit of The War will be a political setup differing from that of Russia in name only." War would destroy the chance of human liberty. "There will be a resurrection, for the spirit of freedom never dies. But its coming will take time and much travail."[24]

Chodorov vs. the Neoconservatives

Written at the height of the Cold War, those words reflected the widespread feeling that it was only a matter of time before World War III broke out. As America entered the decade of the fifties, the anticommunist crusade was the one overwhelming fact of American politics, right and left. In this forbidding landscape, Chodorov's isolation was virtually complete.

This bleak vision of the future, added to the fact that his little periodical had not permitted him to do more than eke out a precarious living, could only have been demoralizing; and it was under these pressures, both ideological and financial, that in January of 1951 he merged *analysis* with the weekly *Human Events*, which had been started by the veteran Old Rightists Frank Hanighen, Felix Morley, and William Henry Chamberlin. There he found employment for four years, where he was an associate editor.

But the conservative movement of which Chodorov had been an early avatar was changing. That the war against communism would bring totalitarianism in through the back door—the same argument John T. Flynn and others had made against FDR's war drive—was not something the Right wanted to hear. Chodorov tried to uphold the tradition of the Old Right in his articles for *Human Events*, but in the summer of 1954, although his contributions would continue over the years, he took up a new position as editor of the *Freeman*, a monthly magazine put out by the Foundation for Economic Education (FEE).

Almost immediately, the conservative-libertarian schism over the question of the Cold War became a burning issue. In an editorial, "The Return of 1940?," Chodorov went on the attack, declaring that "already the libertarians are debating among themselves on the need of putting off the struggle until after the threat of communism, Moscow-style, shall have been removed, even by war." This new war madness would lead to the same results as the old madness, circa 1940: conscription, centralization, war collectivism, confiscatory taxation, and a bloated parasitocracy, all financed by mountains of debt. "All this the 'isolationists' of the 1940s foresaw," he concluded,

> not because they were endowed with any gift of prevision, but because they knew history and would not deny its lesson: that during war the State acquires power at the expense of freedom, and that because of its insatiable lust for power the State is incapable of giving up any of it. The State never abdicates.[25]

This immediately brought a rejoinder from William Schlamm—and the first debate between paleoconservatives and neoconservatives erupted in the November 1954 issue of the *Freeman*.[26]

Schlamm, the primordial neocon, was one of the guiding spirits behind the founding of *National Review*. A German immigrant, he had been a Communist Party member at the age of sixteen. In his twenties, he was editor of the Communist newspaper *Rote Fahne*. When the Comintern declared that the Social Democrats, and not Hitler, were the real fascists in Germany, he transferred his allegiance to the left-wing anti-Stalinist *Die Weltbuhne*. When war broke out, he fled to the United States, where he wrote for the *New Leader* and rose to become Henry Luce's chief foreign policy advisor at Time, Inc. As he made the turn right-ward, he exhibited little or no interest in economic matters, confining himself almost exclusively to the anticommunist issue.

The Chodorov–Schlamm debate was soon joined by William F. Buckley Jr., who took Chodorov to task in the *Freeman*. The question before conservatives was "what are we going to do about the Soviet Union?" On one side were what Buckley called the "containment" conservatives, typified by Chodorov, who were more concerned about the internal threat posed by conscription than the (alleged) external threat posed by the USSR. On the other side were the "interventionist conservatives," who wanted to roll back communism by military means. "The issue," declared Buckley, "is there, and ultimately it will separate us." What he meant was that those who failed to take the cold-warrior line would be drummed out of the conservative movement. Two years earlier he had revealed his true hand in an article, "A Young Republican's View," in which the youthful Buckley enunciated his conservative credo. While paying lip service to the anti-statism of Mencken and Nock, and attacking the Republican Establishment for failing to come up with an alternative to statism, he launched into what was to be the keynote of the New Right: because the inherent and "thus far invincible aggressiveness of the Soviet Union" poses an immediate threat to national security, "we have to accept Big Government for the duration—for neither an offensive nor a defensive war can be waged . . . except through the instrument of a totalitarian bureaucracy within our shores." Forget about opposition to confiscatory taxation: conservatives, he wrote, must become apologists for "the extensive and productive tax laws that are needed to support a vigorous anti-Communist foreign policy," not to mention the "large armies and air forces, atomic energy, central intelligence, war production boards and the attendant centralization of power in Washington—even with Truman at the reins of it all."[27]

This was the question put before the Right, as the Cold War tightened its grip on the American consciousness: would conservatives become the champions of central planning, high taxes, and war-production boards, or would they show the proper disdain for Buckley's prescription and return to their Old Right roots?

Chodorov answered his critics in a series of spirited polemics, and the debate continued in the pages of the *Freeman*. If the war against communism was such a righteous cause, then why, Chodorov wanted to know, was it necessary to institute conscription? The war against communism would, he thought, ultimately turn out to be a war to communize America.[28]

The irony was lost on his opponents. Their steady barrage of criticism continued, and this soon had its effect. A controversy erupted among the trustees of FEE. Leonard E. Read, the founder and chief theoretician at FEE, was eager to avoid anything that might alienate contributors. Shortly after this public tiff with Schlamm and Buckley, Chodorov was ousted as editor of the *Freeman*.

By then, he was sixty-eight and in failing health—but by no means inactive. Chodorov turned to the writing of his memoirs, *Out of Step*, and worked on organizing the Intercollegiate Society of Individualists (ISI).[29] The Society had grown out of an article he wrote for *Human Events*, "A Fifty Year Project," emphasizing the strategy of implanting libertarian ideas on the college campus as a way of preserving the Remnant.[30]

In 1961, he suffered a massive stroke from which he never really recovered. By then, he was living in a nursing home. On December 28, 1966, Frank Chodorov died. He was seventy-nine.

He had carried on the traditions of Mencken, Nock, and the old classical liberals who had opposed two world wars and the threat of a third. Stubbornly sticking to his libertarian credo, he never compromised and never gave up. His was the spirit of the Old Right, preserved through a period of nearly unrelieved darkness. His life was a testament to the ideal of liberty.

As the advocates of a new interventionism once again make their case before the conservative public, Chodorov's warnings against a Byzantine Empire of the West—of corporate conglomerates with transnational connections and no qualms about using the political means to secure their economic interests—seem freshly minted. He lost the first round of the debate with those early neocons, Buckley and Schlamm, not because his arguments were less than compelling, but because he was finally silenced. As the second round of the great debate reaches a fever pitch, perhaps the rediscovery of Chodorov by a new generation of conservatives will make for a different outcome.

6

COLONEL MCCORMICK
AND THE *CHICAGO TRIBUNE*

> *Roosevelt advisors ... applauded lustily such declarations as:*
> *The important thing is to put an end [to criticism of the Roos-*
> *evelt Administration] by whatever means may be necessary....*
> *Get [McCormick] on his income tax or the Mann Act. Hang*
> *him, shoot him, or lock him up in a concentration camp.*
> —New York Daily News, *March 30, 1942*

INSOFAR AS THE IDEA OF the "Remnant" paints a picture of a tiny mi-nority utterly bereft of mass influence, it is false. Although in retreat before the onslaught of the New Deal and the Cold War, the political and cultural forces that embodied the values and traditions of the Old Right were still intact, if somewhat reduced. Furthermore, the Remnant was not powerless as long as Colonel Robert McCormick, publisher of the *Chicago Tribune*, drew breath.

Robert Rutherford McCormick was born on July 30, 1880, the scion of the famous Medill–Patterson–McCormick clan of Chicago. The man the Eastern media berated as an "Anglophobe" was educated in an English boarding school, went on to Yale, and came home to Chicago in 1902, where he ran for city council and won. He was attracted to a career in politics and soon became a force in the Illinois Republican Party. But death in the family and the prospect that the *Tribune* might be sold—not to mention defeat at the polls—spared him such a fate.

McCormick served in the Illinois National Guard, where he secured a commission as a colonel and fought Pancho Villa on the Mexican border. He volunteered during World War I and served with great distinction, commanding a battalion with the First Division.

The Colonel's Tribune: Americanism Unrepentant

Although not in the direct line of succession at the Tribune Company, an alcoholic brother and the distinctly leftist opinions of his cousin, young Joe Patterson—who was later to found the *New York Daily News*—were major factors in propelling him into control of the *Tribune*.

The two-fisted and flamboyant Chicago of the twenties, city of Al Capone and Big Bill Thompson, was reflected in the *Tribune*. Bright with color and violent in its opinions, McCormick's newspaper was the first to use color rotogravure. A good sports section and popular original comics such as "Moon Mullins" and "Winnie Winkle" won it a wide readership. Circulation doubled in a decade: 436,000 in 1920 to 835,000 in 1930, with Sunday sales over a million.

From his aerie atop the gothic Tribune Tower, the Colonel surveyed his kingdom and championed his cause: the Midwestern and distinctly American values of individualism and republicanism against the European import of socialism; the robust nationalism of the heartland against the insipid Anglophilia of the cosmopolitan eastern elite.

As the archenemy of the New Deal, McCormick's *Tribune* was the great voice and organizer of the Old Right movement in America. And a mighty weapon it was. In 1943, McCormick boasted that "the *Tribune* today, as for many years in the past, has the largest circulation of any standard-sized newspaper in this country. The only larger circulation is that of an associated publication, the *New York News*." The two newspapers "had not always seen eye-to-eye on domestic questions, but they have seldom diverged on matters of foreign policy." McCormick noted the "striking fact that these two publications, leaders in the opposition to internationalism, are also the two most widely read newspapers in the United States. Likewise, the *Washington Times-Herald* [also part of the McCormick-Medill family empire], which has taken the same line, has a larger circulation than any other newspaper published in the national capital," and "that isn't accidental," he assured his readers. "It proves that what the people of this country want in their newspapers is forthright, unashamed Americanism."[1]

Colonel McCormick's Americanism was the program of the unrepentant Old Right. His thundering editorials skewered the New Deal, the Communists, the war party, and "burocrats,"[2] refusing to be silenced even in the face of government harassment, censorship, and the threat of prosecution for treason. Against the rise of internationalism, he upheld the values and program of an American nationalism that was neither militaristic nor expansionist—and he dared to utter the forbidden phrase, "America first," even after Pearl Harbor.

Although the *Tribune* had always been staunchly Republican, McCormick editorially congratulated FDR on his election and graciously wished him well. McCormick cheered when the new president cut $400 million worth of federal employees out of the budget, and he threw his hat in the air when Roosevelt called for repeal of the Volstead Act.

But the honeymoon was short. As government agencies began to proliferate and federal spending began to skyrocket, McCormick went on the offensive. The *Tribune* was soon characterizing Roosevelt as the "American Kerensky."

McCormick was a fighting editor who readily admitted that "yes, certainly, we do use every weapon we can find."[3] Two of his heaviest guns were the political cartoonists Joseph Parrish and Carey Orr. The *Tribune* featured a cartoon on the front page, and the New Dealers lived in terror of the deft pen strokes of Parrish and Orr. Frank C. Waldrop, in *The Colonel of Chicago*, relates the fact that "[i]t was no idle rumor that men who knew their business took care to stay out of harm's way, if possible, on days that Mr. Roosevelt, Mr. Ickes and other dignitaries of quick-firing temperament, had been depicted."

Battling the New Deal

While the colonel's opposition to the New Deal was initially equivocal—the *Tribune* attacked social security and the Tennessee Valley Authority, but did not much object to the Securities and Exchange Commission—what finally enraged McCormick was the National Recovery Administration (NRA), which he saw as the prelude to fascism. In "A Warning from Germany," the Colonel reviewed the events of the past weekend, in which Hitler's "Night of the Long Knives" had solidified Nazi rule.[4] In order to prevent the same thing from happening in the United States, he said, Americans must prevent the rise of a dictator. And the one unerring early warning signal of any prospective dictatorship is an attack on the independence of the press. The Colonel strongly suspected that the cartelization of the economy and the corporatist imposition of industry-wide "codes" were not the only similarities between the New Deal and the European despotisms of Mussolini and Hitler. When the NRA's Blue Eagle fastened its talons on the newspaper industry, McCormick's undying enmity for FDR and all his works was born.

At the annual meeting of the directors of the American Newspaper Publishers Association (ANPA), held in New York City, the Colonel threw down the gauntlet:

> [U]nder the First Amendment the press cannot be compelled to accept special governmental control. There is a distinct difference between general laws, such as building and factory laws which govern all forms of activity, and a special law applied to the publishing profession. Obviously a government cannot suppress publication by a general law without at the same time suppressing all activities and bringing national life to immediate termination, while special laws can be enacted to suppress publication, as they have been enacted almost all over the civilized globe.[5]

Roosevelt and NRA chief, General Hugh Johnson, further provoked the Colonel when they stonewalled on the publishers' petition to explicitly guarantee their First Amendment rights under the NRA code. The *Tribune* had in the past energetically defended not only its own First Amendment rights, but also those of other publications—such as the *Saturday Press* of Minneapolis, Minnesota, which was shut down by city officials after charges were printed in the paper that these same officials were in league with organized crime.[6]

As McCormick lashed out at FDR inside the hall, 250,000 true believers in the Blue Eagle paraded down Fifth Avenue, banners flying and in an ugly mood. This was the first indication that Roosevelt and his NRA mobs were getting ready to move against their opponents in the press, just as they had intimidated the business community, and the Colonel did not have much trouble persuading the publishers that the freedom of the press was something that needed to be defended. While they agreed to accept a code of "fair" business practice—over McCormick's objections—ANPA demanded that the government incorporate in the NRA code a declaration guaranteeing freedom of the press. That summer in Washington, the NRA staged a propaganda campaign of unprecedented proportions, with marches, rallies, threats of boycott—and worse—for those who failed to cooperate. General Johnson, the bluff and blustering bureaucrat in charge of the NRA, told Malcolm W. Bingay, editorial director of the *Detroit Free Press*, that the National Industrial Recovery Act was the "new Constitution of the United States."[7]

The newspaper publishers, having sent a delegation to Washington, discovered to their horror that the administration refused to include any provision in the NRA code guaranteeing the rights that had been paid for in blood by so many Americans on countless battlefields. Bainbridge Colby, an attorney who attended the negotiations as the representative of ANPA, described the battle with the administration:

> On one side of the table sat the Administrator (General Hugh S. Johnson), now a well-known figure, with his formidable expression and his somewhat over-confident tone, a fair embodiment of the new evolution of governmental power and authority. . . . He turned to me at one stage in the discussion, saying, "Now, Mr. Colby, you and I are both lawyers. What is this freedom of the press you are talking about?"[8]

The president, in approving the NRA code, declared that all this talk of freedom of the press was "pure surplusage."[9] The newspaper publishers, with McCormick in the lead, called for a national gathering of all publishers to alert the country to the danger. Rather than face such wrath, which might have surpassed the fury provoked by his court-packing scheme, Roosevelt backed down. On February 24, 1933, the president finally signed an amendment to the NRA code, which forbade "the imposition of any requirements that might restrict or interfere with the constitutional guarantee of the freedom of the press."[10]

But Roosevelt and his allies were far from beaten in their efforts to tame the press. They merely effected a strategic retreat and waited for their chance—which was not long in coming.

"Draft Roosevelt and He'll Draft You!"

It was the war question that, above all, engaged the Colonel as the European cauldron boiled over, and his position enraged his enemies to such a fever pitch that they were soon demanding that he should be either "interred or interned," as one pro-war journalist put it. Aligning himself with America First—a slogan perfectly suited to his political philosophy and temperament—McCormick took his stand:

> This is not our war. We did not create the Danzig situation. We did not sign the treaty of Versailles. The peace America made with Germany did not contain another war. The United States did not take spoils. It did not divide up colonies. It had nothing to do with the remaking of Europe which sowed war on nearly every frontier of the new map.
>
> France and Great Britain are not weak nations. They are great empires. Their pooled resources are enormous.
>
> We may think their side is the better side. But it is their war. They are competent to fight it. Great pressure will be brought to bear on the United States. Americans will be told that this is their fight. That is not true. The frontiers of American democracy are not in Europe, Asia or Africa.[11]

Interventionist organizations proliferated. For the Anglophile elite, there was the Century Club in midtown Manhattan, where Henry Luce, Dean Acheson, Morgan partner Thomas W. Lamont, and playwright Robert Sherwood met over lunch to discuss how they were going to dragoon the United States into saving their beloved British Empire. There was the relatively moderate Committee to Aid the Allies, led by America's favorite country editor, William Allen White, of the *Emporia Gazette*, and the more radical Fight for Freedom Committee, which advocated immediate entry into the war. As the liberal swing toward militarism and interventionism was gearing up, the anti-war Right was rising to the challenge. The journalist John T. Flynn, banished from the *New Republic*, was welcomed to the pages of the *Tribune*, which serialized his book, *Country Squire in the White House*.

Popular sentiment was still on the side of the isolationists, as it was right up until Pearl Harbor, and Roosevelt campaigned on a pledge to keep us out of war. McCormick was not taken in; Roosevelt's quarantine speech did not bode well for the cause of peace. As the conscription bill passed over McCormick's fierce opposition, the *Tribune* ran a cartoon on the front page with the caption "Draft Roosevelt and He'll Draft You!" The president, said the Colonel, was "working up a series of war scares" to rationalize running for a third term. Bowing to widespread antiwar sentiment, Roosevelt piously proclaimed that "your boys are not going to be sent into any foreign wars"—at the very moment when he was making secret agreements with Churchill to get the U.S. in at the earliest opportunity.

When Japan joined the Axis, the *Tribune* blamed the scrap-steel embargo and placed the responsibility for "U.S. departures from strict neutrality" on Roosevelt's doorstep:

> For the first time in our history a foreign alliance against us has been perfected. When and if it suits their purpose to do so, they will make war on us. So far as pretexts for war are concerned they have them already.
>
> Mr. Roosevelt now has the critical international situation which, in his reckoning, his third term candidacy requires. He has it because he made it. Logically, his position today corresponds closely to that

of the man who poisoned his mother and father and then pleaded
for mercy on the ground that he was an orphan.[12]

During the battle over Lend-Lease, McCormick pulled out all
the stops. Roosevelt, Harold Ickes, and the New Deal gang were "fat
old men, senile hysterics . . . able bodied men in bombproof public
positions who devote their every energy to stirring up wars for other
men to fight."

If the attacks on the New Deal economic platform in the press—in
the Hearst papers as well as the *Tribune*—had motivated the administration to make a tentative effort in the direction of controlling the media,
then the *Tribune*'s angular stance on the war question gave this talk a
new urgency. In the spring of 1941, Marshall Field III, the department-
store magnate, began to talk about starting a rival to the *Tribune*. When
Roosevelt got wind of it, a visit to the White House was arranged. Field
received the president's full backing and encouragement.

Meanwhile, the European situation was heating up. The *Tribune*,
having predicted the dissolution of the Hitler–Stalin Pact, editorialized
that "the German declaration of war has cut the ground from under
the war party in this country." Britain would now get some relief and
the Germans would have great difficulty fighting a two-front war. The
initial feeling in Washington and around the country was to let the
totalitarians kill each other off. But Winston Churchill's radio broadcast
pledging all-out aid to Russia and calling on Britain's "friends and allies"
to follow suit was soon driving the debate in this country. McCormick
took up the cudgels:

> Our war birds . . . may try . . . to welcome [the invasion] as reason
> for getting into war. To other Americans, to the majority of them,
> it presents the final reason for remaining out. . . . Should we aid
> Stalin to extend his brutalities to all of Finland, to maintain his grip
> on the Baltic states, or to keep what he has of Poland and Rumania?
> Should we enter the war to extend his rule over more of Europe
> or, having helped him to win, should we then have to rescue the
> continent from him?[13]

The Colonel foresaw that the only result of an alliance with the Soviets would be the postwar tragedy of a communized Eastern Europe. A crusade to save Europe and the world would bring on a new threat rising from the ashes of the old—one created by the very people who now inveighed against the totalitarian menace to democracy.

The conversion of the Communists and fellow travelers to the cause of "antifascism" lent the interventionist movement a new impetus—and a new political slant. Every bout of war hysteria needs a couple of hate objects close at hand. As Hitler was 3,000 miles away in Berlin—though, from the tone of the interventionist campaign, one would have thought he was about to invade Brooklyn—the searchers after American "fifth columnists" inevitably seized on the Colonel. Here was a hate object both the New Deal liberals and their friends in the Communist Party could agree on.

The liberal-Left alliance soon came together in a campaign of vilification organized by the Fight for Freedom Committee, which held a mass meeting in Chicago on July 29, 1941, devoted to the topic "What Is Wrong with the *Chicago Tribune*?" The crowd, about 3,500, screamed their hatred for the Colonel, who was denounced by the speakers as a tool of Hitler. Frank J. Gagen, a member of the FFF group, proposed a resolution to "end the un-American monopoly now enjoyed by the *Chicago Tribune* and . . . give positive encouragement to those individuals . . . now contemplating to provide Chicago with another morning newspaper." The crowd roared its approval and then streamed out into the street, where they demonstrated their anti-Nazism by making bonfires with bundles of early morning *Tribunes*.[14] The FFFers also initiated a boycott using direct mail; the campaign was a flop and McCormick mocked them with a full page headlined THE TRIBUNE ACCEPTS THE CHALLENGE, touting his circulation (1,064,342 daily, 1,220,962 on Sundays) as far above all competitors.

When the destroyer *Greer* was attacked while helping a British patrol plane target a German U-boat, the debate turned bitter. Keeping the facts from the American people, the president claimed it was a clear case of German "piracy." In addition, "the incident," said Roosevelt, "is not isolated, but is part of a general plan. . . . Hitler's advance guards—not only his avowed agents but also his dupes among us—have sought to make ready for him footholds in the New World, to be used as soon as he has gained control of the oceans." There was no doubt in anyone's mind that the "dupes" the president was referring to were America First and the *Tribune*.

Lindbergh's Des Moines speech added fuel to an already volatile fire. The *Tribune* sought to disassociate itself from the eccentric aviator, but it was too late to pull photographs of Lindbergh and an accompanying story in the magazine section of the paper. The editors could only append a note saying that the *Tribune* did not endorse his recent remarks.

McCormick would have no truck with anti-Semitism. Deploring the Nazis in an editorial, he pointed out that the number of Jewish employees on the *Tribune* was roughly proportional to the population of Chicago—and included two of his ablest editorial writers. But hatred of Hitler could not determine U.S. policy. "The case for American participation in the war does not rest on detestation of Hitler. If it did, our navy, with the consent of the whole nation, would have started across the Atlantic the day Poland was invaded."[15]

Lindbergh's speech, which enraged the interventionists, gave America First a black eye and raised the decibel level of the debate to an unbearable cacophony. But even this did not compare with the furor over the *Tribune's* revelation of Roosevelt's secret "Victory Plan."

Goading the War Party: The Victory Plan Affair

It all started one day in December 1941, when an aide to Army Air Corps General Henry H. Arnold called Senator Burton Wheeler (D-MT), a leading America Firster, and asked if he wanted to see a copy of a document which set out the war plans of the Roosevelt administration in elaborate detail. Wheeler said that he would.

That evening, the captain delivered a large parcel wrapped in brown paper. He said that the massive document, of which only five copies existed, would have to be returned to the War Department by morning.

Joseph Gies, in *The Colonel of Chicago*, relates that "as Wheeler leafed through it his blood pressure rose."[16] To understand why, keep in mind that right up until the attack on Pearl Harbor, the president had reiterated his determination—"again and again and again"—to keep us out of war. But the document Wheeler was reading undercut that fabrication so completely, and abruptly, that the leader of the antiwar forces in the Senate could hardly believe his eyes. He called *Tribune* reporter Chesly Manly and together they examined the massive document.

Manly had first incurred the president's wrath several months earlier, when the *Tribune* ran stories by him and Walter Trohan correctly reporting the highlight of the famous "Atlantic Charter" meeting between Roosevelt and Churchill: the president's pledge to the king's first minister to bring the Americans into the war. At a press conference, the president complained of reading stories about his meeting with Churchill that were "vicious rumors, distortions of facts, and just plain dirty falsehoods."[17] The "Victory Plan" document confirmed these "falsehoods" to be the absolute truth. As Manly's story, headlined FDR'S WAR PLANS, put it in the next morning's *Tribune*, the "Victory Plan" was

> a blueprint for total war on a scale unprecedented in at least two oceans and three continents, Europe, Africa, and Asia.
>
> The report expresses the considered opinion of the Army and Navy strategists that "Germany and her European satellites cannot be defeated by the European powers that now fight her." Therefore, it concludes, "if our European enemies are to be defeated it will be necessary for the United States to enter the war, and to employ a part of its armed forces offensively in the western Atlantic and in Europe and Africa."[18]

The story identified July 1, 1943, as the date for "the beginning of the final supreme effort by American land forces to defeat the mighty German army in Europe."

The explosion that followed was almost but not quite equal to the one that would rock the nation a few days later, on December 7. Congress was in an uproar, the press besieged the White House—and the FBI besieged Chesly Manly, who steadfastly refused to divulge his sources. The surrealistic quality of this scene is underscored by Joseph Gies, who points out that a similar story buried in the *Wall Street Journal* had beaten the *Tribune* to the punch in October. That *Journal* story, which detailed the facts and figures in the Victory Plan, revealed that the military was planning a land war, and that such a war would take "one of every three men between the ages of eighteen and forty-five."[19]

The War Department denied everything, while the pro-war press played the story down. The *New York Times* gave it a one-column head on page one: PUT VICTORY COST AT 120 BILLIONS. James Reston's story said that the plan called for equipping an expeditionary force to invade the European continent—but somehow neglected to mention that this expeditionary force would consist of an army of ten million *Americans*.

While the White House was stonewalling, the New Dealers were seething with plans to take the Colonel down. One faction wanted to indict McCormick for conspiracy. In a cabinet meeting, Attorney General Francis Biddle suggested that an indictment could be drawn up under the Espionage Act of 1917. Harold Ickes inquired whether McCormick was still an officer in the reserve and suggested that he might be subject to court martial. Nobody knew the answer; Roosevelt told Henry Stimson to go look it up. In the end, however, it was decided to hold off prosecution. This enabled Roosevelt to issue a liberal-sounding statement magnanimously proclaiming that "the right to print the news in unchallenged"—while Biddle and his legal attack dogs bided their time.

After Pearl Harbor: The Search for Treason

Pearl Harbor ended the activities of the organized anti-interventionist movement: the national committee of America First voted to disband and pledged unconditional support for the war effort. The Colonel, too, gave his support to the war effort. "It is," said the *Tribune*, "a war for national existence, and for individual freedom, and prosperity, and happiness. It comes home to every man's hearth; it touches him nearly in all the relations of life, is a part of his daily thoughts and his secret prayers. For the time it is the universal business."

But McCormick's support was not unconditional:

> We are not of those who believe that, because the country is in danger and all private interests are threatened, or because military power overrides the civil law, it is the province of journalism of the better sort to keep silence when incompetency undertakes the management of public affairs, or hold its peace when unblushing rascality under the guise of patriotism is doing its deadly work.[20]

It didn't take long for the rascality to begin. In late March of 1942, at a meeting sponsored by the Overseas Writers Association and attended by many government officials, a panel including three former *Tribune* employees attacked McCormick and Joe Patterson, publisher of the *New York Daily News*, in terms that one expected to hear in Moscow or Berlin but not in Washington, D.C. John O'Donnell's *Daily News* column recounts the incident in vivid detail:

> Roosevelt advisors . . . applauded lustily such declarations as: The important thing is to put an end [to criticism of the Roosevelt Administration] by whatever means may be necessary—be as ruthless as the enemy. . . . Get him on his income tax or the Mann Act. Hang him, shoot him or lock him up in a concentration camp.[21]

One of the speakers, George Seldes, did not dispute this description of the event but for the bracketed summation. He did not want to hang all opponents of Roosevelt—just two who happened to own newspapers. Shortly afterward, the journalistic lynch mob—Seldes, William L. Shirer, and Edmond Taylor—went to Attorney General Biddle and requested that he find grounds, any grounds, for indicting McCormick and Patterson.[22] Archibald MacLeish, the "poet laureate of the New Deal" and Librarian of Congress, gave the lynch party his blessings when he told the ANPA that certain of their members were guilty of treason.

A blizzard of abuse was heaped on the Colonel and the *Tribune*—a torrent of editorials, press conferences, protest meetings, pamphlets, speeches, newspaper ads, and even a few books, all on a single theme: the absolute necessity of rooting out the "traitors" in our midst, especially McCormick. As the fury reached its height, Roosevelt made his first move.

The administration had long been interested in Marshall Field's *Chicago Sun*, having actively encouraged the department-store tycoon to start a competing morning daily on the Colonel's home turf. The *Sun*—launched amid the high hopes of the anti-*Tribune* crowd—was, at best, only a nuisance as far as McCormick was concerned. One of Field's biggest problems was the lack of an Associated Press franchise. The *Tribune* had the area franchise, and Field would have needed McCormick's approval had he bothered to ask for a waiver—which he never did. Instead, Roosevelt called in Attorney General Biddle and told him, "We have a friend in Chicago for whom we must get the Associated Press service. We have also got an enemy of the New Deal in Chicago who has the AP service and won't let our friend have it. Is the law such that we can make the Associated Press serve our friend?"[23]

The next year, government lawyers brought suit against the Associated Press under the Sherman Anti-Trust Act. The case ended three years later with a Supreme Court decision, in 1945, effectively abolishing the franchise system. Before this issue was revolved, however, the government assault on the *Tribune* escalated to a new level. On June 7, 1942, the front page of the *Tribune* incited the New Deal totalitarians to once again try their hand at silencing their greatest enemy. That day, the two-column headline was NAVY HAD WORD OF JAP PLAN TO STRIKE AT SEA. The story, without a byline, said, "The strength of the Japanese forces with which the American navy is battling somewhere west of Midway island . . . was well known in American naval circles several days before the battle began."[24]

The story went into intricate detail on the makeup of the Japanese fleet, down to the identities of ships, their tonnage, and other specific information matched by no other journalistic account. The only other account which it truly resembled was that contained in a secret dispatch written by Admiral Nimitz, sent May 31. This dispatch contained a closely guarded secret which gave the United States an inestimable advantage throughout the war: the American cryptographers had broken the Japanese naval code. As far as U.S. Naval Intelligence was concerned, the *Tribune* story gave this vital secret away.

Convinced that, at last, they had a case against the Colonel, the president's henchmen sought to indict the author of the piece, Stanley Johnston, as well as J. Loy (Pat) Maloney, the *Tribune's* managing editor, and "such other individuals as are implicated in the unauthorized publication of a newspaper article," i.e., McCormick himself, for violation of the Espionage Act.

The smear machine then went into high gear. Walter Winchell, the gossip columnist–laureate of the New Deal, declared to the nation that the *Tribune* had betrayed vital national secrets to the enemy and was consciously working for the victory of the Axis powers.

In the summer of 1942, it was announced that a grand jury would be convened. At the suggestion of Harold Ickes and Ben Cohen, Roosevelt appointed a Republican to prosecute the case, William D. Mitchell, who had been Hoover's attorney general. McCormick's answer was unequivocal:

> The attack on the *Tribune* is now in the open. An administration which for years has been seeking by one sly means or another, but always with complete futility, to intimidate this newspaper has finally despaired of all other means and is now preparing criminal prosecutions. . . . The charge is as false as it is petty and we welcome the opportunity which may come to us to prove how false and petty it is.
>
> We take pride in the knowledge that the administration was moved to this action because of its previous failures to scare us or cajole us into surrender of our independence. . . .
>
> For years they have tried to harass us, to alienate our readers, to weaken our influence, always without success. They encouraged the organization of a rival newspaper with results that to them were cruelly disappointing. And now, all else having failed, they are threatening criminal action.[25]

McCormick's one regret was that the government was going after Maloney and Johnston, two patriotic Americans whose record of distinguished military service was unimpeachable. Not only did Johnston cover the battle of the Coral Sea—his story about it scored a scoop for the *Tribune*—but he was a participant. The only correspondent present, he helped rescue wounded men when the aircraft carrier *Lexington* was hit and sunk. As the government was filing its charges of treason, Johnston's recommendation for a Navy Cross was on an admiral's desk.

In a front-page, unsigned piece, the *Tribune* went after Biddle, emphasizing Johnston's distinguished war record—and contrasting it with that of the attorney general, whose military service started on October 23, 1918, and ended on November 29 of the same year.

The outcome of this dramatic confrontation was anticlimactic: barely a month after the administration sought an indictment against the *Tribune* for espionage, the government's case was dismissed by the jury as entirely without substance. What happened was that Mitchell had to eventually confront the military strategists with the following question: was the navy prepared to inform the jury of the essential fact of the case, i.e., that the Japanese code had been broken? If so, the secret would be out. If not, then the government had no case.

After initial assurances that they would back up the prosecution 100 percent, the military brass backed down, leaving Biddle, Ickes, and Roosevelt in the lurch. But even if the brass had not backed down, it is highly doubtful that Mitchell could have gotten a conviction, even at the height of the war hysteria. The reason is that, incredibly, *the Japanese code had remained unchanged and decipherable*, even after Congressman Elmer Holland (D-PA)—who had once called Joe and Cissy Patterson[26] "America's No. 1 and No. 2 exponents of the Nazi propaganda line"—loudly declared,

> It is public knowledge that the *Tribune* story . . . tipped off the Japanese high command that somehow our Navy had secured and broken the secret code of the Japanese Navy. . . . Three days after the *Tribune* story was published the Japs changed their code.[27]

But Holland was wrong—the Japanese never changed their code, not even after his statement.[28]

The campaign to silence the *Tribune* did not end with the collapse of the government's case. Indeed, it accelerated, with Adlai Stevenson and the Chicago chapter of the Union for Democratic Action—the forerunner of Americans for Democratic Action—leading the charge. The UDA published a 72-page pamphlet, *The People versus the Chicago Tribune*, which made John Roy Carlson look like the epitome of objectivity and fairness. Accusing the Colonel of betraying military secrets, and "delighting the Axis" because it doubted the administration's line on the *Greer* incident, these leading lights of liberalism called for "all justified legal steps" against anyone obstructing the war effort—a category which the UDA obviously meant to include McCormick.[29]

The *Chicago Sun* took out ads accusing the *Tribune* of treason, which the New York papers, the *Times* and the *Herald Tribune*, refused to run. There were rumblings in Canada that the *Tribune's* paper mill, which McCormick had the foresight to buy before the war, would be confiscated—a possibility vehemently opposed by the unions, because the Colonel treated his workers quite well.

Far from being cowed by all this opposition, the Colonel seemed to thrive on it. Through the darkest days of Roosevelt's wartime quasi-dictatorship, anathemas were hurled from the Tribune Tower without respite. A few months before the ill-fated indictment, a *Tribune* editorial asked, "Who are the fascists here?"

> They are not the small fry, the scrambled wits represented by such organizations as the Silver Shirts and other nuisances. They are influential and they are in authority. They try to conceal their true selves by calling the opposition Fascist, and there never was a stranger distortion of the truth than that.
>
> The left wing radicals who are promoting the state controlled economy to endure after the war are Fascist in thought and act.[30]

In calling for sedition trials and suppression of publications, yesterday's American liberals were today's American brownshirts. Echoing the famous aphorism of Randolph Bourne that war is the health of the state, the *Tribune* averred that "war has put the country in the vise of authority. People do not say no to Leon Henderson. . . . Let's call things by their right names," thundered the *Tribune*. "If the word 'Fascist' is a reproach, let it be worn by the planners whom it fits."[31]

Robert McCormick, American Nationalist

Inveighing against wartime controls, New Deal boondoggles, Communists, and Willkieites, the *Tribune* stood like a rock against the temper of the times. While other voices of the Old Right were muted or silenced, McCormick would not submit. As the war reached its climax, the *Tribune* published Garet Garrett's "The Mortification of History," an essay that perfectly expressed McCormick's defiance:

> If you say, "I am first of all an American," you have to be careful. It may be misunderstood. You might have said, "I am for America first." And the American who says that will be denounced in his own country and by his own government. That is not enough. He will be denounced also in Great Britain, Russia, and China, all accusing him of one thing.
>
> He is an isolationist.
>
> But what is that? An isolationist is one who is said to have sinned against the peace and well being of the whole world. He is held responsible for the necessity now to mortify American history by rewriting it to a theme of guilt and atonement.[32]

In fact, said Garrett, there had never been any such thing as genuine American isolationism. This was a straw man, a device used by internationalists to obliterate even the possibility of a healthy American nationalism. From the Monroe Doctrine to the expansionism of Teddy Roosevelt, to the Wilsonian idealism that dragged us into the "war to end war," it was hardly the spirit of "isolationism" that infused American history, said Garrett:

If you say of this history that its intense character has been nationalistic, consistently so from the beginning until now, that is true. Therefore, the word in place of isolationism that would make sense is nationalism. Why is the right word avoided?

The explanation must be that the wrong one, for what it is intended to do, is the perfect political word. Since isolationism cannot be defined, those who attack it are not obliged to define themselves. What are they? Anti-isolationists? But if you cannot say what isolationism is neither can you say what anti-isolationism is, whereas nationalism, being definite, has a positive antithesis. One who attacks nationalism is an internationalist.

The use of the obscurity created by the false word is to conceal something. The thing to be concealed is the identity of what is speaking.

Internationalism is speaking.

It has a right to speak, as itself and for itself; but that right entails a moral obligation to say what it means and to use true words.[33]

As the end of the war came within sight and the internationalists of both parties began to project their vision of an Anglo-American imperium to police the postwar world, the *Tribune*'s sardonic reply, "States Across the Sea," was the Colonel at his best. To the adherents of Union Now—who wanted to repeal the American Revolution and merge with the British Empire—McCormick suggested that our overseas allies might want to utilize Article IV of the U.S. Constitution and apply for admission to the Union. "Great Britain could come into the Union, for example, as four states, England, Scotland, Wales, and Ireland," he wrote. The many economic benefits would be enhanced by the political bonus because "membership in our Union would give the British an opportunity to rid themselves, once and for all, of the incubus of their nobility and the aristocratic system that goes with it." Of course, "Britain would have to give up its king," but since he had no real power it would be no real loss. Scoring a direct hit on his old enemies, the Anglophiles of the Eastern Establishment, McCormick wrote:

Certainly the handkissers and Tories in this country should welcome
the closer relationship if only because it would strengthen their
representation in Congress. They should look forward pleasurably
to more intimate social and political ties with their English friends,
particularly as the new relationship would be that of equals, living
within the same political system.[34]

The editorial cause widespread comment and accounts for some
of his reputation as an alleged "Anglophobe." While he did not conceal
his disdain for the Tory "handkissers" who infested the upper echelons
of the American ruling elite, McCormick had enormous respect for the
British leadership. On the occasion of Churchill's visit to the United
States in the spring of 1943, a *Tribune* editorial bade him a gracious
welcome, noting the eloquence of his speeches. The source of his
oratorical power, said the *Tribune*, was

love for his country, pride in its history and achievements, and
determination to add to its glories.

Americans look in vain for the same quality of patriotism in the
speeches of our latter-day leaders. Here the talk is not of preserving
the American heritage of freedom . . . but of whittling away our
Constitution and disposing of our birthright. Mr. Churchill has
said that he did not become the king's first minister to preside over
the dissolution of the empire, but who of those in high places in
this country has made a parallel declaration as an American? Who
in Washington has announced a purpose to use our victory for the
strengthening of our security in the time to come? The talk is of a
far different sort; it concerns what we shall give up and give away,
not what we shall keep.[35]

The chief evidence that McCormick was motivated by hatred of
the British was a series of muckraking articles, in which the *Tribune*
writers traced the influence of Rhodes scholars on the American foreign-
policy establishment. This account was framed in the context of Cecil
Rhodes's announced goal, which was to return the ex-colonies of the
U.S. to the British Empire.[36] But this was American nationalism, not

Anglophobia; love of America, not hatred of Perfidious Albion. That Churchill was for Britain First, McCormick could well understand. What he could not understand was how or why some *Americans* could put and keep Britain First, even after the defeat of the Axis powers.

The Postwar Era: Twilight of the Old Right

As the U.S. entered the postwar era, McCormick kept up his fighting stance. NATO, the Marshall Plan, the Fair Deal, the Cold War—all were staunchly opposed by the Colonel, who placed his bets on Senator Robert A. Taft to take back the GOP from the "me too" internationalists and restore the republic.

With FDR's death, Harry Truman became the *Tribune's* least favorite politician. When Colonel McCormick's second wife, Maryland, found wallpaper with a motif of horses she intended to hang in their dining room, Richard Gies tells us that "the Colonel demurred. Pointing to a horse prominently facing away from the viewer, he said he didn't want to have to look at Harry Truman every night at the dinner table."[37]

When Taft lost the GOP nomination to Eisenhower in 1952, McCormick went on the Tribune-owned radio station, WGN, and suggested that "the time has come to organize another party," which he called the American Party:

> I swallowed Willkie in '40, Dewey twice in '44 and '48, candidates foisted upon the majority by sharp practice, but now that the Democrats have taken over our party by voting in Republican primaries by the ruse of falsehood and corruption . . . I will be imposed upon no longer.

Eisenhower, he said,

> is the candidate of effeminates like the All-Slops and Childses, the Fleesons, the Schiffs, and the Luces, who are urging him to denounce American-minded senators and support the "free" world.

They use that word with falsehood on their tongues. They mean for him to support socialism in Europe as a prelude to bringing it here.[38]

He tried to persuade General Albert C. Wedemeyer—the probable source of the *Tribune's* "Victory Plan" scoop—to run as the presidential candidate of a new American Party, but without success.

In *The Twenty-Year Revolution: From Roosevelt to Eisenhower*, Chesly Manly succinctly expressed the *Tribune* line during the Eisenhower years. The American republic, he said,

> is threatened by revolutionary forces which, if not checked, will cause its downfall. The primary menace is that our economy, already gravely overstrained, will be ruined by taxing and spending, ostensibly for defense against a foreign foe. Remote control of this country's purse strings, and not the thermonuclear bomb, is the No. 1 weapon in the Kremlin's arsenal.[39]

The United States, he maintained, could defend itself with air power without bankrupting the country. If Europe was unwilling to defend itself, then no American army on European soil could save it. Like McCormick, Manly was embittered by his experience in the GOP and advocated the creation of a new party. "We must have a political realignment in this country," he wrote, "and a new political party, to express the will of millions of Americans who have been effectively disfranchised by a system which asks them to choose between New Deal Democrats and New Deal Republicans." With a program of halting and reversing the growth of government, getting Communists and pro-Communists out of the State Department, getting the U.S. out of the UN, and enacting the Bricker Amendment, the American Party envisioned by McCormick and Manly would bring about a realignment and restore the old Republic.

But it was not to be. Colonel McCormick's death on April 1, 1955, marked the decline of the Old Right's influence on mass public opinion in America. The *Tribune* remained very conservative for many years; but in the face of the postwar liberal-internationalist consensus, the paper's fiery defense of American independence, free enterprise, and sheer Yankee cussedness was soon diluted. Without the Colonel riding herd on them, the Tories, the Socialists, and the globalists were free to trample American values, which they proceeded to do with impunity. Bereft of its major voice, the political influence of the Old Right waned, and the new globalism of the Cold War fastened on the nation its deadening embrace.

And yet, the Old Right was not dead: it merely went underground. Reduced in numbers and influence, still it persisted—and waited for the day when conditions would prove more favorable. It would be a long wait: nearly forty years before the Cold War ended and the world was ready for the Old Right's revival. In the meantime, a few men and women of heroic character struggled to push back the encroaching darkness.

7
The Postwar Old Right

I see the Communist International as finally defeated now. Defeated, I mean, in the sense that France was ruined in the early 1800s; or that springtime begins in December. It is a curious fact in history that effects continue in Time after their cause no longer exists.
—Rose Wilder Lane, Letter to Jasper Crane, 1953

THE POSTWAR TRIUMPH OF LIBERAL internationalism did not go unopposed: a vocal but increasingly beleaguered remnant of nationalist Republicans held out against the liberal dream of a globalized welfare state. The Old Right had its voice in Congress, in the person of Senator Robert A. Taft. The son of President William Howard Taft and a staunch opponent of the New Deal who had been a leader of the anti-interventionists in Congress prior to Pearl Harbor, Taft became the focal point of the postwar Republican isolationists. While he often compromised his position, much to the detriment of his cause, his was the most influential challenge to the Truman–Churchill doctrine of Cold War.

In 1946, when Churchill declared that an "iron curtain" had descended across Europe and rallied the American president and public around yet another crusade to make the world safe for what remained of the British Empire, he was answered by Taft at the Kenyon College "Symposium on English-Speaking Peoples." Taft's speech, "Equal Justice and Law," disputed Churchill's premise that the English-speaking peoples had indeed preserved the heritage of classical liberalism, which must now be defended against the relentless Communist menace. The war years had given rise to a new American philosophy of government, he said, which looked to state power and not social power as the motor of human civilization. The U.S., Taft believed, was repeating the very mistakes that had led to war. A harsh peace, including war-crimes trials, extended military occupation, and the dropping of the atomic bomb on Hiroshima and Nagasaki, all had contributed to the atmosphere of postwar barbarism that would lead, perhaps, to a new conflagration. Taft surveyed the postwar scene and was appalled: the concept of international law had given way to brute force and the "principle" of might makes right. Following in the footsteps of British imperialism, the Americans under Truman were establishing themselves as the world's policemen. "This whole policy," thundered Taft,

> is no accident. For years we have been accepting at home the theory that the people are too dumb to understand and that a benevolent Executive must be given power to describe policy and administer policy. . . . Such a policy in the world, as at home, can only lead to tyranny or to anarchy.[1]

The Old Right in the GOP

The Taft wing of the Republican Party, which had opposed the New Deal and U.S. meddling in European wars, was now fighting Truman's "Fair Deal" continuation of the same agenda. When the president announced his Truman Doctrine and rushed aid to the Greek and Turkish governments, Taft denounced it as the beginning of a policy that would divide the world into zones of influence. As Leonard Liggio puts it, the Taft wing "feared that Truman's program would create a cartelized, monopolistic American economy based on government contracts which, whether or not a Cold War remained, would create an undemocratic domestic atmosphere."[2] The leading Taftite in the House, Representative George Bender (R-OH), lashed out against the Truman Doctrine as a continuation of the British policy of imperialism and cynical "balance of power" politics. "I believe," Bender declared,

> that the White House program is a reaffirmation of the nineteenth century belief in power politics. It is a refinement of the policy first adopted after the Treaty of Versailles in 1919 designed to encircle Russia and establish a "Cordon Sanitaire" around the Soviet Union. It is a program which points to a new policy of interventionism in Europe as a corollary to our Monroe Doctrine in South America. Let there be no mistake about the far-reaching implications of this plan. Once we have taken the historic step of sending financial aid, military experts and loans to Greece and Turkey, we shall be irrevocably committed to a course of action from which it will be impossible to withdraw. More and larger demands will follow. Greater needs will arise thorough the many areas of friction in the world.[3]

When Henry Wallace was attacked for going to Europe and speaking out against the Truman Doctrine, urging Europeans to resist the idea of dividing the world into two armed camps, Bender was one of the few members of Congress to rise to his defense when many on both sides of the aisle were demanding the revocation of Wallace's passport. If Churchill could come to the U.S. and make propaganda in favor of launching a war to preserve the British Empire, said Bender, then Wallace could travel to Europe in order to make speeches in favor of peace.

Bender saw Truman's foreign policy as a rationale for peacetime military conscription, the militarization of the U.S. economy, and an endless flow of U.S. dollars to South American dictators. He denounced the Voice of America as "nothing more or less than the propaganda arm of the Truman Doctrine." Bender was supported by such staunch Old Right Republicans as Rep. Howard Buffett of Omaha, Nebraska, who had been Senator Taft's midwestern campaign manager in 1952, Rep. Ralph W. Gwinn of New York, Rep. Frederick C. Smith of Ohio, and Rep. H. R. Gross of Iowa, all Republicans who were pro–free market at home, anti-interventionist abroad, and who loudly and uncompromisingly opposed conscription.

Opposed to the Old Right GOPers were the internationalist Republicans, primarily from the East, best represented by Governor Thomas E. Dewey of New York, who won the party's presidential nomination in 1948. With their help, Truman was able to push through a whole series of measures which upped the Cold War ante: aid to Greece and Turkey, the Marshall Plan, NATO, and the prostration of the U.S. State Department to the "China Lobby." As Leonard Liggio points out, "Although the internationalist Republicans supported the bipartisan foreign policy and foreign aid, under the leadership of Senator Vandenberg and . . . Dewey, they conditioned their support for the Marshall Plan upon the Administration's inclusion of aid to nationalist dictator Chiang Kai-Shek."[4]

Taft was a great believer in party "unity," and he refused the remonstrations of Bender and *Human Events* editor Felix Morley to break with Vandenberg and take a more militant stance. Thus, although critical of the Truman foreign policy, Taft wound up voting for the draft and the Marshall Plan, limiting his efforts regarding the latter to an amendment reducing the appropriation. But he drew the line when Truman introduced the NATO Treaty for the Senate's approval. In a major speech, "The Future of the Republican Party," Taft declared that the GOP should take the position that there was "no greater tragedy than war." A war would be just only if it was necessary "to protect the liberty of our people." The foreign policy of the Truman administration, he said, "had adopted a tendency to interfere in the affairs of other nations, to assume that we are a kind of demigod and Santa Claus to solve the problems of the world, and that attitude is more and more likely to involve us in disputes where our liberty is not in fact concerned." He warned that "[i]t is easy to skip into an attitude of imperialism where war becomes an instrument of public policy."[5]

Taft argued that there were other ways to stand up to the Soviets than to sign on to the doctrine of collective security. The NATO Treaty "obligates us to go to war if at any time during the next twenty years anyone makes an armed attack on any of the twelve nations." Taft was one of thirteen "Nay" votes on the treaty, because, he explained, U.S. military power was sufficient to deter any attack, and the cost of NATO would be "incalculable." The alliance would not only represent an incredible drain on the U.S. economy, but also posed a threat to the Constitution, which had invested Congress with the power to declare war. Taft would not vote to "give the President . . . unlimited power to go out and arm the world in time of peace."

While formally supporting Truman's actions, Taft's reaction to the Korean War can only be described as critical support, with the emphasis on the critical. Truman, he averred, had invited war by sending the wrong signals. On January 12, 1950, Secretary of State Dean Acheson had declared that Korea was *not* a vital U.S. interest, a stunt similar to the one pulled by Ambassador April Glaspie in her contacts with the Iraqis forty years later. "Is it any wonder that the Korean Communists took us at the word given by our Secretary of State?" Taft asked in a speech to the Senate. Again, he accused Truman of trampling on the Constitution. A dangerous precedent had been set: the president had usurped the power granted only to Congress. With remarkable fore-sight, Taft argued that "If the President can intervene in Korea without Congressional approval, he can go to war in Malaya or Indonesia or Iran or South America." Unless the Senate stood up to the president on this issue, "we would have finally terminated for all time the right of Congress to declare war."[6]

Taft waffled between support and criticism of Truman's conduct of the war, constantly undercutting his own anti-interventionist arguments and those of his more radical followers. Aside from the tremendous pressure applied by Eastern finance capital on the delegates to the Republican convention, this hedging was chiefly responsible for his failure to win the 1952 GOP presidential nomination—a failure which eventually led to the passing of the Old Right as a political force within the Republican Party.

The Revisionists: Getting the Truth Out

But Taft's wishy-washy stance was not shared by such stalwarts as Rep. Howard Buffett, who developed a theory that the U.S., and not the Communists, had been the real instigators of the Korean "police action." In *The Betrayal of the American Right*, Murray Rothbard reveals that Buffett

> had been told by Senator Bridges (R., N.H.) that Admiral Roscoe Hillenkoeter, head of the CIA, had so testified in secret before the Senate Armed Services Committee at the outbreak of the war. For his indiscretion in testifying, Admiral Hillenkoeter was soon fired by President Truman and was little heard from again in Washington. For the rest of his life, Buffett carried on a crusade to have Congress declassify the Hillenkoeter testimony, but without success.[7]

This iconoclastic impulse to get to the bottom of things was characteristic of the postwar American Right. Historical revisionism was a major theme, as a look at the list of titles put out by such Old Right book publishers as Caxton, Devin-Adair, and Henry Regnery will confirm. The main figure in this school was the indefatigable Harry Elmer Barnes, whose *Perpetual War for Perpetual Peace*,[8] an anthology of the major revisionist historians, summarized their case against the court historians of World War II. Charles Beard's *President Roosevelt and the Coming of the War: A Study in Appearances and Realities*[9] posed a major challenge to the sanctity of the official mythology, while Charles Callan Tansill's *Back Door to War*[10] traced the trail of diplomatic deception that led to the war with Japan. Along with the Tansill volume, Regnery also brought out William Henry Chamberlin's *America's Second Crusade*[11] and Frederic R. Sanborn's *Design for War*.[12]

The school of historical revisionism, which had had such success with the liberal intelligentsia after World War I, found itself under attack from this same group in the wake of World War II. "It may be said with great restraint," says Barnes in his introduction to *Perpetual War for Perpetual Peace*, "that, never since the Middle Ages have there been so many powerful forces organized and alerted against the assertion and acceptance of historical truth as are active today to prevent the facts about the responsibility for the second World War and its results from being made generally accessible to the American public."[13] The venerable Charles A. Beard accused the Rockefeller Foundation and the Council on Foreign Relations of trying to head off, "if they can, a repetition of what they call in the vernacular 'the debunking journalistic campaign following World War I.' "[14]

George Morgenstern, an editorial writer for the *Chicago Tribune* and author of *Pearl Harbor: Story of a Secret War*,[15] expressed the foreign-policy outlook of this group in an article for the conservative weekly *Human Events*, in which he traced the longing for empire back to the Spanish-American War, the days when "the sinister Spaniard provided a suitable punching bag." In spite of the fact that the Spanish government had agreed to the American terms,

> we wound up with a couple of costly dependencies, but this was enough to intoxicate the precursors of those who now swoon on very sight of the phrase "world leadership."
>
> McKinley testified that in lonely sessions on his knees at night he had been guided to the realization that we must uplift and civilize and Christianize the Filipinos. . . . This sort of exalted nonsense is familiar to anyone who later attended the evangelical rationalizations of Wilson for intervening in the European war, of Roosevelt promising the millennium . . . of Eisenhower treasuring the "crusade in Europe" that somehow went sour, or of Truman, Stevenson, Paul Douglas, or the *New York Times* preaching the holy war in Korea.
>
> An all-pervasive propaganda had established a myth of inevitability in American action: all wars were necessary, all wars were good. . . . Intervention began with deceit by McKinley; it ends with deceit by Roosevelt and Truman. Perhaps we would have a rational foreign policy . . . if Americans could be brought to realize that the first necessity is the renunciation of the lie as an instrument of foreign policy.[16]

The all-pervasive character of cold-war hysteria was reflected in the fact that Morgenstern's views were already in the process of becoming a minority on the Right. After the resignation of Felix Morley as editor, such ideas were infrequently found in the pages of *Human Events*.

Swan Song of the Old Right:
The Fight for the Bricker Amendment

The swan song of the Old Right as a nationally organized force was the campaign to enact the Bricker Amendment. Authored by Senator John W. Bricker, an Ohio Republican who had been the GOP vice presidential nominee in 1944, the amendment was a last desperate effort to preserve American independence against the encroachment of international agencies. Introduced into the Senate in 1951, Bricker's proposed amendment to the Constitution read as follows:

> Section 1. A provision of a treaty which conflicts with this Constitution shall not be of any force or effect.
>
> Section 2. A treaty shall become effective as internal law in the United States only through legislation which would be valid in the absence of treaty.
>
> Section 3. Congress shall have power to regulate all executive and other agreements with any foreign power or international organization. All such agreements shall be subject to the limitations imposed on treaties by this article.
>
> Section 4. Congress shall have power to enforce this article by appropriate legislation.

Mobilizing to support Bricker, conservatives built a grand coalition which included all the major veterans groups, the Kiwanis Clubs, the American Association of Small Business, many women's groups, as well as the conservative activist organizations of the time, such as the Freedom Clubs and the Committee for Constitutional Government. The conservative press joined in the campaign; writing in *Human Events*, Frank Chodorov made the argument for the amendment in terms of unabashed nationalism:

> The proposed amendment arises from a rather odd situation. A nation is threatened by invasion, not by a foreign army, but by its own legal entanglements. Not soldiers, but theoreticians and visionaries attack its independence and aim to bring its people under the rule

of an agglomeration of foreign governments. This is something new in history. There have been occasions when a weak nation sought security by placing itself under the yoke of a strong one. But, here we have the richest nation in the world, and apparently the strongest, flirting with the liquidation of its independence. Nothing like that has ever happened before.[17]

The breach in our defenses, said Chodorov, is in Article VI of the Constitution, which provides that "[a]ll Treaties . . . shall be the supreme Law of the Land . . . any Thing in the Constitution to the contrary notwithstanding." At the time of the Founders, the division between foreign and domestic policy was clear enough; there was never any intention, as Jefferson wrote, to enable the president and the Senate to "do by treaty what the whole government is interdicted from doing in any way."

But as the concept of limited government was eroded—and under pressure from the endless stream of pacts, covenants, and executive agreements issuing forth from the United Nations and its American enthusiasts—the chink in our constitutional armor widened. Just as the growth of administrative law had threatened to overthrow the old republic during the darkest days of the New Deal, so under Truman and Eisenhower the burgeoning body of treaty law threatened to submerge and subvert U.S. sovereignty.

Executive agreements had created administrative law of a new type; treaties which sought to regulate domestic economic and social behavior to a degree never achieved by the Brain Trusters. If the New Deal had failed to completely socialize America, to conservatives it often seemed as if the United Nations was determined to finish the job. According to the UN Declaration of Human Rights, human beings were endowed with all sorts of "rights," including the right to a job and the right to "security." There were, however, certain significant omissions, chief among them the right to own and maintain private property. Another equally glaring omission was the unqualified right to a free press, the regulation of which was left up to member nations. When three Supreme Court justices, including the chief justice, cited the

UN Charter and the NATO Treaty in support of their argument that Truman had the right to seize the steel mills, conservatives went into action—and the fight for the Bricker Amendment began in earnest.

The Eisenhower administration, and particularly the State Department, went all out to defeat the amendment. Leading the opposition was Secretary of State John Foster Dulles—the man who had said, two years earlier, that "the treaty power is an extraordinary power, liable to abuse," and warned that "treaties can take powers away from Congress and give them to the President. They can take powers from the states and give them to the federal government or to some international body and they can cut across the rights given to the people by their Constitutional Bill of Rights." Hammered with this quote by Clarence Manion, dean of the University of Notre Dame Law School, Dulles could only take refuge in the argument that *this* president would never compromise U.S. sovereignty.[18]

Although the Bricker Amendment started out with fifty-six cosponsors, it eventually went down to defeat in the Senate, 42–50, with 4 not voting. (A watered-down version, the "George proposal," lost by a single vote.) The defection of Senators William Knowland (CA) and Alexander Wiley (WI) from conservative Republican ranks on this occasion was particularly significant, and marked the beginning not only of Wiley's chairmanship of the Senate Foreign Relations Committee, but also the beginning of the breakup of what had been the Taft wing of the GOP.

The defeat of the Bricker Amendment, combined with the deaths of Taft (1953) and McCormick (1955), signaled the virtual demise of the Old Right as a political force on the national scene. The near-complete absence of any visible movement against the twin evils of statism at home and globalism abroad was perhaps responsible for the deep pessimism of such libertarians as Chodorov. This was understandable, given the tenor of the times, but, as it turned out, not quite justified. For even as the all-pervasive propaganda of collectivism and Cold War was achieving something close to unanimity, when everything and everyone was being absorbed into that many-tentacled monster, the so-called "Vital Center," the seeds of dissent had already been planted and were soon to sprout into a rebirth of the American individualist tradition.

Although a bit thin in the postwar years, the ranks of the Remnant were reinforced by Ludwig von Mises, the émigré economist and founder of the radical free market "Austrian" school of economics, whose monumental *Human Action*[19] was to become the libertarian equivalent of Marx's *Capital* in future years. Two of his books, *Bureaucracy*[20] and *Omnipotent Government*,[21] were published at this time. More significant in terms of notoriety was the publication, in 1944, of Friedrich von Hayek's bestselling *The Road to Serfdom*.[22] Arguing that fascism, communism, Nazism, and Social Democracy all came from the same root, and that the economic and ideological antecedents of Hitlerism were present in the Weimar Republic—a theme pursued by John T. Flynn in *As We Go Marching*, which came out that same year—the book's popularity sent shock waves through the Liberal Establishment.

Nineteen forty-three was a banner year for right-wing individualist authors. Three important works on libertarian themes came out, all by women authors: *The Discovery of Freedom*[23] by Rose Wilder Lane, *The God of the Machine*[24] by Isabel Paterson, and *The Fountainhead*[25] by Ayn Rand.

The remarkable story of Rose Lane is perhaps the most enchanting of the three; certainly it is the most novelistic. The story of her life captures the heroic spirit of the movement that fought the New Deal, survived the war years, and lived to fight another day.

Rose Wilder Lane: The Transformation

Rose Wilder Lane was born in 1886 on a South Dakota homestead claim. She grew up in Mansfield, Missouri, the daughter of Laura Ingalls Wilder, whose *Little House on the Prairie* novels for children continue to be bestsellers. After graduating from high school, she went to work for Western Union, a job which took her to San Francisco, where she eventually found a position with the *San Francisco Bulletin*.[26]

Shortly after the First World War, Lane traveled to Russia, the

Balkans, and the Near East on behalf of the American Red Cross as an investigator and writer. Already she was sympathetic to left-wing ideas, and it was due only to circumstance, rather than intention, that Lane did not join the Communist Party. Soon after the founding of the party, she came down with influenza and nearly died. Her reduced financial condition then forced her to take a job in Europe. "Nevertheless," she said, "I was at heart a communist,"

During this time she wrote *Henry Ford's Own Story* (1917); *White Shadows in the South Seas*, coauthored with Frederick O'Brien (1919); and her first novel, *Diverging Roads*, which was published as a serial in *Sunset* magazine. In 1920, she published *The Making of Herbert Hoover*, and in 1925, *He Was a Man*, a fictionalized biography of Jack London, in additional to the first of her popular Ozark novels, *Hill Billy*; a second Ozark novel, *Cindy*, was published in 1928.

In those days, John Reed was organizing the Communist Party of the United States—and Rose Wilder Lane was there as the conspirators met in secret session. They were on their guard against the ever-present threat of police attack, for that was the era of the infamous "Palmer Raids," named after the attorney general who carried them out. As she tells it in her remarkable memoir and manifesto, *Give Me Liberty*,

> I remember the room as a small room, with perhaps sixty men and women in it. There was an almost unbearable sense of expectancy, and a sense of danger. The meeting had not begun. A few men gathered around Jack Reed were talking earnestly, urgently. He caught sight of the man with me, and his tenseness broke into Jack Reed's smile, more joyous than a shout. He broke loose from the others, reached us in half a dozen strides and exclaimed, "Are you with us!"
>
> "Are you?" he repeated, expectant. But the question itself was a challenge. This was a risky enterprise. Jack Reed, as every communist knows, did not leave his own country later; he escaped from it. Federal agents, raiding police, might break in upon us at that moment. We knew this, and because I shared the communist dream I was prepared to take risks and also to submit to the rigorous party discipline. But the man beside me began a vague discussion

of tactics; evaded; hesitated; questioned and demurred; finally, with a disarming smile, doubted whether he should risk committing himself, his safety was so valuable to The Cause. Jack Reed turned on his heel, saying, "Oh, go to hell, you damn coward."[27]

Give Me Liberty is a seminal document in the history of the Old Right. It served as a manifesto for an activist group of libertarian and conservative publicists, businessmen, and intellectuals brought together by its publication in the *Saturday Evening Post*. This was not just another personal memoir detailing the author's disillusionment with communism; it was a powerful testament to the positive ideal of liberty. Here she recalls the incident that planted the seeds of doubt:

> I was in Transcaucasian Russia at the time, drinking tea with cherry preserves in it and trying to hold a lump of sugar between my teeth while I did so. It's difficult. My plump Russian hostess and her placid, golden-bearded husband beamed at me, and a number of round-cheeked children stared in wonder at the American.[28]

The year was 1920, the Bolshevik coup was four years old, and the village was solidly Communist—at least on the surface. Rose Wilder Lane was no ordinary tourist but a proud partisan come to stand shoulder to shoulder with the workers and peasants of the New Russia. She was therefore puzzled to discover that her enthusiasm for the Soviet regime was not shared by her peasant hosts. "My host astounded me by the force with which he said that he did not like the new government," she wrote.

> I could hardly believe that a lifelong communist, with the proofs of successful communism thick about us, was opposed to a communist government. He repeated that he did not like it. "No! No!"
>
> His complaint was government interference with village affairs. He protested against the growing bureaucracy that was taking more and more men from productive work. He predicted chaos and suffering from the centralizing of economic power in Moscow. These were not his words, but that was what he meant.

This I said to myself is the opposition of the peasant mind to new ideas, too large for him to grasp. Here is my small opportunity to spread a little light. . . . I drew for him a picture of Great Russia, to its remotest corner enjoying the equality, the peace and the justly divided prosperity of his village. He shook his head sadly.

"It is too big," he said. "Too big. At the top, it is too small. It will not work. In Moscow there are only men, and man is not God. A man has only a man's head, and one hundred heads together do not make one great head. No. Only God can know Russia."[29]

Thus, a simple Russian peasant summed up Ludwig von Mises's theory of the impossibility of economic calculation under socialism—and accurately predicted the downfall of such an unworkable system.

It seemed to Rose Lane that the man had a point. "It is quite true that many heads do not make one great head; actually, they make a session of Congress. What, then, I asked myself dizzily, is the State?"

She had achieved world fame as a writer; her articles appeared regularly in all the major magazines of the day, including the *American Mercury*, *Good Housekeeping*, the *Saturday Evening Post*, and *Harpers*. According to Roger MacBride, she "was said to be the second highest paid author (after Somerset Maugham) in the United States." Her novel *Let the Hurricane Roar* (1933) was a bestseller, and is still in print. She also wrote short stories, a volume of which was published as *Old Home Town* (1935). It was the "Red Decade," Rose was a literary success, and she had no good reason to go against the overwhelmingly pro-Soviet trend which dominated the American intelligentsia—except that the seeds of doubt planted during her tour of the Workers Paradise had germinated and finally sprouted in the form of *Give Me Liberty*. Written in her unique prose style, at once intensely visual and cerebral, the original title of this piece as it appeared in the *Saturday Evening Post*, "Credo," describes its significance as the manifesto of a generation of proto-libertarian activists.

Like Shachtman and Burnham a few years later, Rose Lane observed that the Communist revolution had "concentrated economic power in the hands of the State, the commissars, so that the lives, the livelihoods, of common men were once more subject to dictators." The gains made against the power of the church and the aristocracy had been "lost by the collectivist economic reaction." The Soviet system—and socialism itself—was, then, profoundly *reactionary*, a throwback to an earlier era which had to be fought by all true radicals. Her analysis went far beyond the superficial revision of Marxism promulgated by Shachtman, however, or the world-weary brutality of Burnham's neo-Machiavellian rationale for power. Instead of positing some highly artificial theoretical construct, such as the theory of a "degenerated workers' state," and embellishing it with all sorts of qualifications and abstruse modifications, Rose Lane got down to first principles. Quite unlike her opposite numbers in the Future Neocons of America contingent, she did not hop on the Roosevelt bandwagon and then drift helplessly and aimlessly toward the morass of the "Vital Center." Instead of singing the song of "The God That Failed" and joining the great liberal consensus, Lane dared to challenge the central premise of statism. Instead of blaming Lenin "because he did not establish a republic," she pointed out that it would not have made any difference if he had. Since "the government of multitudes of men must be in the hands of a few men," therefore "the fact that a few men ruled Russia would not have been altered."

> Representative government cannot express the will of the mass of the people, because there is no mass of the people; The People is a fiction, like The State. You cannot get a Will of the Mass, even among a dozen persons who all want to go on a picnic. The only human mass with a common will is a mob, and that will is a temporary insanity.[30]

In the intellectual atmosphere of the Red Decade, this radical statement of libertarian principle was electrifying, and helped galvanize the group that eventually came to form around Leonard Read and his Foundation for Economic Education (FEE). William C. Mullendore, Orval Watts, James C. Ingrebretsen, and others involved in the publishing venture that put out *Give Me Liberty*, Pamphleteers, Inc., would go on to become the core group of FEE. Rose's fiery voice, raised in defense of liberty, provided much of the impetus for the embattled group of intellectuals who were in the vanguard of the anti–New Deal forces.

Give Me Liberty reflects many of the same themes expressed by Garet Garrett; his concept of the American character as almost intrinsically anti-statist rebounds through this essay, and there is every reason to believe this influence was direct. She knew Garrett well; they worked together on the *Saturday Evening Post*. In a letter to Jasper Crane, she wrote,

> The European peasants want, and get, "protection"—tariffs—but American farmers fought the "protective tariff" from 1800 to 1896; while the "infant industries" became the "soulless corporations" and the Trusts. Even as late as 1933, when Garet Garrett and I drove all over the Midwest, the farmers in general were not wanting AAA or any other Federal interference.[31]

She relates her Midwest experience in *Give Me Liberty*:

> In Kansas I met a rabble-rousing New Dealer from Washington who took me to a farmers' meeting where he spoke with real conviction and eloquence. The audience listened absolutely noncommittal, until he worked up to an incandescent peroration: "We went down there to Washington and got you all a Ford. Now we're going to get you a Cadillac!" The temperature suddenly fell below freezing; the silent antagonism was colder than zero. That ended the speech; the whole audience rose and went out. The orator later said to me, "Those damned numbskulls! The only thing to use on them is a club."

Lane's celebration of the American spirit, far from being the expression of some narrow form of nationalism, was framed by her concept of the coming World Revolution of liberty and capitalism, which she foresaw so clearly in the dark days of the New Deal. "Forty years ago," she wrote,

> America's parrot-intellectuals were ceaselessly repeating, "Germany is fifty years ahead of us in social legislation."

Blind to America and worshipping Europe, these reactionary pseudo-thinkers shifted American thought into reverse, in an effort to catch up with the Kaiser's Germany. They called it "liberal" to suppress liberty; "progressive" to stop the free initiative that is the source of all human progress; "economic freedom," to obstruct all freedom, and "economic equality" to make men slaves.

In our ignorance, we could not see that the Kaiser's Germany and the Communist International were merely two aspects of the Old World's reaction against the new, the American, principle of individual liberty and human rights. American leaders of thought, whom we respected, told us that the Communist reaction was the world revolution.

That was the lie that deceived us. Americans are world revolutionists. . . . Three generations of Americans have been creating a new world, the modern world. It is our tradition, our heritage, the unconscious impulse of our lives, to destroy the old, to create the new. Our ignorance betrayed us; we believed labels. We wanted the ancient thing that was marked "New."

The New Deal took root twenty-five years ago in American colleges and in the New York slums where, in danger of police violence, we listened to such ignorant idealists as Jack Reed. We dreamed we were world-revolutionists. We were reactionaries, undermining the real world revolution at its source, in our own country.[32]

Rose Wilder Lane was an optimist. With the New Deal triumphant all around her, with the militant statism of Germany and Russia on the march, she saw it all as a temporary reaction, equal and opposite to the two great victories over the aristocracy and the power of the Established Church. But the pendulum, she fervently believed, was bound to swing the other way. In a letter to Jasper Crane, she criticized Garet Garrett for what she saw as his pessimism:

Yes, I read Garet's last book. I like him very much and admired him; he wrote marvelously, even with flashes of genius. We never agreed in principle. He said that I am a mystic ruined by materialism, and that he was a materialist ruined by mysticism. (I don't agree with that, either.) He spoiled everything he wrote, for me, by always putting into it some contradictory flaw that threw away his basic position. I mean that he tried to fight for individualism on an always semi-collectivist basis. And above all, he was profoundly a pessimist. . . . Garet's *The Revolution Was*, for example, is a great bit of reporting, a piece of remarkable insight, and a great, most lamentable, detriment to the real existing Revolution. Its effect is to discourage any impulse to act for the human rights that, Garet says, are already lost, hopelessly lost. . . . There's nothing to do now, but sit and keen, wail with Garet for the happy past that is no more and can never be again. That attitude irritates me to near the point of frenzy. Not only that it's false but that it's so damned absurd. And Garet's presentation of it is so cleverly effective.[33]

Rose Lane was a fighter, and she didn't have much patience with the tragic sense-of-life. She fought the New Deal and the war drive to the bitter end, defiant and utterly unreconciled to the notion that "the Revolution was." In *her* mind, it was a *counter*revolution, and only an episodic one. At the end of *Give Me Liberty*, she declares: "A half-century of backsliding makes our country less than it might have been. But a world revolution cannot be won without encountering a reaction against it. This last decade of reactionary national socialism hampers all Americans." Yet "individual Americans," she believed, "are ending the reactionary period here."[34]

Because she opposed communism more consistently than any ordinary conservative, Lane saw that it was essentially a rear-guard action, a futile attempt to turn back the clock and use the state to obstruct the material and spiritual progress of the human race. This long-range optimism stayed with her all her long life. Nearly twenty years after the publication of *Give Me Liberty*, in a 1953 letter to Jasper Crane, this farsighted woman predicted the demise of communism and the end of the Cold War.

If our perspective were long enough, perhaps we might see that the present confrontation of the USSR and the USA was made inevitable in 1776. Every action produces an equal and opposite reaction. The world Revolution was, is, intrinsically an attack on the whole Old World; on its basis, its philosophy, its concept of man and the universe. Of course there was a reaction, and—given communication between this country and Europe—this reaction produced effects here.

The real conflict *is* between Revolution and Reaction, centered now in this country and in Russia. And actually the Nazis could not—did not win, or hope to win, a war without Russian support. The latest fighting in Europe and in Asia was instigated in Russia. And it seems to me to be what the Communists say it is—essentially a *defensive* action. Not defensive in a military, but in a political sense. The men in the Kremlin do not *dare* let Americans come any nearer; they are afraid of Paine's "army of principles." They are terrified of the effects of American success upon their subjects, if their subjects even suspect or guess what living in this country is like. *They have made a trap and are caught in it.*[35] I do not believe that they dare to risk a military decision. . . . and I believe they do not dare risk anything like peace. The latest fighting showed them that in war their armies will desert; in peace, their subjects will starve, or (if the Iron Curtain is removed) be "Americanized." I see the Communist International as finally defeated now. Defeated, I mean, in the sense that France was ruined in the early 1800s; or that springtime begins in December. It is a curious fact in history that effects continue in Time after their cause no longer exists; I suppose because people's concepts of things are changed so slowly. Everyone goes on acting *as if* a Great Power that once existed, still exists, when it doesn't.[36]

The Korean War had broken out. The confrontation between the U.S. and the Communist bloc was looming large on the world stage, threatening to immolate the world on the altar of the Cold War—and Rose Wilder Lane was predicting the removal of the Iron Curtain and confidently anticipating the time when "[d]eprived of faith in the Comintern, intellectuals really have nowhere to go but to individualism;

and when that is fashionable among the Little Groups of Serious Think-ers, there'll be a great day coming."

Liberty Under Siege: The War Years

In the meantime, however, the going was rough. World War II, during which the Old Right was forced by wartime censorship and controls to go underground, put her optimism to the ultimate test.

In 1938, she bought a farm in Danbury, Connecticut, where she lived for the next quarter century. With the death of Albert Jay Nock, Lane took his place as the editor and chief writer for the National Economic council's *Review of Books*, which provided her with just enough to eke out a living. As a protest against the confiscatory rate of taxation and an act of resistance to the New Deal, she gave up writing fiction and reduced her income to the absolute minimum.

She opposed rationing and refused to get a ration card. If we were going to adopt national socialism in an effort to defeat it, she, for one, would have no part of it. Determined to make herself totally self-sufficient, she made good use of the skills acquired when she was a young girl in the Ozarks. To defy Roosevelt and the New Order in America, she would churn her own butter and cheese, bake her own bread, keep a cow, tend a small flock of chickens, raise a pig or two, can vegetables and jams and jellies, and store them in her cellar for the long, dark winter ahead. Anything but cooperate with, and thus sanc-tion, the tyranny of wartime controls. "I have no ration card and shan't have one," she wrote in a letter to Mary Paxton Keeley.

> Every time the radio says, "You must get your ration card," I turn purple with rage and snap it off; no radio lives to say must to me. I do not believe in rationing, in principle; I am certain it causes more shortages than it relieves.[37]

Since there was little occasion for her to express her opposition in public, she sought to register her protest in her own private way. But if she thought this would spare her the scrutiny of the authorities, she miscalculated. In the spring of 1943, she was listening to a radio program by the commentator Samuel Grafton, who solicited the opinion of his audience on the question of whether to extend the social security system. Always ready to speak up on behalf of the cause, she sent off a postcard bearing the following polemic:

> If school teachers say . . . "We believe in Social Security," the children will ask, "Then why did you fight Germany?" All these "Social Security" laws are German, instituted by Bismarck and expanded by Hitler. Americans believe in freedom, [not in] being taxed for their own good and bossed by bureaucrats.[38]

The postcard, deemed "subversive" by an inquisitive local postmaster, was copied and sent to the Federal Bureau of Investigation. In a typical example of bureaucratic bungling, her name was miscopied, and so the authorities were searching for a "C. G. Lang." Since no one by that name was listed as being at her address, the state police were called in to do the footwork. The rest of the story is told by a newspaper account of the incident, which dramatizes the oppressive authoritarianism of the war years—and what strength of character was required to defy it:

> Two weeks later she was digging dandelions from her lawn, when a State Police car stopped at her gate. A State Trooper, uniformed and armed, walked up to her. He said that he was investigating subversive activities for the FBI, and asked her whether anyone in her house had sent a postcard to Samuel Grafton.
>
> She said that she had sent one. The State trooper leafed through a sheaf of papers clipped to a board, found a typed copy of the words she had written, held this before her eyes and asked sternly if she had written those words.
>
> She said, "Yes, I wrote that. What have the State Police to do with any opinion that an American citizen wants to express?"
>
> The trooper said, more sternly, "I do not like your attitude."
>
> A furious American rose to her full height. "You do not like my attitude! I am an American citizen. I hire you, I pay you, and you have the insolence to question my attitude? The point is that I don't like your attitude. What is this—the Gestapo?"

The young State Trooper said hastily, "Oh no, nothing like that. I was not trying to frighten you."

"You know perfectly well that your uniform and your tone would frighten a great many Americans in this neighborhood who remember the police methods in Europe. You know, or you should know, that any investigation of opinions by the American police is outrageous!"

"Oh, come now," the trooper protested, "At least give me credit for coming to you, instead of going around among your neighbors and gathering gossip about you. I only want to know whether you wrote that postcard."

"Is that a subversive activity?" she demanded.

Somewhat confused, the trooper answered, "Yes."

"Then I'm subversive as all hell!" she told him. "I'm against all this so-called Social Security, and I'll tell you why." And for five minutes she told him why. "I say this, and I write this, and I broadcast it on the radio, and I'm going to keep right on doing it till you put me in jail. Write that down and report it to your superiors."[39]

The National Economic Council, an Old Right group based in New York, printed up an account of the incident, and *What Is This, the Gestapo?* was circulated throughout the country. Local newspapers picked up the story, and Rose was suddenly a celebrity. She used the occasion to make the same point emphasized by John T. Flynn and others: that the war was being won on the battlefield and lost at home; that Americans were defeating national socialism in the trenches and succumbing to it in their own country. This was the message she delivered to the Danbury Lions Club, when her newfound celebrity gave her the opportunity to speak her mind. It was the message she sent in a letter to none other than J. Edgar Hoover himself, in which she conceded it was necessary, in wartime, to take certain measures—but was adamant on the necessity of keeping them strictly within the limits of "American principles."

> To this end, whenever a policeman or an investigator puts so much as a toe of his boot across the line protecting any American citizen's

> right to free thought and free speech, I regard it as that citizen's duty
> to refuse to permit this, and to raise a loud yell.[40]

The FBI, never all that punctilious about sticking to American principles, was not impressed. Its file on her was enormous, eventually growing to be over one hundred pages.[41]

An American Manifesto: The Discovery of Freedom

Rose's defiance began rather than ended with acts of personal resistance. Aside from writing voluminous letters to a circle of friends and fellow libertarians, during this time she was also writing *The Discovery of Freedom*, which took the themes of *Give Me Liberty* and expanded them into a systematic view of the history of the human race.[42] The theme was expressed in the subtitle of the book: *Man's Struggle Against Authority*. Her central idea was that the whole of human history was the story of human energy pulling at its restraints. American history, she wrote, is "an unprecedented fury of human energy, attacking the non-human world, and making this earth more habitable for human beings."

But why was this attack so successful here, in America? It was not a matter of wealth or natural resources; other places were richer, with more bounty to be had in the forests and under the ground. The answer, Lane thought, must be in the people themselves. Some quality of character, some intangible but fierce energy that drove them to achieve a standard of living, a height of civilization, without precedent in the history of the world. She believed this unique quality was generated because Americans had rejected the Old World way of looking at things as static, limited, unknowable. Only twice before had the "pagan" concept of man, as a plaything controlled by forces outside his control, been challenged. Christians had made the first attempt; Jesus had taught the value of the individual soul and the notion of self-responsibility against the "pagan" notion of mortals manipulated by fickle and childish gods. The Saracens had rediscovered the same principle and established a sophisticated and technically developed civilization, which was not surpassed until the beginning of the industrial revolution. However, both efforts suffered form distortions and internal contradictions, and so did not last. Europe passed into the long, dark night of feudalism, from which the only escape was by sea, westward, to the New World.

It was on this virgin soil that the third attempt was made, and we are living it. The bounty of a continent, released by the untrammeled energy of a free people, created a World Revolution which, Lane predicted, would sweep the earth. "World Revolution is a revolutionary change in men's minds, in their view of the nature of this universe and the nature of man. The Revolution is a struggle of knowledge against blind superstition; it is the American revolutionary recognition of the fact that individuals are free, pitted against the ancient pagan superstition that Authority controls individuals."[43]

The Discovery of Freedom has had much more influence than indicated in its small sales at the time of publication. Down through the years, it has been reprinted again and again, to enlighten yet another generation of fighters and delight them with its vivid style and insight into the nature of man and the mythology of power. While in 1943 the book was not a financial success, it was and is an intellectual tour de force, the power of which is not diminished by the years.

Deprived of a national audience, Lane poured her energy into her correspondence with a growing circle of like-minded people all across the nation; her complete letters would doubtless fill half a dozen fat volumes. Of the small portion that has, so far, been published, what we can glean is that she was a *movement* type; that is, she in no way saw herself as a lone voice crying in the wilderness, but as a frontline fighter in a larger movement. She closely followed current events and was actively involved in what remained of the Old Right during the fifties. Writing to Jasper Crane about the upcoming presidential election, she declared her support for the third-party effort of T. Coleman Andrews, who ran on the Constitution ticket in 1956:

> Dear Mr. Crane, it's fantastic how well we agree in fundamentals and how frequently we diverge on surface matters. Now I am serious about the Coleman Andrews Party, and I shall change my plans

in order to be here to vote for the splinter Republican candidate, Vivian Kellems, in Connecticut.[44] I agree with you, of course, that these movements "won't get very far," (at least, not soon) and I also agree completely with the statement of the Andrews Party's Vice Presidential candidate on Fulton Lewis's broadcast last Friday: Americans have had no vote since 1932, the choice has been between Tweedledum and Tweedledee, "and I'm against both of them," he said; and this new ticket on the ballot in twenty-eight states is, (1) an opportunity for Americans to register a choice, and (2) an experiment to find out what actual support there is in these States for American Constitutional Government.

That is the opportunity that I have been longing for, all these years; and I welcome with the greatest joy this offer of a way to *register* my own political philosophy—to "stand up and be counted," as one who believes what I believe.[45]

In 1951, Lane became eligible for social security. She refused to cooperate even to the extent of getting a social security number. At this time, the National Economic Council, which had been her mainstay, decided to deduct social security payments from her salary—this in spite of the fact that, as a nonprofit educational organization, it could have chosen to opt out. Rose ceased work on the *Review of Books*. But her letter-writing did not cease. In 1963, she wrote a series on needlework which appeared in *Woman's Day* and was collected into a book, *The Woman's Day Book of American Needlework*. In 1965, when she was 75, the magazine sent her to Vietnam as a war correspondent. She bought a home in Harlingen, Texas, where she spent her winters. Finally retired at the age of 82, she was still restless, still looking for new horizons to explore, and eagerly looked forward to a planned trip around the world. Not long before the ship was set to sail from New York, Rose Wilder Lane died in her sleep.

Her indomitable spirit lived on in the movement she helped to keep alive through the nadir of the forties, through the lean years of the Cold War, and the degeneration of the conservative movement. She kept the torch of freedom aloft, made sure that it did not sputter out—and dreamed of a day when it would flare into a brightness that would light up the world.

Rose Lane's importance as a central figure in the Old Right and the early libertarian movement lies in her revolutionary optimism and her fighting spirit, which inspired her fellow Old Rightists at a time when it seemed all was lost. She redefined the Nockian–Chodorovian "Remnant"—from a lonely band of idealists who did not dare hope to effectively oppose the tide of collectivism, to the combative and growing "Hard Right" which took root in the fifties. When Rose Lane died, it was no longer a Remnant, but a full-fledged *movement* slowly but steadily gathering its strength for the great burst of exponential growth that was to usher in the decade of the sixties. The seeds planted by Lane and her fellow Old Rightists in the previous decades had taken root and were about to blossom forth. Soon those who followed would harvest the crop—a bounty brought forth in good measure through the labors of a wise and patient gardener such Rose Wilder Lane.

Isabel Paterson *and* The God of the Machine

That Lane was not a lone figure, a voice crying in the wilderness, was illustrated by the publication, in 1943, of another book preaching the virtues of individualism and capitalism: *The God of the Machine*, by Isabel Paterson. Paterson was a columnist for the *New York Herald Tribune*, the author of many novels, well-known in Old Right circles, and as brilliant as she was abrasive. The theme of her book is strikingly similar to that of *The Discovery of Freedom*: the U.S. is the product of a free, uninhibited, but wonderfully self-disciplined *energy*. This energy is controlled by individual human beings. Authority, as embodied in the state, is an illusion: it can only impede the energy flow, delay and retard the human attack on the physical world that makes civilization possible. In explaining the rise of England and her colonies to world prominence, Paterson put it in the context of her central thesis:

> The balance of power fell to England because England allowed the
> energy to flow most freely, which is to say that England conceded
> the most liberty to the individual by respecting private property and
> abandoning by degrees the practice of political trade monopolies.
> Of course England did not desist from the granting of monopolies
> all at once, and it was the remains of monopoly which precipitated
> the American Revolution; but free enterprise had enough leeway
> to beat Spain and France hands down.[46]

Although Paterson's engineering metaphor—in which she makes
the analogy between the proper functioning of society and the smooth
operation of a machine—is, at times, intrusive and confusing, as often
as not it is brilliantly illuminating.

Paterson's fierce individualism was a central theme of the book.
"There is no collective good," she wrote. "Strictly speaking, there is not
even any common good. There are in the natural order conditions and
materials through which the individual . . . is capable of experiencing
good. Let it be asked, is not sunlight a common good? No; persons do
not enjoy the benefit by community, but singly. A blind man cannot
see by community."[47]

Paterson's analysis of the co-dependent rise of big business and big
government is particularly cogent. The Civil War, she wrote, "prompted
the Federal Government to finance railroads, by land grants and cash
subsidies. With this the era in which business was charged with corrupting politics was well under way."[48] But in fact it was politics that
had corrupted business, such as Standard Oil, which employed the
political means in pursuit of profits. The response of the "reformers"
was to assail the profit motive and enlarge the political power, when the
only sensible course was to strictly *limit* the power of government—by
abolishing its power to grant monopoly.

The excellent chapter, "The Fatal Amendments," which describes
the process by which the gains of the American Revolution were rolled
back, is Paterson at her best. Here she attacks the repressive wartime
atmosphere by pointing to "extensions of the political power by simple
usurpation."

A sedition trial is such usurpation; there is no authority for it in the Constitution, and there was wrathful protest on the first occasion; now it is accepted casually, with little comment except suggestions to enlarge it, frequently at the behest of alleged "liberals."[49]

The militarization of society, conscription, sedition trials—these are the inevitable consequences of state intervention in the economy.

The military state is the final form to which every planned economy tends rapidly. But military force consists of energy drawn from production, and yielding no return. . . .Energy flowing through the channels of private civilian life is self-sustaining, self-augmenting and self-renewing. Energy flowing into the military channel is used up, it produces nothing, not even maintenance of its own transmission line. An army may occasionally seize supplies from the enemy, but these are quickly consumed.[50]

The most potent chapter in what is really a collection of essays is "The Humanitarian with a Guillotine," a frontal assault on the do-gooder morality of collectivism. At a time when Stalinism was a respectable political persuasion, like being a Democrat or a Republican—when, indeed, apologias for torture, mass murder, and dictatorship were common in certain influential circles—Paterson sought some plausible explanation for the phenomenon. Averring that "[m]ost of the harm in the world is done by good people, and not by accident, lapse, or omission," how, she asked, could the alleged ends of the humanitarians contrast so sharply with their means?

If the primary objective of the philanthropist, his justification for living, is to help others, his ultimate good *requires that others be in want*. His happiness is the obverse of their misery. If he wishes to help "humanity," the whole of humanity must be in need. The humanitarian wishes to be a prime mover in the lives of others. He cannot admit either the divine or the natural order, by which men have the power to help themselves. The humanitarian puts himself in the place of God.[51]

But this presents certain problems. To begin with, not everyone *wants* to become an object of charity. Secondly, how is one to judge conflicting claims? The humanitarian ethic demands that one do "good" for others. The question, then, arises, Who or what determines the nature of the "good"? "Of course," says Paterson, "what the humanitarian actually proposes is that *he* shall do what he thinks is good for everybody. It is at this point that the humanitarian sets up the guillotine."

If this denunciation of altruism brings to mind the egoism of Ayn Rand, then the reason is that the two were friends. Rand wrote the third libertarian book of 1943, *The Fountainhead*, a best-selling novel about the struggle of an idealistic young architect to preserve his integrity in a profession rife with parasites, social climbers, schemers, and other second-handers. Although it was published in May of 1943, a discussion of the enormous impact of this book and its author does not really belong in an account of this period. Rand's influence did not really peak until much later, with the publication of *Atlas Shrugged* and the founding of an organized movement dedicated to propagating her ideas.[52] A discussion of Rand and her philosophy of "Objectivism" therefore properly belongs in our survey of the sixties.

Louis Bromfield: Old Right Jeffersonian

In spite of the bland uniformity of the American Right enforced by the Cold War, the America First–libertarian current continued to register its colorful dissent. A good example is the novelist and screenwriter Louis Bromfield, whose 1954 book, *A New Pattern for a Tired World*, is the passionate protest of an unreconstructed Old Rightist.[53]

Bromfield was a bestselling author of the twenties and thirties, who won a Pulitzer in 1926 and lived abroad in France and India. In 1938, he returned to the United States to live in the rural area of Richland County, Ohio, where he was brought up. There he purchased Malabar Farm and started a new phase in what had been a varied and colorful career: that of the independent small farmer and political polemicist. Although Bromfield continued to write fiction, clearly his nonfiction

of later years—the books on agricultural technique as well as the quasi-
novel *The Farm*—meant more to him.[54] There are premonitions of his
ideological stance in some of his fiction, as well as in earlier nonfiction
books such as *Brass Tacks*[55] and especially *Pleasant Valley*,[56] but his
views did not fully crystallize in print until he wrote *A New Pattern for
a Tired World*.[57] Here he makes the case for free trade, free markets, and
a noninterventionist foreign policy based on economic cooperation. As
an example of the libertarian tendency in the Old Right, Bromfield is
unique. In him the twin tendencies of nationalism and libertarianism,
which sometimes conflicted on the Right, were in perfect harmony.

As the Cold War cast its paralyzing influence over the national
consciousness, Bromfield attacked the emerging national security state
as "government by propaganda and pressure." He was appalled by the rise
of a militarist bureaucracy and declared that "the armed forces represent
our greatest bureaucracy and our most powerful all-pervading lobby."
As in the totalitarian states of Nazi Germany, Fascist Italy, and Soviet
Russia, this bureaucracy unleashed a constant barrage of propaganda.
It was a propaganda of fear, "a propaganda against peace and for more
and more forced military service and arms appropriations." Aside from
"politicians, generals, and captive journalists," the real motive power
behind the war scare was a group of

> Americans suffering from what might best be described as "a
> Messiah complex," who feel a compulsion to save the world and
> constantly to meddle in the affairs of other peoples and nations,
> regardless of whether, as is more and more the case, this interfer-
> ence is actually resented.
>
> The Messiah complex is peculiarly an Anglo-Saxon disease
> which at times can border upon the ecstatic and the psychopathic.
> It existed strongly among the English people who sent missionar-
> ies everywhere in the world although they took care to have them
> accompanied by traders. In the United States we are inclined to
> send the missionaries, unaccompanied however by traders, and
> to spread money and welfare broadcast in return for no material
> rewards whatever and frequently with small benefits or none at all

to the *great masses* of the people in the nations we are supposed to be aiding.[58]

Bromfield remarks that more than one foreigner has said that "we are the only nation in the world that exhibits all the annoying traits and practices of imperialism without asking for any of the rewards of imperialism." As Garet Garrett put it in *Rise of Empire*, published a few years previously, America rules "the Empire of the Bottomless Purse," in which "everything goes out and nothing comes in."

Bromfield excoriated the architects of "containment" who pushed the United Nations on a war-weary world and brought us the Korean War. "Today," said Bromfield, "our policies and actions are determined by a strange mixture of hazy impractical idealism and of militarism promoted by a campaign of calculated fear." The globalist pipe dreams of utopian do-gooders ignored the real problems confronting us, which were no longer military or political but economic. The answer was not in the United Nations, or in any political scheme of alliances and aid to foreign governments.

> These problems cannot be solved by the wholesale bestowal and distribution of American wealth, in the old-fashioned concept of Lady Bountiful passing from cottage to cottage with her basket well laden with the luxuries of the Castle. They cannot be solved by the arbitrary bestowal or imposition of political "democracy" with the touch of a fairy wand, or by brutal assault of tanks and guns upon peoples who have little conception or understanding of or even words in their languages for democracy, freedom, liberty and human dignity.[59]

Bromfield warned against the influence of those who owed their allegiance overseas, either to Moscow or London. The problem with U.S. foreign policy, he said, is that it is designed to serve the decadent colonial powers of Europe, especially Great Britain. In the midwestern tradition of Colonel McCormick and the *Chicago Tribune*, Bromfield saw an Anglophilic eastern elite as the main source of our problems, starting with "Franklin D. Roosevelt, whose sympathies and traditional background were European, and in particular, British." This England First policy was continued under Truman and Eisenhower and accentuated by Dean Acheson, the American secretary of state cited by Bromfield as "the best Foreign Minister Great Britain has had in the last generation." The policy of the Anglophiles had been to "build up European industry, restore the old colonial empires which cannot be restored, and build European defenses against the ramshackle Soviet Empire." Beyond this influence, extending back to the New Deal days, was that of the Communist fellow travelers, who were "everywhere in government, boring, operating, influencing, moulding policies," and creating a general confusion which served Soviet rather than American interests. The effect of these influences, said Bromfield, "like that of much of the military propaganda coming from the Pentagon and the Truman chiefs of staff, was to stress the immense power and threat of Russia (a strongly debatable attitude) while at the same time operating paradoxically so that this same Russian power would benefit."[60]

Bromfield's view of the Soviets as atavistic throwbacks to a neo-medieval condition is underscored by the fact that he invariably referred to the Soviet Union as "ramshackle." Like Rose Wilder Lane, Bromfield believed that dynamic American capitalism was the vanguard of a world revolution, of economic and technological changes that meant the inevitable end of the old national patterns of statism and imperialism. Soviet Russia, he said, "appears superficially to be a modern state," but in reality is an economic cripple. Aside from the inherent inability of socialism to produce material abundance, "the Soviet Sparta" was diverting its resources into the dead end of military expenditures. Such a policy could lead only to economic disaster.

Bromfield believed that we were in the midst of a World Revolution, although he, unlike Lane, resisted the impulse to capitalize. "The world revolution now in progress," he wrote, "is not only the struggle for freedom and independence of formerly exploited nations. It is a spontaneous and inevitable regrouping, geographically, politically and economically, upon a new and basic economic pattern, of the nations and peoples of the world."

The key to this regroupment, he believed, would be the land masses where population was low or reasonable, and where natural resources existed in quantities sufficient to maintain "the interior markets of a prosperous, self-contained and dynamic economy." At bottom, Bromfield's opposition to the Eurocentric foreign policy of the Anglophiles in the State Department was rooted in his view of American interests as *hemispheric*. Bromfield looked to South and Central America, especially Brazil, as well as Canada, as the nucleus of a hemispheric free trade zone. He believed "that our own future lies in this immensely rich Western Hemisphere rather than in a divided Europe hampered economically in countless ways or in a chaotic Asia." The dynamo driving the economic motor of the New World is a capitalism that is competitive, vital, and capable of generating a large middle class. This he contrasted with the mercantilist, cartelized state capitalism of decadent Europe, in which economic privileges and state-granted franchises were kept within a very small closed circle.

As nationalist revolutions rocked the Third World, Bromfield counseled a policy of strict nonintervention; it was not our duty to bail out the dying colonial empires. In terms reminiscent of John T. Flynn, he also warned against growing U.S. involvement in Vietnam:

> The battle in Indo-china is not altogether a battle against Communists and Red China. In it are engaged countless Indo-Chinese, of all the small individual nationalities represented in the Indo-Chinese area, who hate French domination more than Chinese domination and many who are fighting not *for* the Red Chinese but *against* domination and exploitation by the French. Yet there are even those, principally in the armed forces of the U.S., who would, if they dared, advocate drafting American boys from Ohio, Iowa, Kansas and elsewhere and sending them into this struggle where they or the nation itself have no proper place and where our intervention can only serve to do us tragic harm in the long run.[61]

While the nascent New Right was fulminating against the Communist menace and demanding the mobilization of all our resources in a relentless crusade to stamp it out, Bromfield was proclaiming the death of communism:

Indeed the very simplicity and crudity of the Communist appeal is working toward the defeat of Communism throughout the world and tending more and more to reduce the leadership of Marxian Communism to the proportions of a world-wide psychopathic cult.[62]

To ally with the dead empires of Europe could only help the cause of the Soviet imperium, which was itself as outmoded and doomed as the French, the British, the Dutch, and the Portuguese colonial systems:

Imperialism, colonialism and all forms of overseas or foreign exploitation, including especially the half-feudal system of conquest, hostages, purges and economic rape set up by Russia and her satellites, belong to the barbaric past, regardless of the fact that they still exist in more or less vestigial form in the twentieth century. They are dead, slain by the declining economic and military status and generally increasing impotence of the key European colonial nations . . . and by the rising nationalism of peoples everywhere. The antiquated Russian pattern of conquest contains within itself the seeds of its own destruction, and the more the pattern expands the more this will be true.[63]

The Old Right in the Fifties

Bromfield's book made virtually no impression on conservatives when it came out. A number of independent individuals and groups shared his values, however, and held up the banner of the Old Right during that quiescent decade, an era of seeming decline. The Taft wing of the GOP lost out and crashed on the rocks of the Cold War; the liberal "consensus" dominated the political and intellectual life of the nation. But amid the ruins of what had once been a mass movement, things were stirring. Aside from the voices of seemingly isolated figures such as Rose Wilder Lane, Isabel Paterson, Chodorov, Flynn, and Garrett, a renewed movement was silently coalescing without fanfare or much of a national presence.

In her volume of letters to Jasper Crane, Rose Wilder Lane gives a delightful account of a local Old Right group's run-in with the school board of Danbury, Connecticut, and her own efforts to take on resident special interests and their political lackeys, and then she gives us an overview of the state of the Old Right in the fifties:

> I think the time has come for local *work*, local *action* of this kind. The mill-run of Americans is individualist, decent, moral, honest. And not as innocently trustful of Government, and therefore as inattentive to it, as Americans have been for two or three generations. A right action in opposition to the gangster politicians gets active support now. And I think these amorphous local groups will be desperately needed, before this inflation is over.

Yet she tempered her inherent optimism with a note of caution and a sense of the movement's limitations:

> The difficulty is communication. That can't be overcome on a national, or even probably a State, scale without organization and money, but it can be overcome locally, without them. . . . the necessity is to reach "the masses," to break through the resistance of the VIPs. And State and National organization depends on the VIPs, has to be financed (and therefore controlled) by them. There aren't enough non-socialist VIPs anywhere to support an organization.[64]

Not enough to support an organization of political activists, but there *was* in existence one major institution for the preservation, propagation, and development of Old Right–libertarian ideas and scholarship, and that was the Foundation for Economic Education, based in Irvington-on-Hudson, in New York. Founded in 1946 by Leonard E. Read, FEE was meant to be a center for the advanced study of libertarian thought. Read had been head of the Los Angeles Chamber of Commerce, and he gathered around him Dr. Orval Watts, who had been the chamber's chief economist; F. A. Harper of Cornell University; Dr. Paul Poirot; and a group of free-market economists.[65]

FEE published books and pamphlets, and financed scholarly research, in addition to putting out the *Freeman*, a magazine, and periodic anthologies titled *Ideas on Liberty*. For a while, it seemed to fulfill its early promise as a center of uncompromising Old Rightism shot through with a decidedly radical libertarianism. Indeed, one of the early controversies on the staff was between those who wanted to severely limit government and those who would not be averse to doing away with it altogether. FEE was also staunchly anti-interventionist, hostile to militarism, and vocal in its opposition to the Korean War. In his pamphlet *Conscience on the Battlefield*, Read put himself in the role of an American soldier dying on the Korean battlefield, and imagined an inner monologue taking place inside the mind of this young casualty. When the soldier's conscience indicts him for being "responsible for the death of many women and children during this military campaign," the soldier answers that "we had to stop Communist aggression and the enslavement of people by dictators." His conscience then asks, "Did you kill these people as an act of self-defense? Were they threatening your life or your family? Were they on your shores, about to enslave you?"[66]

In 1951, FEE published F. A. Harper's *In Search of Peace*, which faced the issue of the Cold War head on. We were embarked on a world crusade to minimize and even roll back Russian influence because of the Russians' Communist ideology, said Harper. "But if it is necessary for us to embrace all these socialist-communist measures in order to fight a nation that has adopted them—because *they* have adopted them—then why fight them? Why not just join them in the first place and save all the bloodshed?"[67]

Even blunter was Dean Russell, a member of the FEE staff, who declared,

> Those who advocate the "temporary loss" of our freedom in order to preserve it permanently are advocating only one thing: the abolition of liberty. In order to fight a form of slavery abroad, they advocate a form of bondage at home! However good their intentions may be, these people are enemies of your freedom and my freedom; and I fear them more than I fear any potential Russian threat to my liberty. These sincere but highly emotional patriots are clear and present threats to freedom; the Russians are still thousands of miles away.[68]

Russell wanted to pull "our troops and military commitments back into the Western Hemisphere and [keep] them there." By "turning ourselves into a permanent garrison state and stationing conscripts all over the world," he said, "we are rapidly becoming a caricature of the thing we profess to hate."

FEE's adherence to the Old Right principle of noninterventionism, which carried on the rich tradition of the America First Committee, did not, however, last through the decade. In November 1954, the Chodorov–Schlamm controversy hit the pages of the *Freeman*, after which the former was ousted from his post as editor. As Murray Rothbard puts it, Chodorov was

> a man of stubborn independence and integrity, [who] would not submit to any form of mental castration; with Chodorov gone, Leonard Read could return to his long-standing policy of never engaging in direct political or ideological controversy, and the *Freeman* proceeded to sink into the slough of innocuous desuetude in which it remains today.[69]

Aside from FEE, there were other organizations which kept the Old Right tradition alive. Clarence Manion, dean of the Notre Dame law school, headed up "For America," which advocated the abolition of the draft and called on the U.S. to "enter no foreign wars unless the safety of the United States is directly threatened." For a time, the right-wing Congress of Freedom was heavily influenced by Old Right libertarians. There was a small constellation of Old Right organizations such as the Committee for Constitutional Government—which had played a key role in fighting FDR's court-packing scheme—and the National Economic Council, as well as the various conservative third-party movements, which culminated in the presidential campaign of T. Coleman Andrews in 1956.

Characteristic of this period was Thomas H. Barber's book, *Where We Are At*, which simply and cogently made the case for economic freedom, individual rights, and a noninterventionist foreign policy.[70] Barber attacked the planned society and decried the collectivist scheme of "special privileges for everyone" to be enforced by all-powerful bureaucrats. Hard money, the necessity of laissez-faire, the need to undo the usurpations of administrative law and restore to Congress the power co-opted by the executive; these familiar themes run throughout his book. Written in a down-to-earth style, *Where We Are At* has a section titled "What Can We Do About It?" which captures the perspective of a grassroots activist:

> It does not matter much what the particular means is, that will fan to flame the deep love of liberty that glows in the heart of every true American. For though history shows that mankind seldom recognizes its own foolishness while indulging in it, it also shows that when things get so bad that man has to think deeply, he eventually straightens himself out. Today, anyone who talks to thoughtful people in any section of the country about our government, will realize from the indignation and bitterness expressed that we are just about at the turning point.
>
> We don't need any great national leader for this. What we need is to have groups of energetic citizens spring up in towns and villages all over the country and make an intensive drive to break down legal privilege and the excessive bureaucracy. The chances are they will find an Augean stable to clean up right at home. Soon they will get in touch with similar groups elsewhere; county groups will get busy, then state groups, eventually a national group.[71]

Silently bubbling just beneath the surface of the "Vital Center," the libertarian current of the Old Right gathered strength throughout the placid fifties. Groups of local activists carried on the good fight, in tandem with a small but growing number of intellectuals. So that, by the time the sixties dawned, these scattered small groups were starting to coalesce into something with the potential to become a national force.

The Smearmongers: Bell, Hofstadter, and Adorno

While the growth and initial development of this movement had little effect on the national political scene, it did not go unnoticed by the mandarins of the "Vital Center." For *any* challenge to the welfare-warfare state stood as a reproach to their analysis that we had reached "the end of ideology"—and that the history of ideas had culminated in the postwar smugness of certain New York–based social-democratic intellectuals.[72]

In an anthology of essays edited by Daniel Bell, *The New American Right*,[73] a panel of sociologists advanced the proposition that the so-called radical rightists were not merely wrong, but were also representative of a social pathology, profoundly disturbed and potentially dangerous. This was a continuation of the old Carlson-type smear job, updated and stamped with the imprimatur of sociological "science." In the liberal utopia of the postwar post–New Deal era, *all* dissent was deemed pathological.

These mandarins of the Sensible Center were, at least three of them, ex-radicals of one stripe of another. The book's editor, Daniel Bell, was a prominent socialist. In the early fifties, he testified before the House Committee on Un-American Activities on behalf of Shachtman's Independent Socialist League. Richard Hofstadter, another soldier-sociologist enlisted in the war against "extremism," had been a member of the Communist Party. Seymour Martin Lipset had once been a member of Shachtman's Workers Party. He later became a Shermanite and left the party with Selznick, Kristol, and the others.

According to these prototypical neocons, the end of ideology was upon us. As Daniel Bell, author of a book of that title, put it, this meant that polarity in American politics was a thing of the past. In the dawning era of the welfare-warfare state, he wrote, "There is no coherent conservative force . . . and the radical right is outside the political pale, insofar as it refuses to accept the American consensus." By the Great Consensus, of course, he meant the New Deal, the internationalization of the welfare state and the elevation of collective security above and beyond American sovereignty. All dissent from these three sacred principles was deemed by the contributors to Bell's volume to be evidence of "status resentment." This psychological phenomenon, it seems, is part of the very structure of capitalist society; or, as Bell puts it, it is the fate of rootless moderns "whose status aspirations have been whipped up to a high pitch by our democratic ethos and our rags-to-riches mythology."[74]

In the midst of postwar prosperity, when it appeared that the productive power of the American economy had solved the problem of material want, Hofstadter posited that political conflict had become primarily a fight for status, "an arena into which status aspirations and frustrations are, as the psychologists would say, projected. It is at this point that the issues of politics, or the pretended issues of politics, become interwoven with and dependent upon the personal problems of individuals."

Thus, all explanations of dissent from the postwar Grand Consensus were attributable to "the personal problems of individuals." What John T. Flynn had called the "Smear Bund" was operating at full capacity, this time speaking with the authority of the social "scientist."

Drawing from the methods and conclusions of Theodore Adorno and his disciples, who melded psychoanalysis with Reichian-Marxist jargon, the new smearmongers of the sociological school launched a vicious ad hominem attack. According to Richard Hofstadter, the "radical rightists" of the postwar period were not really conservative in any sense of the word: they were, instead, "pseudoconservatives" who "succeed in concealing from themselves impulsive tendencies that, if released in action, would be very far from conservative." What especially baffled Hofstadter and his fellow liberals was, "Why do the pseudo-conservatives express such a persistent fear and suspicion of *their own government?*"—a question which, today, seems more than a little naïve. Hofstadter's portrait of the pseudoconservative is of an obstreperous ingrate who, for some reason, is not teary-eyed with gratitude for the privilege of inhabiting Hofstadter's liberal utopia. Included among the disrupters of the peace are opponents of the income tax, supporters of the Bricker Amendment, and, of course, McCarthyites. The pseudocon's chief sin is that

> he believes himself to be living in a world in which he is spied upon,
> plotted against, betrayed, and very likely destined for total ruin.
> He feels that his liberties have been arbitrarily and outrageously

invaded. He is opposed to almost everything that has happened
in American politics for the past twenty years. He hates the very
thought of Franklin D. Roosevelt.[75]

Hofstadter is unwilling to entertain the notion that anyone could
seriously hate the very thought of FDR—although he is willing to concede
that it may have "important economic and political causes." Certainly,
he says, "wealthy reactionaries try to use pseudo-conservative organizers,
spokesmen and groups to propagate their notions of public policy." But
their motives are naturally mercenary, as are those of the organizers, who
"often find in this work a means of making a living." What motivates
the rank-and-file pseudocon to "expend so much emotional energy and
crusading idealism upon causes that plainly bring them no material
reward"? In the mechanical materialist world posited by Adorno and his
disciples, in which humankind is a soulless automaton animated by the
interplay of unconscious desires with early toilet training, such passion
can only be evidence that something is terribly wrong.

Billing his essay as a discussion "of the neglected socio-political
elements in pseudo-conservatism," Hofstadter rules out the possibility
that one could honestly oppose the liberal utopia. The best way for the
postwar liberals to dispose of the Old Right opposition was to deny that
any such opposing ideology existed. What existed, they asserted, was
not ideology but psychopathology. Opposition to the "reforms" of the
New Deal and any trace of a belief in the traditional American concept
of less government were evidence of mental illness.

The theoretical framework for this campaign of character assassination was Adorno's *The Authoritarian Personality*, cited by several
contributors to this anthology of smears, including Hofstadter.[76] However, there is no real discussion of Adorno, his methods, or his politics,
except in a few brief footnotes.

Adorno was a Marxist sociologist and theoretician who set out to
define the parameters of the fascist mentality, or the mentality that might
readily revive fascist ideology in the postwar world. He did not bother
to hide his political bias. In the prevailing intellectual atmosphere, it
was hardly necessary.

Here he describes his methodology: while "we do not pretend that psychology is the cause and ideology is the effect," says Adorno, "we try to interrelate both as intimately as possible, guided by the assumption that ideological irrationalities . . . are concomitant with unconscious psychological conflicts. We combed through the interview material with particular attention to such irrationalities."[77]

Adorno utilized questionnaires, psychological tests, and extensive interviews to ferret out incipient fascism in his subjects. A "high" score on the various scales—which purport to quantify everything from anti-Semitism to political conservatism—meant that the subject was a potential storm trooper.

Here is one telling example of an "ideological irrationality," Adorno-style: the case of "M105, a prelaw student high on all scales, who stresses his conservative background while admitting overt fascist leanings." Adorno then quotes M105's interview as proof of the subject's "overt" fascism:

> Naturally, I get my Republican sentiments from my parents. But recently I have read more for myself, and I agree with them. . . . We are a conservative family. We hate anything to do with socialism. My father regretted that he voted for FDR in 1932. Father wrote to Senator Reynolds of South Carolina [sic] about the Nationalist Party. It's not America First, it's not really isolationist, but we believe that our country is being sold down the river.

Adorno's profound analysis is that the subject evidences a "father fixation," this being the chief characteristic of all fascists everywhere. He further berates the subject for saying that "America is fighting the war but we will lose the peace if we win the war. I can't see what I can possibly get out of it." Here, Adorno drops the psychoanalytical window dressing and attacked poor M105 in explicitly political terms for using "a phrase familiar with fascists when they were faced with the defeat of Germany and the German system and yet somehow wished to cling to their negative Utopia."

Adorno's politics suffuse his "scientific" study. He makes no attempt to either hide or defend his stereotypically Marxist view of fascism as the doings of the "enraged petit-bourgeois"; it is simply assumed. As he puts it,

> The goal toward which the pseudoconservative mentality strives—diffusedly and semi-consciously—is to establish a dictatorship of the economically strongest group. This is to be achieved by means of a mass movement, one which promises security and privileges to the so-called "little man" (that is to say, worried members of the middle and lower middle class who still cling to their status and their supposed independence), if they join with the right people at the right time. . . . Roosevelt and the New Deal particularly are said to have usurped power and to have entrenched themselves dictatorially.[78]

Opposition to Roosevelt is evidence, according to Adorno, of a "usurpation complex" and is rooted in a deep subconscious fear that our parents are not our "real" family. This Freudian gobbledygook is mixed with a generous dose of outright political denunciation. In addition to being "rigid" and unfeeling, high-scorers

> want no pity for the poor, neither here nor abroad. This trait seems to be strictly confined to high scorers and to be one of the most differentiating features in political philosophy. . . . Abolition of the dole, rejection of state interference with the "natural" play of supply and demand on the labor market, the spirit of the adage "who does not work, shall not eat" belong to the traditional wisdom of economic individualism and are stressed by all those who regard the liberal system as being endangered by socialism. At the same time, the ideas involved have a tinge of punitiveness and authoritarian aggressiveness which makes them ideal receptacles of some typical psychological urges of the prejudiced character. . . . The mechanism of projectivity is also involved: the potentially fascist character blames the poor who need assistance for the very same passivity and greediness which he has learnt not to admit to in his own consciousness.[79]

Opposition to labor unions, according to Adorno, is derived from "the lack of an adequately internalized identification with paternal authority during the Oedipus situation." For literally hundreds of pages, Adorno and his co-workers continue this running commentary—and not even the "low scorers" are safe from their withering scorn. M711, described as an "easy-going low-scorer," is attacked by Adorno for saying that Roosevelt's program had the potential to evolve into fascism. Asked if he approved of FDR's program of wide-ranging state interference in the private sector, M711 said no: "I don't. There, again, that could be a road to a fascist state eventually." The poor man, intones Adorno, is "apparently unaware of the progressive function this interference had under Roosevelt. . . . In spite of his leftist ideology, this man shows symptoms of a confusion which may make him the prey of pseudo-progressive slogans of fascist propaganda."

The most telling example of Adorno's rabid leftism is in his treatment of the issue of taxation. This is an area, we are told, "of the utmost importance for the formative processes of fascism." In a statement which surely sums up the writer's ultra-left brand of psycho-sociological "science," he declares that "[t]he man who bangs his fist on the table and complains about heavy taxation is a 'natural candidate' for totalitarian movements." Such antisocial sentiments are proof of Nazi sympathies, because "[t]he Nazis knew very well how to exploit the complex of the 'taxpayer's money.'"

Even more ludicrous is the method by which the various "scales" were arrived at. The participants were asked to complete a series of questionnaires, the results of which were used to quantify and correlate such things as conservatism, "ethnocentrism," and anti-Semitism. Subjects were asked to indicate their level of agreement with the following statements:

> He is indeed contemptible who does not feel an undying love, gratitude, and respect for his parents.
>
> Every person should have a deep faith in some supernatural force higher than himself to which he gives total allegiance and whose decisions he does not question.
>
> What this country needs is fewer laws and agencies, and more courageous, tireless, devoted leaders whom the people can put their faith in.

No sane, decent person could ever think of hurting a close friend
or relative.[80]

To agree with any or all of these statements, says Adorno, is to exhibit not "merely a realistic, balanced respect for valid authority but an
exaggerated, all-out, emotional need to submit." Love of family, religious
devotion, a desire for less government and more leadership—Adorno
says that all these core American values are evidence, not of the virtu-
ous society but of "authoritarian submission." Why are these admirable
sentiments proof of a willing "subservience of the individual to the
state"—and even a reflection of "important aspects of the Nazi creed"?
Because, says Adorno, these are middle-class values.

> It is a well-known hypothesis that susceptibility to fascism is most
> characteristically a middle-class phenomenon, that it is "in the cul-
> ture" and, hence, that those who conform the most to this culture
> will be the most prejudiced.[81]

This disdain and fear of the middle class, particularly the lower
middle class, is shared by Hofstadter, who sneers that, although pseudo-
conservatism is to be found in all classes, "its power probably rests largely
upon its appeal to the less educated members of the middle classes."[82]

In "The Dispossessed," Daniel Bell views the rise of the Radical
Right through the prism of an ideology that is by now familiar to the
reader. Citing "[t]he new nature of decision-making," whereby all decisions will be made by government in consultation with a growing army
of scientific and technical experts, he writes,

> The spread of education, of research, of administration, and of gov-
> ernment creates a new constituency, the technical and professional
> intelligentsia, and while these are not bound by some common
> ethos to constitute a new class, or even a cohesive social group, they
> are the products of a new system of recruitment for power (just as
> property and inheritance represented the old system), and those who
> are the products of the old system understandably feel a vague and
> apprehensive disquiet—the disquiet of the dispossessed.[83]

Although stylistically this analysis owes much to Burnham's *The Managerial Revolution*, it would be more accurate to say that this was a page from Max Shachtman's book, even down to the question of whether the rising managerial elite constitutes a class. For Bell, the socialist, and his Shachtmanite confreres, the battle against the Radical Right was a class struggle. Just as in the days of their radical youth, the enemy was still the middle class—business in general, especially small business—but, instead of championing the cause of the slumbering proletariat, they did battle on behalf of a new managerial aristocracy of technicians, administrators, scientists, and bureaucrats. In short, they aligned themselves with *power*.

This anti-populist theme—of a wise and benevolent elite versus the ignorant and potentially dangerous masses—permeates the book. The contribution of David Riesman and Nathan Glazer, "The Intellectuals and the Discontented Classes," is typical in its approach. The right-wing eruption, a bump on the road to the liberal utopia, is due to the fact that "many who were once among the inarticulate masses are no longer silent: an unacknowledged social revolution has transformed their situation. Rejecting the liberal intellectuals as guides, they have echoed and reinforced the stridency of right-wing demi-intellectuals— themselves often arising from those we shall, until we find a less clumsy name, call the ex-masses."[84]

Peter Viereck's contempt for "the lower classes" who have dared to rise above their station renders his contribution to the Bell anthology nearly incoherent. Viereck claimed to be a "New Conservative"— "meaning non-Republican, non-commercialist, non-conformist"—but in fact his cranky and somewhat idiosyncratic brand of "conservatism" amounted to abject conformism to the liberal orthodoxy of the day. The son of the pro-German George Sylvester Viereck—who was a propagandist for the Kaiser during World War I, and jailed for his activities on behalf of Hitler during World War II—young Peter's ideological evolution is a prime candidate for psychoanalysis. Vehemently disassociating himself from his father's extreme nationalist views, he ricocheted toward a conservatism that was internationalist, cosmopolitan, and anti-populist. His *Conservatism Revisited*, the first postwar book to use the term conservative in its title, gave the word new visibility; also due to the effect of Russell Kirk's *The Conservative Mind*, the label was affixed to a movement where it has stuck ever since. As much as it titillated the liberals to entertain an opening to the Right, it is easy to see how Viereck's version of conservatism—which held up the figure of Klemens von Metternich, the famous diplomat and symbol of the ancien régime, as a role model—confirmed the liberal view of the world as divided between "progressives" and "reactionaries." Viereck, from their point of view, was a "good" reactionary, perhaps because he had the capacity to describe himself, as he did no one occasion, as a "conservative socialist."[85] This was a conservative after their own hearts. Attacking McCarthyism as "the revenge of the noses that for twenty years of fancy parties were pressed against the outside window pane," Viereck attacked the resurgent Radical Rightists because, through the instrument of McCarthy, they had become "revolutionaries of savage direct democracy."

> "Conservative" is no proper label for western Old Guard Republicans, nor for their incongruous allies among the status-craving, increasingly prosperous, but socially insecure immigrants in South Boston and the non-elite part of the west. What all these groups are at heart is the same old isolationist, Anglophobe, Germanophile revolt of the radical Populist lunatic-fringers against the eastern, educated, Anglicized elite.[86]

Educated at Harvard and Oxford, and a professor at Mount Holyoke College, Viereck hated capitalism, the lower classes, McCarthyism, and all forms of populism, and saw himself as a spokesman for the elite. This was the only sort of "conservative" the postwar Left-Liberal Establishment was willing to tolerate.

A whole subgenre of hate-the-Right scare books was created during the midfifties and early sixties: the tireless team of Arnold Forster and Benjamin Epstein, of the Anti-Defamation League, churned out diatribes on the order of John Roy Carlson's *Under Cover* with clocklike regularity. The Forster–Epstein method was identical to Carlson's: lump known anti-Semites in with nationalists, libertarians, and, as they put it, "extreme political reactionaries who are unable or unwilling to recognize the bigots among those joining their movement." That Gerald L. K. Smith and other minor prophets of race hate met with little success in Old Right circles did not impress the ADL, whose published reports on the activities of the Congress of Freedom seemed more shocked at the group's rejection of the United Nations and the income tax than by any real potential for becoming a center of anti-Semitic agitation.[87]

As relentless as the campaign of vituperation was, it had little effect. Not only did the movement grow, it proliferated in diverse forms: libertarian, traditionalist, and "fusionist," as represented by, respectively, the *Freeman*, the writings of Russell Kirk, and *National Review*. The prediction of the liberal mandarins that the Right was an atavism destined for the dustbin of history was not fulfilled. As the sixties dawned, far from heralding the "end of ideology," the new decade would soon make it clear that the era of ideology was just beginning.

8
Birth of the Modern Libertarian Movement

For the libertarian, the main task of the present epoch is to . . . discover who his friends and natural allies are, and above all, perhaps, who his enemies are.
—Murray N. Rothbard

T HE SIXTIES WERE YEARS OF rebellion and reaction, division and realignment, destruction and renewal. Along with the rest of American society, the American Right underwent a similar catharsis. While the chief players on the Left were the would-be revolutionaries of Students for a Democratic Society and the Black Panthers, on the Right the main actors in the ideological drama were the conservative intellectuals grouped around William F. Buckley Jr.'s magazine, *National Review.*

Heresy Hunt: The National Review *Purges*

When *National Review* was founded in late 1955, Buckley and his circle initially refrained from criticizing or even differentiating themselves from the rest of the right-wing movement in this country. But it wasn't long before the so-called "New Right" began to show its true colors. Whereas the Old Right had been a diverse and loose coalition of free-market libertarians, old Progressive isolationists, and the few remaining Jeffersonian Democrats, coexisting in a working alliance against the New Deal, Buckley and the *National Review* crowd soon put an end to this peaceable kingdom. In a series of polemics, they sought to purge American conservatism of every dissident group and subgroup.

Their first target was Ayn Rand and her followers. In 1957, Rand's massive *Atlas Shrugged* was published, and this gave rise to the Randian movement, which swept the college campuses and acquired a devoted following. Buckley assigned the job of hatchet man to the ex-Communist Whittaker Chambers, who had once been at the center of a Soviet espionage ring and whose sensational accusations against Alger Hiss had become a right-wing cause célèbre. Instead of attacking individualism and laissez-faire directly, Chambers resorted to the same old tricks: he *red-baited* Rand! "Randian man, like Marxian man, is made the center of a Godless world," he intoned, opining that it was not hard to imagine what the triumph of Rand's philosophy would have to mean: "To a gas chamber, go!" This cheap smear did nothing to stem Rand's influence; if anything, quite the opposite. Young conservatives looking from something more substantial than moth-eaten appeals to tradition and "transcendence" were drawn to the Randian philosophy for precisely the reason Chambers condemned it: Rand's idealism and her commitment to reason. In spite of Rand's growing influence among right-wing youth, the interdict had served its purpose: to wall off the main body of the conservative movement from the burgeoning ranks of the Randians.

Next on Buckley's hit list was the John Birch Society. In the early sixties, *National Review* went after JBS founder Robert Welch, ostensibly over his embarrassing public pronouncements to the effect that Eisenhower was an agent of the Communist conspiracy. According to an infamous "Scoreboard" issue of *American Opinion*, the Birch magazine, the United States was 60–80 percent Communist-dominated—an evaluation which struck the editors of *National Review* as dangerous to the future of the conservative movement. Aside from the idiosyncrasies of Robert Welch, however, the real issue was the primacy of conducting the Cold War—not at home, as the Birchers would have it, but abroad, in vast armaments and foreign-aid programs, as well as in the jungles of Southeast Asia. To look on these projects with suspicion, as Welch and the JBS did, was to be guilty of the mortal sin of "isolationism." The penalty was excommunication from the Buckleyite church of the Respectable Right.

The third target group was the nascent libertarian movement, of which the free-market economist and theoretician Murray N. Rothbard was the leading figure. Although *National Review* had for years promoted what it called "fusionism"—a fusion of the libertarian concern for economic and personal freedom with the conservative reverence for tradition—in fact this was nothing but ideological window-dressing. All talk of the free market and individualism was mere rhetoric, reserved for purely ceremonial occasions, designed to prettify *National Review's real* preoccupation: the holy war against communism. As if to underscore this point, the rites of excommunication were performed by Frank S. Meyer, the leading advocate of this phony "fusionism," in an article, "The Twisted Tree of Liberty," which—without naming them—read Rothbard and his circle out of the conservative movement.[1]

In the broad conservative movement, said Meyer, "there are and have been many different groupings, holding varying positions within the same broad outlook. Some have emphasized the menace of international communism; others have emphasized the danger of the creeping rot at the heart of our own institutions." In spite of a tendency on the part of some to "over-stress" one of these two aspects of conservative doctrine, up until this point there had been no current on the Right which "directly and explicitly opposes itself to the defense of freedom from either its domestic or foreign enemies."

Here, of course, was the signal that anathemas were about to be pronounced. Meyer took on the new heretics with the same zealous disregard for the truth that had characterized previous *National Review* purges. "Recently, however," he continued,

> there has arisen for the first time a considered position, developed out of the "pure libertarian" sector of right-wing opinion, which sharply repudiates the struggle against the major and most immediate

contemporary enemy of freedom, Soviet Communism—and does so on grounds, purportedly, of a love of freedom. These "pure libertarian" pacifists applaud Khrushchev, support the Fair Play for Cuba Committee, join the Sane Nuclear Policy Committee, and toy with the tactic of a united front with Communists "against war." They project themselves as the true representatives of the Right, attacking the militantly anti-Communist position of the leadership of American conservatism as moving towards the destruction of individual liberty because it is prepared to use the power of the American state in one of its legitimate functions, to defend freedom against Communist totalitarianism.[2]

It was only natural for Meyer, who was once a top leader of the American Communist Party, to engage in a little redbaiting. The origin of the charge that libertarians "applaud Khrushchev" was in Rothbard's refusal to go along with the right-wing opposition to the 1960 summit conference and Khrushchev's visit to the U.S. Some members of Rothbard's libertarian group, in search of a way to express their opposition to the consolidation of an American Empire, *did* join SANE—but found its rather prim brand of peace mongering to be wholly inadequate. And so, for preferring détente to the risk of nuclear war, libertarians were accused by Meyer and *National Review* of being a front for the Fair Play for Cuba Committee. This smear was all the more odious because Meyer knew perfectly well that Rothbard (with whom he had worked under the auspices of the Volker Fund) was so far from being a Communist that the distance could only be measured in light-years.

Buried in all these hysterical charges, however, was the lie at the heart of Meyer's argument: the idea that an anti-interventionist current "has arisen for the first time" on the Right. Thus, the Old Right tradition of Garet Garrett, John T. Flynn, McCormick's *Tribune*, and the America First Committee was consigned to the Orwellian "memory hole." In Meyer's book, it never happened, although how, in that case, Rothbard and his band of libertarians could "project themselves as the true representatives of the Right," surpasses all understanding.

Not content with redbaiting them, Meyer sought to explain libertarian opposition to an internationalist foreign policy as an opportunistic adaptation to left-liberalism:

> [T]hey offer tempting fleshpots: the opportunity at one and the same time bravely to proclaim devotion to individual freedom, championship of the free-market economy, and opposition to prevailing Liberal welfare-statism, while comfortably basking in the sunshine of the Liberal atmosphere, which is today primarily the atmosphere of appeasement and piecemeal surrender.[3]

Yet it was the administration of John F. Kennedy, a liberal regime if ever there was one, that was risking war with the Soviet Union over Cuba—and was getting us deeply entrenched in Vietnam. In fact, the "liberal atmosphere" in which Rothbard and his fellow libertarians were supposed to be basking was thoroughly and militantly interventionist and internationalist, just as virtually all liberals had been since the days of FDR.

With the purging of these disparate heretics from the conservative "mainstream," the betrayal and homogenization of the American Right was complete. Straining at the bit to get on with their holy war against the Soviet Union, the New Right was on the march and focused on a single goal: *power.*

The story of the conservative movement after this ritual cleansing is well-known: the Goldwater campaign of 1964, the growing Buckleyite influence, the capitulation to Richard Nixon, and finally the rise of the Reagan wing of the GOP, which culminated in the conservatives winning the White House in 1980.

The history of the heretics, on the other hand, is far less known— and far more relevant now that the conservative consensus has broken down in the wake of the Cold War's end. For the New Right of Bill Buckley and *National Review,* after more than a decade in power, has ended in failure. Eight years of Reaganism and four years of Bush failed to achieve a political realignment—and the pendulum has swung the other way. In this context, it is time to reexamine the history of the modern conservative movement, to take a second look at the purges, and to ask whether some key factor, some ingredient essential to victory, was discarded along the way.

The John Birch Society

Not since the furious campaign of calumny directed against the America First Committee has a group on the Right had to endure such a barrage of negative publicity as the John Birch Society—and with little if any justification.

After being the target of smears directed against 1964 Republican presidential candidate Barry Goldwater, membership in the society peaked in the late sixties, and then began a slow decline. The death of Robert Welch's successor, Congressman Larry McDonald, in the 1983 downing of Korean Air Lines flight 007, plunged the group into a series of murky internal disputes, and in the eighties the society drastically cut back its operations. The fall of communism has been disorienting, to say the least. The society is hard put to explain to its members how the Kremlin went from exercising 60–80 percent control over American political life to being overthrown in Russia—especially since the leadership had been telling them that Communist influence had been growing. Perhaps in anticipation of this development, in later years Welch downplayed the Communist conspiracy and started harping on the existence of a mysterious group of "Insiders" centered in the Council on Foreign Relations, a theme taken up and expanded on by the post-Welch leadership. But this shadowy stand-in for the Kremlin is no substitute for the real thing. Today, with only a fraction of the membership, income, and influence it once enjoyed, the John Birch Society is a shadow of its former self.

The JBS can be seen as a radical extension—one might even say a bit of an *over*extension—of a tendency in the Old Right best represented by John T. Flynn, whose conspiracy theories, forcefully expressed in his later writings, were rooted in his experiences in the America First Committee. As a leading opponent of the war drive, Flynn and his New York branch of the AFC were subjected to a smear campaign of relentless ferocity. In a useful study of Flynn's career, Michele Flynn Stenehjem notes the effect of John Roy Carlson's *Under Cover* on the embattled Flynn:

> The most important reason for Flynn's intense anger over the Carlson book, however, concerned the America Firster's conspiracy theory. Many of the same persons that had been staunch nonin-terventionists in 1941 were currently criticizing both Roosevelt's financing of the war, and his initial steps toward postwar global commitments. Flynn asserted in early 1944 that Roosevelt and for-eign agents, working through Carlson and others, had now resumed their orchestration of old smears in order to discredit and intimidate critics of the President's current policies. *Under Cover*, Flynn was convinced, was only part of a larger conspiracy "to frighten legitimate American patriotism underground."[4]

In concert with other ex-AFCers, Flynn launched his own private investigation of the Carlson book and its origins. The idea was to drum up support for a congressional probe. In the winter of 1944, he hired a researcher and together they set out to identify the existence of a "conspiracy which has put not only this book but others out for a very definite purpose," as he said in a letter to his researcher. In uncovering the author of *Under Cover*, Flynn discovered that Carlson's sponsors were "acrawl with fellow travelers," and that Carlson had published a number of articles in Communist periodicals. Carlson was, he contended, "an instrument in their hands."[5]

The hoped-for congressional investigation of the Communist-interventionist connection fell through, in late 1944, when its chief sponsor, Martin Dies, declined to run for reelection. Unable to find an outlet for his views, it was at this point that Flynn, as Stenehjem tells us, was led to "the nadir of pessimism and despair. . . . He was convinced that he was being deliberately silenced in favor of supporters of the President."

Flynn's despair was shared, in a general sense, by the Old Right remnant, and this translated into a defensive posture. Confronted with the onslaught of the New Deal and driven underground by the war,

Flynn and his dwindling band of ex-America Firsters saw themselves as fighting a last, desperate battle to save the old republic before it was too late.

This same sense of fighting against almost overwhelming odds permeated the propaganda and public pronouncements of the JBS since its founding. Flynn's *While You Slept* was reprinted by the society's publishing arm, and Welch recommended some of his other books in an extensive bibliography published in the period before the society's founding. It is easy to explain the Birchers' affinity for Flynn, with his caustic wit and investigative instincts, but there was one important difference between them: while Flynn was convinced that Communist penetration of government during the New Deal and the war years was substantial, he did not go quite as far as Welch and his followers. Flynn was convinced that Roosevelt knew about Communist penetration of such government agencies as the Office of War Information and the Censorship Board and that he used the Communists to smear his political opponents and drive them out of public life—but the president himself was not a Communist. "All this was possible for one reason and one reason only," he wrote, "because the President of the United States countenanced these things, encouraged them and in many cases sponsored them, not because he was a Communist or fascist or held definitely to any political system, but because at the moment they contributed to his own ambitions."[6]

The Birch Society did not make such subtle distinctions. Welch's sensational charge that President Eisenhower was a conscious agent of the Communist conspiracy effectively discredited the group in the public eye. The society's pariah status merely served to confirm the Birchers' worst suspicions and reinforced their own sense of hopelessness and isolation. This pessimism was ultimately self-defeating and eventually led the society into a cul-de-sac. For, if the United States is 60–80 percent Communist-controlled, then there is little incentive to fight: the battle is practically over.

But a debilitating pessimism was hardly a sufficient reason for an all-out assault on the order of the one launched against the society by *National Review*. The real reason for Buckley joining with the liberals in a smear campaign of massive proportions was that the Birchers refused to fall into line behind the cold-war foreign policy of the New Right. In an article in the *JBS Bulletin*, Welch denounced the Vietnam War as a Communist ploy to entice us into an unwinnable land war in Asia, and suggested that the Birch slogan against the United Nations— "Get US Out!"—could easily be applied to the Southeast Asian morass. The expulsion of the Birchers, then, was part of the continuing purge of the Old Right from the precincts of the "respectable" conservative movement, a necessary adjunct to the New Right's campaign to refocus conservatives on one overriding goal—defeating communism abroad by military means.

Whatever its other peccadilloes, the society has lived up to its Old Right heritage by sticking to its noninterventionism right up to the present day. When President George Bush went to war against Iraq in the name of a "New World Order," the society took out newspaper ads declaring, "Mr. President, stop using our nation's military forces to build your 'New World Order' and BRING THE TROOPS HOME!"

The JBS was inveighing against the New World Order *years* before George Bush popularized that sinister phrase. For more than thirty years, the smear brigade derided these concerns as the perfervid fantasies of discredited "conspiracy theorists." When the plans of the internationalists for a world government backed by U.S. troops and tax dollars unfolded on the front pages of our newspapers, the society crowed, "JBS—Ahead of its time!"—and justifiably so.[7]

The other two heresies cast into the outer darkness by the guardians of New Right orthodoxy did not suffer isolation and decline, as did the Birchers. Instead, both the Randians and the libertarians flourished after being cast out, building substantial independent organizations outside the conservative movement. Unencumbered by the ideological baggage that gave rise to a characteristic and debilitating pessimism in conservative circles, both groups started out with high hopes and high energy.

Ayn Rand: The System-Builder

Any account of the modern libertarian movement must begin by acknowledging the enormous influence of novelist-philosopher Ayn Rand. The growth and development of the movement was given a huge impetus, in 1957, with the publication of Rand's one-thousand-page novel, *Atlas Shrugged*. This paean to the virtues of capitalism, egoism, and the supremacy of reason was viciously attacked by left-liberal reviewers, who could hardly believe that anyone would dare to advocate individualism and capitalism in *moral* terms—and in the form of a popular novel, at that!

In spite of a hostile critical reception, *Atlas Shrugged* was a bestseller, and the Randian movement took off. During the writing of the novel, which had taken her some fourteen years, Rand had attracted a circle of followers, and in January 1958, a few months after the publication of *Atlas Shrugged*, her two chief disciples, Nathaniel and Barbara Branden, founded the National Branden Institute (NBI). Starting out on the Brandens' dining-room table, NBI soon acquired its own quarters, first on East 35th Street, in New York City, and eventually in the Empire State Building, where it came to occupy an entire floor. The purpose of NBI was to present Rand's philosophy, which she insisted on calling "Objectivism," in the form of lecture courses, starting with "Basic Principles of Objectivism," given by Nathaniel Branden. Other courses were soon added: "The Economics of a Free Society," "Basic Principles of Objectivist Psychology," "The Esthetics of the Visual Arts," and "Principles of Efficient Thinking," to name a few. The Brandens then added a publishing outlet, NBI Press, and created the NBI Book Service, which offered students a list of approved books. They also established NBI Art Reproductions, which sold prints of paintings by members of the Randian inner circle, several of whom were aspiring artists, including Rand's husband, Frank O'Connor.

In January of 1962, the first issue of the *Objectivist Newsletter* was published. The lead article by Rand made it clear that Objectivism was not a political ideology, but a philosophical *system* which one had to either accept or reject in its entirety. "Objectivism," wrote Rand, is a philosophical movement; since politics is a branch of philosophy, Objectivism advocates certain political principles— specifically, those of *laissez-faire* capitalism—as the consequence and the ultimate practical application of its fundamental philosophical principles. It does not regard politics as a separate or primary goal, that is: as a goal that can be achieved without a wider ideological context.[8]

This was the basis of Rand's growing popularity on the nation's college campuses. Not just the idea of a consistent system which encompassed the whole of life; Marxism could make a similar claim—so, for that matter, could Scientology, psychoanalysis, spiritualism, and Swedenborgianism. What gave Objectivism such appeal, especially to the young, was best expressed in a passage from *The Fountainhead*, in an exchange between the hero, Howard Roark, an aspiring young architect, and the dean of his college, who is about to expel him for his unorthodox ideas. After the dean launches into a long and windy speech, in which he declares that there has been nothing new in the field of architecture since the Parthenon, Roark answers him:

> "But you see," said Roark quietly, "I have, let's say, sixty years to live. Most of that time will be spent working. I've chosen the work I want to do. If I find no joy in it, then I'm only condemning myself to sixty years of torture. And I can find the joy only if I do my work in the best way possible to me. But the best is a matter of standards—and I set my own standards. I inherit nothing. I stand at the end of no tradition. I may, perhaps, stand at the beginning of one."[9]

Although this passage appears in a work of fiction, it clearly expresses Rand's own view of her relationship to the history of ideas. As she gathered a group around her, Objectivism's chief appeal was that this was something unprecedented. Like Howard Roark and the goddess Athena, Rand sprang forth fully armed from the head of Zeus—or so went the official mythology, a fiction maintained to this day by a new generation of acolytes.

After the publication of *Atlas Shrugged* and the birth of the organized Objectivist movement, Rand was emphatic in denying any connection whatsoever with "the so-called conservatives." Although she was bitterly opposed to communism and politically indistinguishable from many on the extreme Right, she energetically denounced all conservatives as ineffective dolts who did more to discredit capitalism than to defend it.

In the ten years of its existence as an organized movement, Objectivism grew so rapidly that it looked, for a while, as if it might some day become a force to be reckoned with. By the midsixties, NBI was giving lecture courses via tape transcription in eighty cities across the country, and they were getting ready to export Objectivism as far away as Pakistan. The *Objectivist Newsletter*, once a modest four-pager, adopted a magazine format and became the *Objectivist*. But in October of 1968, the readers of the *Objectivist* were stunned to learn that the Objectivist movement was no more. In an article, "To Whom It May Concern," Rand denounced both Nathaniel and Barbara Branden, and declared that NBI had been dissolved. Although Rand's explanation of the break was maddeningly vague, the real reason was a very personal conflict that, in any other movement, would not have spelled its end. It was only because Objectivism claimed to be a total worldview, a prescription for moral and psychological perfection, that the details of Nathaniel Branden's affair with the much older Rand became public knowledge.[10]

The Randian influence grew at a fantastic rate during a time of cultural anomie, the sixties, in which it was fashionable to despise any and all traditions, and to pretend that we could or should abolish history and start anew. The Objectivist movement pandered to this trend by claiming to be something entirely new under the sun. This was a deliberate deception, a cheap marketing technique which deluded Rand's young—and generally not very widely read—followers into isolating themselves from the corrupting influence of competing ideas, and accepting Rand's word, and the word of her leading followers, as gospel. *I inherit nothing.* And, therefore, everything must be created from scratch: philosophy, metaphysics, ethics, economics, politics, esthetics. In the Randian Cultural Revolution, nothing and no one was spared—with the single exception of Aristotle, the only thinker to whom she ever acknowledged an intellectual debt.

Did Rand Invent Individualism?

This claim to utter uniqueness is a lie on two levels. To begin with, for her disciples to claim that Rand inherited nothing from the Western tradition of classical liberalism is simply a confession of ignorance so abysmal that it could only be excusable in the very young. It does not take a whole lot of research to uncover the fact that there is ample precedent for her ethical and political views not only in Nietzsche, but also in Mencken, Nock, Rose Wilder Lane, Chodorov, Isabel Paterson—and, indeed, in the entire tradition of nineteenth-century classical liberalism. Paterson's *The God of the Machine*, particularly the chapter "The Humanitarian with the Guillotine," is infused with a theme, tone, and spirit that ought to give readers and admirers of Rand's work a shock of déjà vu. Observing that most of the mass murder in the modern world has been carried out in the name of a supposedly idealistic "humanitarianism," Paterson asks,

> Why did the humanitarian philosophy of eighteenth century Europe usher in the Reign of Terror? It did not happen by chance; it followed from the original premise, objective and means proposed. The objective is to do good to others as a *primary* justification of existence; the means is the power of the collective; and the premise is that "good" is collective.
>
> The root of the matter is ethical, philosophical, and religious, involving the relation of man to the universe. The fatal divergence occurs in failing to recognize the norm of human life. Obviously there is a great deal of pain and distress incidental to existence. Poverty, illness, and accident are possibilities which may be reduced to a minimum, but cannot be altogether eliminated. . . . Ills are marginal. They can be alleviated from the marginal surplus of

production; otherwise nothing at all could be done. Therefore it cannot be supposed that the producer exists only for the sake of the non-producer, the well for the sake of the ill, the competent for the sake of the incompetent; nor any person merely for the sake of another.[11]

There is no question that Rand was personally acquainted with both Lane and Paterson—in the case of the latter, they were friends for many years. In her not-quite-hagiographic book, *The Passion of Ayn Rand*, ex-acolyte Barbara Branden admits that Rand and Paterson "were running a friendly race to see who would finish [her book] first." She then goes on to give the official Randian view of their relationship:

> Ayn had spent many evenings explaining her moral philosophy to Pat,[12] clarifying and specifying the rationale behind it, and how it applied to human action; during their early discussions, Pat had argued against a morality of self-interest, but after months of often angry discussions, had finally been convinced. Now, she asked Ayn if she might include in her own book a defense of Ayn's moral theory as opposed to humanitarianism. Ayn agreed immediately. She later explained, "I felt pleased and flattered that Pat wanted to use my ideas. She told me that for certain reasons—she hated a lot of footnotes—she would rather not mention by name in her book. My consideration was only that the more the ideas are spread, the better, and that it would be wonderful to have them presented in a nonfiction book. I was totally idea-centered. So I told her, 'By all means, I don't want any credit.'"[13]

The Passion of Ayn Rand is, in large part, based on an earlier and entirely uncritical biographical sketch originally published just as the Rand cult was getting off the ground.[14] Great hunks of the former work were thrown into this hopelessly overwritten memoir, and the result was an indigestible stew. Purpled with endless paragraphs of overwrought prose, the tone of the book oscillates from wide-eyed adulation to embittered denunciations of its subject, often on the same page, and contradictions abound. Based largely on extensive interviews with Rand,

Passion relies almost exclusively on Rand's recollection of the facts, as well as their interpretation—except when it comes to the period after the founding of the Objectivist movement, where Barbara Branden has her own axe to grind. Thus she writes that Paterson's book

> contains a paraphrasing of Ayn's ideas. Today a reader of Ayn Rand would recognize the source of certain ideas in that chapter; but then, with *The Fountainhead* newly published, readers could legitimately assume that Isabel Paterson was the source of these radical new moral concepts.

Forgetting that she was supposed to be "totally idea-centered," Rand complained to her biographer that "[i]t was only after the book came out . . . that I realized Pat had done something enormously improper. And she had a name, I did not; had she mentioned me, it could have helped me professionally."[5]

While Barbara Branden's book is generally unreliable, often the newer material inadvertently gives us a glimpse of the truth, as when Rand's friend, Mimi Sutton, is quoted on the subject of Rand's relationship with Paterson:

> Isabel Paterson was a dowdy woman, with no charm whatever. . . . But Ayn was entranced with her. They'd sit up until four or five in the morning—and Ayn would be sitting at the master's feet. One night, when they were talking, I went to bed, but I could hear the conversation, and it was as if Pat were the guru and teacher—and Ayn *didn't do that*. Ayn would be asking questions, and Pat would be answering. It was very strange.[6]

As the two women tried out new ideas on each other, in the wee hours of those mornings that dawned half a century ago, who is to say who learned what from whom? Typically, Ms. Branden, the Randian spin doctor, tells us that while "it seems clear that Ayn's early relationship with Pat did have a strong element of student to teacher," this was "not in the realm of philosophy," but was confined to politics and history. How does she know this? In spite of her claim to have achieved some sort of perspective on her mentor, Ms. Branden takes Rand's word for it, in this matter as in so many others.

In their books, lecture courses, and other public pronouncements, the Randians have always claimed that the Objectivist ethics is an entirely original contribution to the history of philosophy. But as George H. Smith points out in his book of essays, *Atheism, Ayn Rand, and Other Heresies*, the central tenet of the Randian ethics—the notion that the concept of value is contingent on the existence of life—is hardly the trailblazing work of an original theorist. Nietzsche was such an obvious influence that Rand had to acknowledge it (if only to denounce him) in her introduction to the twenty-fifth anniversary edition of *The Fountainhead*. As Smith points out, it was Nietzsche who said, "When we speak of values we do so under the inspiration and from the perspective of life." Herbert Spencer is another obvious influence. As Smith puts it,

> Rand's theory of ethics is based on natural law, an approach that was exceedingly popular for many centuries (we find it in the ancient Stoics, for instance). As natural law ethics fell into disfavor, Rand was one among a minority of philosophers (mainly Aristotelians) who attempted to resurrect this tradition—although here, as elsewhere, Rand labored under the misapprehension that she was giving birth to a new approach rather than breathing life into an old one.[17]

Smith's theory is that Rand misunderstood Aristotle's ethics and never bothered to read Spencer or the others. According to him, Rand—laboring in ignorant bliss—simply cooked up her philosophical system on her own. This is possible of course—but considerably *less* credible if we take some new evidence of her sources into account.

The Rand-Garrett Connection: "Who Is Henry Galt?"

There is a second, and deeper, level on which the assertion of Rand's utter uniqueness is a lie. The Randian claim to have given birth to a philosophy without antecedents, which amounts to an Objectivist version of the Virgin Birth, is proved false by the fact that Rand's novel, *Atlas Shrugged*, bears such a strong resemblance to Garet Garrett's 1922 novel, *The Driver*, that there arises a real question as to whether Rand passed the boundaries of acceptable behavior in "borrowing" a little too much. Here I want to emphasize the fact that I mean "acceptable behavior" by *her* standards; that is, the sort of behavior one might expect from someone who makes a virtue out of inheriting nothing.

In spite of Rand's high-powered narrative, as a literary work *Atlas Shrugged* is eventually overwhelmed by its extreme didacticism. The story, set in the United States of the not-too-distant future, relates what happens when the men of ability go on strike. The leader of the strike, one John Galt, is described as being little short of a god, and the whole thing—with its square-jawed industrialists, including Henry Rearden, a steel magnate, and Dagny Taggart, lady president of a transcontinental railroad—has the air of a religious text. The characters do not speak; they *speechify*, at great length and on every subject under the sun: the meaning of money, the meaning of sex, the meaning of life and morality. At the end of the book, as civilization is collapsing and the lights of New York City blink out, Galt commandeers the airwaves and delivers a climatic tirade which goes on for *sixty pages*. Not even Rand's considerable talents as a dramatist managed to carry it off.

The Driver also has a character named Galt: Henry M. Galt. Like *Atlas Shrugged*, *The Driver* also takes place against the backdrop of great American industries, initially the railroad industry and eventually branching off into other areas. Henry Galt is a Wall Street speculator—like Rand's Galt, Henry is a genius who takes over the bankrupt Great Midwestern Railroad and turns it into a mighty empire. Along the way, he is persecuted and attacked by his fellow businessmen and by government. In the end, his enemies conspire to put him on trial for violation of the Sherman Anti-Trust Act. At the trial, he defends his profits and his right to them in terms reminiscent of an Ayn Rand hero. Like *Atlas Shrugged*, *The Driver* is a paean to the entrepreneur as creator, and Galt is portrayed in language Rand might have used to describe Hank Rearden (who undergoes a similar trial), Francisco d'Anconia, Ellis Wyatt, or any of the other members of the Randian pantheon.

The ready explanation of Galt's rise in a few years to the role of Wall Street monarch is that he was a master profit maker. The way of it was phenomenal. His touch was that of genius, daring, unaccountable, mysteriously guided by an inner mentality. And when the results appeared they were so natural, inevitable, that men wondered no less at their own stupidity that at his prescience. Why had they not seen the same opportunity?

His associates made money by no effort of their own. They had only to put their talents with the mighty steward. He took them, employed them as he pleased, and presently returned them two-fold, five-fold, sometimes twenty-fold.[18]

Compare this to the following passage from *Atlas Shrugged*, in which Rand is describing the entrepreneurial prowess of one of her characters:

Midas Mulligan had once been the richest and, consequently, the most denounced man in the country. He had never taken a loss on any investment he made; everything he touched turned into gold. "It's because I know what to touch," he said. Nobody could grasp the pattern of his investments: he rejected deals that were considered flawlessly safe, and he put enormous amounts into ventures that no other banker would handle. Through the years, he had been the trigger that had sent unexpected, spectacular bullets of industrial success shooting over the country.[19]

As Carl G. Ryant notes, the hero of *The Driver* bore more than a passing resemblance to E. H. Harriman, the speculative and financial genius who began his career as an errand boy and rose to challenge J. P. Morgan for control of the nation's railroads.[20] Harriman, in turn, is a dead ringer for Nathaniel Taggart, grandfather to Dagny and founder of Taggart Transcontinental, who is described in *Atlas Shrugged* as "a penniless adventurer who had come from somewhere in New England and built a railroad across a continent, in the days of the first steel rails."

The clearest evidence, albeit circumstantial, that Rand did indeed read *The Driver* is the fact that a stylistic device used throughout

Atlas Shrugged also occurs in *The Driver*. While it is plausible that two different authors could come up with a similar name for their main character, and even that the two novels might express similar themes, it is too much to believe that use of the same rhetorical device could also have occurred by happenstance. *Atlas Shrugged* opens with the question "Who is John Galt?" and the phrase recurs throughout the book. John Galt does not make an appearance until the last third of the novel; he is the mystery man, the unseen shaper of large events. In *The Driver*, a similar motif is employed. Henry M. Galt is introduced as a man of mystery, whose secret gradually unfolds. The narrator first meets him on a train, where they get into a political discussion, and then he turns up again:

> "Who is Henry M. Galt?" I asked suddenly, addressing the question to the three of them collectively. I expected it to produce some effect, possibly a strange effect; yet I was surprised at their reactions to the sound of the name. It was as if I had spilled a family taboo. Unconsciously gestures of anxiety went around the table. For several minutes no one spoke, apparently because no one could think just what to say.[21]

The same phraseology evokes a very similar emotional reaction in the opening lines of *Atlas Shrugged*:

> "Who is John Galt?"
> The light was ebbing, and Eddie Willers could not distinguish the bum's face. The bum had said it simply, without expression. But from the sunset far at the end of the street, yellow glints caught his eyes, and the eyes looked straight at Eddie Willers, mocking and still—as if the question had been addressed to the causeless uneasiness within him.

As in *Atlas Shrugged*, so in *The Driver*: Henry Galt plays the behind-the-scenes manipulator of great events, as he secretly buys up Great Midwestern stock, gradually taking control. At one point he goes out into the field to research his reorganization plan. "Three days after he set out on this errand," writes Garrett, we began to receive messages by telegraph from our operating officials, traffic managers, agents and division superintendents, to this effect:

"Who is Henry M. Galt?"

A Galt hangs over both novels, mysterious and powerful, certainly no ordinary mortal but a heroic figure, larger than life. Both suffer for their greatness, but triumph in the end. The portrait of Henry Galt in *The Driver* is one of a man who carries the whole country on his shoulders. Garrett describes him as "a colossus emerging from the mist," surely an image that conjures visions of Atlas holding up the world. If Ayn Rand didn't read *The Driver*, then this surely makes the case for the pseudo-mystical concept of synchronicity.

Rand's intellectual and artistic debt to Garet Garrett is underscored by yet another strange coincidence. For it isn't only *Atlas Shrugged* that contains echoes of Garrett's long-forgotten novel. In Garrett's book, Henry Galt has a daughter, Vera, who bears more than a passing resemblance to Dominique Francon, bitch goddess of The *Fountainhead*. To illustrate, here is how Rand describes the effect of Dominique's laughter on the listener:

> Then Keating heard her laughing; it was a sound so gay and so cold that he knew it was best not to go in. He knew he did not want to go in, because he was afraid again, as he had been when he'd seen her eyes.[22]

The laughter of Garrett's Vera has the same effect on the narrator of *The Driver*:

> She leaped to her feet, evading me, and laughed with her head tossed back—an icy, brilliant laugh that made me rigid. I could not interpret it. I do not know yet what it meant. Nor do I comprehend the astonishing gesture that followed.

Taken by itself, this juxtaposition proves nothing; certainly it does not prove that these two frigid women, aloof and exulting in their own sterile freedom, are anything but sisters in spirit. The proof comes a few paragraphs later. For the "astonishing gesture that followed" is similar to a scene in *The Fountainhead*, where Dominique throws the priceless statue of a Greek god down an air shaft. In *The Driver*, Vera Galt does the same thing to a costly African sculpture for similarly perverse reasons. As Vera makes this dramatic gesture, she remarks that "[s]o many things turn ugly when you look at them closely," a sentiment which could easily have been uttered by Dominique. These two haughty, languid ladies, with their icy laughter and imperious beauty, embody the tragic sense of life; Dominique and Vera are literary twin sisters, hewn from the same archetype.

The official version of the origins of Dominique, as given by Barbara Branden, is that the creative process that gave birth to the character was arrived at "by introspection." "Dominique," said Rand, "is myself in a bad mood." But in light of Vera in *The Driver* and our new perspective on Rand, this explanation hardly seems adequate.

From the overwhelming mass of evidence, it is clear that Rand was influenced by Garrett. The similarities between *The Driver* and *Atlas Shrugged* are too numerous and too detailed to be coincidence. This is not a question of plagiarism. What is really at issue is the authenticity of Rand's claim to stand not at the end but at the beginning of a tradition. *The Driver* proves beyond the shadow of a doubt that this is untrue. The only question is whether this was a conscious lie on Rand's part.

Ayn Rand's leading ex-disciple, the psychologist Nathaniel Branden, attributes the remarkable similarity to Rand's subconscious; she was not, he said in a brief interview, the sort of person who would have been capable of appropriating names, themes, and certain fictional devices without acknowledging the source. My own theory is that Ayn Rand knew perfectly well what she was doing, and did not regard it as appropriating anything. For *The Driver* is like a crude, one-dimensional schematic drawing of *Atlas Shrugged*, not in terms of the plot—although there are some similarities—but thematically. I believe Rand never acknowledged Garrett as a source for two reasons.

First, because she probably considered him to be a minor writer whom she certainly did not intend to imitate or plagiarize, but only to *improve* on. For her, Garrett's work was a takeoff point, a stimulus which led her to the question "Wouldn't it be interesting if . . . ?" Secondly, at the time she read *The Driver*—perhaps soon after she arrived in the United States, in 1926—she was far more friendly to conservatives. In her mind, Garrett doubtless represented the best of the conservative defenders of capitalism and individualism; a bit clumsy, perhaps, but well-meaning. It was only later that, after the founding of the Randian cult, she began to denounce conservatives with special virulence. There was, then, an *ideological* reason for withholding the information: the necessity, as she saw it, of distancing herself from the conservative movement. She failed to acknowledge her intellectual debt because Garrett was a well-known figure of the Old Right, one of the hated conservatives.

Certainly there was plenty of opportunity for her to acknowledge Garrett's unmistakable influence. She might have done it in her article "What is Romanticism?" where she briefly analyzes the "slick magazine" fiction popular before World War II. Indeed, there is a passage in this essay, in which she discusses

> a class of writers whose basic premise, in effect, is that man possesses volition *in regard to existence, but not to consciousness*, i.e., in regard to his physical actions, but not in regard to his own character. The distinguishing characteristic of this class is: stories of unusual events enacted by *conventional* characters. The stories are abstract projections, involving actions one does not observe in "real life," the characters are commonplace concretes. The stories are Romantic, the characters Naturalistic. Such novels seldom have plots . . . but they do have a form resembling a plot: a coherent, imaginative, often suspenseful story held together by some one central goal or undertaking of the characters.
>
> The contradictions in such a combination of elements are obvious; they lead to a total breach between action and characterization, leaving the action unmotivated and the characters unintelligible. The reader is left to feel: "These people couldn't do these things!"[23]

If there ever was a description of *The Driver*, then this is it. As Henry Galt returns from a hard day of empire-building, he sits down to dinner with Mrs. Galt, his perfectly conventional wife, and his daughters, Vera and the good-natured Natalie. There is also Grandma Galt, the stern family matriarch, whose single interest in life seems to be the price of stock in the Great Midwestern Railroad; every night she asks Henry the price, and every night he dutifully replies. How Rand must have snorted in derision when she first read it! For it is the exact opposite of her own literary aesthetic, which dictated that the Randian pantheon be peopled by gods and heroes, unencumbered by such unromantic phenomena as mothers, wives, and children.

I am willing to admit that, in spite of all the evidence to the contrary, Nathaniel Branden's theory that the Garrett material was sitting in Rand's subconscious could well be true. I just do not think it is very likely. In spite of my inclination to give Rand the benefit of every doubt, there are just too many details one would have to overlook in order to believe she read *The Driver* and promptly forgot all about it.

While not plagiarism in the legal sense, the unacknowledged and—in my view—*conscious* use of Garrett's work as a starting point for her own, does, *in this case*, constitute intellectual fraud. It is fraud because Rand spent so much time denying not only her own past, but also the value of any and all tradition. Especially in view of the fact that the "official" biographical essay, written in the sixties by Barbara Branden, and based on extensive interviews with Rand, has a long account of the writing of *Atlas Shrugged* that makes no mention of Garrett, Rand's silence on this subject amounted to a deliberate deception.

On the other hand, this is not a case of word-for-word plagiarism, as with Martin Luther King's doctoral dissertation. It is a case of denying one's own roots, curiously akin to Rand's bizarre attitude toward the concept of family. As *The Passion of Ayn Rand* relates,

> It was a phenomenon to which she seemed monumentally indifferent. "It's not *chosen* values," she would often say when the issue arose in conversation. "One is simply born into a family. Therefore it's of no real significance."[24]

Ms. Branden attributes this to "oblivious [ness] to the fact that there could be a love not tied to intellectual values." But, as we have seen, neither did she acknowledge a kinship that *was* tied to intellectual values, such as her obvious affinity for the ideas first expressed in *The Driver*.

This kinship is reflected not only in the work of these two Old Right figures, but also in the general pattern of their respective careers; like Rand, Garrett rose from nothing to become a successful writer. Both fought against the collectivist spirit of the age at a time when it was neither fashionable nor profitable to do so. Both left behind a substantial body of work.

The irony is that Rand's relatively crude nonfiction tirades, with a few exceptions mostly bereft of any art, are still available in any bookstore; on the other hand, the gemlike prose of, say, Garrett's *The American Story* is long out of print, and you would be lucky to find it in a used bookshop. An entire mini-industry has grown up around Rand, in which ex-disciples hawk kiss-and-tell memoirs and her epigones market rival interpretations of the sacred text, while the work and legacy of Garet Garrett is largely forgotten.

Ayn Rand and the Old Right

Ayn Rand vehemently denied her intellectual ancestors, but they have come back to haunt her and her orthodox followers. The legacy of the true individualist tradition in American, of which Rand was a small and somewhat eccentric offshoot, is today being rediscovered. What the Randians and the libertarians who idolized her have come to terms with is the fact that one ought not to feel ashamed, but, instead, *honored* to stand at the end of such a great and glorious tradition.

Rand borrowed freely—but selectively—from her Old Right colleagues, including the tenets of individualism and capitalism but discarding their fierce opposition to a U.S. foreign policy of global intervention. Although there are vague sentiments in some of her essays that indicate she may not have thought U.S. entry into World War II was the best course, these references are few, scattered, and cryptic. The cold-war hysteria that gripped the conservative movement in the post-war period was nowhere more virulent than in the person of Ayn Rand and the Objectivist movement; she once claimed it would be morally permissible to launch a massive invasion of *any* Communist country, the only restraining factor being the practicality of such a step. This typically hopped-up Randian dogma distorted the libertarian movement in its formative years, and accounts—at least in part—for the peculiar lack of response from these circles to the collapse of communism and the end of the Cold War.

Today's Randian dogmatists emphasize the later writings, *Atlas Shrugged* and her nonfiction: there is almost no mention of the early works, such as her 1936 novel, *We the Living*;[25] a novelette, *Anthem*;[26] and her plays, notably *Night of January 16th*, first produced in 1934. Yet, in purely literary terms, the youthful Ayn Rand was by far the better dramatist.[27]

We the Living is a beautifully wrought story set in Soviet Russia, which dramatizes a fervent anticommunism not by hitting the reader over the head with speeches, but in three unforgettable characters: Kira Argounova, the young anticommunist firebrand; Leo Kovalensky, the languid and slightly decadent Russian aristocrat; and the austere Andrei Taganov, the young Communist idealist. In the end, Taganov's suicide symbolizes the death of Marxist egalitarianism as a moral ideal—but we don't need any fifty-page speeches to tell us that. As Rand the novelist and playwright calcified into Rand the philosopher and leader of an organized movement, she lost what was her greatest asset: her unusual ability to translate moral and political ideas into fictional terms without slipping into didactic mode.

Anthem is a novelette set in the far future, in which collectivism has eliminated the word "I" from the language and society has reverted to a primitive state. The story chronicles the hero's rediscovery of the forbidden word—and, in a characteristic Randian dramatic flourish, also the rediscovery of the electric light. The image of the light bulb glowing with electricity as the symbol of the ego rediscovered, linking science and progress with individualism, is a masterful feat of integration. *Anthem*, which attracted no attention at the time of its publication, is the most underrated of Rand's novels, a powerful parable written with the start simplicity of a Greek myth or a biblical story.

Ayn Rand's crowning achievement was *The Fountainhead*. No matter how she came to imagine Dominique's statue-smashing scene, *The Fountainhead* is a masterful novel and will endure long after Rand's critics are buried and forgotten. There is a timeless quality to the book, a modernity about the characters and the story, which will continue to make the reading of the novel a rite of passage for many years to come.

Unfortunately, one cannot say the same thing about *Atlas Shrugged*, which reads today like a period piece. With all its talk of railroads and heavy industry, *Atlas Shrugged* has not aged very well. Nor has the movement it spawned—the Rand cult, and, to a large degree, the wider libertarian movement—seemed to have aged very gracefully. For the hordes of young people who were converted to the Objectivist creed were urged to cut all ties, to renounce family, tradition, religion, culture; even Mozart was deemed to be "anti-life" and therefore verboten. The typical Randian cadre, therefore, lived in a void, alienated from and deeply suspicious of anything and everything outside the Objectivist canon—a condition which seems to have persisted even unto the nineties. As the end of the Cold War brings debate and the promise of a realignment on the Right, as old alliances shift and new ones form, such groups as the Libertarian Party and the Objectivist sect continue to float in a void, unaware of and indifferent to the turmoil around them. If revealing the Ayn Rand–Garet Garrett connection accomplishes nothing else, then perhaps it will begin to reconnect the libertarian movement to its Old Right roots.

I would be the last to deny Ayn Rand's achievement as a writer and a force for liberty. But her life and work must be seen in context; that is, in the context of a larger movement, the Old Right, of which she was a part. Rand's arrogant and ultimately self-defeating insistence on standing aloof from this tradition was an error that her libertarian admirers would be foolish to repeat.

At the end of *Atlas Shrugged*, John Galt and his fellow strikers come down from the mountains, ready to rebuild civilization. "The road is cleared," says Galt. "We are going back to the world." Now that the myth of Ayn Rand's uniqueness has been exploded, once and for all, perhaps her latter-day followers will come back to the world—and, in the process, discover the secret of their lost heritage.

Murray Rothbard: The Paradigmatic Libertarian

The self-immolation of the objectivists did not mean the destruction of the libertarian movement.[28] For there was another wing of the movement, one which—unlike its Randian cousin—did not deny its Old Right heritage. Murray N. Rothbard and his circle saw themselves as the continuators of a glorious tradition. In contrast to the Randians, who limited themselves to reading the works of Rand and the few books on the officially approved recommended reading list, Rothbard and his group were widely read academics who encouraged libertarians to investigate, understand, and appreciate their own history.

Rothbard had been briefly associated with the Objectivist movement, but he was soon repelled by the cultish aspects of the New York Randians. Born in 1925, Rothbard's libertarian affiliations preceded the Randian movement by a decade. He grew up in New York City, in a left-wing atmosphere, and was converted to libertarianism after coming in contact with FEE and Frank Chodorov's *analysis*. Rothbard then started to attend seminars given by the great Austrian economist Ludwig von Mises at New York University, and became a devoted Misesian. He earned a doctorate in economics at Columbia University, and in 1952 he received a grant from the Kansas City–based Volker Fund to write a textbook on Austrian economics, which eventually became his monumental *Man, Economy, and State*.[29] His association with the Volker Fund as an analyst lasted a decade, during which he sought out, evaluated, and assisted libertarian scholars. Devoted to the libertarian Old Right tradition of strict noninterventionism and opposition to the welfare state, at the time Rothbard saw himself as an extreme "rightist," that is, a radical partisan of the Taft wing of the Republican

Party. In the midfifties there was little outlet for views of this kind, but Rothbard searched them out and found a niche at the magazine *Faith and Freedom*, published by the Rev. James W. Fifield's Spiritual Mobilization movement, a right-wing group headquartered in Los Angeles, California. The defeat and dissolution of the Taft group led him to various right-wing third parties, but these proved ephemeral, as did his association with Fifield. Rothbard's staunch opposition to the Cold War—which was increasingly eccentric on the Right—soon resulted in his dismissal from *Faith and Freedom*.

In the meantime, a group of libertarians known as the Circle Bastiat began to form in the New York area, and this became the nucleus of a libertarian faction in Students for America, a conservative youth group. This, however, was only a prelude to a new phase in the development of the embryonic libertarian movement, a new turn that would soon propel Rothbard and his group into heretofore uncharted territory.

The Old Right Meets the New Left

In 1964, after a brief stay in the *National Review* orbit and an even briefer sojourn in the Objectivist movement, Rothbard and his small group founded a quarterly magazine, *Left and Right*, in an effort to break out of their political isolation and reach out to the New Left. With the rise of the student rebellion symbolized by the Berkeley Free Speech Movement and the burgeoning opposition to the Vietnam War, the non-Randian wing of the libertarian movement saw its chance to have an impact. The first issue of *Left and Right* featured Rothbard's stirring manifesto, "Left and Right: The Prospects for Liberty." This remarkable document attempted to reorient libertarian thought away from the pessimism of the Remnant by harking back to the optimism of nineteenth-century liberalism. The problem, said Rothbard, is that

> [t]oo many libertarians mistakenly link the prognosis for liberty with that of the seemingly stronger and supposedly allied conservative movement; this linkage makes the characteristic long-run pessi-

mism of the modern libertarian easy to understand. But this paper
contends that while the short-run prospects for liberty at home and
abroad may seem dim, the proper attitude for the libertarian to take
is one of unquenchable long-run optimism.[30]

Libertarian pessimism was due to a case of amnesia: the partisans
of liberty had forgotten their historical legacy, the great liberal revolutions that destroyed European feudalism and aristocratic privilege.
The victory of the society of contract over the society of status, even
if only partial, had effected a revolution in human affairs. Classical
liberalism was

> the party of hope, of radicalism, of liberty, of the Industrial Revolu-
> tion, of progress, of humanity; the other was conservatism, the party
> of reaction, the party that longed to restore the hierarchy, statism,
> theocracy, serfdom, and class exploitation of the Old Order.[31]

Nineteenth-century liberalism declined because of "an inner rot."
"For with the partial success of the liberal revolution in the West," wrote
Rothbard, "the liberals increasingly abandoned their radical fervor and
therefore their liberal goals, to rest content with a mere defense of the
uninspiring and defective *status quo.*" Having abandoned natural rights
for utilitarianism, and adopted Spencerian evolutionism, or Social Dar-
winism, the classical liberals were led into the delusion that progress
toward human liberty was inevitable and automatic.

What Rothbard was proposing was a radical shift in perspective
which, he said, was necessary for victory; a paradigm shift that would
provide the theoretical underpinning for a libertarian alliance with
the New Left.

> Thus, with liberalism abandoned from within, there was no longer
> a party of hope in the Western world, no longer a "left" movement
> to lead a struggle against the State and against the unbreached
> remainder of the Old Order. Into this gap, into this void created by
> the drying up of radical liberalism, there stepped a new movement:
> socialism. Libertarians of the present day are accustomed to think

of socialism as the polar opposite of the libertarian creed. But this is a grave mistake, responsible for a severe ideological disorientation in the present world. As we have seen, conservatism was the polar opposite of liberty; and socialism, while to the "left" of conservatism, was essentially a confused, middle-of-the-road movement. It was, and still is, middle of the road because it tries to achieve liberal *ends* by the use of conservative *means*.[32]

Conservatives had deluded themselves into believing that America was a laissez-faire utopia before the New Deal. This myth, he explained, holds that the evil

Roosevelt, influenced by Felix Frankfurter, the Intercollegiate Socialist Society, and other "Fabian" and Communist "conspirators," engineered a revolution which set America on the path to socialism, and further on beyond the horizon, to communism.[33]

There was, said Rothbard, ample precedent for the usurpations of the New Deal in the policies of William Howard Taft, Woodrow Wilson, and Herbert Hoover. In support of his thesis, he cited Dr. Gabriel Kolko's *The Triumph of Conservatism*, which traced the origins of American state capitalism to the reforms of the Progressive Era.[34] These measures were pushed through by big-business interests such as J. P. Morgan and his heirs, who "realized that monopoly privilege can be created only by the State and not as a result of free-market operations." Big business hailed Wilson's war collectivism and welcomed the Interstate Commerce Commission, the Federal Trade Commission, the Federal Reserve, and agricultural subsidies with open arms. They didn't want free competition in free markets, but privileges doled out by an all-powerful state, in which hierarchy and monopoly would stifle all challenges to their dominance. These were the real roots of the problem, a web of controls and government-business "partnership" that would blossom into the New Deal. A few liberals, like Flynn, rebelled; but the great majority, as we have seen, went along with the new trend.

The New Deal did not expropriate industry, but cartelized it and exacerbated a preexisting trend toward state-monopoly capitalism. Rothbard quotes R. Palme Dutt—the Marxist theoretician of the Comintern's "Third Period"—in support of the thesis that the New Deal followed the fascist pattern of right-wing collectivism. Its purpose, said Dutt, was to "move to a form of dictatorship of the war type." Shorn of its "progressive" rhetorical veneer, the New Deal meant subsidies for big business, state-regulated and planned cartels, all financed by inflation and fixed wages. Roosevelt's program was "the reality of the new Fascist type of system of concentrated State capitalism"[35]

Rothbard might just as easily have cited John T. Flynn's *As We Go Marching*—although perhaps a quote from an obscure right-wing author might not have fitted in with the new turn. For Rothbard was convinced that the rising antiwar movement and the just-developing New Left were fertile fields for harvesting a whole new crop of eager young libertarians. Thus his aim was to show that the view pushed by the Right, that American business was the innocent victim who had been put upon by evil socialist college professors, was utterly false. (Ayn Rand was peddling this view, both in her romanticization of the industrialists in *Atlas Shrugged* and in the title of one of her speeches: "America's Persecuted Minority: Big Business.")

Rothbard then turns his attention to the cadre of his own movement, trying to draw from the past a lesson for today. He points to the fact that, in the twenties, Nock and Mencken were considered extreme "leftists" who opposed the conservative brand of statism represented by Coolidge and Hoover:

> [W]hen the New Deal succeeded Hoover, on the other hand the milk-and-water socialists and vaguely leftist interventionists hopped on the New Deal bandwagon; on the left only such libertarians as Nock and Mencken . . . realized that Roosevelt was only a continuation of Hoover in other rhetorical guise. It was perfectly natural for the radicals to form a united front against FDR with the older Hoover and Al Smith conservatives. . . . The problem was that Nock and his fellow radicals, at first properly scornful of their newfound allies, soon began to accept them and even don cheerfully the formerly despised label of "conservative."

The root error of these two influential Old Rightists, says Rothbard, was in their unrelenting despair:

> There had always been one grave flaw in the brilliant and finely honed libertarian doctrine hammered out in their very different ways by Nock and Mencken: Both had long adopted the great error of pessimism. Both saw no hope for the human race ever adopting the system of liberty. Despairing of the radical doctrine of liberty ever being applied in practice, each in his own personal way retreated from the responsibility of ideological leadership. Mencken joyously and hedonically, Nock haughtily and secretively. Despite the massive contribution of both men to the cause of liberty, therefore, neither could ever become the conscious leader of a libertarian movement, for neither could ever envision the party of liberty as the party of hope, the party of revolution.[36]

In this essay, Rothbard meant to meet the challenge of the sixties by undoing the fusion of the thirties; that is, by breaking apart the merger of libertarianism and conservatism which had forged the Old Right. He asked libertarians to see themselves in a new light: as the true revolutionaries, competing with the "middle of the road" centrists who called themselves Marxists for leadership of the student rebellion and the movement against the Vietnam War. It was necessary to break with the Right, said Rothbard, and permissible to ally in this case with the Left because the latter was basically impotent—and, therefore, no real threat. The reason for this is because only laissez-faire can organize society into a productive whole, and therefore

> radical deviations cause breakdowns and economic crises. This crisis of statism becomes particularly dramatic and acute in a fully socialist society; hence the inevitable breakdown of statism has first become strikingly apparent in the countries of the socialist (i.e. communist) camp. For socialism confronts the inner contradiction of statism most starkly. Desperately, socialism tries to fulfill its proclaimed goals of industrial growth, higher standards of living for the masses, and eventual withering away of the State—and is increasingly unable to do so. Hence, the inevitable collapse of socialism.[37]

Armed with the Misesian dictum that economic calculation—and, therefore, any sort of planning—would be impossible under socialism, Rothbard predicted the implosion of the Communist bloc over twenty years before the Great Revolution of 1989. Convinced of the case for long-term optimism, Rothbard did not hesitate to risk the contamination of consorting with the Left. What was there to fear from an ideology that was doomed to failure? From the vantage point of this new perspective, the main task of the libertarian in the decade of the sixties was

> to cast off his needless and debilitating pessimism, to set his sight on long-run victory, and to set out on the road to its attainment. To do this, he must, perhaps first of all, drastically realign his mistaken view of the ideological spectrum; he must discover who his friends and natural allies are, and above all perhaps, who his enemies are.

In the second issue of the journal *Left and Right*, Rothbard wrote an article praising the New Left for its opposition to bureaucracy and the centralized national-security state in its fight against the state-controlled educational system, epitomized by Clark Kerr; and most especially its fervent opposition to the war in Vietnam. However, the turn to the New Left did not last very long. By the summer of 1969, SDS and the New Left had burned themselves out in an orgy of violence and self-destruction. By that time, however, the ranks of the libertarian movement had swelled, in spite of a few defections to the Left. *Left and Right* folded, to be replaced by the more frequently published *Libertarian Forum*. Rothbard and his group trained their sights on a new target: the right-wing youth group, Young Americans for Freedom (YAF).

Libertarianism Comes of Age

YAF had been formed by the Buckley crowd in 1960 and functioned as the youth section of the New Right. But the influence of libertarian ideas on America's conservative youth was considerable, and there Rothbard saw an opening. In addition, the extreme sectarianism of the Objectivist leadership had sent many of Rand's followers in search of some alternative, and the Rand–Branden split accelerated the process; increasing numbers of ex-Randians were won to the revivified libertarian movement.[38] Many of them joined YAF and built up a large and very vocal Libertarian Caucus. Things came to a head at YAF's August 1969 convention, held in St. Louis, where there was a showdown over the issues of the draft and the Vietnam War. When one young libertarian YAFer set his draft card ablaze, the convention went ballistic and the libertarians walked out. New organizations were formed: on the East Coast, the Society for Individual Liberty, and in the West, the California Libertarian Alliance.

In 1971, the New York Times Magazine took note of the new phenomenon with a feature article on the "Freedom Conspiracy," a libertarian youth group at Columbia University, as an example of a new and exciting movement that would, perhaps, take the place of the New Left as the new ideological force on campus. Out of that spate of publicity, Rothbard got a contract to write a book on libertarianism. For a New Liberty: The Libertarian Manifesto was published in 1973.[39]

The Libertarian Party had already made its first appearance on the scene, in 1972, and run its first presidential candidate, university professor John Hospers. Although Hospers was on the ballot in only two states and received about 5,000 votes, the Libertarian Party did achieve the coup of receiving one electoral vote: that of Virginia elector Roger MacBride, who had bolted from the GOP column. This libertarian movement took off, with the Libertarian Party as its chief vehicle.

The seventies ushered in a new era for libertarianism nationally; no longer the marginal Remnant, precariously preserving the canons of a dying tradition, the movement was growing rapidly. The Libertarian Party's 1976 presidential candidate, Roger MacBride, won over 200,000 votes and established the Libertarians as America's up-and-coming third party.

During the late seventies, the libertarian movement recruited two people whose vast wealth would catapult libertarianism into the spotlight: Charles and David Koch, brothers who owned Koch Industries, one of the largest family-owned companies in the nation. With their personal wealth estimated upward from $500 million, the Kochs were in a position to provide the libertarian movement with financial support. Soon a whole panoply of institutions and publications sprang up: the Cato Institute, *Inquiry* magazine (a biweekly), *Libertarian Review* (a monthly), a student affiliate, Students for a Libertarian Society (SLS), and a host of scholarly endowments and think tanks. Headquartered in San Francisco and operating under the watchful eye of Koch advisor, Edward H. Crane III, this nexus of libertarian institutions presided over a burgeoning movement.

For a while, things went well. *Inquiry* received some favorable attention under the editorship of Williamson Evers; *Libertarian Review*, with a smaller circulation, was meant to be a "movement" periodical, and it too flourished with Roy A. Child's Jr. at the helm. In 1978, the Libertarian Party's candidate for governor of California—Ed Clark, a corporate lawyer for ARCO—polled an amazing five percent of the vote, the highest vote for a third-party candidate in many years. As the eighties dawned, it seemed as if the libertarian movement was headed for a future of exponential growth.

Then the whole thing came crashing down.

Those halcyon days of the late seventies were not, apparently, as trouble-free as appeared on the surface. For while there were as yet no public displays of internal strife, privately the leaders of the movement were at each other's throats. Well before the 1980 presidential campaign of Ed Clark turned into a factional free-for-all, differences over strategy had become apparent. A dispute within SLS over the question of whether nuclear power could exist in a free society took on all the ferocity of blood feud, with the adults egging on their student proxies. Then, as the 1980 presidential campaign got underway, Rothbard went public with his criticisms. As he tells it

> [i]n the spring of 1979, a fateful—and fatal—shift took place in the direction and strategic vision of our leading libertarian institutions: foundations, youth movements, journals, etc. The shift was a classic leap into opportunist betrayal of our fundamental principles. The major architects of that shift . . . seized control of the Clark campaign from its very inception, and, in recent weeks, have stepped up their pattern of betrayal at an accelerating pace.

Rothbard defined this opportunist strategy as the "'quick victory' model." "The reasoning," he wrote, "goes something like this":

> All this principle stuff is just a drag on the machinery. We can gain
> a rapid and enormous leap forward in votes, money, membership,
> and media influence. But to gain these great goals we must quietly
> but effectively bury these annoying principles, which only put off
> voters, money, influence, etc. It is too slow to get votes and support
> by holding high the banner of libertarian principle and slowly con-
> verting people to it; far quicker to abandon our own principles and
> adopt the program dear to the hearts of those who might bring us
> votes, money, and influence.[40]

Rothbard was furious with the LP leadership. For years he had labored in the vineyards, shepherding his libertarian flock through hard times, and slowly building up a sizeable cadre of articulate and principled activists. Now the leaders of the movement wanted to throw it overboard for some dubious "get-rich-quick" scheme. He charged that "the opportunists have targeted as their constituency young, middle-class liberals, the sort of articulate people who tend to mould voter opinion, the sort of people who read the *New York Times* and watch CBS News" and "better yet . . . the sort of people who *write* the *New York Times* and *make* CBS News. All they care about," said Rothbard,

> is finding some plausible libertarian-sounding rationale for a posi-
> tion which will suck in the votes and support of the media and the
> media-oriented constituency.
>
> For example: how are white, middle-class youth to be sucked in
> to supporting Clark? Easy. What has been the biggest, in fact virtu-
> ally the *only*, issue animating this group for the last several years?
> Hysterical and ill-informed opposition to nuclear power *per se*. So:
> we promise them No nukes.
>
> How about the sort of white, middle-class liberal women who
> read the *New York Times*, etc.? Clearly, their issue for years has been
> the ERA, so Clark, Crane, and their allied opportunist institutions
> come out vigorously for this amendment.

What are the other basic views of the media constituency? Mainly they are soft liberals: that is, they favor the welfare state, but worry about its high costs, and wish for some sort of mild reduction in Big Government. So: Clark has now promised that welfare *will not* be cut in a libertarian regime: in one version, until private institutions take up the welfare burden (fat chance!) or, in another, until "full employment" is achieved (no chance at all). So, middle-class liberals are assured: No Welfare Cuts. No "Goldwater extremism" here.[41]

It was an increasingly bitter Rothbard who, confronted with the systematic sell-out of the movement he had done so much to create, determined that he would not stand by silently. When Ed Clark went on national television and was asked by interviewer Ted Koppel to sum up the LP program, Clark answered: "Low-tax liberalism"—and the Libertarian Party rank-and-file was in an uproar.

On Election Day, Ed Clark polled some 900,000 votes; a respectable sum, to be sure, but considerably less than the party faithful had expected—and far less than their leaders had promised. The leadership blamed it all on the presence of independent candidate John Anderson in the race; but Rothbard had anticipated this, writing a few months before the election that Anderson had co-opted the Clark strategy of running for the benefit of the liberal media. Anderson, said Rothbard,

> is the media's darling, and Clark is bound to remain a humble suitor left standing in the wings. This, then, accounts for the panic and near-hysteria on the part of the Clark managers over the Anderson candidacy. Anderson, they wail, has taken away "our" constituency. Tough. It couldn't have happened to a more deserving group of guys. It is indeed poetic justice for a group of people to sell their souls for a mess of pottage and then not even get the pottage.[42]

While the dispute was heated and shot thorough with more than a hint of strong personalities in conflict, Rothbard's objections to the Clark strategy could not be dismissed out of hand as the result of a personal grudge. The curmudgeonly Rothbard had always been a populist, and his conception of building a movement was light-years removed from that of Clark's handlers, who thought they could pull it off with smoke and mirrors. What he had once hoped for in the Clark campaign was a means to build a grassroots movement; what he had gotten was an all-out effort to impress the editorial board of the *New York Times*. When Clark and his campaign staff balked at calling for repeal of the income tax—an idea well outside the boundaries of "respectable" liberal opinion—Rothbard started a war of words that marked the end of the Libertarian Party as a viable electoral force.

The factional battle reached its climax at the Libertarian Party's 1983 presidential nominating convention, in which Earl Ravenal, the candidate of the Cato group, was defeated by David Bergland, a California attorney, supported by Rothbard and a diverse coalition. The Cato people—virtually half the party's activists and most of the money—walked out. The Bergland campaign was a disaster, garnering a mere 250,000 votes and almost no attention.

In 1988, the Libertarian Party rebounded somewhat, nominating ex-congressman Ron Paul of Texas, and receiving some 420,000 votes. But once again internal disputes took center stage; some LPers were disturbed by Paul's cultural conservatism, which clashed with their own neo-hippie values and lifestyle.

Rothbard's break with the Libertarian Party was originally precipitated by the shabby treatment Paul received at the hands of his LP critics, and by the decisive defeat of his principal supporters at the party's subsequent national convention. In a more fundamental sense, however, the actual cause of the split was a "real world" event, which had nothing whatever to do with the LP's convoluted internal politics: the death of communism.

Split on the Right

At first glance, the two events seem entirely unrelated: and yet, if we put Rothbard's break with the Libertarian Party in the context of his strategic views as outlined in *Left and Right: The Prospects for Liberty*, it is clear that they are intimately related. Discussing the circumstances that had led libertarians to ally themselves with conservatives, Rothbard wrote,

> By the end of World War II, it was second nature for libertarians to consider themselves at an "extreme right-wing" pole, with the conservatives immediately to the left of them—hence the great error of the spectrum that persists to this day. In particular, the modern libertarians forgot (or never realized) that opposition to war and militarism had always been a left-wing tradition which had included libertarians. Thus when the historical aberration of the New Deal period corrected itself and the "right wing" was once again the great partisan of total war, the libertarians were unprepared to understand what was happening and tailed along in the wake of their supposed conservative "allies." The liberals had completely lost their old ideological markings and guidelines.[43]

With the end of the Cold War, however, the advocates of total war have no one to make war *on*. A new movement is growing on the Right which opposes the concept of the U.S. as the world's policeman, attacks foreign aid, and calls on America to "come home." These are the paleoconservatives, and their rise signaled to Rothbard that it was time for another major turn: time to re-cement the ties that the alliance with the New Left had sundered and to recreate the Old Right coalition. For the main danger to liberty in the nineties, argues Rothbard, comes not from the extreme Right or the extreme Left, but from the old Social Democracy, the Mensheviks, who survived their Bolshevik rivals by adopting a "neoconservative" disguise. The neocon–social democrats are bad, from a Rothbardian perspective, on virtually every issue: they are pro-interventionist "almost as a high principle," and they are pledged to keep the New Deal virtually intact, preserving the welfare state while, perhaps, tinkering a bit around the edges. "In short," wrote Rothbard,

> on all crucial issues, social democrats stand against liberty and tradition, and in favor of statism and Big Government. They are more dangerous in the long run than the Communists not simply because they have endured, but also because their program and their

rhetorical appeals are far more insidious, since they claim to combine socialism with the appealing virtues of "democracy" and freedom of inquiry. For a long while they stubbornly refused to accept the libertarian lesson that economic freedom and civil liberties are of a piece; now, in their second line of retreat, they give lip service to some sort of "market," suitably taxed, regulated, and hobbled by a massive welfare-warfare State.[44]

The old conservative consensus of the Reagan years is finished, and an internecine war as bitter as the blood feuds now wracking the Soviet Union is splitting the Right. In response to the takeover of leading conservative institutions by neocon operatives, and a systematic campaign to smear all opposition to the new orthodoxy, a leading paleoconservative, Patrick J. Buchanan, has already sounded the clarion call to arms. In the summer of 1991, he reported in his syndicated column on an article by Old Right scholar Paul Gottfried which contends that the neocons "now control the money spigot of the American Right" and have systematically smeared their opponents as "racists" and "fascists." Buchanan asks, "Who are they, and what do they believe?" His answer:

> Ex–Great Society liberals, almost all of them, they support the welfare state and Big Government. They are pro-civil rights and affirmative action, though anti-quota. They are pro-foreign aid, especially for Israel. . . . Many are viscerally hostile to the Old Right, and to any America First foreign policy. They want to use America's wealth to promote "global democracy" abroad and impose "democratic values" in our public schools.
>
> They have openly embraced "Big Government Conservatism," (an oxymoron if ever there was one) and globalism, neither of which has roots in the movement. They have introduced the nastiness of the far Left into the arguments of the Right. While they may control its foundations, they have never won the movement's heart; and they do not have its young. Though in Washington their apparatchiks seem everywhere, in number they are few. Like the fleas who con-

clude they are steering the dog, their relationship to the movement has always been parasitical.

Buchanan concludes by recommending to his fellow conservatives a good dose of flea powder:

> With the unifying issue of anti-Communism fading, the deep disagreements between the neocons and traditional conservatives are surfacing. And the time to split the blanket has probably arrived. Before true conservatives can ever take back the country, they are going to have to take back their movement.

The neoconservatives may have a lock on the big money and access to the media, but in the ranks of the Right a rebellion is brewing. Who and what are these rebels who call themselves paleoconservatives? What is the nature of this new movement, which is rising to challenge the neocons and displace the old cold-warrior conservatism of Bill Buckley's *National Review*?

At the beginning of this chapter, we raised the question of whether some ingredient essential to the success of the conservative movement had been lost in the *National Review* purges. At this point the answer is clear. For the one trait the various excommunicates share, in spite of their many differences, is that each can trace their lineage back to the Old Right tradition so eagerly buried by the Buckleyites. This, then, is the missing ingredient, the essential factor thoughtlessly discarded. It is no surprise, therefore, that a new movement on the Right has arisen to reclaim what has been lost.

9

The Paleoconservative Revolt

Most of us "neo-isolationists," a disparate, contentious lot, are really not "neo" anything. We are old church and old right, anti-imperialist and anti-intervention-ist, disbelievers in Pax Americana. We love the old republic, and when we hear phrases like "New World Order," we release the safety catches on our revolvers.
— *Patrick J. Buchanan*

The end of the Cold War and the subsequent identity crisis of conservatism has produced a fascinating phenomenon on the Right: paleoconservatism. The prefix *paleo,* according to *Merriam-Webster's Dictionary,* means *old* or *ancient* and "is used to denote remote in the past." In the context of the crisis of conservatism, it means getting back to first principles and uncovering the buried legacy of the Old Right. This development could transform and revitalize the conservative movement in the nineties—and, perhaps, change the face of American politics.

When the Communist empire collapsed like a house of cards, some conservatives looked for new enemies to conquer. But others were reminded of the original concept of the Right's anticommunist crusade as a *temporary* expedient, an extended but necessary diversion from the main task of building a free society. And they began to wonder whether America's alleged moral obligation to right every wrong, patrol every disputed border, and dole out an ever-increasing amount of foreign aid to would-be "democrats" had become an intolerable burden. Although other deep fissures would soon crack the veneer of conservative unity, it was a foreign-policy issue—the Iraq war—that heralded the coming split.

Paleoconservatism is not an ideology, i.e., a self-conscious and fully integrated worldview, but only a prelude to one. It is surely self-conscious, in that its proponents see themselves as a movement intent on preserving basic principles against the neoconservative incursion. And yet it is not fully integrated; it implies more than it says. As the most well-known, and certainly the leading paleoconservative commentator, 1992 Republican presidential hopeful Patrick J. Buchanan embodies both the self-consciousness and the ambiguity that characterize this new insurgency on the Right.

Patrick J. Buchanan: Putting America First

Buchanan is the tough-talking, street fighting conservative polemicist who served two Republican presidents and whose verbal fireworks on CNN's *Crossfire* made him a media star. Blunt, fearlessly honest, quick to entangle his opponents in arguments of Jesuitical complexity, has become a hero to a new generation of young conservative activists.

The facile explanation of Buchanan makes him out to be a blue-collar Bill Buckley, but in fact the two are opposites. Unlike Buckley, who still defends a conservative orthodoxy that crumbled with the Berlin Wall, Buchanan is a rebel. Against the globalist pretensions of the neoconservatives, who want to export "democracy" to every Third World hellhole on earth—no matter how distant or how hellish—he has raised the banner of a new American nationalism. While such champions of empire as Jack Kemp and columnist Charles Krauthammer see the end of the Cold War as an opportunity to institutionalize America's manifest destiny as nursemaid to the world, Buchanan raises the battle cry of the *New* New Right: *"America, Come Home!"*

In a remarkable essay penned in response to Krauthammer's proclamation of a "new universalism" in the neoconservative journal the *National Interest*, Buchanan outlines what he calls "a New Nationalism." Not nationalism of the imported European variety, a rationale for imperial ambitions and military adventurism, but a tendency toward introspection; a celebration, not of empire, but of America's republican virtues. Attacking ideological special-interest groups which substitute "an extra-national ideal for the national interest," he writes that "each sees our national purpose in another continent or country; each treats our Republic as a means to some larger end." For Buchanan, the American Republic is an end in itself. Citing George Washington's Farewell Address, he questions the wisdom of virtually every U.S. intervention, from the conquest of the Philippines to World War II. "For a century after Washington's death," he writes, "we resisted the siren's call of empire. Then, Kipling's call to 'Take up the white man's burden' fell upon the receptive ears of President William McKinley, who came down from a sleepless night of consulting the Almighty to tell the press: 'God told me to take the Philippines.' We were launched."[1]

But, says Buchanan, the great crusade to cleanse the world of tyrants violated the natural inclinations of most ordinary Americans, who resisted sending soldiers overseas prior to both world wars. Would-be empire-builders and world-savers therefore had to invent some compelling reason, some makeshift ideology, in order to justify the spilling of American blood.

> "To make the world safe for democracy," we joined an alliance of empires, British, French and Russian, that held most of mankind in colonial captivity. Washington's warning proved prophetic. Doughboys fell in places like the Argonne and Belleau Wood, in no small measure to vindicate the Germanophobia and Anglophilia of a regnant Yankee elite. When the great "war to end war" had fertilized the seed bed that produced Mussolini, Hitler and Stalin, Americans, by 1941, had concluded a blunder had been made in ignoring the wise counsel of their Founding Father.[2]

Although he bows in the direction of the militant anticommunism that made him Oliver North's most passionate defender, it is clear Buchanan has learned the lesson of the great anticommunist revolution of 1989. "From Berlin to Bucharest to Beijing," he writes, "as Lord Byron observed, 'Who would be free, themselves must strike the blow.' "[3]

Projecting the demise of communism in the Soviet Union—before the event—and positing the withdrawal of the Red Army from Central Europe, Buchanan called for the total withdrawal of U.S. troops from the NATO nations. He celebrates the fact that "the day of the realpoliticians, with their Metternichian 'new architectures,' balance-of-power stratagems, and hidden fear of a world where their op-ed articles and televised advice are about as relevant as white papers from Her Majesty's Colonial Office, is over."[4]

In raising the banner of noninterventionism, of "a new foreign policy that puts America First, and not only first, but second and third as well," Buchanan is challenging the global mind-set that has long dominated American foreign policy. Calling for U.S. withdrawal from a South Korea perfectly able to defend itself, he asks, "If Kim Il Sung attacks, why should Americans be first to die?" And then he declares, "It is time we began uprooting the global network of 'tripwires,' planted on foreign soil, to ensnare the United States in the wars of other nations, to back commitments made and treaties signed before this generation of American soldiers was even born."[5]

Buchanan was quick to challenge the wisdom of mobilizing America's military might on behalf of the emir of Kuwait. While holding no brief for the Iraqi dictator, he dared to challenge those who compared Saddam Hussein to Hitler. "Recall that Hitler, after annexing Austria and establishing a 'protectorate' over Czechoslovakia, overran Poland, Norway, Denmark, Belgium, Holland, France, Yugoslavia, Greece, the Baltic states, and drove 1,000 miles into the Soviet Union—in two years. . . . And Saddam Hussein? For all his bluster, he has thus far managed the land grab of a tiny, defenseless kingdom, not half the size of Denmark."[6]

On the August 24, 1990, broadcast of *The McLaughlin Group*, the weekly must-see PBS program for the nation's political junkies, Buchanan brought out the big guns, denouncing the war drive in no uncertain terms. In a somewhat snide account of the split in the conservative ranks over the war issue, *Time* magazine quoted Buchanan as saying, "There are lots of things worth fighting for, but an extra 10 cents for a gallon of gas isn't one of them."[7]

In spite of the fact that he had been keeping his criticism of the war party rather low-key in the first weeks of the Gulf crisis, Buchanan was viciously attacked by the *New Republic*'s Morton Kondracke on *The McLaughlin Group* for not joining in the orgy of war hysteria. Pat's erstwhile friends in the conservative movement also piled on. In an editorial, "Come Home America?" the editors of *National Review* scolded Buchanan for forgetting that "isolationism is always contextual." While conceding that "a careful rethinking of the American role abroad is certainly called for," the editors were horrified by the prospect of telling our European allies that they had better start paying for their own defense. But, they spluttered, "No European head of government wishes to see a precipitate withdrawal of American forces." What they want to see is the free ride they've been getting at Uncle Sam's expense extended into the indefinite future. According to *National Review*, U.S. troops "represent a guarantee of regional stability, and for the smaller nations, a hedge against a resurgent Germany."[8] In other words, U.S. troops are going to be the guarantors of the new European order, serving as a peacekeeping force to mediate the disputes of the Germans and the Poles, the Czechs and the Slovaks, the Hungarian and the Romanians, the Serbs and the Croatians. As for the alleged danger of "a resurgent Germany"—why didn't they mention this when they were cheering the downing of the Berlin Wall? Even Soviet propagandists prior to the fall of communism had long since ceased to speak as if the Germany of the Federal Republic were the reincarnation of the Third Reich. Why did *National Review* pick up where *Pravda* had left off?

"Questions should be asked," they say, "but not answered on the basis of a predisposition toward isolationism or interventionism." What this really means is that there is no reason to prefer peace over war, or a war in defense of the homeland over a colonial adventure. In this view, it doesn't matter whether we are spilling American blood to defend our own shores, to "make the world safe for democracy"—or to make the world safe for the sheik of Araby. Now that communism has collapsed, yesterday's professional anticommunists are telling us that "[i]solationism is contextual." What, then, *is* the context? Today, the United States is unchallenged in its role as the only superpower, threatened by none, respected and feared by its enemies, and admired and emulated by its many friends throughout the world. It is the conservative globalists, not Buchanan, who are ignoring the context.

This attack by *National Review* was as nothing compared to the vicious assault launched by the neocons and their allies in the media once Buchanan's presidential bid took shape. In its mindless ferocity and utter disregard for truth, the neocon smear campaign against Buchanan rivaled that conducted by the Popular Front left-liberals against John T. Flynn. The only difference is that it was far less successful.

The Smear Campaign

Every war in American history has provoked a domestic witch-hunt against dissent, and the Iraq war proved to be no exception. In World War I, it was Eugene Debs and the Left who were rounded up and jailed; prior to World War II, the anti-interventionist America First Committee was smeared with the "pro-Nazi" brush. The Korean War and the onset of the Cold War witnessed the onslaught of McCarthyism, while the Vietnam War provided the raison d'être for a domestic covert operation aimed at disrupting the antiwar movement.

In each case, the interventionists carefully prepared public opinion to accept the idea of a public lynching. The propaganda mills were churning overtime to convince the average American that the enemy represented such a dire threat to our survival as a nation that it was necessary to root out potential "fifth columnists." As the Iraq war got underway, the well-oiled propaganda machine of the interventionists singled out its most vocal and fearless opponent for a particularly vicious and unrelenting attack.

When Pat Buchanan dared to stand virtually alone against the war hysteria, and raise his voice in protest against the criminal prospect of American boys dying in a war to make the world safe for Arab emirs, the word went out in pro-war circles: *Get Buchanan!* After a few preliminary skirmishes launched in the pages of *National Review* and the *New Republic*, Buchanan's neoconservative enemies brought out the big guns. *New York Times* columnist A. M. Rosenthal, having tired of trying to convince his readers that German reunification meant the reincarnation of the Third Reich, turned his attention to the home front. Quoting Buchanan to the effect that "there are only two groups that are beating the drums for war in the Middle East, the Israeli Defense Ministry and its amen corner in the United States," Rosenthal screeched that this is "blood libel" and constitutes "venom about Jews."[9]

Rosenthal claimed that he "did not address the Buchanan situation before because it was so distasteful. I was sick at the thought of the Buchanian nastiness I would have to recount." The truth is that Rosenthal and his warmongering friends were sick at the thought of a well-known and articulate opponent with access to the media—and, in desperation, launched a smear campaign that made the worst of Joe McCarthy's antics seem relatively tame.

Rosenthal's litany of Buchanan's alleged acts of anti-Semitism dissolves under even the most cursory analysis. He waxes indignant that "in one column, he [Buchanan] denounced five people for supporting military action against Iraq—all Jews, including me." The proper answer to this is, *so what*? If Rosenthal was going to go on the record as advocating an all-out air war against Iraq, did he imagine that his Jewishness immunized him against all criticism? In fact, Buchanan attacked Rosenthal, Kissinger, Richard Perle, and the "let's flatten Iraq" crowd because they are warmongers, *not* because they are of the Jewish faith. Rosenthal's vile smear was a brazen attempt to equate antiwar sentiment with anti-Semitism.

According to Rosenthal, Buchanan defends "war criminals" because he dared suggest that the trial and conviction of John Demjanjuk as a Nazi criminal was *a case of mistaken identity*—a position which has no more to do with anti-Semitism than Rosenthal's smear campaign has to do with truth. As for Buchanan's charge that Congress is "Israeli-occupied territory," the irony is that the veracity of this was proven even as the Rosenthal smear saw print. In its rush to war, the Bush White House thought it would have no trouble pushing a multibillion-dollar arms sale to the Saudis through Congress—and was rudely reminded of the power of the Israeli lobby, which forced the president to back down. Apparently not even war hysteria is enough to neutralize the power of AIPAC.

The most absurd—and potentially the most dangerous—of Rosenthal's assertions is that Buchanan's concern over the "de-Christianization" of America was really a "code-word" for anti-Semitism. In other words, *all* the many critics of secularism are anti-Semites, along with all critics of the Gulf War—an equation that should make the *real* anti-Semites jump for joy.

Rosenthal accused Buchanan of "demeaning the Holocaust," but in fact it was Rosenthal who was doing the demeaning. By invoking the slaughter of millions as the justification for smearing a man whose only "crime" was to speak out against the war hysteria, Rosenthal cheapened the memory of the Holocaust.

The hate campaign against Buchanan soon took on the characteristics of a lynch mob. Rosenthal's allies, not content to smear Buchanan's good name, contacted newspaper editors and threatened them with dire consequences if they continued to carry Buchanan's column. The *New York Post*, a cheap tabloid that caters to its readers' appetites for grisly murders, society scandals, and every other form of crass sensationalism, joined the fracas, echoing Rosenthal's libel and adding a few of its own. The purpose of this lynch mob, described by Buchanan in a column, was "to frighten, intimidate, censor, and silence: to cut off debate; to so smear men's reputations that no one will listen to them again; to scar men so indelibly, that no one will ever look at them again without saying, 'Say, isn't he an anti-Semite?' "[10]

The purpose of the "Get Buchanan" campaign was aptly summed up in a *San Francisco Chronicle* headline over an Associated Press story: "Forget Iraq—Columnists Warring Over Jews and U.S. Policy."[11] This, of course, is exactly what the pro-war crowd was counting on. They didn't—and don't—want to debate the pros and cons of a U.S.-imposed New World Order. Instead, it suited their purposes perfectly to focus on the alleged motives of their critics. The idea was to divert attention away from the *real* issue of whether we had any legitimate interests in starting a war with Saddam Hussein.

Rosenthal's smear-job was just the opening shot. As the war hysteria mounted, the neocons stepped up their attack. For sheer viciousness, nothing surpassed the hate campaign unleashed in the *New Republic*. "No, he is not like Hitler," said the editors; but "Hitler," they intoned, "cannot be allowed to set the standard."[12] Thus, the stage was set to smear *anyone* who dared identify the existence of a powerful Israeli lobby—let alone criticize it—as the moral equivalent of a Nazi.

The editors of the *New Republic*—or, at least, the publisher—thought that Buchanan's anti-war stance "drips with hostility to Jews" because he listed the four most prominent and strident advocates of a U.S. first strike, all of whom happen to be Jewish, while writing that the victims of this war are likely to be "kids with names like McAllister, Murphy, Gonzales, and Leroy Brown." No, Buchanan was *not* "suggesting that kids with names like Rosenthal have never died for this country," as the *New Republic* asserts—only that some individuals (including one named Rosenthal, whom the *Nation* calls one of "Israel's personal messengers to the *New York Times*") couldn't wait for the shooting to start. Martin Peretz and his cadre of character assassins hoped to pin the "anti-Semite" label on Buchanan before he began to mobilize conservatives against Bush's war. The reality, however, is that Buchanan's remarks merely reflected the widely held view that the interests of the United States and Israel were diverging.

The pro-war intelligentsia, led by the *New Republic*, had by this time worked itself up into a frothy-mouthed frenzy, and was no longer either willing or able to distinguish fantasy from reality. Their analogy of the manufactured "crisis" in the Middle East as equivalent to pre–World War II Europe—a gross exaggeration, to say the least—was now blown up into a full delusional system. Not only was Saddam Hussein supposed to be a latter-day Hitler, but "Charles Lindbergh has found an heir" in Pat Buchanan.[13] In their eagerness to put the clock back and land us in a time when the world was on the brink of mass destruction, the interventionist smear mongers left out more than a few details. In his notorious Des Moines speech, Lindbergh spoke of what he saw as undue Jewish "ownership and influence" over the media. Buchanan has made no such charge. Lindbergh was, in the words of Ronald Radosh, an advocate of a "corporatist collectivist state," while Buchanan is a free marketeer who believes in strictly limited government.

For insisting that the prosecution of John Demjanjuk was a case of mistaken identity, suggesting that the Justice Department ought to have better things to do than track down everyone who ever served in the German army, and pointing out that the department's Office of Special Investigation had long since outlived its original function, the *New Republic* called him a "Holocaust revisionist." Never mind that Buchanan does *not* deny the Holocaust, but merely questions the political agenda of those who have made a career out of using it as a bludgeon against their political opponents. In the Martin Peretz school of character assassination, such distinctions are routinely ignored. The idea is to bury your opponent in a mudslide of such proportions that he will never dig himself out.

The *New Republic*'s diatribe was based almost word-for-word on a hit piece widely circulated by the Anti-Defamation League of B'nai B'rith.[14] As "evidence" of Buchanan's supposed anti-Semitism, the ADL offered up columns which allegedly "deny the Jewish centrality of the Holocaust" and quote Buchanan as writing "[f]ilms, books, plays speak of Hitler's pogrom: *no one denies it*; what is being resisted is a systematic campaign to exclude all others from the honor roll of the dead." [Emphasis added.] *This* is anti-Semitism? The ADL also stupidly denounced Buchanan for expressing his pro-life views "by equating abortion to the Nazi war crimes," never once realizing that this, for Buchanan, is a terrible indictment, his way of remarking on the gravity of the Nazi crimes—and, by the way, effectively *refuting* the outrageous charge that he is a "Holocaust revisionist."[15]

Unlike the persecution and blacklisting suffered by John T. Flynn and Garet Garrett, the campaign against Buchanan had very limited success. The poisonous farrago of lies, distortions, and innuendo spread by Rosenthal and the neocons backfired. When asked, on *The McLaughlin Group*, whether they gave any credence to the charges against Buchanan, his journalist colleagues—Eleanor Clift of *Newsweek*, Jack Germond of the *Baltimore Sun*, and Fred Barnes—came to his defense.[16]

The Iraq war was a turning point for Buchanan and for the emerging paleoconservative tendency, exposing the faultlines in what used to be the conservative united front. For the first time, many on the Right came to question in public the globalist doctrine of America as the world's policeman. Not only Buchanan but a plethora of right-wing journalists, publicists, and activists came out against Bush's war for the New World Order: newspaper columnists Charley Reese and Joe Sobran; publisher Henry Regnery; Phil Nicolaides, a former deputy director of Voice of America; William Niskanen, head of the Council of Economic Advisors under Reagan; the prominent free-market economist Robert Hessen; and many others. Particularly eloquent was Reese, whose depth of passion reflected the deep split in the ranks of the Right:

> Several prominent conservatives, among them Reed Irvine of Accuracy in Media, have actually advocated using nuclear weapons against Iraq. As a colleague, Joseph Sobran so correctly put it, that is advocating mass murder of innocent civilians.
>
> What have Iraqi schoolchildren ever done to America conservatives that they deserve to be incinerated, horribly maimed, and poisoned with radiation? Are you afraid of children? Do you hate people just because you don't know them? I'm sorry anybody ever called me a conservative. Don't do it anymore. I don't wish to be associated with people who think the price of oil is worth mass murder of children. I don't want to be associated with anyone who is so weak-brained as to be so easily manipulated into joining a lynch mob.[17]

While crystallizing a noninterventionist faction of conservatives, the Iraq war also underscored the existence—and power—of the small group of neoconservatives. If a movement is in large part defined by its enemies, then the prominence of the neocons in the attempted lynching of Pat Buchanan did much to draw the line of demarcation for the paleoconservatives.

But it is not enough to have enemies. A successful ideological movement must have a positive program, a coherent and consistent self-concept. Buchanan has done much to provide both, especially on the key issue of foreign policy. While the clownish Dan Quayle burbled about "the McGovern–Buchanan Axis" and complained that "[t]here is a strain of neo-isolationist sentiment in our party," Buchanan drew his own line in the sand:

> Most of us "neo-isolationists," a disparate, contentious lot, are really not "neo" anything. We are old church and old right, anti-imperialist and anti-interventionist, disbelievers in Pax Americana. We love the old republic, and when we hear phrases like "New World Order," we release the safety catches on our revolvers."[18]

The Trade Issue: Nationalism and Liberty

After the Iraq war, Buchanan turned his attention to the home front, denouncing the Bush sellout on the tax issue and bemoaning the fact that "the Republican Party has made a separate peace with the welfare state. Whatever disposition there was in the Reagan era to roll back Great Society socialism, it has dissipated if not disappeared." The only hope, he wrote, is the taxpayers: "The permanent tax revolt is capitalism's last best hope." Buchanan got more radical on economic issues as the issue of the Iraq war faded, calling for the abolition of the federal income tax and attacking such liberal Republicans as California governor Pete Wilson.[19] However, this increasingly libertarian tendency was in conflict with some aspects of Buchanan's ardent nationalism.

The nationalism of the Old Right was, and is, in large part a celebration of the American character: of individualism, of initiative, of the pioneer virtues. However, there is another, anti-libertarian aspect to this nationalist spirit in Buchanan's writings, expressed in his contention that "a foreign policy that looks out for America First should be married to an economic policy that considers first the well-being of our own workers." There has always been a strain of protectionist sentiment among conservatives, and the Old Right was particularly prone to it. Having revived the Old Right with all its virtues, Buchanan has also resurrected its major flaw. Thus, he writes,

On one foreign policy issue, virtually all of America's men of words, columnist and commentator, Left and Right, are agreed: Free trade must remain a pillar of U.S. economic and foreign policy.

The unanimity, methinks, is coming to an end. Events conspire against the consensus. T. S. Eliot once said that there are no true lost causes, because there are no true "won" causes. The endless battle between free traders and protectionists is about to re-erupt. . . .[20]

Noting Pat Choate's best-selling *Agents of Influence*, which details how top U.S. officials "have gone geisha for the economic Empire of the Rising Sun," Buchanan continues,

Critics may dismiss Mr. Choate's book as "Japan-bashing." But it has touched a chord. Suspicion of Japan is not only related to race, or the performance of the imperial army in the Bataan Death March, but to a sense that Tokyo's trade policy in 1990 is a bastard child of Hirohito's imperial policy in 1940. It is related to a sense that Japan's invasions of U.S. markets have been plotted at the highest levels in Tokyo with the same thoroughness with which Admiral Isoroku Yamamoto plotted Pearl Harbor, that Japan's objective is to go the "economic road" to acquire hegemony in Asia and the world her army and navy were unable to win half a century ago.

What kind of "imperial policy" is it that inundates an "enemy" nation, not with bombs and troops, but with low-priced, high-quality VCRs, automobiles, and computer chips—thus *raising* the standard of living? If this is Japanese "imperialism," then we need *more* of it! If Japanese companies are wining "hegemony" in Far Eastern and American markets, it is because their products are superior, cheaper, and thus more desirable. What kind of "hegemony" is this? It is, in fact, the hegemony of the *consumer*, in America and around the world.

Buchanan raises the bogeyman of Japan's "subsidized cartels," which supposedly have an unfair advantage over their U.S. competitors. But this is a canard spread by American liberals and trade unionists, who want to shut Japan out of U.S. markets in order to create American cartels. If subsidies to business and economic planning didn't work in what used to be the Soviet Union and the formerly socialist countries, then why should they work in Japan? In fact, Japan's economic success is due, not to MITI, but to Japanese upstart companies, as well as cultural factors, such as a strong work ethic, a highly developed sense of company loyalty, and a compulsion to save.

Buchanan knows all this, however:

> But free trade is the one most efficient allocator of goods, runs the economic argument. Undeniably. If Chinese are making tennis shoes for $2 a pair, selling them for $8 a pair, America's poor benefit by not having to pay $20 for shoes made in the U.S.A. . . . But if recession hits hard, amid a perception Uncle Sam has thrown open markets to foreigners who are closing theirs, the argument from efficiency will not carry the house. The arguments of the head will lose to the arguments of the heart. Let's take care of our own.

It is often hard to tell what Buchanan really thinks when he falls into his reportorial mode. Is he merely predicting the popular mood, or is he projecting his own opinions? More than likely, a little of both. He goes on to cite William Gill's book, *Trade Wars Against America*, as his source for the myth that

> America thrived during the nineteenth century . . . with no income tax, behind a wall of tariffs that raised 50 percent to 90 percent of all federal revenue, while the Brits, devoted to free-trade principles, lost their economic primacy to the protectionist United States.

The fact is that the British Empire was brought down by the inner rot of socialism and the debasement of its currency. Facts also contradict Buchanan's equation of a foreign policy of America First with building a tariff wall. As Murray Rothbard has shown, historically protectionism and a policy of foreign entanglements and do-gooder meddling have been allied. For example, the tariffs imposed during the twenties were part of an inflationary policy designed to help foreign governments and American exporters:

To supply foreign countries with the dollars needed to purchase American exports, the United States government decided *not* sensibly to lower tariffs, but instead to promote cheap money at home, thus stimulating foreign borrowing and checking the gold inflow from abroad. Consequently, the resumption of American inflation on a grand scale in 1924 set off a foreign lending boom, which reached a peak in mid-1928. It also established American trade, not on a solid foundation of reciprocal and productive exchange, but on a feverish promotion of loans later revealed to be unsound. Foreign countries were hampered in trying to sell their goods to the United States, but were encouraged to borrow dollars. But afterward, they could not sell goods to repay; they could only try to borrow more at an accelerated pace to repay the loans. Thus, in an indirect but nonetheless clear manner, American protectionist policy must shoulder some of the responsibility for our inflationist policy of the 1920s.

Who benefited, and who was injured, by the policy of protection *cum* inflation as against the rational alternative of free trade and hard money? Certainly, the bulk of the American population was injured, both as consumers of imports and as victims of inflation and poor foreign credit and later depression. Benefited were the industries protected by the tariff, the export industries uneconomically subsidized by foreign loans, and the investment bankers who floated the foreign bonds at handsome commissions.[21]

Rothbard cites Professor Frank W. Fetter's observation that "[f]oreign loans were glorified by the same political leaders who wanted bigger and better trade restrictions, entirely oblivious to the problems involved in the repayment of such loans."[22]

In the twenties, those foreign loans were private; today, of course, the United States government has taken on the role of international banker to the underprivileged nations of the world, with a plethora of government-to-government loans and loan guarantees. This is the foreign-aid giveaway that Buchanan relentlessly attacks—and which is supported by the same big-business special interests that ceaselessly agitate for protectionism. *They* know where their true interests lie, even if Buchanan is confused about his.

Although on this issue Buchanan's libertarian impulses are overwhelmed by other instincts, the main tendency of his politics is profoundly anti-statist. On the central issues of the day—foreign policy and the domestic economy—his position is indistinguishable from the Old Right libertarian opposition to big government and empire-building.

In the post–Cold War world, libertarians and authentic conservatives are rediscovering their common Old Right heritage not in order to satisfy some purely scholarly impulse, but out of political necessity. For the fact is that, in the nineties, these two anti-statist tendencies constitute the sole opposition to the welfare-warfare state. When both liberals and neoconservatives were cheerleading George Bush's war for the New World Order, it was only the paleoconservatives led by Buchanan and the libertarians who dared dissent. As the neoconservatives whisper sweet nothings in the ear of the managerial elite, proffering unsolicited advice on how best to make the social democratic status quo more efficient, only the paleoconservatives and their libertarian first cousins call for its overthrow.

Like his Old Right ancestors, Buchanan is culturally conservative: that is, he sees the disintegration of the family and the breakdown of the moral order in society as corrosive and ultimately fatal. For him, liberty is not enough. In this view, the free society is only possible if nurtured by a healthy culture—or, at the very least, a culture which does not seek to destroy its own traditions and its own young. This is enough to differentiate him and his fellow paleoconservatives from the all-too-many libertarians who have confused legalization of drugs and unconventional lifestyles with defending and even advocating such activities.

The New Fusionism and the Old Right Revival

The paleoconservative revolt, which had been bubbling just beneath the surface for some time, erupted in full force in the months prior to the outbreak of the Iraq war. While most of the conservative press marched in lockstep to the war drums beaten by George Bush and the neocons, *Chronicles* magazine, published by the Rockford Institute, let loose with a barrage of withering scorn. Editor Tom Fleming wrote that he could "find no conceivable justification for sending in American boys to die fighting for this or that group of heroic democrats or gangster allies. If the Russian bear has really clipped his claws . . . then the last pretext for American interventionism has been taken away."[23] Striking a posture that is the essence of the nose-thumbing, bad-boy paleo spirit, Fleming declared,

> Better a world torn apart by Husseins and Qaddafis, better a war to the knife between the PLO and the Likud Party, between Zulus and Afrikaaners, than a world run by George Balls and Dag Hammarskjölds, because a world made safe for democracy is a world in which no one dares to raise his voice for fear that mommy will put you away some place where you can be reeducated.[24]

In an issue of *Chronicles* devoted to the timely theme "Conservative Movement, R.I.P.?" Fleming mourned the transformation of American conservatism into "a narrow-minded ideology that justified the high salaries of fundraisers and foundation managers." Nostalgic for the days when Louis Bromfield, Rose Wilder Lane, and Ayn Rand "could all be read with respect by people who looked to George Stigler and Milton Friedman for economic wisdom," he pointed out that "all were anti-Communist, but there was no consensus on the Cold War. The hysteria over containing and/or rolling back the Communists was manufactured almost entirely by ex-Communists who . . . wildly overestimated the abilities of their former co-conspirators." Fleming has little or no use for the new conservative movement where

> Pat Buchanan is regarded as a dangerous bigot, while A. M. Rosenthal of the *New York Times* is celebrated as a great conservative commentator. Welfare is not evil *per se*, and only needs some adjustments—enterprise zones, workfare, and educational choice—to make it an issue that can secure votes for Republicans, jobs for conservatives, and contracts for loyal supporters "in the community."[25]

Fleming calls for a New Fusionism, which combines a love of liberty with the Old Right insight that, as Garet Garrett put it, "the revolution was," or as Fleming says:

> It is too late to think about conserving. There is not much left of the old Republic, which has been bloated into a swollen and cancerous empire that threatens to devour all the life and energy that still exists. We don't need to reform the nation; we need to take it back from the occupying army of government officials and managers and interest groups that treat the citizenry like a conquered people.[26]

The "mainstream" conservatives, who are busy thinking up new rationales for welfare in the name of the "opportunity society" and trumpeting the dawn of the New World Order, will (in the short run) enjoy

> a brilliant success. They have a lock on all the money and all the institutions created by the right; they have established a cozy relationship with the leftist establishment media who recognize them for what they are: safe and well-groomed lapdogs who bark but never bite. When the day comes that they are no longer needed, the conservatives will be treated like a lower-class sweetheart picked up for a summer affair. I only hope they're given carfare for the long ride home back to their side of town.[27]

Fleming's acerbic commentary was complemented, in that issue of *Chronicles*, with a fascinating analysis of the conservative movement—past, present, and future—by Samuel Francis, syndicated columnist and deputy editorial page director of the *Washington Times*, whose prose is one of the chief assets of the magazine. "Beautiful Losers: The Failure of American Conservatism" is a perceptive critique and history of the conservative movement, the theme of which is nearly identical to that of this book: American conservatism is a failure, and the roots of that failure are to be found within itself—an internal rot that has led those who today call themselves conservatives "to accept at least the premises and often the full-blown agenda of the left."[28] The egalitarian and globalist premises of the neoconservatives now define what Francis calls the "permissible right." This tame pseudo-conservatism masquerades in a variety of guises: the "Big Government conservatism" touted by Fred Barnes, Jack Kemp's "progressive conservatism," Newt Gingrich's "opportunity society," the "cultural conservative" rationale for welfarism peddled by Paul Weyrich, or the so-called "New Paradigm" of ex-Bush White House aide James Pinkerton. Whatever their differences, they are variations on the theme of big government in the service of "the enhancement of economic opportunity through one kind or another of social engineering."

The problem with these varieties of neoconservatism is that they are concerned with mere process and not with ultimate ends. The Right, says Francis,

> tacitly concedes the goals of public action to its enemies and quietly comes to share the premises on which the goals of the left rest. Eventually, having silently and unconsciously accepted the premises and goals, it will also come to accept even the means by which the left has secured its dominance, and the very distinction between "right" and "left" will disappear.[29]

Thus, the neoconservative "End of Ideology" will come to pass and the entire American political spectrum will be subsumed under what Arthur Schlesinger Jr. hailed as the "Vital Center," i.e., a general and indeed virtually unanimous consensus in favor of social democracy at home and imperial globalism abroad.

Correctly identifying the neoconservative incursion as the source of the internal rot of modern conservatism, Francis is somewhat confused by the history of the problem. He cites none other than our old friend James Burnham as the one who first identified the "ideo-neurological reflexes and knee-jerks of the left" in neoconservative doctrine. Yet he does not seem to realize that Burnham himself was the virtual embodiment of that doctrine. It was Burnham, after all, who dismissed Old Right political goals as impractical, and, as Francis notes, was disdainful of conservative economic doctrine as "obsolescent."

Francis also failed to understand the true role of William F. Buckley Jr., and *National Review*. "The Old Right," Francis tells us, was "composed mainly of the organized conservative resistance formed in the mid-1950s and centered around *National Review.*" In fact, as we have seen, Buckley and his crowd *displaced* the Old Right in a series of ruthless purges. Francis criticizes the Buckleyites for seeking "accommodation with the new managerial-bureaucratic establishment rather than to challenge it." But in fact, the New Right of Buckley and Burnham was never about anything other than *preserving* the status quo, which they were perfectly content to defend so long as the nation's resources were mobilized in a monomaniacal crusade to wipe out communism. In spite of this confusion, Francis homes in on a key point to be made about the evolution of the Right:

> The crucial episode in the assimilation occurred during the Vietnam War, which the Old Right in general supported on the grounds of anticommunism. The war was itself a result of misconceived liberal policies and was effectively lost by liberal mismanagement, and there was no good reason for the right (even the anticommunist right) to support it. Yet, as the New Left mounted an attack on the war and broadened the attack to include the bureaucratized university and parts of the leviathan state, the right's response was to defend not only the war itself and sometimes even the liberal policies that were losing it, but also the liberal power centers themselves. The Old Right critique of containment, mounted by anti-interventionists such as Robert Taft and John T. Flynn, and by anti-communist interventionists such as Burnham, was forgotten, as was much of the Old Right cultural critique of the domestic liberal regime.[30]

This odd error over the role of Buckley and Burnham is peripheral, however, and not really important to the central argument of the Francis piece that the Right has been corrupted by the neoconservative invasion of its ranks.

> It was at this point that the Old Right began to join forces with the emerging neoconservative elements, whose concern was entirely with defending the liberal managerial system, foreign and domestic, and which never had the slightest intention of dismantling it. The

result of the coalition between the Old Right and neoconservatism has been the adoption by the right of Wilsonian-Rooseveltian globalism and its universalist premises, the diffusion of those premises within the right in defense of what are actually the institutions and goals of the left, and the gradual abandonment of the Old Right goals of reducing the size and scope of centralized power. By swallowing the premises of the left's globalist and messianic foreign policy, the right has wound up regurgitating those same premises domestically.[31]

There remains the question, then, of what is to be done? Clearly, Francis believes that something *can* be done. The principal error of the conservative movement, he says, has been to identify itself with an incumbent elite; his prescription is to "rectify that error by a radical alteration of the right's strategy." Abandoning the illusion that it represents an establishment to be " 'conserved,' a new American Right must recognize that its values and goals lie outside and against the establishment and that its natural allies are not in Manhattan, New Haven, and Washington, but in the increasingly alienated and threatened strata of Middle America."

In short, what is needed, says Francis, is a populist revolt. Not a movement of intellectuals directed at the elite, not an attempt to preserve what has already been destroyed, but a grassroots movement against the welfare-warfare state.

How can such a revolt take shape? How can a revolution against a managerial elite that has ruled America since the postwar era be organized and led to victory? Now that we have examined the history not only of the Old Right, but of its neoconservative antithesis; now that we have traced and come to understand how and when the American Right was betrayed and led astray, we can turn to that all-important question.

10
Taking Back America

> No doubt the people know they can have their Republic
> back if they want it enough to fight for it and to pay the
> price. The only point is that no leader has yet appeared
> with the courage to make them choose.
>
> —Garet Garrett

A S AMERICA ENTERS THE POSTCOMMUNIST era, the future appears
to be the British model: social democracy at home and do-good
imperialism abroad. A number of paleoconservative writers have used
the term "welfare-warfare state," a phrase I have employed throughout
this book because it emphasizes the co-dependence of socialism with a
policy of imperialism or globalism. While King George the Geopoliti-
cian played power politics in the Persian Gulf, the inside-the-Beltway
crowd was extending the welfare state at home—and President Clinton
will almost certainly accelerate both trends. In Bill Clinton's America,
and for the foreseeable future, the budget of the United States will be
divvied up among subsidies for big business, officially approved victim
groups, and foreign-aid recipients, all competing for their "fair share" of
the pie. And in the center of it all will be Washington, D.C., the bloated
imperial capital of a "republic" rife with more pomp and circumstance
than any royal court in history.

With the end of the Cold War, the political pressure to reduce
military spending is irresistible. A major component of the welfare-
warfare state, the great jobs-creation machine of the defense industry,

is in danger of running down. If, however, we are going to have a New World Order—if U.S. troops will now enforce United Nations Security Council edicts from Mogadishu to Sarajevo—then the rationale for military spending is restored. Instead of making nuclear missiles, our war industries will be put to work making what we need to police the world: jet fighters, small arms, and camouflage for every terrain. Fueled by public debt and confiscatory taxation, the jobs-creation machine will be brought sputtering to life, with the armed forces and "national service" absorbing most of the excess unemployed. Like the British in their heyday, we will export our unemployed (and unemployable) to distant outposts of empire. Having crippled American business by taxing and regulating it nearly out of existence, bureaucrats will dole out government subsidies for favored industries in the name of "competitiveness." This program of militarism and repackaged central planning is how the Left intends to resuscitate the thoroughly discredited theory of socialism and sneak it in through the backdoor. The polite word for this system is corporate statism, that is, statism which operates for the benefit of certain corporate interests. A more accurate term is fascism. Not the uniformed, goose-stepping variety, but homegrown American fascism of the sort foreseen by John T. Flynn. The advocates of this system will not, of course, call it fascism, says Flynn,

> although some of them frankly see the resemblance. But they are not disturbed, because they know that *they* will never burn books, *they* will never hound the Jews or the Negroes, *they* will never resort to assassination and suppression. What will turn up in their hands will be a very genteel and dainty and pleasant form of fascism which cannot be called fascism at all because it will be so polite and virtuous.[1]

In describing the authors of this fascist system, Flynn elicits in the contemporary reader a sense of déjà vu:

> Many of these men are ex-socialists or academic or parlor pinks who had never become outright socialists. This gentry, numerous in New York City, used almost all of the socialist diagnosis of the

evils of capitalism and, when on that subject, seemed to be talking the doctrine of socialism. But they always held themselves a little above socialism. They were a kind of radical elite. They flourished on the circumference of the radical movements, never quite forming part of them. The black history of Moscow settled their hash as potential communist philosophers. But it did not end their careers as radical aristocrats. They began to flirt with the alluring pastime of reconstructing the capitalist system. And in the process of this new career they began to fashion doctrines that turned out to be the principles of fascism.

Today, more than half a century later, the triumph of Flynn's "radical aristocrats" is complete. The fact that they have immigrated from left to right makes little difference. Yesterday they were New Deal liberals, today they are "neoconservatives," but the result of their powerful influence has the same effect: to preserve and expand the specifically American form of incipient fascism which is the welfare-warfare state.

The Martyrdom of the Middle Class

Before we can begin to answer the question of how to oppose the welfare-warfare state, we must ask and answer yet another question: who benefits and who loses from such a system?

The beneficiaries are, first of all, the managerial and corporate elite. They get first dibs on the loot and dole out what's left to the special interests. In principle, this is no different from the bread and circuses of the late Roman Empire, the New Deal, the Fair Deal, or the Great Society. Our modern radical aristocrats have made one original contribution to this familiar pattern, however, and that is the new science of victimology. This innovation gauges one's right to "entitlements" on the basis of how "oppressed" one is—the more you are victimized, the more you are subsidized. The Washington of the nineties is ruled not by Congress or even the president, but by the lobbyists of every group aspiring to victimhood, competing for the right to rob the taxpayers blind.

Taxed by the patricians for the benefit of the growing underclass, the great American middle class is being ground underfoot. It is they who will bail out the Soviets and bail out the banks, feed Somalia, and meet the payroll of the National Endowment for the Arts. It is their sons and daughters who will be displaced by affirmative-action programs, their values which are mocked and defiled by federally funded "artists"—and their taxes which will pay for the whole sorry mess. Every special interest has a Washington lobbyist. But who will defend the American middle class? They alone are without a voice or a champion. Of course, there are various single-issue taxpayer groups that monitor federal spending and raise questions on specific issues at congressional hearings. But by their nature they cannot voice the populist yearnings of the oppressed taxpayer in any general sense. At any rate, such groups are outgunned and vastly outnumbered in Washington, since both parties have been taken over by welfare statists.

The Democratic Party has long been the captive of the special interests. What really rigs the game against the long-suffering middle class, however, is that the Republican Party, their ostensible defender, has itself fallen prey to the depredations of the right-wing social democrats. In a natural alliance with the old Rockefeller wing of the GOP, the neoconservatives have invaded the Republican Party, and are now getting ready to position one of several potential candidates for 1996.

The Problem: The Great Sellout

The problem is not just in the Republican Party, but in the conservative movement. The American Right is in a wretched state. Just how wretched is indicated in a surrealistic article by neocon godfather Irving Kristol, which proclaims George Bush to be the leader of the conservative movement. The Kristol epistle to the readers of the *Wall Street Journal*, written in the summer of 1991, describes the proceedings of a by-invitation-only conference sponsored by *National Review.*

Kristol does not reveal the names of the movement leaders assembled in solemn conclave to decide the future course of the American Right. But he lets it be known, without quite saying it, that anybody who is or aspires to be anybody in the conservative movement was asked to join this esteemed company. As this assembly of worthies convened, "most of those attending regarded themselves as conservatives first and Republicans second." However, according to Kristol, a strange transformation was effected by the end of this little convention.

> By the end of the meeting, a significant reversal had occurred. It turned out that, under current circumstances, most were Republicans first and conservatives second. George Bush may not have disarmed Saddam Hussein, but he has in large measure disarmed the conservative movement.[2]

Gauging the mood of the meeting, Kristol then focuses on the two issues of foreign policy and abortion. On the former, he detects virtual unanimity:

> Foreign policy was simply not mentioned. The media have been full of stories of how the end of the cold war has generated a sharp division among conservatives, with some committed to "exporting democracy," others urging a new "realism" based on our national interest, and still others trying to revive a version of pre–World War II isolationism. These divisions of opinion are real enough, but they seem not to have had any noticeable political repercussions.

If foreign policy was not even *mentioned*, then one can think of several prominent conservatives who were not invited—which leads us to doubt if the attendees were picked from a pool any broader than the editorial board of the *National Interest*.

Kristol blurs the sharp division on this question by inventing a third, centrist position, the so-called "new realism," which would base U.S. policy on an unspecified interpretation of the national interest. In fact, there is no third alternative somewhere between internationalism, Muravchik-style, and nationalist noninterventionism. Either the foreign policy of the United States is predicated on the defense of U.S.

territory against external military threats, or it is concerned chiefly with other things. There is no middle ground. By counterpoising realism to so-called "isolationism," is Kristol telling us that a foreign policy that puts America first is somehow based on something *other* than national self-interest? In fact, "realism" is a smokescreen for a less messianic interventionism; the difference is one of style, not substance.

Kristol prefers to imagine that the America Firsters of the paleo persuasion are just a small group; he dismisses them as "by far the smallest faction." This shows just how far removed these alleged conservative "leaders" are from their rank-and-file. There is *no* constituency on the Right for the New World Order. And as for "exporting democracy," enthusiasm for such a cause seems limited to those few who will directly benefit: i.e., the publicists, activists, and intellectuals in the neocon orbit, and their friends and hangers-on. In short, this is not exactly a mass movement.

Pat Buchanan was far closer to the conservative sensibility on the question of the New World Order when he wrote,

> Excuse me, this is not conservatism, it is Trilateralism; the foreign policy of David Rockefeller, not Robert Taft. Where in the Constitution is the U.S. Government authorized to send Marines to die for "international order"? Why should they die for "order" and "stability" when the disorder and instability of '89 produced the greatest advances for freedom in half a century? As for the Near East, it has been the scene, for decades, of war and assassination, riot and revolution, the least stable region of the world. To stand before these powerful tides, and say, thus far and no further, is utopianism, not conservatism.[3]

Kristol also dismisses the issue of abortion, because the states will settle that, and then asks what is left of the conservative agenda. The answer, which not even he could evade, is Bush's betrayal of his "no-new-taxes" pledge. When the conversation gets around to this sore subject, Kristol admits to hearing a murmur or two of dissent—and he has an answer for that one, too:

But what's done is done, and the issue today is what strategy makes the most conservative sense. A small minority argued that conservatives could not and should not try to live with that budget agreement. Could not, because the Democrats are already busy subverting the agreement and will put Republican congressmen in the impossible position of voting against popular legislation (health care, veterans' benefits, etc.). Should not, because the economy is in so sickly a condition that tax reform, both of the income tax and capital gains tax, is a precondition both of recovery from the current recession and of future economic growth.

Naturally, "every conservative nerve responded favorably to this Reaganesque approach." But while their hearts said one thing, as Kristol tells it, their heads said quite another. On second thought, says Kristol, it wasn't such a bad budget deal after all; because, you see, "it was not a deal in which nothing was gained . . . namely, severe restrictions on congressional spending over the next several years."

And, besides, "what's done is done." This phrase sums up Kristol's strategic vision: the welfare state is an accomplished fact, and conservatives must reconcile themselves to the social democratic status quo.

In the name of mythical "restrictions" on the budget—which faded as fast as they were announced—the neocons told conservatives that it was futile to put up a fight and that they had no choice but to go along with the Bush program of more new taxes. Kristol's argument boiled down to this: having betrayed his pledge, his party, and the legacy of his predecessor, President Bush was then owed the loyalty of all conservatives in making sure the terms of the deal were strictly observed.

If, as Kristol asserts, Congress was "once again engaged in its familiar strategy of taxing and spending," then conservatives should have and did oppose it because they oppose such policies on principle, not out of any sense of loyalty to President Bush. For it was George Bush who made the taxing and the spending possible, by caving in to the Democrats in the name of a "kinder and gentler" America—and paving the way for future tax hikes. Not only that, but he unleashed American regulatory agencies on American business. Under Bush, the Food and Drug Administration and the Environmental Protection Agency ran amok, while the so-called Clean Air Act and the Americans with Disabilities Act imposed billions in extra costs and eliminated untold thousands of jobs.

Why did conservatives owe Bush their loyalty when he betrayed them on the vital issue of taxes? Because, says Kristol, the president "is now the leader of the conservative movement within the Republican Party. He is not their leader of choice, but he is their leader."

Conservatives, it seems, *never* have a choice. One way or another they are always put in a position of having to suppress their real impulses, at least for the time being, in the interests of some greater good.

Even before his humiliating defeat, the idea that George Bush ever could have been the leader of the conservative movement was patently absurd. In touting this transparently nonsensical proposition, Kristol was essentially telling conservatives that the best thing they could do was to commit suicide—that is, to abolish their movement and dissolve into the Bushian Popular Front.

Most conservatives rejected Kristol's counsel for the same reason they will reject the neoconservatives' bid for leadership of the Right: a healthy instinct for self-preservation. Tainted by the failure of the man they proclaimed the "leader" of the conservative movement, the neocons' future is dim. In spite of their access to millions in foundation money, no amount of money can cover up their intellectual bankruptcy. Nor can it hide the fact that the paleoconservatives represent the true traditions of the Right; not the heritage of Trotskyism-gone-sour, as exemplified by James Burnham, Max Shachtman, and Irving Kristol, but the libertarian populist legacy of the Old Right.

The Nockian "Remnant" kept alive the legacy of laissez-faire and America First when those words were almost the intellectual equivalent of high treason. They preserved that heritage against the time when a revived Old Right should gather the strength to challenge the usurpers. Now that movement, whose very memory had been nearly wiped out and forgotten, is making a resurgence. The battle for the mantle of the Right has begun, and—in spite of the neocons' advantages, not the least of which is financial—authentic conservatives have a good chance to take back their movement from the interlopers.

A great disadvantage of the neoconservatives is their small numbers. For all of Irving Kristol's talk about how the paleos represent "by far the smallest faction," in fact the neocons are the smallest—and, what's more, are likely to remain so. They have never really been interested in building a mass movement. It isn't their style. Instead, they have concentrated on recruiting the elite; placing sympathizers in key positions in the media, government, and academia. Their technique is adapted to manipulating the levers of power and is not suited to building or leading a populist grassroots movement. Elitists in every way, the neocons detest all forms of populism on principle.

In contrast, the paleoconservative program—free markets, low taxes, no affirmative action, no foreign aid, and a foreign policy of America First—is populist to the core. It is a direct appeal to the disenfranchised middle class, a bold and even revolutionary call to arms against the welfare-warfare state. The energy, the vitality, the fervor is all on the paleo side. Did Irving Kristol seriously expect conservatives to go to the barricades for the president's sellout budget amendment—or for the president himself? Certainly such a program was not going to win over the conservative youth; neither, in the long run, will it find much favor among their elders.

The Solution: Take Back Our Movement

After a decade in power, why has the conservative movement failed to make so much as a dent in the growth of big government? This is the question asked at the very beginning of this book, and at this point the answer is readily apparent: *because opponents of the welfare-warfare state long ago lost control of the conservative movement.* The advent of "Big Government conservatism," of conservative mis-leaders who unashamedly sell out for perks and proximity to power, has disoriented and nearly destroyed the American Right and the Republican Party as a cohesive political force. The very idea of George Bush as a man of the Right, let alone its leader, mocks the very concept of American conservatism. Irving Kristol was able to get away with it only as long as the vacuum of leadership on the Right allowed the neoconservatives free reign.

The presidential campaign of Pat Buchanan changed all that. Eight weeks before the New Hampshire primary, Buchanan and his sister, Angela Bay Buchanan, decided it was time to take back their movement and their party—and they made history. Regularly drawing thirty percent of the GOP primary vote against a sitting Republican president, Pat Buchanan took the message of less government and a foreign policy of American First to the people. The Buchanan campaign transformed what had been a growing tendency among a few conservative intellectuals into a movement with a mass base. While the presumed presidential contenders favored by the neoconservatives—Bill Bennett, Jack Kemp, and Texas senator Phil Gramm—tried to sell Kristol's Bush-is-the-king line to rank-and-file conservatives, Buchanan took on the president in New Hampshire, effectively routing King George and his Tory Republicans with thirty-seven percent of the vote.

The paleo revolt is not to be stopped. Before the revolt can become a revolution, however, paleoconservatives must forge a program and devise a strategy. Before they can begin the fight to roll back big government, authentic conservatives must unite behind a campaign to take back America. To take it back from the empire-builders and international do-gooders, and their foreign lobbyist allies, who milk the American taxpayer for billions in foreign aid each year. To take it back from the career "victims" who have used the power of the state to entrench and expand their special privileges. To take it back from the bureaucrats, the special interests, and the politicians who are feeding at the public trough and draining the country dry. To take it back from the corporate, professional, and managerial elites who have seized the reins of power, in the culture as well as in the government, and who threaten what remains of the old republic.

Counterpoised to the British model of a do-gooding, tax-eating bureaucracy at home and a do-gooding, foreign aid-devouring overseas empire, paleoconservatives hold up the distinctly *American* model of limited government at home and strictly limited foreign entanglements—limited, that is, to trade agreements. This was once the majority sentiment in America, and it can be again. But it will not happen without a battle—and a self-conscious paleoconservative movement that honors its Old Right heritage, knows its enemies, and has not forgotten how to fight.

As we contemplate the prospect of a protracted conflict, a war on the Right for the mantle of authentic conservatism (and control of the Republican Party), paleoconservatives would do well to ponder what Garet Garrett says in the final paragraphs of *Rise of Empire*:

> The positions in the lost terrain that have been named are vital. To serve the Republic they must all be stormed and captured. Others are important, but if these are taken the others can wait; but there is still one more, the last and highest of all, and as you approach it you may understand the serpent's sardonic grin. The slopes are steep and barren. No enemy is visible. The enemy is in yourself. For this may be named the Peak of Fortitude.
>
> What you have to face is that the cost of saving the Republic may be extremely high. It could be relatively as high as the cost of setting it up in the first place, one hundred and seventy-five years ago, when love of political liberty was a mighty passion, and people were willing to die for it.
>
> When the economy has for a long time been moving by jet propulsion, the higher the faster, on the fuel of perpetual war and planned inflation, a time comes when you have to choose whether to go on and on and dissolve in the stratosphere, or decelerate. But deceleration will cause a terrific shock. Who will say, "Now!" Who is willing to face the grim and dangerous realities of deflation and depression?
>
> When Moses had brought his people near to the Promised Land he sent out scouts to explore it. They returned with rapturous words for its beauties and its fruits, whereupon the people were shrill with joy, until the scouts said: "The only thing is, this land is inhabited by very fierce men."
>
> Moses said: "Come. Let us fall upon them and take the land. It is ours from the Lord."

> At that the people turned bitterly on Moses, and said: "What a prophet you have turned out to be! So the land is ours if we can take it? We needed no prophet to tell us that."
>
> No doubt the people know they can have their Republic back if they want it enough to fight for it and to pay the price. The only point is that no leader has yet appeared with the courage to make them choose.[4]

Whether a Moses will step forward with the courage to make the country choose is something no one can predict. What we can know is that such an event is far more likely in the not-too-distant future than it was when Garet Garrett's words saw print. *Rise of Empire* was published in 1952, a watershed year for the Old Right. That was the year Wall Street stole the Republican presidential nomination from Robert A. Taft and handed it to Ike, the genial internationalist. With the death of Taft a year later, there was no leader such as Garrett pined for because, after a brief postwar burst of activity, the movement for a free society was entering a dormant stage. The leader that Garet Garrett hoped for, longed for, could not exist in a vacuum. *Rise of Empire* was a letter to the future, a time capsule to be opened on the day when Garrett's message could be heard.

That day dawned with the downing of the Berlin Wall; the collapse of communism liberated not only the peoples of Eastern Europe and the Soviet Union, but also American conservatives. The Cold War froze the conservative movement, locked it into a rigid posture, and effectively ended all debate on the Right. Today, it is no longer an act of thoughtcrime for conservatives to advocate a policy of nonintervention, nor is it a "hate crime" to utter the formerly forbidden words: "America first."

It is a great advance, yet we have far to go. As Garrett said, we need leadership; but this presupposes an organized movement, which assumes a common program and a set of fundamental principles. This is the task of the New Fusionism: to hammer out a common platform and a strategy to win. Before the dialogue can even begin, it is first of all necessary to give such a movement a sense of history, a sense of its roots and its place in the world. That is what I have tried to do in this book.

Having established this common history and regained a sense of intellectual community, the New Fusionists can then begin to build a movement to take back their party and their country. To be sure, there are divisions: over trade policy, legislating morality, and questions of strategy and tactics. No doubt these will be discussed, openly and vigorously. To reconcile liberty and tradition, to balance American nationalism against the requirements of a free market and a free society, to present a radical and positive alternative to the right-wing social democrats who have taken over the conservative movement and hijacked the Republican Party—these tasks will not be accomplished overnight.

But more than half the battle is already won. Paleoconservatives and Old Right libertarians certainly know what they are against: big government, confiscatory taxation, foreign aid, the New World Order. More importantly, we have a general idea of what we are for: free markets, tax rollbacks, and a noninterventionist foreign policy that puts America first. There is even some preliminary general agreement on the subject of strategy and tactics; by its very nature, the paleoconservative revolt embodies a resurgent populism, a grassroots rebellion against an arrogant managerial elite.

Garrett envisioned it forty years ago: an aroused citizenry finally rising against their tormentors and taking back their republic. For him it was a hope, a cry of anguish, and a message for the future—which *had* to be brighter. Today that vision is within the realm of the possible, if only we have the courage to fight for it. Then, perhaps, we can begin to take back the positions in the lost terrain, to storm and capture them one-by-one—until, finally, we have scaled the Peak of Fortitude.

THE OLD RIGHT AND THE TRADITIONALIST ANTIPATHY TO IDEOLOGY

Scott P. Richert

I N HISTORICAL TERMS, FIFTEEN YEARS may not be enough time to establish the worth of a book, but in the modern world it is certainly long enough to determine whether a book is bound for the dustbins of history (as are most books published today). As this republication attests, Justin Raimondo's *Reclaiming the American Right: The Lost Legacy of the Conservative Movement* has cleared that first hurdle, and it is well on its way to being considered a classic of American political conservatism, on the order of those works of Albert Jay Nock and John T. Flynn and Garet Garrett which are discussed herein.

Even classics cannot please everyone all of the time, however, and in these few pages, I will address a few omissions and interpretations that make *Reclaiming the American Right* somewhat less than completely satisfying from a traditionalist conservative standpoint. As will become clear, my remarks are not meant to detract from Raimondo's accomplishment but simply to provide one answer to his call, in his penultimate chapter, for a New Fusionism by accounting for elements of modern American conservatism that are missing or downplayed in his book, as well as by extending his argument in at least one way that he may not have considered.

I first read *Reclaiming the American Right* shortly after it was published, and returning to it today I am struck, as I was then, by the depth of Raimondo's historical research and understanding. It is not easy, when writing about people whose work has strongly influenced your own, to refrain from the impulse toward hagiography—trimming out sordid details, overemphasizing arguments that foreshadow your own work, downplaying certain writings or political positions that make the subject's thought seem less than completely consistent and coherent. But Raimondo has the historian's love for detail and narrative, and he knows that the history of a person, no less than the history of a country or nation, rarely moves in a straight line. Those figures on the Old Right whom he has chosen to cover have received their due, and then some. Others revered by many traditionalist conservatives have not—most notably James Burnham, to whom Raimondo dedicates the first chapter of the book (but whom he considers the intellectual godfather of the "New Right," clustered around *National Review*, and thus not a figure to be admired), and Russell Kirk, to whom Raimondo dedicates no more than a few words here and there.

Which brings us to the question of interpretation. When he moves beyond historical description and attempts to make his broader argument, Raimondo is concerned primarily, I would argue, with the creation of an ideology of the true American Right, in order to rectify the lack of one in times past. He admits as much early in his introduction, when he does not simply note but laments the "traditionalist antipathy to ideology." "There has been," he writes, "no equivalent of Marxist ideology on the right, no overarching system that defined the commonality of American conservatism, and this is even truer today, with the end of the cold war and the dissolution of the old conservative consensus."

Historically, Raimondo is correct. What lesson, however, should we draw from that fact? Russell Kirk and other traditionalist conservatives have argued that ideology is, by its very nature, a distortion of reality, an attempt to force organically developed historical institutions to conform to an abstract system. Assuming that they are correct, it is hard to conserve something that you are actively engaged in distorting. That is why Kirk argued that conservatism is "the negation of ideology." Properly understood, Kirk declared, conservatism is "the defense of [an objective universal] moral order against its ideological adversaries of both the Left and the Right."

The Power of Ideology

While approaching this question from different angles, Kirk and Raimondo agree, however, on at least one thing: ideology is a powerful force. It can—and does—wreak destruction on everything that conservatives hold dear. And it puts those who uphold tradition, and oppose ideology, at a distinct disadvantage, as Raimondo himself notes: "The traditionalist antipathy to ideology put the neoconservatives in an excellent position. It gave them the intellectual advantage of a positive program as against the aloof mysticism of a few, like Kirk, that could only appeal to a few rarefied souls. Having surrendered the vital realm of ideology to various and sundry ex-Leninists, what was left of the old conservative movement slowly faded out of the picture."

Traditionalist conservatives do not have to agree with Raimondo's characterization of Kirk or endorse his view that rejecting the siren song of ideology amounted to the surrender of a "vital realm" to recognize the essential truth of this argument. Back in the 1980s, the Third Generation of young conservatives who used to gather at the Heritage Foundation in Washington, D.C., often claimed that what separated conservatives from liberals is that conservatives read and engage in rational argumentation, while liberals memorize talking points that they are unwilling—indeed, unable—rationally to defend. But when has the development of public policy ever depended primarily on the strength of rational argument? The fact that many of those young conservatives were not particularly well read or able to engage in rational argument themselves merely proved the point: modern ideological politics, like modern science from the time of Bacon and Descartes, is more about power than it is about reality.

Those who embrace a distorted view of reality—whether ideologues or psychopaths—often find themselves holding a certain power over those who stubbornly cling to reality in all of its fullness. Once you have reduced reality to a series of sound bites or a handful of defining principles, you enjoy a certain freedom of action that the person who is always saying, "Yes, but . . ." does not have. But what lesson should those who recognize this fact draw from it? In his recent book *Conservatism in America: Making Sense of the American Right*, Paul Gottfried echoes Justin Raimondo, before going even further by placing much of the blame for the rise of the neoconservatives upon Kirk himself. Under the influence of Kirk and his best-known work, *The Conservative Mind*, Gottfried argues, traditionalist conservatives failed to present a viable ideological alternative to the neoconservatives, and this failure ensured the latter's triumph.

I do not agree with this argument, but, for the moment, let's concede the point and assume that, after World War II, the heirs to the Old Right should have coalesced around an ideological agenda that could have offered an alternative to neoconservatism. What might it have looked like? Raimondo offers this vision:

> [T]he Old Right used to argue in terms of an American exceptionalism, a largely unspoken but all-pervasive assumption that the New World is and ought to be exempt from the vicissitudes ordinarily visited upon the Old. . . . This American exceptionalism animated the Right's case for limiting the power of the state, both at home and abroad. . . . Based on the bedrock American political values of individualism, anti-statism, and the kind of foreign policy envisioned by Washington in his Farewell Address, the laissez-faire credo of the Old Right was founded on this reverence for "a revolution exemplary."

There is much that is very good about this vision, and this is not the place to quibble about the use or definitions of such terms as *individualism*, *laissez-faire*, or even *American exceptionalism*. Toward the end of his life, in addition to work on natural law that remained sadly unfinished, Kirk dedicated much of his public efforts to critiquing the rise of an

American foreign policy (advanced primarily by the neoconservatives) that was destructive of civilization both abroad and at home. But his argument was that such a foreign policy was inherently ideological, and that traditional American foreign policy was not. So, too, the traditional American attachment to ordered liberty, Jeffersonian decentralism, and limited government. Conservatives valued such things, Kirk believed, not because they form an ideology to which we rationally subscribe or a blueprint for limited government, but because they were formed by, and form, the historical heritage of the country and nation and, even more broadly, the civilization to which we belong.

Here we see the point at which traditionalism and Raimondo's vision of conservatism most diverge, for Raimondo argues that "the very heart of the American conservative soul" is a "nationalism that was unlike any other. Unique in that it was founded neither in ancient folk dances, nor religion, nor ethnicity, but in an abstract and revolutionary idea inextricably bound up with the American character: the idea of liberty."

For the traditionalist, such a claim is bound to bring to mind the "propositional nation" or "credal nation" view of America associated most often with Harry Jaffa, a disciple of political philosopher Leo Strauss, and more broadly with modern neoconservatism. True, the proposition that the Straussians and neocons find at the heart of "the American experiment" is equality, not liberty, but the form—"an abstract and revolutionary idea bound up with the American character"—is the same.

The trouble that traditionalists have with abstract and revolutionary ideas is that they are, well, abstract and revolutionary. Indeed, the more abstract they are, the more revolutionary they are. There is no single "idea of liberty." I have one; Justin Raimondo has one; and John Podhoretz has one. And I dare say that no two of the three completely coincide (though one of the three may not overlap at all with the other two). President George W. Bush, in his second inaugural address, may have used the word freedom more often than any other word, and he undoubtedly would regard it as a synonym for liberty; but his vision of freedom is very different from, and less traditionally American than, Justin Raimondo's understanding of liberty.

Which brings us around to where Raimondo and Kirk once again converge, because Raimondo, despite his own words, is not really talking about an abstract idea of liberty but a peculiarly American one that is rooted in the traditions of the American people. Those traditions, however much they may diverge in historical particulars from the traditions of Europe, are themselves rooted in the broader traditions of European (particularly Anglo-Saxon) civilization. We value limited government, for instance, not because it is some platonic ideal, or because it conforms to the (abstract) libertarian ideal of nonaggression, but because it is part of our historical experience, and our historical experience has shown us its value (even if we have been made aware of its value most often in its absence).

The way that we understand our liberty—as abstract or historically rooted—becomes most important when that liberty is under attack. Raimondo rightly faults the "New Right"—the postwar conservatives clustered around *National Review*—for being so concerned with the threat of international communism that they were willing to curtail traditional American liberties:

> While paying lip service to the anti-statism of Mencken and Nock, and attacking the Republican Establishment for failing to come up with an alternative to statism, [William F. Buckley] launched into what was to be the keynote of the New Right: because the inherent and "thus far invincible aggressiveness of the Soviet Union" poses an immediate threat to national security, "we have to accept Big Government for the duration—for neither an offensive nor a defensive war can be waged . . . except through the instrument of a totalitarian bureaucracy within our shores". . . . This was the question put before the Right, as the cold war tightened its grip on the American consciousness: would conservatives become the champions of central planning, high taxes, and war production boards, or would they show the proper disdain for Buckley's prescription and return to their Old Right roots?

We know which road they took, and, unfortunately, it was not the one less traveled by. Buckley prevailed in his argument that America needed to curtail the liberty of her citizens in order to save it (an argument being advanced by self-described conservatives again, fifty years later, in the face of another external threat). The ideological nature of the American conservative anticommunism of the second half of the twentieth century would quickly convince the conservative Catholic historian John Lukacs, himself an émigré from Communist Hungary, to begin referring to himself as an "anti-anticommunist." But what Lukacs (and, at least toward the end of his life, Kirk) recognized is that this ideological anticommunism was the flip side of an understanding of liberty that was also ideological. In other words, the problem was not, as Raimondo assumes, that *National Review* was insufficiently attached to an abstract idea of liberty, but that the idea of liberty to which American conservatives had become attached in the Cold War era *was* abstract, ideological, and thus not organic and historically American. It was, to use an analogy that Russell Kirk developed in a lecture he frequently delivered in his later years, more like the Rights of Man than the Bill of Rights.

The chief lights of Raimondo's Old Right were not more committed to an "abstract and revolutionary" idea of liberty than Raimondo's New Right was; they were *less so,* and that made all of the difference. When you are defending something real, you are unlikely to take a cavalier attitude toward that which you are defending; when you are defending something abstract, you are much more likely to make compromises. A man might die to defend his family; he is much less likely to do so to defend an abstract concept of "the family" (and for good reason). For the Old Right, the liberty that they defended was as real as the Alamo was to Crockett, Bowie, and Travis; for the New Right, it was a debating point that they could revise or even concede as necessary in order to win the debate. And winning the debate meant taking, or increasing their hold on, the reins of power.

The European Virus

In one sense, Raimondo fully understands this. He laments what he calls the "European virus"—an obsession with power, especially the power of the state. He argues that, for ex-communist conservatives, "the content of their ideology had indeed changed; but not, in many cases, its *form*"—that form being a "universalist and globalist" outlook "imprinted with the European mind-set which could not imagine or allow the limits of power."

What was being created in the United States, however, was a new totalism that was more a creature of modern ideology than of anything particularly European. True, European conservatives (especially post-Christian ones) were more likely to defend the modern state, and even the Christian Right in Europe believed in a role for the state that was more extensive than that traditionally held by Americans (though European Christians, especially Catholics, also believed the state to be limited in important ways by the Christian moral order and the principle of subsidiarity).

The question, in both Europe and America, was where the locus of power would lie. For four centuries, the tendency had been toward the centralization of power, aided, as Emory University professor of philosophy Donald Livingston has shown in his 1998 book *Philosophical Melancholy and Delirium: Hume's Pathology of Philosophy,* by the rise of ideologies that attacked traditional, organic institutions and, in so doing, destroyed them as independent bases of power. Families, guilds, agrarian communities, the church herself—all those things that constituted the "little platoons" that Edmund Burke saw as essential to the preservation of traditional social order and liberty—all were attacked, undermined, scattered. And in their absence, or in their weakened state, the power they once held accrued to the centralized (and centralizing) state.

The Old Right, by European lights, seems positively egalitarian, but a prototypical individualist such as Ayn Rand (as Raimondo makes clear) did not believe that all men are created equal—much less that they should end up that way. When Richard M. Weaver, in *Ideas Have Consequences,* laments the loss of distinction and hierarchy, he points out that, rather than leading to an increase of individual liberty, such a loss increases the power of the state: "The state, ceasing to express man's inner qualifications, turns into a vast bureaucracy designed to promote economic activity. It is little wonder that traditional values, however much they may be eulogized on commemorative occasions, today must dodge about and find themselves nooks and crannies if they are to survive at all. Burke's remark that the state is not 'a partnership in things subservient only to gross animal existence' now seems as antiquated as his tribute to chivalry."

Weaver was far more skeptical of capitalism than Raimondo is; even so, we can see another point of contact between the traditionalist insistence that man is more than *Homo economicus* and Raimondo's more libertarian vision when Raimondo, discussing the late Samuel Francis, attacks the dominant trends in recent conservatism: "This tame pseudo-conservatism masquerades in a variety of guises; the 'Big Government' conservatism touted by Fred Barnes, Jack Kemp's 'progressive conservatism,' Newt Gingrich's 'opportunity society,' the 'cultural conservative' rationale for welfarism peddled by Paul Weyrich, or the so-called 'New Paradigm' of ex–Bush White House aide James Pinkerton. Whatever their differences, they are variations on the theme of big government in the service of [in the words of Sam Francis] 'the enhancement of economic opportunity through one kind or another of social engineering.'"

This elevation of the state in the name of the individual extends across the entire Right today. We see so-called libertarians—some, obscenely, regarding themselves as the intellectual heirs of Mencken and Flynn, Rose Wilder Lane and Ayn Rand—using the federal courts to press Fourteenth Amendment lawsuits aimed at overturning state and local laws, with the ostensible purpose of increasing individual liberty, but with the ultimate effect of increasing the power of Washington. And of course, many conservatives have been happy to support military ventures abroad that consolidate power, and destroy traditional liberties, here at home.

Ideology and the Destruction of Tradition

Raimondo is right: the new conservative ideology destroyed nearly all that the Old Right stood for. But the problem was not that the wrong ideology won, but that ideology won at all. There is a reason why, in their essentials, the two major political parties in the United States so resemble each other today. The substance of their ideologies may be different (though increasingly less so); but as ideological organizations, they both stand against tradition and for centralized power.

Ideological systems must be imposed from the top down. Of necessity, "blueprints" for the government of fifty states and 300 million people cannot deal with the multitudinous variations that arise organically at the level of the several states, much less at the local or family levels. Everything must be reduced to the lowest common denominator, which, in the case of government, does not mean the lowest level of society, but the highest level of government. Such programs only become feasible when the traditional institutions that stand between man and the centralized state are wiped out, thus making all men truly "individuals"—which is another way of saying, making all men equal, at least in relation to the state. Thus, the ideological conservative's answer to the liberal assault on the family and states' rights reflected in *Roe v. Wade* is not a return to the status quo ante (which would strengthen both the family and states and local communities), but a human life amendment to the U.S. Constitution that would, in essence, make the federal government, not God, the ultimate arbiter of when human life begins.

In this sense, the fate of the Old Right was sealed, not with U.S. entry into World War II, or with the hijacking of the conservative movement by ideological anticommunism, but at the very beginning of the modern age of ideology. The defense of liberty and tradition is a positive good, but it is not, as Raimondo points out, akin to the kind of "positive program" possessed by the neoconservatives (or liberals, or Marxists). It is easier to convince the public to support doing *something* than it is to convince the public that, if it is not necessary to do something, it is necessary not to do something.

With each advance of the "positive program," power is increasingly centralized, and the erstwhile decentralized loci of power are correspondingly weakened. In other words, the process of centralization is self-perpetuating, and, with the countryside having been laid waste during the inexorable march to the future, it is increasingly hard to turn back.

Several people, including Thomas Jefferson, are often credited with having declared that "eternal vigilance is the price of liberty," but the man who really uttered the sentiment, Irish orator John Philpot Curran, actually said something much less abstract and, hence, more interesting: "It is the common fate of the indolent to see their rights become a prey to the active. The condition upon which God hath given liberty to man is eternal vigilance; which condition if he break, servitude is at once the consequence of his crime and the punishment of his guilt."

It is not that conservatives in the latter half of the twentieth century could not conceive of limits on the power of the centralized state; for decades, they prattled on endlessly about reducing the size of government, cutting taxes, overturning regulations, restoring states' rights. Out in the heartland, voters believed the rhetoric and ushered in the "Reagan Revolution" and the "Contract with America." But ensconced in government offices and think tanks in the Washington–New York corridor, the leaders of the conservative movement never had more than an abstract attachment to such ideas. The struggles of a blue-collar family to make ends meet on two incomes (let alone one), or of a factory owner to make payroll when he finds most of his gross income being eaten up by social security and Medicare taxes and the costs of adhering to safety regulations, are simply not as real to them as *power*, and never have been.

A New Type of Power Politics

The problem for the defenders of true liberty, then, is how to keep power from flowing to the center, into the hands of the defenders of abstract liberty, and—even more pertinent today—how to reverse the flow of power, to return it to the lowest levels of society, where it belongs. Even if we grant the best of intentions to those who promised us a "New Federalism," we must admit that the deck was stacked from the beginning, because they intended to use the power of the federal government to "empower" states and communities and families. Once you have slipped on the ring, however, you find yourself in thrall to its power, and your transformation into Gollum has begun. Why give power to others that can be used to undercut your own? So every attempt to do so became half-hearted: states and localities and families could only be given a certain autonomy *if that autonomy rested firmly upon the power of the federal government.*

What is needed is the return of alternative loci of power—not through the actions of, but in opposition to, the central state. "Individual rights" are not enough; an "abstract and revolutionary idea" of liberty is not enough. The defense of liberty requires removing certain things from the federal purview altogether—to remove, say, the family from the realm of modern ideological politics.

In other words, what is necessary is the use of power by certain interests on their own behalf against the forces of modern ideological politics. Thus the traditionalist conservative emphasis on culture—a word barely used in *Reclaiming the American Right.* If Weaver and Kirk and other traditionalists are correct, and the loss of distinction and hierarchy and tradition and Christianity increase, rather than decrease, the power of the state, Raimondo's libertarian focus on the individual may be misplaced. The individual *qua* individual is no match for the power of the centralized ideological state; but the *person*—that is, the human being in the context of his family, community, nationality, faith—just might be.

It is precisely here that Raimondo's treatment of James Burnham's power politics seems a bit too one-sided. Raimondo never mentions Burnham's most conservative, and most consistently underrated, work, his 1959 book *Congress and the American Tradition.* Stepping outside of traditional discussions of the separation of powers, Burnham makes a persuasive argument that the structure of the legislative branch, as the Framers of the Constitution conceived it, was intended to prevent the sovereignty of the several states from being subsumed into the sovereignty of the federal government—which, he rightly recognized, meant the power of the executive branch. The problem is that the evolution (or devolution) of the American constitutional system—both through formal amendments, such as the Seventeenth, which provided for the direct election of U.S. senators, and through the growth of the population beyond the bounds that could be foreseen by the Framers and the concomitant destruction of traditional culture—have weakened this role of Congress and, consequently, allowed the executive branch to usurp not only the powers of Congress per se but also of the states and their citizens.

"Real human beings," Burnham argued, "are not statistical abstractions, not political Common Denominators. They make a living by this or that kind of work, occupy house or palace or apartment or shanty, dwell in mountain or plain or city, belong to this Church or that, like change or stability, seek glory or wealth or peace or pleasure. Each in his specificity is different from every other. . . ." It is this specificity that distinguishes "the people" from "the masses," and the "citizen" from "mass-man," who, Burnham notes, "cannot be other than a 'subject.'" It is through the loss of this specificity that liberty itself is lost, and America heads down the road to despotism. The only certain bulwark against dictatorship, then—at least within the context of the American constitutional system—is the revival of those intermediary institutions and attachments that separate a citizen from a subject.

Despite his criticisms of Burnham, Raimondo, in his penultimate chapter, "The Paleoconservative Revolt," praises the analysis of the late Samuel Francis, the long-time Washington editor for *Chronicles: A Magazine of American Culture* and Burnham's greatest disciple. He tries to separate that analysis from its roots in Burnham's thought, but it really cannot be done (as Francis would have been the first to admit). Nor is there any need to do so: when power is properly decentralized, those who love the organic liberty that Americans have historically enjoyed can better resist the centralizing force of the state. That is why Francis called for, in Raimondo's words, "Not a movement of intellectuals directed at the elite, not an attempt to preserve what has already been destroyed, but a grassroots movement against the welfare-warfare state."

A New Fusionism

What is needed, Raimondo declares, is what Thomas Fleming, in the May 1991 issue of *Chronicles*, called a "New Fusionism" between the libertarian heirs of the Old Right and the paleoconservative heirs of traditionalism. But while Raimondo, in his final chapter, outlines the goals of such an effort, a strategy for victory remains elusive. If the battle is fought on the playing field of national ideological politics, where the partisans of liberty have been consistently defeated for sixty years, there is little reason to believe that the New Fusionist coalition will be successful—and many reasons, fifteen years and four presidential elections after the initial publication of *Reclaiming the American Right*, to believe it will not be.

For such a grassroots movement to succeed, its members must forsake the politics of ideology, stressing (as Raimondo does) the common history of the New Fusionists but recognizing that that history forms a tradition in itself. Rather than attempting to "reconcile liberty and tradition," we need to recover the traditional roots of liberty and recognize that liberty without tradition cannot long survive, because it leads to atomization and the destruction of those institutions and attachments which alone can act as brakes on the power of the central state. We need to acknowledge, in other words, that there is something worthwhile in religion, ethnicity, even ancient folk dances. There is a reason why the totalist state, which is so destructive of human liberty, hates all of those things, too.

In *Reclaiming the American Right*, Justin Raimondo delivers a clarion call in defense of the American history of liberty; fifteen years after his book was published, it is more than time for his conservative counterparts to respond in kind with a robust defense of the traditional institutions of Western civilization. Those traditions alone made possible the liberty that we once enjoyed and, Deo volente, may someday enjoy again.

WHY THE OLD RIGHT WAS RIGHT:
A FOREIGN POLICY FOR AMERICA

David Gordon

J USTIN RAIMONDO ENABLES US TO understand his program of "taking back America" through a historical account of its genesis. In like fashion, I suggest, one can obtain a better understanding of Justin Raimondo by looking at his intellectual pedigree. Here, one figure stands out: the great Austrian economist and libertarian theorist Murray Rothbard. Raimondo for many years worked closely with Rothbard as a libertarian activist. He has chronicled their activities in his outstanding biography of Rothbard, *Enemy of the State*.[1]

In writing *Reclaiming*, Raimondo made use of a then unpublished manuscript by Rothbard, "The Betrayal of the American Right"; he cites it several times in the book. Rothbard's manuscript provided the conceptual framework for Raimondo's work, and *Reclaiming* is best viewed as an outstanding elaboration and extension of Rothbard's account. Fortunately, the Ludwig von Mises Institute has recently published Rothbard's manuscript, and we can now grasp the foundations of Raimondo's narrative.[2]

Rothbard takes the principal enemy of liberty to be a powerful state, and war has been the chief means by which the state expands and consolidates its power.[3] Accordingly, he supports a noninterventionist foreign policy: only when threatened with attack should a nation go to war. Rothbard contends that the Old Right, the American conservative movement that opposed the New Deal, favored this course of action: "In brief, the Old Right was born and had its being as the opposition movement to the New Deal, and to everything, foreign and domestic, that the New Deal encompassed: at first, to burgeoning New Deal statism at home, and then later, in the '30s, to the drive for American global intervention abroad" (2).

As readers of Raimondo's book have discovered, in the 1950s, a very different notion of foreign policy, advocated principally by William F. Buckley Jr. and his fellow editors of *National Review*, came to prevail among American conservatives. This new view emphasized the primary importance of engaging in a worldwide struggle against Soviet Russia.

Rothbard made clear the basis of his opposition to *National Review* foreign policy in an essay, "For a New Isolationism," written in April 1959; the magazine did not publish it. To those who favored a policy of "liberation" directed against the Communist bloc, Rothbard raised a devastating objection: "In all the reams of material written by the Right in the last decade, [1949–59] there is never any precise spelling-out of what a policy of ultrafirmness or toughness really entails. Let us then fill in this gap by considering what I am sure is the *toughest possible* policy: an immediate ultimatum to Khrushchev and Co. to resign and disband the whole Communist regime; otherwise we drop the H-bomb on the Kremlin . . . What is wrong with this policy? Simply that it would quickly precipitate an H-bomb, bacteriological, chemical, global war which would destroy the United States as well as Russia."

To this dire picture, proponents of "rollback" would of course respond that the Communists would surrender: Rothbard dissents, for reasons that will be discussed in detail later. Suffice it to say that he thought it obvious that since "the destruction of the United States would follow such an ultimatum, we must strongly oppose such a policy."

If "liberation" leads to national suicide, what is the alternative? Rothbard suggests a return to "the ancient and traditional American policy of isolationism and neutrality." But is this not open to a fatal objection? "But, I [Rothbard] will hear from every side, everyone knows that isolationism is obsolete and dead, in this age of H-bombs, guided missiles, etc." How can America shun involvement in European power politics if Russia has the ability to destroy us? No longer can we retreat to Fortress America.

To this position Rothbard has a simple response: *"a program of world disarmament up to the point where isolationism again becomes militarily practical."* If this policy were carried out, America would be safe from foreign attack: no longer would we need to involve ourselves in foreign quarrels. Mutual disarmament was in Russia's interest as well, so a disarmament agreement was entirely feasible.

Ever alert for objections, Rothbard anticipates that critics will charge that a Fortress America would be saddled with crushing military expenses and be cut off from world trade. Not at all, he responds: "this argument, never very sensible, is absurd today when we are groaning under the fantastic budgets imposed by our nuclear arms race. Certainly . . . our arms budget will be less than it is now. . . . The basis of all trade is benefit to *both* parties." (These quotations are from an unpublished memorandum by Rothbard.) Even if a hostile power controlled the rest of the world, why would it not be willing to trade with us? Unfortunately, Rothbard's arguments did not have any effect on his bellicose antagonists, and he and *National Review* soon parted ways.

The foreign policy Rothbard supported adhered closely to the American tradition. In his classic 1928 memorandum on the Monroe Doctrine, Undersecretary of State J. Reuben Clark notes that it was long-standing American policy to avoid involvement in European power politics. Pointing to conflicts with France in the 1790s, Clark remarks, "It was now again demonstrated to American statesmen that political affiliations and associations with European powers, no matter what their origin nor how benevolent their purpose, always involved us in difficulty. As Washington was to say some three years later, 'Europe has a set of primary interests which to us have none or a very remote relation.'"[4]

The claim that American foreign policy in the eighteenth and nineteenth centuries was noninterventionist is, one would have thought, uncontroversial; but one eminent neoconservative writer has ventured to deny it. Robert Kagan has attempted an impossible task; and, predictably, he fails. In *Dangerous Nation*, a history of American foreign policy from the colonial period to the onset of the Spanish-American War, he argues that the standard account of American diplomatic history is grievously in error.⁵ America did not, Kagan contends, break sharply in the twentieth century with a fixed policy of nonintervention in European power politics. Quite the contrary; American policy has always been actively interventionist. "The pervasive myth of America as isolationist . . . rests on a misunderstanding of America's foreign policies in the seventeenth, eighteenth, and nineteenth centuries."

How can Kagan say this? Until the twentieth century, America carefully avoided involvement in European wars, just as the "myth" suggests. Conflicts with European nations, e.g., the quasi-war with France in the 1790s and the War of 1812, came about only in response to interference with America's rights as a neutral power; and in the nineteenth century, America avoided involvement in any European conflicts whatever. America's policy was clear and straightforward: America shunned the constant struggle for mastery in Europe but, to a lesser extent, claimed dominance in the Western hemisphere. Classic documents—Washington's Farewell Address, Jefferson's First Inaugural, and Monroe's 1823 Message to Congress—enunciated this policy. If Kagan wishes to deny that American foreign policy was ever in this sense isolationist, must he not erase the clear historical record?

He does his best to do exactly that. He gives a lengthy account of American expansion across the continent: in support of the constant hunger of Americans for land, he shows, the United States government was often quite willing forcibly to challenge the powers of Europe. He complains that diplomatic historians have wrongly separated this saga of expansion from their accounts of foreign policy. These historians classify expansion as a domestic affair; and, by so doing, they can claim that American foreign policy was isolationist. But they pass over the fact that this "domestic" expansion involved conflicts with foreign powers. If they took this fact into account, they would have to abandon their thesis of American isolation.

Kagan here ignores the point at issue. The "isolationist" thesis is that America deliberately avoided involvement in European power politics. No one contends that the makers of American foreign policy embraced pacifism in all circumstances. Americans were no doubt quite willing to fight for control of the American continent, but what has this to do with the standard picture that Kagan professes to challenge? Kagan embeds the isolationist thesis within the larger and implausible claim that America has in all cases followed a passive course of action. He triumphantly refutes this implausible claim and acts as if he has lain to rest the standard account of American isolation. Our author, one must say, has a peculiar way of handling historical evidence. In his Farewell Address, George Washington wrote, "Europe has a set of primary interests which to us have none; or a very remote relation. Hence she must be engaged in frequent controversies, the causes of which are essentially foreign to our concerns. Hence, therefore, it must be unwise in us to implicate ourselves by artificial ties in the ordinary vicissitudes of her politics, or the ordinary combinations and collisions of her friendships and enmities."

Is not this classic defense of nonintervention inconvenient for Kagan's thesis? He responds by denying that Washington's statement expressed a permanent policy. Rather, he had in mind the immediate need to avoid undue partiality toward France and enmity toward Britain. This is certainly an application of Washington's principle; but Kagan offers no evidence whatever against reading the address as the statement of general principles it professes to be.

Thomas Jefferson confirmed and extended Washington's view of foreign affairs in his First Inaugural, supporting "peace, commerce, and friendship with all nations, entangling alliances with none." Readers who guess that Kagan will dismiss this too as an affair of the moment are in for a surprise. He does not mention the First Inaugural at all.

If Washington and Jefferson leave Kagan unfazed, the Monroe Doctrine is for him mere child's play. In his message to Congress on December 2, 1823, James Monroe stated, "Our policy in regard to Europe, which was adopted at an early stage of the quarrels which have so agitated that quarter of the globe, nevertheless remains the same, which is, not to interfere in the internal concerns of any of its powers. . . ." Kagan acknowledges that Monroe said this, but he stresses instead

Monroe's sympathy for Greek independence and Spanish liberalism. "His [Monroe's] message was not a declaration of hemispheric isolationism. In important respects, it was a statement of international republican solidarity" (174). Again, Kagan misses the essential point. Monroe did not propose to go beyond his expression of sympathy. He renounced any policy of forcible interference in European affairs, and that made all the difference. Prince Metternich might well consider America "dangerous," but this was not because he expected American armed intervention in Europe. Rather, he feared that the American example would inspire European rebels who wished to overturn monarchism. Metternich's secretary, Friedrich von Gentz, by contrast thought that the American Revolution differed fundamentally from the destructive French Revolution. Kagan omits any mention of Gentz's famous essay on the subject.

The foreign policy that Rothbard and Raimondo favor may be in the American tradition, but should we adopt it today? Critics may claim that isolation from world power politics was suitable for a minor country but is no longer fitting for the world's foremost military nation. We have already encountered this view in Rothbard's memorandum. (Walt Whitman Rostow takes exactly this line in his *The United States in the World Arena*.)[6]

Is our traditional policy still viable? To help answer this vital question, I should like to call attention to a neglected book by the eminent political scientist Eric Nordlinger. This book, *Isolationism Reconfigured*,[7] very usefully supplements Raimondo's account of non-interventionism. Nordlinger offers a detailed theoretical defense of the policy that Raimondo has described through an account of some of its leading advocates.

During most of the long historical period that Nordlinger covers, one fact has remained constant; and this is the linchpin of his case for American isolation. Because of our geographical position, natural resources, and military strength, the United States since the early nineteenth century has always been in a position to resist invasion without difficulty. To do so of course requires a strong defense capacity: Nordlinger does not argue his case on pacifist grounds. But, given military technology that equals or surpasses that of rivals, the advantage lies naturally with the defense.

"A national strategy does not entail any less of a commitment to research and development than strategic internationalism," he writes. "Without it there is no knowing how science and technology can make for yet greater security, and it is the only way to guard against others forging beyond us in ways that would detract from our security" (49).

One advantage of isolation should excite little controversy. It is much cheaper than a policy of "entangling alliances," as Thomas Jefferson aptly termed interventionism. Like Earl Ravenal, one of the few "defense intellectuals" to support isolation, Nordlinger maintains that the drastic cuts in the defense budget under isolation would redound greatly to the advantage of our economy, through lowering the deficit and releasing funds for private spending and investment.

But this of course does not suffice to make the case for isolation, as opponents of the policy will be quick to point out. How does Nordlinger defend his principal thesis, viz., that isolation can better promote American security than interventionism? He does so, in large part, by an ingenious reversal of an influential argument for intervention of worldwide scope.

According to the view Nordlinger combats, a state's security depends on its credibility. The world of nations is one of constant struggle for power; and to maintain its existence amidst this strife, a country must acquire a reputation for resolve. If it is known to fulfill scrupulously its commitments, other nations will be deterred from threat or invasion. "The more frequently the United States undertakes and fulfills defensive obligations," proponents of this view allege, "the greater its current credibility. Insofar as the fulfillment of defense commitments involves major efforts and great sacrifices, the other side will be all the more convinced of our high resolve" (116).

As Nordlinger notes, the distinguished economist Thomas Schelling has probably been the most influential supporter of this argument. He went so far as to claim "that most of the globe is central to our security for subjective, political reasons" (117).

To enable a state to secure credibility, Schelling and other theorists have devised elaborate models detailing how states should threaten and respond to threats. Nordlinger confronts the models with an elementary fact. The intentions of others are very difficult to gauge. But the strategic minuets of move and countermove devised by defense specialists depend on accurate perceptions of intention: if what was intended as a gesture of conciliation is judged a threat, for example, trouble obviously looms. Why then engage in such futile exercises?

One might in part reply to Nordlinger that not all strategic analysis does in fact depend on knowledge of intention. Some strategies dominate others; i.e., following them makes one better off regardless of what others do. But in the main our author is clearly right. To judge that because a nation has kept its commitments, it will be likely to do so in the future is precisely to assess intention.

If, though, we take Nordlinger's advice and abstain from the strategic duels of Schelling and company, does not disaster threaten? If we do not make commitments, we shall not obtain credibility; and then other nations will not hesitate to threaten us. Here exactly lies the point at which Nordlinger executes his remarkable reversal of the credibility argument.

It is not, he says, by constant commitments that one best builds credibility. On the contrary, a nation that maintains a strong defense capability but refrains from foreign entanglements has made its intentions crystal clear. Since, almost by definition, a nation places extreme value on its territorial integrity, no problem exists of convincing others that it will fight if attacked. And there is no need to fight for others in order to enhance a credibility that was not first laid on the line.

Nordlinger's argument echoes the wise words of the great Conservative prime minister Lord Salisbury. In "The Egyptian Question," a speech delivered in Edinburgh in November 1882, he remarked: "We have heard a great deal about prestige. I detest the word: I should rather say 'military credit.' Military credit stands in precisely the same position as financial credit. The use of it is to represent a military power, and to effect the objects of a military power without recourse to arms. . . . It is the same with a military nation [as a financial power] that is careful to preserve its military credit. If it does so, it may, without shedding a drop of blood or incurring one penny of expenditure effect all the objects which, without that military credit, can only result in much waste of blood and treasure."[8]

An isolationist, then, is not a player who always concedes the point to an opponent, but rather someone who does not play the game of international power politics at all. In making this distinction, Nordlinger deftly avoids a common accusation against isolationists: they are, it is charged, appeasers who ignore the lessons of the Munich Conference, where Britain and France surrendered the Sudetenland to Germany in a futile effort to stave off war. (In discussions of noninterventionist foreign policy, the pre–World War II period is ubiquitous.)

This charge is untrue, Nordlinger responds. Isolation entails disengagement from world politics, not participation in them in a particular fashion. "It was Britain and France, not a disengaged America, that pressured Czechoslovakia to concede much of its territory to Hitler at Munich. Without being at all bellicose, isolationism does not involve significant concessions to opponents, with whom there are few interactions and few political-military treaties and agreements" (5).

In my view, the Old Right foreign policy triumphantly withstands critical examination. But our choices do not consist only of isolation and the neoconservative policy of continual intervention. Political "realists" such as John Mearsheimer, who by no means favor a noninterventionist foreign policy, warned against neoconservative plans to invade Iraq.[9] These amateur warriors have more in mind than the invasion of Iraq, disastrous though this has been. Some, such as Norman Podhoretz, contend that the worldwide spread of democracy will ensure peace. The American mission must be to overthrow dictatorial regimes, especially in the Middle East. Of course this policy of what Charles Beard aptly termed "perpetual war for perpetual peace" cannot work.

An early and unfortunately influential exposition of the neoconservative position was David Frum and Richard Perle's *An End to Evil.*[10] These authors maintain that the conquest of Iraq is an excellent beginning to the world war against terror, but we must be careful lest bureaucracies in the military and State Department cause our crusade to stumble. A number of other countries require a regime change. Iran is no democracy: voters can select only which Islamic extremist they wish to represent them. What is worse, Iran supports terrorism: "Iran foments Palestinian terrorism against Israel, using terror to undermine every attempt to encourage an Israel-Palestine peace" (105). Why not then get rid of a government so hostile to our interests? "Above all, Iran's dissidents need . . . us to make clear that we regard Iran's current government as illegitimate and intolerable and that we support the brave souls who are struggling to topple it" (112).

And why stop there? Syria must also replace its government with one more to our liking. But we must be fair: we should first approach the present regime with demands for change. Only if the government rejects these should we take action. I venture to suggest that acceptance is unlikely. The requirements include this: "We expect Syria to cease its campaign of incitement against Israel, which only nourishes the culture of suicide bombing" (115). Can Frum and Perle really think that a Syrian government that ceased to be anti-Israel could maintain itself in power? Their list of demands recalls the Sudeten German leader Konrad Henlein's summary of Hitler's instructions for negotiations with the Czech authorities: "We must always demand so much that we can never be satisfied."

Our authors foresee an objection to their plans. They wish to replace various Arab governments. But will not doing so require permanent American military occupation of the countries concerned? Frum and Perle oppose "radical Islam." Well and good; but what if the people in the occupied countries favor it?

Their response staggers belief. When the Arab populations see the wonders that democracy has brought a "free" Iraq, they will embrace with ardor the policies that we want. "[W]e have given Iraqis a chance to lead the Arab and Muslim world to democracy and liberty." Fortunately, "Iraq does not have to attain perfection to challenge the region with the power of a better alternative" (168). The Communists, by their own declaration, did not invade Hungary in 1956 or Czechoslovakia in 1968; they "liberated" these countries from evil. Frum and Perle have learned their lessons well.

But I must not give a misleading picture of this book. Frum and Perle have much more in mind than changes in various Arab governments. North Korea, along with Iran and Iraq, is part of the axis of evil. It too gets the treatment: demands almost certain to be rejected followed by military action. If North Korea does not immediately surrender all its nuclear material and close its missile bases, then "decisive action" follows. This "would begin with a comprehensive air and naval blockade" (103). Such action would prepare the way for "a preemptive strike against North Korea's nuclear facilities" (104). If we are fortunate, China will finish the job for us by forcibly replacing the North Korean government.

But China should not be complacent. Frum and Perle have plans for the Chinese as well. France, by the way, has not been behaving in a fashion appropriate to a subservient ally. While military action is not yet on our authors' agenda, France must be punished for disobedience. I shall leave the details of these schemes to readers of the book. Their policy can be summarized in the slogan "Shout, and swing a very big stick."

Podhoretz is another extreme proponent of the same position. Like Frum and Perle, he maintains that we must install democracies throughout the Middle East. Bush's "new approach" aimed "to make the Middle East safe for America by making it safe for democracy."[11] This is no Utopian idea, since the states of that region "had all been conjured into existence less than one hundred years ago out of the ruins of the defeated Ottoman empire in World War I. . . . This being the case, there was nothing 'utopian' about the idea that such regimes—which had been planted with shallow roots by two Western powers [Britain and France] and whose legitimacy was constantly challenged by internal forces both religious and secular—could be uprooted with the help of a third Western power and that a better political system could be put in their place" (144–45).

Of course Podhoretz's argument is wrong: it does not follow from the instability of a government that a successor regime can be easily established, but this is not the problem to which I now wish to call attention. If Podhoretz is to be believed, millions of Muslims aim to destroy us. In a democracy, will these people not vote for governments that will endeavor to carry out their radical programs? Given their numbers (once more, if Podhoretz is right about them) they are often likely to have a decisive voice in elections. The effect of Podhoretz's democratic remedy is likely to be an intensification of the problem it is supposed to cure. Does Podhoretz think that the radical Islamic views he fears flourish only in undemocratic regimes? If so, he once again offers nothing to support his position.

He does mention the problem in one place: "Yes, elections brought Hamas to power in the Palestinian Authority, gave the terrorists of Hezbollah a place in the Lebanese government, and awarded the terrorists of the Muslim Brotherhood seats in the Egyptian parliament" (211). His response is to cite two Middle Eastern writers who praise elections as a sign that the ballot box has replaced tyranny. In other words, the answer to the problem that voters may establish hostile regimes is that Democracy is a Good Thing.

Another effort to defend the neoconservative crusade for democracy fares no better. Lawrence Kaplan and William Kristol contend that the "strategic value of democracy is reflected in a truth of international politics: Democracies rarely, if ever, wage war against one another."[12] Given this premise, is not the conclusion obvious? We have only to establish democracy everywhere and the millennium is at hand. But why accept the premise? Our authors appeal to Kant: "[When] the consent of citizens is required to decide whether or not war should be declared, it is very natural that they will have a great hesitation in embarking on so dangerous an enterprise" (105, quoting Kant).

Kant's point gives our authors no help. In modern "democracies," the executive usually decides unilaterally on military action: I do not recall, for example, that a declaration of war from Congress, much less a popular referendum, preceded our crusade against Hitler redivivus, Saddam Hussein. Further, Kant here says nothing about our authors' claim that democracies are unlikely to do battle with other democracies. He is making a general claim that democracies are less bellicose than other regimes: one has only to glance at a list of modern wars to see that the claim is false.

But perhaps our authors can do better than Kant. Is it not simply a well-confirmed fact that democracies do not fight one another but settle disputes peacefully? Our authors do not cite the Yale political scientist Bruce Russett, but he, among others, has published data that purport to establish this "fact" as ironclad. (By "democracy" in the following I mean, roughly, "a representative government with some civil liberties.")

I do not think it wise to use this alleged fact as a basis for policy. Until the twentieth century, very few democracies existed, and generalizations about their behavior seem unlikely to prove robust. If the few democracies that have so far existed have not gone to war with each other, why does it follow that a world transformed into democratic states would be likewise pacific? Would the conflicts between Israel and the Arab states go away if all the regimes in question became democratic?

Those enamored of a belligerent foreign policy often use another argument besides the appeal to "democratic peace theory." They contend that if we firmly confront hostile dictatorships, they will beat a hasty retreat. Nonintervention is a course of weakness that will only encourage our enemies to aggrandize themselves. Murray Rothbard has given the best response to this view.

Rothbard called this argument "The Accepted Picture." Of it he trenchantly observed, "Answer me this, war hawks: when, in history when, did one State, faced with belligerent, ultra-tough ultimatums by another, when did that State ever give up and in effect surrender before any war was fought? When?"[3] Rothbard's rhetorical question rests upon a simple point of psychology. The supposed "bully" cannot surrender to an ultimatum lest he be overthrown. "No head of State with any pride or self-respect, or who wishes to keep the respect of his citizens, will surrender to such an ultimatum" (170). Both the Gulf War and our current Iraq war perfectly illustrate Rothbard's contention. Faced with an overwhelming show of force, Saddam Hussein did not back down. Rothbard's apt generalization explains Saddam's seemingly irrational response.

But have we not forgotten something? Once again, World War II returns. Does not the failure to confront Hitler over Czechoslovakia in 1938 lend support to this thesis of the anti-appeasers? (It should be noted that our earlier claim that the Munich settlement was an example of intervention rather than nonintervention does not speak to this argument. Here the contention is that a particular sort of intervention, namely the threat of war, will in fact avert war.)

Rothbard's response illustrates his ability to counter an opposing argument at its strongest point. "Neither was World War II in Europe a case where toughness worked. On the contrary, Hitler disregarded the English guarantee to Poland that brought England and France into the German-Polish war in September 1939" (170).

We must acknowledge that among American conservatives, the noninterventionist position of Rothbard and Raimondo has not triumphed, despite that position's deep roots in the American tradition and its inherent reasonableness. This edition of *Reclaiming the American Right*, one may hope, will usher in a return to sounder conservative principles.

SELECTED BIBLIOGRAPHY

THE FOLLOWING IS BY NO means a complete compilation of published material on every aspect of the Old Right. It omits, for the most part, the literature in the scholarly journals on the subject. Nor is it an all-inclusive compendium of works cited in this volume. For those wishing to acquaint themselves with the subject of the Old Right, and the political evolution of the conservative movement in the postwar era, it is a good beginning.

Barnes, Harry Elmer, ed. *Perpetual War for Perpetual Peace*. New York: Greenwood Press, 1953.

———. *Revisionism: A Key to Peace, and Other Essays*. San Francisco: Cato Institute, 1980.

Beard, Charles A. *President Roosevelt and the Coming of the War, 1941: A Study in Appearances and Realities*. New Haven: Yale University Press, 1948.

Branden, Barbara. *The Passion of Ayn Rand*. Garden City, NY: Doubleday, 1986.

Branden, Nathaniel. *Judgment Day*. Boston: Houghton Mifflin Co., 1989.

———. *Who is Ayn Rand?* With a biographical essay by Barbara Branden. New York: Random House, 1962.

Bromfield, Louis. *A New Pattern for a Tired World*. New York: Harper, 1954.

Carlson, John Roy. *The Plotters*. New York: E. P. Dutton & Co., 1946.

———. *Under Cover.* New York: E. P. Dutton & Co., 1943.

Burnham, James. *The Managerial Revolution.* New York: John Day, 1941. Paperback edition, Indianapolis: Anchor Books, 1960.

Chamberlin, William Henry. *America's Second Crusade.* Chicago: Henry Regnery Co., 1950.

Chodorov, Frank. *The Income Tax: Root of All Evil.* New York: Devin-Adair, 1954.

———. *One is a Crowd: Reflections of an Individualist.* New York: Macmillan, 1940.

———. *Out of Step: The Autobiography of an Individualist.* New York: Devin-Adair, 1962.

———. *The Rise and Fall of Society.* New York: Devin-Adair, 1959.

Cole, Wayne S. *America First: The Battle Against Intervention, 1940–41.* Madison: University of Wisconsin Press, 1953.

———. *Charles A. Lindbergh and the Battle Against Intervention in World War II.* New York: Harcourt Brace Jovanovich, 1974.

Doenecke, Justus D., ed. *In Danger Undaunted: The Anti-Interventionist Movement of 1940–41 as Revealed in the Papers of the America First Committee.* Stanford: Hoover Institution Press, 1990.

———. *The Literature of Isolationism: A Guide to Non-Interventionist Scholarship, 1930–1972.* Colorado Springs: Ralph Myles, 1972.

———. "The Literature of Isolationism, 1972–1983: A Bibliographical Guide," *Journal of Libertarian Studies* 7, no. 1 (Spring 1983): 152–84.

———. *Not to the Swift: The Old Isolationists in the Cold War Era.* Lewisburg, PA: Bucknell University Press, 1979.

Flynn, John T. *As We Go Marching.* New York: Doubleday, 1944.

———. *Country Squire in the White House.* New York: Doubleday, 1940.

———. *The Decline of the American Republic.* New York: Devin-Adair, 1955.

———. *The Epic of Freedom.* Philadelphia: Fireside Press, 1947.

———. *God's Gold: The Story of Rockefeller and His Times.* New York: Harcourt Brace & Co., 1932.

———. *Graft in Business.* New York: Vanguard Press, 1931.

———. *The Lattimore Story.* New York: Devin-Adair, 1953.

———. *McCarthy: His War on American Reds.* New York: America's Future, 1954.

———. *Meet Your Congress.* New York: Doubleday, 1944.

———. *Men of Wealth.* New York: Simon & Schuster, 1941.

———. *The Road Ahead: America's Creeping Revolution.* New York: Devin-Adair, 1953.

———. *The Roosevelt Myth.* New York: Devin-Adair, 1948. Revised edition, Garden City, NY: Garden City Publishing, 1956.

———. *While You Slept: Our Tragedy in Asia and Who Made It.* New York: Devin-Adair, 1951.

Garrett, Garet. *The American Omen*. New York: E. P. Dutton, 1928.

———. *The American Story*. Chicago: Henry Regnery Co., 1955.

———. *The Blue Wound*. New York: Putnam's, 1921.

———. *A Bubble That Broke the World*. Boston: Little, Brown, 1932.

———. *The Cinder Buggy: A Fable in Iron and Steel*. New York: E. P. Dutton, 1923.

———. *The Driver*. New York: E. P. Dutton, 1922.

———. *Ex America*. Caldwell, ID: Caxton, 1952.

———. *Harangue: The Trees Said to the Bramble, "Come Reign Over Us."* New York: E. P. Dutton, 1927.

———. *Ouroboros: or, The Mechanical Extension of Mankind*. New York: E. P. Dutton, 1926.

———. *The People's Pottage*. Caldwell, ID: Caxton, 1953.

———. *The Revolution Was*. Caldwell, ID: Caxton, 1952.

———. *Rise of Empire*. Caldwell, ID: Caxton, 1952.

———. *Satan's Bushel*. New York: E. P. Dutton, 1924.

———. *A Time is Born*. New York: Pantheon, 1944.

———. *Where the Money Grows*. New York: Harper, 1911.

———. *The Wild Wheel*. New York: Pantheon, 1952.

Gies, Joseph. *The Colonel of Chicago*. New York: E. P. Dutton, 1979.

Goddard, Arthur, ed. *Harry Elmer Barnes: Learned Crusader*. Colorado Springs: Ralph Myles, 1968.

Hamilton, Charles H., ed. *Fugitive Essays: Selected Writings of Frank Chodorov*. Indianapolis: Liberty Press, 1980.

Hayek, Friedrich. *The Road to Serfdom*. 1944. Chicago: University of Chicago Press, 1956.

Holman, Frank E. *The Story of the Bricker Amendment: The First Phase*. New York: Committee for Constitutional Government, 1954.

Judis, John B. *William F. Buckley Jr.: Patron Saint of the Conservatives*. New York: Simon & Schuster, 1988.

Lane, Rose Wilder. *The Discovery of Freedom: Man's Struggle Against Authority*. New York: John Day, 1943.

———. *Give Me Liberty*. Los Angeles, Pamphleteers, 1945.

Liggio, Leonard. *Why the Futile Crusade?* New York: Center for Libertarian Studies, 1978.

MacBride, Roger Lea, ed. *The Lady and the Tycoon: The Best of Letters between Rose Wilder Lane and Jasper Crane*. Caldwell, ID: Caxton, 1973.

Manion, Clarence. *The Conservative American*. Shepherdsville, KY: Victor Publishing Co., 1966.

Martin, James J. *American Liberalism and World Politics*. 2 vols. New York: Devin-Adair, 1964.

Manly, Chesly. *The Twenty-Year Revolution: From Roosevelt to Eisenhower.* Chicago: Henry Regnery Co., 1954.

Mises, Ludwig von. *Bureaucracy.* New Haven: Yale University Press, 1944.

———. *Human Action.* New Haven: Yale University Press, 1949.

———. *Omnipotent Government.* New Haven: Yale University Press, 1955.

Morgenstern, George. *Pearl Harbor: The Story of the Secret War.* New York: Devin-Adair, 1947.

Nash, George H. *The Conservative Intellectual Movement in America Since 1945.* New York: Basic Books, 1976.

Nock, Albert Jay. *The Memoirs of a Superfluous Man.* Chicago: Henry Regnery Co., 1969.

———. *Our Enemy, the State.* 1935. Caldwell, ID: Caxton, 1946.

Oppenheimer, Frank. *The State.* New York: Bobbs-Merrill, 1914.

Paterson, Isabel. *The God of the Machine.* New York: Putnam, 1943.

Patterson, James T. *Congressional Conservatism and the New Deal.* Lexington: University of Kentucky Press, 1967.

———. *Mr. Republican: A Biography of Robert A. Taft.* Boston: Houghton Mifflin, 1972.

Pettingill, Samuel B. *Jefferson: The Forgotten Man.* New York: America's Future, Inc. 1940.

———. *Smokescreen.* New York: America's Future, 1940.

Radosh, Ronald. *Prophets on the Right: Conservative Critics of American Globalism.* New York: Simon & Schuster, 1975.

Rand, Ayn. *Anthem.* 1938. Revised edition, Los Angeles: Pamphleteers, 1946. Paperback edition, New York: New American Library, 1946.

———. *Atlas Shrugged.* New York: Random House, 1957.

———. *The Fountainhead.* New York: Bobbs-Merrill, 1943.

———. *We the Living.* New York: Macmillan, 1936. Paperback edition, New York: New American Library, 1959.

Rockwell, Llewellyn H. *The Case for Paleolibertarianism, and Realignment on the Right.* Burlingame, CA: Center for Libertarian Studies, 1990.

Rothbard, Murray N. *The Betrayal of the American Right.* Auburn, AL: Ludwig von Mises Institute, 2007.

———. *For a New Liberty: The Libertarian Manifesto.* New York: Macmillan, 1972.

———. *Left and Right: The Prospects for Liberty.* San Francisco: Cato Institute, 1978.

Ryant, Carl G. *Profit's Prophet: Garet Garrett (1878–1954).* Selinsgrove, PA: Susquehanna University Press, 1989.

Sanborn, Frederic R. *Design for War.* Chicago: Henry Regnery Co., 1951.

Bibliography

Stenehjem, Michelle Flynn. *An American First: John T. Flynn and the America First Committee*. New Rochelle: Arlington House, 1976.

Tansill, Charles Callan. *Back Door to War*. Chicago: Henry Regnery Co., 1952.

Tebbel, John. *George Horace Lorimer and the* Saturday Evening Post. New York: Doubleday, 1948.

Notes

Introduction to the 2008 Edition

1. Robert Nisbet, *The Present Age: Progress and Anarchy in Modern America* (New York: Harper & Row, 1988; rpt. ed., Indianapolis: Liberty Fund, Amagi Books, 2003), 51–52.

2. On this issue, see George W. Carey, ed., *Freedom and Virtue: The Conservative/Libertarian Debate*, rev. ed. (Wilmington, DE: ISI Books, 1998). This work contains essays by prominent traditionalists and libertarians that deal with various aspects of their philosophical divide. The attention focused on this issue was the outgrowth of an article that appeared in *National Review* (January 1962) that questioned the sources of William F. Buckley's conservatism.

3. The seventh and revised edition of *The Conservative Mind: From Burke to Eliot* (Washington, D.C.: Regnery Publishing) was the last edition and appeared in 1985.

4. A prime example of the more expansive understanding of conservatism that emerged is Bruce Frohnen's *Virtue and the Promise of Conservatism: The Legacy of Burke and Tocqueville* (Lawrence, KS: University Press of Kansas, 1993).

5. Robert Nisbet, *Conservatism: Dream and Reality* (Minneapolis: University of Minnesota Press, 1986), 2. In this brief work, Nisbet offers, if anything, a more expansive view of conservatism than does Kirk.

6. See Russell Kirk and James McClellan, *The Political Principles of Robert A. Taft* (New York: Fleet Press, 1967).

7. See, for example, Robert Nisbet, *The Quest for Community: A Study in the Ethics of Order and Freedom* (New York: Oxford University Press, 1953; rpt ed., San Francisco: Institute for Contemporary Studies, 1990).

Introduction

1. Rose Wilder Lane, *Give Me Liberty* (Los Angeles: Pamphleteers, 1945).
2. Garet Garrett, *The American Story* (Chicago: Regnery, 1955), 19.
3. John Judis, *William F. Buckley Jr.: Patron Saint of the Conservatives* (New York: Simon & Schuster, 1988), 130.
4. Russell Kirk, *The Neoconservatives: An Endangered Species*, (Washington, D.C.: Heritage Foundation, 1988).
5. Llewellyn H. Rockwell, *The Case for Paleolibertarianism, and Realignment on the Right* (Burlingame, CA: Center for Libertarian Studies, 1990), 21.
6. I mean to include the neoconservatives under the broad rubric of the New Right, although, in a much narrower sense, they came later than the founding of *National Review*.

Chapter 1: *James Burnham: From Trotsky to Machiavelli*

1. See Alan M. Wald, *The New York Intellectuals: The Rise and Decline of the Anti-Stalinist Left from the 1930s to the 1980s* (Chapel Hill, NC: University of North Carolina Press, 1987). See also Irving Kristol, *Reflections of a Neoconservative* (New York: Basic Books, 1983).
2. James Burnham and Max Shactman, "Intellectuals in Retreat," *New International*, (January 1939). See also Wald, *The New York Intellectuals*, 83.
3. There was nothing new about this theory: The ex-Trotskyist Bruno Rizzi, in his *The Bureaucratization of the World* (Paris, 1939), said essentially the same thing, extending his argument to include the corporatist New Deal and European national socialism. Rizzi saw all these phenomena as national variations on a single theme of increased economic and political centralization.
4. James Burnham, "Science and Style," reprinted in full in the appendix to *In Defense of Marxism* by Leon Trotsky (New York: Pathfinder Press, 1971).
5. "Letter of Resignation of James Burnham from the Workers Party," in ibid., 207–13.
6. James Burnham, *The Managerial Revolution* (New York: John Day, 1941), 77–95. The references are to the Indiana University Press/Midland Books edition, published in 1960.
7. See especially Samuel B. Pettingill's *Smokescreen* (New York: Southern Publishers, 1940).
8. James Burnham, *The Managerial Revolution*, 8.
9. George Orwell, "James Burnham and the Managerial Revolution," in *The Collected Essays, Journalism, and Letters of George Orwell*, eds., Sonia Orwell and Ian Angus (New York: Harcourt Brace Jovanovich, 1968), 4:172. Emphasis in original.

10. Burnham, *The Managerial Revolution*, 245.

11. Ibid., 228.

12. Ibid., 229.

13. Ibid., 249.

14. Ibid., 261.

15. James Burnham, *The Machiavellians: In Defense of Freedom* (New York: John Day, 1943).

16. Ibid., 251–56.

17. Ibid., 285.

18. Ibid., 304.

19. Ibid.

20. Cited in Judis, *William F. Buckley Jr.*, 123.

21. James Burnham, *The Struggle for the World* (New York: John Day, 1947).

22. Ibid., 182.

23. Ibid., 221. Emphasis in original.

24. John O'Sullivan, "James Burnham and the New World Order," *National Review*, November 11, 1990.

25. Murray N. Rothbard, *The Betrayal of the American Right*. Auburn, AL: Ludwig von Mises Institute, 2007.

26. Judis, *William F. Buckley Jr.*, 225.

27. Burnham, *The Managerial Revolution*, IX.

28. James Burnham, *The Coming Defeat of Communism* (New York: John Day, 1949).

29. Ibid., 258–59.

30. Ibid.

31. Ibid., 267.

Chapter 2: Max Shachtman: Journey to the West

1. Wald, *The New York Intellectuals*, 175.

2. James P. Cannon, *The History of American Trotskyism* (New York: Pathfinder Press, 1944), 48–59.

3. Max Shachtman, *Behind the Moscow Trials: The Greatest Frame-Up in History* (New York: Pioneer Publishers, 1936).

4. Wald, *The New York Intellectuals*, 173.

5. Trotsky, *In Defense of Marxism*, 64.

6. Wald, *The New York Intellectuals*, 350–51.

7. Shachtman, "Is Russia a Worker's State?" *New International* (December 3, 1940).

8. Trotsky, *In Defense of Marxism*, 8.

9. Shachtman, "Is Russia a Worker's State?"

10. Ibid.

11. Ibid.

12. Irving Howe, *A Margin of Hope* (New York: Harcourt Brace Jovanovich, 1982), 205. Emphasis added.

13. Christopher Lasch, *The Agony of the American Left* (New York: Vintage, 1969), 61–114.

14. Ibid., 93.

15. Tom Braden, "I'm Glad the CIA Is Immoral," *Saturday Evening Post*, May 10, 1967.

16. Lasch, *The Agony of the American Left*, 99. Emphasis added.

17. Ibid.

18. Michael Novak, *The Spirit of Democratic Capitalism* (Lanham, MD: Madison Books, 1991), 32.

19. Ibid.

20. Irving Kristol, *Two Cheers for Capitalism* (New York: Basic Books, 1978), 119. Emphasis added.

21. Paul Gottfried, "Scrambling for Funds," *Rothbard-Rockwell Report*, March 1991.

22. Joshua Muravchik, *Exporting Democracy: Fulfilling America's Destiny* (Washington, D.C.: AEI Press, 1991).

23. Charles Krauthammer, "Universal Dominion: Toward a Unipolar World," *The National Interest*, Winter 1989–90.

24. Ibid.

25. Francis Fukuyama, "The End of History?" *The National Interest*, Summer 1989. In his subsequently published book, *The End of History and the Last Man* (New York: The Free Press, 1992), Fukuyama states that this work "is not a restatement of my original article." In fact, it is an extension of his original thesis, which, less starkly presented, seems to lose much of its elegance.

26. Alexander Kojève, *Introduction to the Reading of Hegel* (New York: Basic Books, 1969), 159.

Chapter 3: Garet Garrett: Exemplar of the Old Right

1. Typical of this willful ignorance is John Judis in *William F. Buckley Jr.: Patron Saint of the Conservatives*, wherein the words "nationalism," "isolationism," "nativism," and "anti-Semitism" are invariably uttered in the same breath.

2. I am indebted to the work of Carl Ryant, whose doctoral dissertation "Garet Garrett's America" (University of Wisconsin, 1968), provided me with valuable information about Garrett's life and career. Ryant's work was published as *Profit's*

Prophet: Garet Garrett (1878–1954) (Selinsgrove, PA: Susquehanna University Press, 1989). Page numbers in subsequent citations refer to the unpublished version.

3. Quoted in ibid., 15.

4. Garet Garrett, *Where the Money Grows* (New York: Harper Brothers, 1911).

5. *The Nation*, December 2, 1911. Quoted in Ryant, 19.

6. Garet Garrett, "Inner Germany," *New York Times Current History*, March 1916, quoted in Ryant, 34.

7. *Saturday Evening Post*, April 3, 1920. (Hereafter *SEP*, followed by the date.)

8. *SEP*, August 14, 1920.

9. Garet Garrett, *The Blue Wound* (New York: G. P. Putnam's Sons, 1921).

10. Ibid., 38–40.

11. Ibid., 40–42.

12. Ibid., 122–23; emphasis in original.

13. Ibid., 81.

14. Ibid., 90–91.

15. See John P. Cregan, ed., *America Asleep: The Free Trade Syndrome and the Global Economic Challenge*, with an introduction by Patrick J. Buchanan (Washington, D.C.: U.S. Industrial Council Educational Foundation, 1991).

16. Garrett, *The Blue Wound*, 72–73.

17. Garet Garrett, *Other People's Money* (New York: The Chemical Foundation, Inc., 1931), 39.

18. Originally published as *The American Omen* (New York: E. P. Dutton & Co., 1928). Reprinted in Garet Garrett, *A Time is Born* (New York: Pantheon Books, 1944), 171.

19. Garrett, *Other People's Money*, 69.

20. *SEP*, December 24, 1921–January 28, 1922.

21. Garet Garrett, *The Driver* (New York: E. P. Dutton & Co., 1922).

22. See Chapter 10, 197–200.

23. Garrett, *The Driver*, 1.

24. Ibid., 4–5.

25. Garet Garrett, *The Cinder Buggy: A Fable in Iron and Steel* (New York: E. P. Dutton & Co., 1923).

26. Garet Garrett, *Satan's Bushel* (New York: E. P. Dutton & Co., 1924).

27. Garet Garrett, "The Trees Said to the Bramble, 'Come Reign Over Us,'" *SEP*, October 2–30, 1926; published in book form as *Harangue: The Trees Said to the Bramble, 'Come Reign Over Us,'* (New York: E. P. Dutton & Co., 1927).

28. Garrett, "The Trees Said to the Bramble," *SEP*, October 9, 1926, 94.

29. Garet Garrett, "The Whirling Pyramid," *New Republic*, December 3, 1920; quoted in Ryant, 90.

30. Garet Garrett, "Alice Economics," *New Republic*, December 29, 1920; quoted in Ryant, 92.

31. Garet Garrett, "As Citizens Thereof," *SEP*, July 19, 1924; quoted in Ryant, 115.

32. Garet Garrett, "Insatiable Government," *SEP*, June 25, 1932; quoted in Ryant, 139–40.

33. Garet Garrett, "Why Some Banks Fail and Others Don't," *SEP*, May 20, 1933; quoted in Ryant, 149.

34. Garet Garrett, "Security," *SEP*, September 9, 1936; quoted in Ryant, 162.

35. Garet Garrett, *The Revolution Was* (Caldwell, ID: Caxton Printers, 1945).

36. Garet Garrett, *The People's Pottage* (Caldwell, ID: Caxton Printers, 1953). Page references to all three essays are to this edition.

37. Ibid., 1.

38. Garet Garrett, *The American Omen* (New York: E. P. Dutton, 1925).

39. Garet Garrett, *Ouroboros; or, The Mechanical Extension of Mankind* (New York: E. P. Dutton, 1926).

40. Garrett, *The People's Pottage*, 19.

41. Ibid., 22.

42. Ibid., 24–25.

43. Ibid., 25.

44. James Burnham, *The Managerial Revolution*, 254.

45. Ibid., 255.

46. Garrett, *The People's Pottage*, 34–35.

47. Ibid., 38.

48. Ibid., 43.

49. Ibid., 44–45.

50. Ibid., 53.

51. Ibid., 63.

52. Ibid., 50.

53. Ibid., 70–71.

54. Ibid., 72.

55. Ibid., 73.

56. Garet Garrett, "And They Were Unprepared," *SEP*, May 22, 1940; quoted in Ryant, 165.

57. Garet Garrett, "Quo Vadis?" *SEP*, July 13, 1940; quoted in Ryant, 167.

58. Garet Garrett, "Burma Road," *SEP*, November 11, 1940; quoted in Ryant, 169.

59. Garet Garrett, "Dream Power," *SEP*, February 8, 1941; quoted in Ryant, 170.

60. Garet Garrett, "Where Goeth Before a Fall," *SEP*, December 27, 1941; quoted in Ryant, 171.

61. Garrett to Hoover, March 15, 1942; quoted in Ryant, 177.

62. Garet Garrett, "The Debacle of Planning," *American Affairs*, October 1947; quoted in Ryant, 195.

63. Garet Garrett, "Laissez-Faire," *American Affairs*, January 1949; quoted in Ryant, 196.

64. Garet Garrett, *The Wild Wheel* (New York: Pantheon, 1952).

65. Ibid., 220.

66. Garet Garrett, *Ex America* (Caldwell, ID: Caxton, 1951).

67. Garrett, *The People's Pottage*, 77.

68. Ibid., 78.

69. Ibid., 64.

70. Ibid., 87.

71. Ibid., 87–88.

72. Ibid., 89–90.

73. Ibid., 118.

74. Ibid., 124.

75. Ibid., 125.

76. Ibid., 126.

77. Ibid., 127.

78. Ibid., 129.

79. Ibid., 139.

80. Ibid., 140.

81. Ibid., 141.

82. Ibid., 149.

83. Ibid., 150.

84. Ibid., 152.

85. Ibid., 155.

86. Ibid., 156.

87. Ibid., 158.

88. Ibid., 158–59.

89. Ibid., 166.

90. Ibid., 169–70.

91. Ibid., 170.

92. Ibid., 172.

93. Garet Garrett, *The American Story* (Chicago: Regnery Co., 1955).

94. Ibid., 394.

95. Those who think they can make the charge of anti-Semitism stick to Garrett should read *The Driver*, Garrett's 1922 novel, in which the character Mordecai, a Jew, is depicted as an admirable example of loyalty to values.

96. Garrett, *The American Story*, 396.

97. Ibid., 88.

98. Ibid., 397.

99. Ibid., 393.

Chapter 4: John T. Flynn: From Liberalism to Laissez-Faire

1. For an in-depth analysis of this sudden switch in political polarity, see James J. Martin's *American Liberalism and World Politics*, 2 vols. (New York: Devin-Adair, 1964).

2. I am indebted to Ronald Radosh's *Prophets on the Right: Profiles of Conservative Critics of American Globalism* (New York: Free Life Editions, 1975), especially the chapters "John T. Flynn and the Coming of World War II," and "John T. Flynn and the Cold War," for much of the factual information in this chapter. Readers of both this book and Radosh's will see where we diverge in our interpretation of those facts.

3. John T. Flynn, *Investment Trusts Gone Wrong!* (New York: New Republic, 1930).

4. John T. Flynn, *Graft in Business* (New York: Vanguard Press, 1931).

5. John T. Flynn, *God's Gold* (New York: Harcourt, Brace & Co., 1932).

6. John T. Flynn, *Country Squire in the White House* (New York: Doubleday, Doran, 1940).

7. Ibid., 83.

8. Ibid., 102.

9. Ibid., 113.

10. Quoted in Radosh, *Prophets on the Right*, 204–205.

11. John T. Flynn, "Recovery Through War Scares," *New Republic*, November 2, 1938.

12. Quoted in Martin, *American Liberalism and World Politics*, 2: 759.

13. Ibid.

14. Ibid., 766.

15. *New Republic*, July 9, 1940; quoted in Radosh, *Prophets on the Right*, 212.

16. Quoted in ibid., 213.

17. *New Republic*, July 22, 1940; cited in Radosh, *Prophets on the Right*, 213.

18. *New Republic*, September 9, 1940; quoted in ibid., 214–15.

19. Martin, *American Liberalism and World Politics*, 2:777.

20. Radosh, *Prophets on the Right*, 218.

21. John Roy Carlson, *Under Cover* (New York: E. P. Dutton, 1943); idem, *The Plotters* (New York: E. P. Dutton, 1946); John T. Flynn, *The Smear Terror* (New York: privately published, 1947).

22. Flynn to Lindbergh, Sept. 15, 1941; cited in Radosh, *Prophets on the Right*, 223–24.

23. Quoted in ibid., 225.

24. John T. Flynn, *The Truth About Pearl Harbor* (New York: privately published, 1944); idem, *The Final Secret of Pearl Harbor* (New York: privately published, 1945).

25. Murray N. Rothbard, *The Betrayal of the American Right*, chap. 3.

26. John T. Flynn, *As We Go Marching* (New York: Doubleday, 1944). Page references are to the paperback reprint (New York: Free Life, 1973).

27. Ibid., 252–53.

28. Ibid., 212–26.

29. Radosh, *Prophets on the Right*, 253–58.

30. John T. Flynn, *The Roosevelt Myth* (Garden City, NY: Garden City Publishing Co., 1948).

31. John T. Flynn, *The Road Ahead: America's Creeping Revolution* (New York: Devin-Adair, 1949).

32. John T. Flynn, *While You Slept: Our Tragedy in Asia and Who Made It* (New York: Devin-Adair, 1951).

33. John T. Flynn, *The Lattimore Story* (New York: Devin-Adair, 1953).

34. John T. Flynn, *McCarthy: His War on American Reds* (New York: America's Future, 1954).

35. Radosh, *Prophets on the Right*, 269.

36. Flynn radio script, May 16, 1954; quoted in ibid., 266.

37. Ibid., 267.

38. Ibid., 272.

Chapter 5: The Remnant: Mencken, Nock, and Chodorov

1. Albert Jay Nock, *The Myth of a Guilty Nation* (New York: B. W. Huebsch, 1922).

2. Francis Neilson, *How Diplomats Make War* (New York: B. W. Huebsch, 1916).

3. Michael Wreszin, *The Superfluous Anarchist: Albert Jay Nock* (Providence: Brown University Press, 1972), 44–45.

4. H. L. Mencken, *Smart Set*, December 1919; reprinted in *A Mencken Chrestomathy* (New York: Knopf, 1949).

5. Albert Jay Nock, *Our Enemy, the State* (New York: William Morrow, 1935); reprinted by Caxton Printers (Caldwell, ID, 1946). Page references are to the Caxton edition.

6. Franz Oppenheimer, *The State* (New York: Free Life Editions, 1976).

7. Ibid., 22.

8. Nock, *Our Enemy, the State*, 162–63.

9. Albert Jay Nock, "Imposter Terms," *Atlantic Monthly*, February 1936; quoted in ibid.

10. Lawrence Dennis, *The Coming American Fascism* (New York: Harper, 1936); idem, *Is Capitalism Doomed?* (New York: Harper, 1932); idem, *The Dynamics of War and Revolution* (New York: Weekly Foreign Letter, 1940).

11. Quoted in Charles Hamilton, ed., *Fugitive Essays* (Indianapolis: Liberty Press, 1980). I am indebted to Hamilton's informative introduction, as well as Murray

Rothbard's *The Betrayal of the American Right*, for biographical information about Frank Chorodov.

12. Albert Jay Nock, *Free Speech and Plain Language* (New York: William Morrow, 1937), 248–65.

13. Hamilton, Fugitive Essays, 12.

14. Frank Chodorov, "When War Comes," *The Freeman*, November 1938; quoted in Hamilton, 17.

15. Reprinted in Frank Chodorov, *Out of Step* (New York: Devin-Adair, 1962).

16. Frank Chodorov, "Socialism Via Taxation," *analysis*, February, March, and April 1946; Hamilton, *Fugitive Essays*, 267–86.

17. Frank Chodorov, "Let's *Teach* Communism," *analysis*, September 1949; Hamilton, *Fugitive Essays*, 165–71.

18. Frank Chodorov, "Commies Don't Count," *analysis*, December 1946; Hamilton, *Fugitive Essays*, 172–98.

19. Ibid.

20. Frank Chodorov, "A Byzantine Empire of the West?" *analysis*, April 1947; Hamilton, *Fugitive Essays*, 337–49.

21. Ibid., 341.

22. Ibid., 343.

23. The similarity of the Nockian class analysis to the Marxist theory is superficial. According to the Leninist followers of Marx, imperialism was inherent in the very nature of capitalism; in other words, capitalism is the policy of imperialism. But Chodorov believed that the chief crime of the capitalists was that they had abandoned capitalism.

24. Frank Chodorov, "A Jeremiad" *analysis*, August 1950; Hamilton, *Fugitive Essays*, 361–44.

25. Frank Chodorov, "The Return of 1940?" *The Freeman*, September 1954; quoted in Hamilton, 24.

26. William Schlamm, "But It Is Not 1940," *The Freeman*, November 1954; quoted in Hamilton, 24.

27. William F. Buckley Jr., "A Young Republican's View," *Commonweal*, January 25, 1952; quoted in Rothbard, *The Betrayal of the American Right*, chap. 12.

28. Frank Chodorov, "A War to Communize America," *The Freeman*, November 1954; Hamilton, *Fugitive Essays*, 371–79.

29. Frank Chodorov, *Out of Step* (New York: Devin-Adair, 1962).

30. *analysis*, October 1950; reprinted in revised form by *Human Events* and as a pamphlet by the National Council for American Education; Hamilton, *Fugitive Essays*, 151–62.

Chapter 6: Colonel McCormick and the Chicago Tribune

1. *Chicago Tribune*, March 1, 1944; reprinted in *Thunderer of the Prairies: A Selection of Wartime Editorials and Cartoons*, 1941–1944 (Chicago: Tribune Co., 1944), 147–50.
2. The *Tribune* went in for a system of "simplified" spelling, rendering the word although into "altho," bureaucrat into "burocrat," etc.
3. Quoted in Richard Gies, *The Colonel of Chicago* (New York: E. P. Dutton, 1979), 214.
4. Frank C. Waldrop, *McCormick of Chicago* (Englewood, NJ: Prentice-Hall, 1966), 222–23.
5. Quoted in Philip Kinsley, *Liberty and the Press* (Chicago: Tribune Co., 1944), 46.
6. A year after the battle with the NRA, McCormick took on another petty tyrant intent on joining the major leagues, Huey Long, when that demagogue decided to tax newspapers which dared oppose his Louisiana reign of terror. McCormick provided the bulk of the funds for the defense of the publisher's rights.
7. Kinsley, *Liberty and the Press*, 47.
8. Ibid.
9. Ibid.
10. Ibid., 48–49.
11. Quoted in Gies, *The Colonel of Chicago*, 151.
12. Ibid., 158.
13. Ibid., 174–75.
14. Ibid., 176.
15. Ibid., 184.
16. Ibid., 188.
17. Ibid., 180.
18. Ibid., 189.
19. Ibid., 186–87.
20. Tribune Co., *Thunderer of the Prairies*, 5–6.
21. John O'Donnel, *New York Daily News*, March 30, 1942; quoted in Gies, *The Colonel of Chicago*, 198.
22. Gies says the third was "probably" Taylor. Ibid.
23. Gies, *The Colonel of Chicago*, 203–4.
24. Ibid., 205–6.
25. Tribune Co., *Thunderer of the Prairies*, 49–50.
26. Publishers of the *New York Daily News* and the *Washington Times-Herald*, respectively.
27. Gies, *The Colonel of Chicago*, 210.
28. Ibid., 210–11.

29. *The People* vs. *the Chicago Tribune* (Chicago: Union for Democratic Action, 1942). A characteristically hysterical assault on McCormick and freedom of the press is found in George Seldes, *Facts and Fascism* (New York: In Fact, 1943).

30. Tribune Co., *Thunderer of the Prairies*, 45–46.

31. Henderson started his political career as a leading exponent of Technocracy and publicist for the crackpot Howard Scott, and wound up working for the NRA as chief statistician. He later became FDR's academic advisor, research director of the Democratic Party, and was made head of the Office of Price Administration during the war.

32. Garet Garrett, "The Mortification of History," Chicago Tribune, September 19, 1943; reprinted as The Mortification of History: Nationalism, Key to America's Greatness (Chicago: Tribune Co., 1943), 1. Page numbers refer to the pamphlet edition.

33. Ibid., 9.

34. Tribune Co., *Thunderer of the Prairies*, 75–78.

35. Ibid., 81–87.

36. Rothbard, *The Betrayal of the American Right*, chap. 10.

37. Gies, *The Colonel of Chicago*, 226.

38. Complete text of the radio address is reprinted as an appendix to Waldrop, *McCormick of Chicago*, 298–303.

39. Chesly Manly, *The Twenty-Year Revolution: From Roosevelt to Eisenhower* (Chicago: Regnery, 1954).

Chapter 7: The Postwar Old Right

1. Leonard Liggio, *Why the Futile Crusade?* (New York: Center for Libertarian Studies, 1978), 23. I am indebted to this informative study for much of the material on the Old Right and the Republican Party.

2. Ibid., 24.

3. Ibid., 24–25.

4. Ibid., 28.

5. Quoted in Radosh, *Prophets on the Right*, 168.

6. Ibid., 174.

7. Rothbard, *The Betrayal of the American Right*, chap. 8.

8. Harry Elmer Barnes, ed., *Perpetual War for Perpetual Peace* (Caldwell, ID: Caxton Printers, 1953).

9. Charles A. Beard, *President Roosevelt and the Coming of the War: A Study in Appearances and Realities* (New Haven: Yale University Press, 1948).

10. Charles Callan Tansill, *Back Door to War* (Chicago: Regnery, 1953).

11. William Henry Chamberlin, *America's Second Crusade* (Chicago: Regnery, 1950).

12. Frederic R. Sanborn, *Design for War* (Chicago: Regnery, 1951).

13. Harry Elmer Barnes, "Revisionism and the Historical Blackout," in Barnes, *Perpetual War for Perpetual Peace*, 10.

14. Ibid.

15. George Morgenstern, *Pearl Harbor: Story of a Secret War* (New York: Devin-Adair, 1947).

16. George Morgenstern, "The Past Marches On," *Human Events*, April 22, 1953; quoted in Rothbard, *The Betrayal of the American Right*, chap. 8.

17. Frank E. Holman, *The Story of the Bricker Amendment: The First Phase* (New York: Committee for Constitutional Government, 1954), 147–152.

18. Clarence Manion, *The Conservative American* (Shepherdsville, KY: Victor Publishing Co., 1966), 106–28.

19. Ludwig von Mises, *Human Action* (New Haven: Yale University Press, 1949).

20. Ludwig von Mises, *Bureaucracy* (New Haven: Yale University Press, 1944).

21. Ludwig von Mises, *Omnipotent Government* (New Haven: Yale University Press, 1955).

22. Friedrich Hayek, *The Road to Serfdom* (Chicago: University of Chicago Press, 1944).

23. Rose Wilder Lane, *The Discovery of Freedom* (New York: John Day, 1943).

24. Isabel Paterson, *The God of the Machine* (New York: G. P. Putnam's Sons, 1943; Caldwell, ID: Caxton Printers, 1968).

25. Ayn Rand, *The Fountainhead* (New York: Bobbs-Merrill, 1943).

26. In 1909, she married Gillette Lane; the marriage ended in divorce in 1918.

27. Rose Wilder Lane, *Give Me Liberty* (Los Angeles: Pamphleteers, 1945); originally published as "Credo" in the *SEP* in 1936, and then expanded into a small book by Longmans, Green & Co. that same year. Page numbers refer to the Pamphleteers edition.

28. Ibid., 8.

29. Ibid., 11.

30. Ibid., 13.

31. Ibid; Roger Lea MacBride, ed., *The Lady and the Tycoon: the Best of Letters between Rose Wilder Lane and Jasper Crane* (Caldwell, ID: Caxton Printers, 1972), 168.

32. Lane, *Give Me Liberty*, 58–59.

33. MacBride, *The Lady and the Tycoon*, 125.

34. Lane, *Give Me Liberty*, 61–62.

35. Emphasis added.

36. MacBride, *The Lady and the Tycoon*, 87.

37. Quoted in William Holtz, "The Woman Versus the State," *Liberty*, March 1991. I am indebted to Professor Holtz's informative article for much of my information on Rose Wilder Lane's wartime struggles.

38. *Washington Post*, August 10, 1943; quoted in Holtz, 46.

39. Quoted in Holtz, 46.

40. Letter to J. Edgar Hoover; quoted in ibid., 47.

41. John Roy Carlson, the professional sneak and agent provocateur, also kept a file on her. In *The Plotters* (282), Carlson says he wrote to Lane under several different pseudonyms. What a correspondence that must have been! "She's even got it in for the Danbury, Conn., Public Service Commission, which regulates the number of taxicabs in town," he writes, dumbfounded by Lane's brand of "subversion."

42. Page references are to the 1972 Arno Press edition of *The Discovery of Freedom*.

43. Lane, *The Discovery of Freedom*, 256.

44. Vivian Kellems was a factory owner, a tax resister, and an activist in the movement to repeal the income tax.

45. MacBride, *The Lady and the Tycoon*, 153.

46. Isabel Paterson, *The God of the Machine*, 62.

47. Ibid., 93.

48. Ibid., 173.

49. Ibid., 166.

50. Ibid., 282.

51. Ibid., 253; emphasis in the original.

52. Ayn Rand, *Atlas Shrugged* (New York: Random House, 1957).

53. Louis Bromfield, *A New Pattern for a Tired World* (New York: Harper Brothers, 1954).

54. Louis Bromfield, *The Farm* (New York: Harper, 1933).

55. Louis Bromfield, *Brass Tacks* (New York: Harper, 1946).

56. Louis Bromfield, *Pleasant Valley* (New York: Harper, 1943).

57. Bromfield, *A New Pattern for a Tired World*, 8.

58. Ibid., 15–16.

59. Ibid., 17.

60. Ibid., 22–24.

61. Ibid., 60.

62. Ibid., 206.

63. Ibid., 91–92.

64. MacBride, *The Lady and the Tycoon*, 48–58.

65. For a fuller discussion of FEE, as well as the William Volker Fund, see Rothbard, *The Betrayal of the American Right*, especially chapters 7 and 9.

66. Leonard E. Read, *Conscience on the Battlefield* (New York: Foundation for Economic Education, 1951); quoted in Rothbard, *The Betrayal of the American Right*, chap. 7.

67. F. A. Harper, *In Search of Peace* (New York: Foundation for Economic Education, 1951); quoted in Rothbard, *Betrayal of the American Right*, chap. 7.

68. Dean Russell, "The Conscription Idea," *Ideas on Liberty*, May 1955, 42; quoted in ibid.

69. Ibid., chap. 11.

70. Thomas H. Barber, *Where We Are At* (New York: Charles Scribner's Sons, 1950).

71. Ibid., 251.

72. See Daniel Bell, *The End of Ideology* (New York: The Free Press, 1960).

73. Daniel Bell, ed., *The New American Right* (New York: Criterion Books, 1955); revised edition, *The Radical Right* (New York: Anchor Books, 1964). Page references are to the Anchor Books edition.

74. Ibid., 84.

75. Ibid., 89.

76. Theodore W. Adorno, ed., *The Authoritarian Personality* (New York: Harper & Row, 1950).

77. Theodore W. Adorno, "Politics and Economics in the Interview Material"; in Adorno, *The Authoritarian Personality*, 654–726.

78. Ibid., 685.

79. Ibid., 699.

80. Ibid., 231.

81. Ibid., 229–31.

82. "The Dispossessed," in Bell, *The Radical Right*, 77.

83. Ibid., 22.

84. David Riesman and Nathan Glazer, "The Intellectuals and the Discontented Classes," in Bell, *The Radical Right*, 108.

85. George H. Nash, *The Conservative Intellectual Movement in America* (New York: Basic Books, 1976), 66.

86. Peter Viereck, "The Revolt Against the Elite," in Bell, *The Radical Right*, 164.

87. See, for example, Arnold Forster and Benjamin Epstein, *Crosscurrents* (New York: Doubleday, 1956), 160–69.

Chapter 8: Birth of the Modern Libertarian Movement

1. Frank S. Meyer, "The Twisted Tree of Liberty," *National Review*, January 16, 1962; reprinted in Frank S. Meyer, *The Conservative Mainstream* (New Rochelle: Arlington House, 1969), 38–43.

2. Ibid.

3. Ibid.

4. Michelle Flynn Stenehjem, *An American First: John T. Flynn and the America First Committee* (New Rochelle: Arlington House, 1976), 169.

5. Ibid., 170.

6. Flynn, *The Roosevelt Myth*, 331.

7. John Birch Society *Bulletin*, January 1991 and March 1991.

8. Ayn Rand, "Choose Your Issues," *The Objectivist Newsletter*, January 1962.

9. Rand, *The Fountainhead*, 25.

10. A good portion of Barbara Branden's *The Passion of Ayn Rand* (Garden City, NY: Doubleday, 1986) gives a blow-by-blow description of the whole messy business. For a *National Enquirer*-style version of this sad story, see Nathaniel Branden's kiss-and-tell memoir, *Judgment Day* (Boston: Houghton Mifflin, 1989).

11. Paterson, *The God of the Machine*, 250–51.

12. Isabel Paterson.

13. Branden, *The Passion of Ayn Rand*, 171–72.

14. Nathaniel and Barbara Branden, *Who is Ayn Rand?* (New York: Random House, 1962).

15. Branden, *The Passion of Ayn Rand*, 182.

16. Ibid., 166. Emphasis in original.

17. George H. Smith, *Atheism, Ayn Rand, and Other Heresies* (New York: Prometheus Books, 1991), 202.

18. Garrett, *The Driver*, 213.

19. Rand, *Atlas Shrugged*, 315.

20. Ryant, *Profit's Prophet*, 33.

21. Garrett, *The Driver*, 151–52.

22. Rand, *The Fountainhead*, 113.

23. Ayn Rand, *The Romantic Manifesto* (New York: World Publishing Co., 1971) 108–9.

24. Branden, *The Passion of Ayn Rand*, 73.

25. Ayn Rand, *We the Living* (New York: Macmillan, 1936). These early works, including a posthumous collection of Rand's first attempts at fiction, have all been reprinted in mass paperback editions.

26. Ayn Rand, *Anthem* (London: Cassell, 1938; rev. ed., Los Angeles: Pamphleteers, 1946).

27. Ayn Rand, *Night of January 16th* (New York: Longmans Green, 1936).

28. Nor did it lessen the influence of Rand's books, which are still selling. While Rand the thinker is growing in influence, the official movement she bequeathed to disciple Leonard Peikoff—today reduced to a tiny sect—is slowly choking on its dogmatism.

29. Murray N. Rothbard, *Man, Economy and State* (Los Angeles: Nash Publishing, 1962).

30. *Left and Right*, vol. 1, no. 1, Spring 1965; reprinted as Rothbard, *Left and Right: The Prospects for Liberty* (San Francisco: Cato Institute, 1979).

31. Ibid., 7.

32. Ibid., 10. Emphasis in original.

33. Ibid., 16.

34. Gabriel Kolko, *The Triumph of Conservatism* (Glencoe, IL: The Free Press, 1963).

35. R. Palme Dutt, *Fascism and Social Revolution* (New York: International Publishers, 1934), 247–51.
36. Rothbard, *Left and Right*, 23–24.
37. Ibid., 26.
38. Although Rand claimed to oppose the Vietnam War, her attitude toward the anti-war movement was to mercilessly denounce it, and redbait all opponents of the war.
39. Murray N. Rothbard, *For a New Liberty* (New York: Macmillan, 1973).
40. Murray N. Rothbard, "Libertarianism versus 'Low-Tax Liberalism,'" *Cadre*, July–August 1980.
41. Ibid.
42. Ibid.
43. Rothbard, *Left and Right*, 24–25.
44. Murray N. Rothbard, "The New Fusionism: A Movement for Our Time," *Rothbard-Rockwell Report*, January 1991, 4. The *Report*, which Rothbard co-edits with Llewellyn H. Rockwell Jr. is the voice of a nascent paleolibertarian movement which seeks to distinguish itself from the Libertarian Party.

Chapter 9: The Paleoconservative Revolt

1. Patrick J. Buchanan, "A New Nationalism," *From the Right*, Spring 1990.
2. Ibid.
3. Ibid.
4. Ibid.
5. Ibid.
6. Patrick Buchanan, "Middle East: The Eagle's Last Scream," *Seattle-Post Intelligencer*, August 21, 1990.
7. "Look Who's Anti-War Now," *Time*, September 9, 1990.
8. "Come Home, America?" *National Review*, August 20, 1990.
9. A. M. Rosenthal, "Forgive Them Not," On My Mind, *New York Times*, September 14, 1990.
10. Patrick Buchanan, "A. M. Rosenthal Pins Scarlet Letter on Me," *Seattle-Post Intelligencer*, September 15, 1990.
11. Associated Press, "Forget Iraq—Columnists Warring Over Jews and U.S. Policy," *San Francisco Chronicle*, September 21, 1990.
12. "Loose Buchanan," *New Republic*, October 16, 1990.
13. Jacob Weisberg, "The Heresies of Pat Buchanan," *New Republic*, October 22, 1990.
14. Anti-Defamation League of B'nai B'rith news release (New York: September 19, 1990).

15. Ibid.

16. The single exception was *New Republic* editor and noxious twit Morton Kondracke, who smeared Buchanan at every opportunity.

17. Reprinted in *New Isolationist*, vol. 1, no. 2, October 1990.

18. Patrick Buchanan, "All 'Neo-Isolationists' Want Is to Get Out of Persian Gulf," *Seattle-Post Intelligencer*, November 16, 1990.

19. Patrick Buchanan, "A Tax Whose Time Has Gone," *Washington Times*, April 17, 1991.

20. Patrick Buchanan, "Raise the Tariff Walls, U.S. Can't Afford to Pay for Free Trade," *Seattle-Post Intelligencer*, November 21, 1990.

21. Murray N. Rothbard, *America's Great Depression* (Los Angeles: Nash Publishing, 1971), 127–29.

22. Frank W. Fetter, "Tariff Policy and Foreign Trade," *Facing the Facts*, ed. J. G. Smith (New York: G. P. Putnam's Sons, 1932), 83; cited in ibid.

23. Thomas Fleming, "Further Reflections on Violence," *Chronicles*, November 1990.

24. Ibid.

25. Thomas Fleming, "The New Fusionism," *Chronicles*, May 1991.

26. Ibid.

27. Ibid.

28. Samuel Francis, "Beautiful Losers," *Chronicles*, May 1991.

29. Ibid.

30. Ibid.

31. Ibid.

Why the Old Right Was Right

DAVID GORDON

1. Justin Raimondo, *Enemy of the State* (Amherst, NY: Prometheus, 2000).

2. Murray Rothbard, *The Betrayal of the American Right* (Auburn, AL: Ludwig von Mises Institute, 2007). Citations to this book will be by page numbers in parentheses in the text.

3. A key book documenting how war permanently increases the power of the state is Robert Higgs, *Crisis and Leviathan* (Oxford: Oxford University Press, 1989).

4. J. Reuben Clark, *Memorandum on the Monroe Doctrine* (Washington, D.C.: United States Government Printing Office, 1928), 14.

5. Robert Kagan, *Dangerous Nation* (New York: Knopf, 2006). Subsequent references to this book will be by page numbers in parentheses in the text.

6. Walt Whitman Rostow, The United States in the World Arena (New York: Harper, 1960).

7. Eric Nordlinger, *Isolationism Reconfigured* (Princeton, NJ: Princeton University Press, 1995). Subsequent references to this book will be by page numbers in parentheses in the text.

8. Mayo William Hesseltine, ed., *Orations from Homer to William McKinley,* (New York: P. F. Collier, 1902), 9276–77. I am grateful to Daniel McCarthy for calling my attention to this speech.

9. George Kennan was the foremost American realist, and his *American Diplomacy, 1900–1950* (Chicago: University of Chicago, 1950) famously warns against "moralism" in foreign policy.

10. David Frum and Richard Perle, *An End to Evil* (New York: Random House, 2004). Subsequent references to this book will be by page numbers in parentheses in the text.

11. Norman Podhoretz, *World War IV: The Long Struggle Against Islamofascism* (New York: Doubleday, 2007), 144–45. Subsequent references to this book will be by page numbers in parentheses in the text.

12. Lawrence Kaplan and William Kristol, *The War Over Iraq: Saddam's Tyranny and America's Mission* (San Francisco: Encounter Books, 2003), 104. Subsequent references to this book will be by page numbers in parentheses in the text.

13. *The Irrepressible Rothbard: The Rothbard-Rockwell Report Essays of Murray N. Rothbard,* ed. Llewellyn H. Rockwell Jr. (Auburn, AL: Center for Libertarian Studies, 2000), 170. Subsequent references to this book will be by page number in parentheses in the text.

Index

H

Index

Wilder, Laura Ingalls, 183
Wiley, Sen. Alexander, 182
Wilkie, Wendell, 21, 169
William F. Buckley Jr.: Patron Saint of the Conservatives (Judis), xix-xx, 339n
Wilson, Gov. Pete, 274
Wilson, Woodrow, 250
Winchell, Walter, 163
Woman's Day Book of American Needlework (Lane), 197
Wood, General Robert E., 117
Workers Council, 28
Workers Party, 8, 14, 31, 39–40. *See also* Shachtman, Max.

Y

Yale Review, 114
Young Americans for Freedom, 253–54
Young Worker, 28

About the Contributors

JUSTIN RAIMONDO is editorial director of Antiwar.com, a senior fellow at the Randolph Bourne Institute, and author of *An Enemy of the State: The Life of Murray N. Rothbard.*

GEORGE W. CAREY (1933–2013) was one of the foremost authorities on the political theory of the American Founding. He taught at Georgetown University for more than fifty years and was the author or editor of many books, including *Freedom and Virtue: The Conservative/Libertarian Debate.*

PATRICK J. BUCHANAN served as a speechwriter and political advisor for President Richard Nixon and as communications director for President Ronald Reagan. A renowned political commentator and syndicated columnist, he is the author of *Day of Reckoning: How Hubris, Ideology, and Greed Are Tearing America Apart.*

SCOTT P. RICHERT is the executive editor of *Chronicles: A Magazine of American Culture*, and author of numerous articles on Catholic moral, social, political, and historical issues.

DAVID GORDON is the editor of *The Mises Review*, senior fellow at the Ludwig von Mises Institute, and contributor to such journals as *Analysis, The International Philosophic Quarterly, The Journal of Libertarian Studies*, and *The Quarterly Journal of Austrian Economics.*